### Section 8—The Java Server Pages (JSP) Technology Model

8.1 Write the opening and closing tags for the following JSP tag types:
- Directive • Declaration • Scriptlet • Expression

8.2 Given a type of JSP tag, identify correct statements about its purpose or use.

8.3 Given a JSP tag type, identify the equivalent XML-based tags.

8.4 Identify the page directive attribute, and its values, that:
- Import a Java class into the JSP page
- Declare that a JSP page exists within a session
- Declare that a JSP page uses an error page
- Declare that a JSP page is an error page

8.5 Identify and put in sequence the following elements of the JSP page lifecycle:
- Page translation • JSP page compilation
- Load class • Create instance • Call jspInit Call _jspService • Call jspDestroy

8.6 Match correct descriptions about purpose, function, or use with any of the following implicit objects:
- request • response • out • session
- config • application • page • pageContext
- exception

8.7 Distinguish correct and incorrect scriptlet code for:
- A conditional statement;
- An iteration statement

### Section 9—Designing and Developing Reusable Web Components

9.1 Given a description of required functionality, identify the JSP page directive or standard tag in the correct format with the correct attributes required to specify the inclusion of a Web component into the JSP page.

### Section 10—Designing and Developing JSP pages Using JavaBean Components

10.1 For any of the following tag functions, match the correctly constructed tag, with attributes and values as appropriate, with the corresponding description of the tag's functionality:
- Declare the use of a JavaBean component within the page. • Specify, for jsp:useBean or jsp:getProperty tags, the name of an attribute.
- Specify, for a jsp:useBean tag, the class of the attribute. • Specify, for a jsp:useBean tag, the scope of the attribute. • Access or mutate a property from a declared JavaBean. • Specify, for a jsp:getProperty tag, the property of the attribute. • Specify, for a jsp:setProperty tag, the property of the attribute to mutate, and the new value.

10.2 Given JSP page attribute scopes: request, session, application, identify the equivalent servlet code.

10.3 Identify techniques that access a declared JavaBean component.

### Section 11—Designing and Developing JSP pages Using Custom Tags

11.1 Identify properly formatted tag library declarations in the Web application deployment descriptor.

11.2 Identify properly formatted taglib directives in a JSP page.

11.3 Given a custom tag library, identify properly formatted custom tag usage in a JSP page. Uses include:
- An empty custom tag • A custom tag with attributes • A custom tag that surrounds other JSP code • Nested custom tags

### Section 12—Designing and Developing a Custom Tag Library

12.1 Identify the tag library descriptor element names that declare the following:
- The name of the tag • The class of the tag handler • The type of content that the tag accepts • Any attributes of the tag

12.2 Identify the tag library descriptor element names that declare the following:
- The name of a tag attribute • Whether a tag attribute is required • Whether or not the attribute's value can be dynamically specified

12.3 Given a custom tag, identify the necessary value for the bodycontent TLD element for any of the following tag types:
- Empty-tag • Custom tag that surrounds other JSP code • Custom tag that surrounds content that is used only by the tag handler

12.4 Given a tag event method (doStartTag, doAfterBody, and doEndTag), identify the correct description of the method's trigger.

12.5 Identify valid return values for the following methods:
- doStartTag • doAfterBody • doEndTag
- PageConext.getOut

12.6 Given a "BODY" or "PAGE" constant, identify a correct description of the constant's use in the following methods:
- doStartTag • doAfterBody • doEndTag

12.7 Identify the method in the custom tag handler that accesses:
- A given JSP page's implicit variable
- The JSP page's attributes

12.8 Identify methods that return an outer tag handler from within an inner tag handler.

### Section 13

13.1 Given a scenario description with a list of issues, select the design pattern (Value Objects, MVC, Data Access Object, or Business Delegate) that would best solve those issues.

13.2 Match design patterns with statements describing potential benefits that accrue from the use of the pattern, for any of the following patterns:
- Value Objects • MVC • Data Access Object
- Business Delegate

# *SCWCD Exam Study Kit*

JAVA WEB COMPONENT DEVELOPER CERTIFICATION

Hanumant Deshmukh
Jignesh Malavia
with Jacquelyn Carter

MANNING
Greenwich
(74° w. long.)

For online information and ordering of this and other Manning books, go to www.manning.com. The publisher offers discounts on this book when ordered in quantity. For more information, please contact:

Special Sales Department
Manning Publications Co.
209 Bruce Park Avenue
Greenwich, CT 06830
Fax: (203) 661-9018
email: orders@manning.com



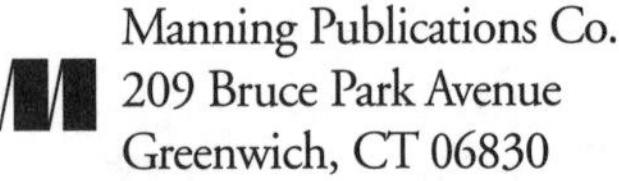

Manning Publications Co.
209 Bruce Park Avenue
Greenwich, CT 06830

Copyeditor: Liz Welch
Typesetter: D. Dalinnik
Cover designer: Leslie Haimes

ISBN 1-930110-59-6

Printed in the United States of America
1 2 3 4 5 6 7 8 9 10 – VHG – 06 05 04 03 02

*To my alma mater, IT-BHU*
*–Hanumant*

*To my parents*
*–Jignesh*

# *brief contents*

## *Part 4 Patterns and filters 343*



## *Appendices*

# *contents*

# *Part 3 Java Server Pages 173*

## *Appendices*

# *preface*

We first started thinking about writing this book when we were preparing to take the Sun Certified Web Component Developer (SCWCD) exam. We had difficulty finding any books that thoroughly covered the objectives published by Sun. The idea continued to percolate during the time we were developing JWebPlus, our exam simulator for the SCWCD. With its successful release, we finally turned our attention to putting our combined knowledge and experience into this book.

We have been interacting with Java Certification aspirants for a long time. Through our discussion forums and our exam simulators, JWebPlus and JQPlus (for SCJP—Sun Certified Java Programmer), we have helped people gain the skills they need. Our goal in this book is to leverage that experience and help you feel confident about taking the exam. This book and the accompanying CD will prepare you to do so; they are all you need to pass with flying colors. Of course, you'll still have to write a lot of code yourself!

### *Who is this book for?*

This book is for Java programmers who want to prepare for the SCWCD exam, which focuses on the Servlet and JavaServer Pages technologies. This book will also be very useful for beginners since we have explained the concepts using simple examples. The text will bring you up to speed even if you are totally new to these technologies. Even expert Servlet/JSP programmers should read the book to ensure that they do not overlook any exam objectives. However, since this book is a study guide, we do not try to cover advanced tricks and techniques for expert Servlet/JSP developers.

### *About the Sun certification exams*

The Java platform comes in three flavors: Standard Edition, Enterprise Edition, and Micro Edition. The figure below shows the certification exams that Sun offers for the first two editions.

The Standard Edition (J2SE) is the basis of the Java platform and is used in the development of Java applets and applications. The standard library includes important packages, such as `java.io`, `java.net`, `java.rmi`, and `javax.swing`. Sun offers two certifications for this platform: the Java Programmer (SCJP) certification and the Java Developer (SCJD) certification. While the Java Programmer certification process consists of only one multiple-choice exam covering the basics of the Java language, the Java Developer certification requires you to develop a simple but nontrivial client server application using the `java.net`, `java.rmi`, and `javax.swing` packages, followed by an essay-type exam on the application.

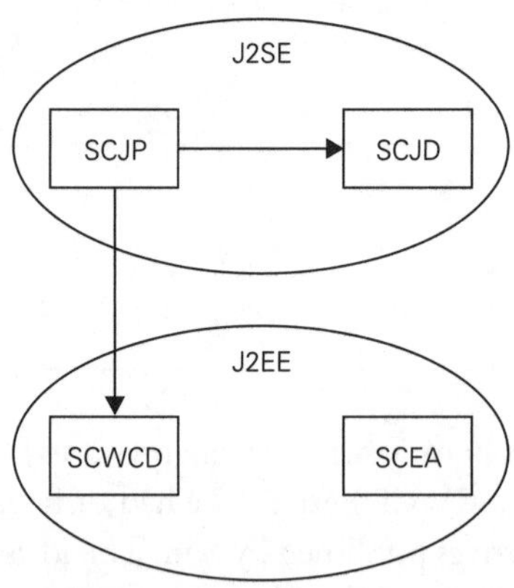


**A roadmap for Sun's certifications in the J2SE and the J2EE platforms. SCJP certification is required before taking the SCWCD exam.**

The Enterprise Edition (J2EE) builds on the Standard Edition and includes a number of technologies, such as Enterprise JavaBeans (EJB), Servlet, and JavaServer Pages, used for building enterprise-class server-side applications. Sun offers two certifications for this platform: the Web Component Developer (SCWCD) certification and the Enterprise Architect (SCEA) certification. The SCWCD certification process is designed for programmers developing web applications using Servlet and JSP technology and consists of one multiple-choice exam. You must be a Sun Certified Java Programmer before you can take this exam. The Enterprise Architect certification is designed for senior developers who are using the whole gamut of J2EE technologies to design enterprise-class applications. The certification process consists of one multiple-choice exam and one architecture and design project, followed by an essay-type exam on the project.

The Micro Edition (J2ME) is an optimized Java runtime environment meant for use in consumer electronic products, such as cell phones and pagers. Sun does not offer any certification for this platform yet.

### *Preparing for the SCWCD*

We believe that studying for a test is very different than just learning a technology. Of course, you also learn the technology when you study for the test. But when you take the exam, you have to show that you understand what the examiner expects you to know about the technology. And that's what makes studying for a test a different ball game altogether. It is not surprising that even people with many years of experience sometimes fail the tests. In this book, we'll teach you the technology while training you for the test.

Here are the things that you will need:

- *A copy of the exam objectives.* It is very important to take a look at the objectives before you start a chapter and after you finish it. It helps to keep you focused. For your convenience, we have included the relevant exam objectives at the beginning of each chapter, as well as in appendix E.

- *A Servlet engine that implements the Servlet 2.3 and JSP 1.2 specifications.* You will need it because we'll do some coding exercises to illustrate the concepts. In this book, we have decided to use Tomcat 4.0 because it is now the official reference implementation for the JSP/Servlet technology and it conforms to the specifications. In addition, it is free and very easy to install and run. Appendix A explains where to get Tomcat (included on the CD) and how to install it. If you are clueless about what Tomcat is, don't worry. Chapters 1 and 2 will bring you up to speed.
- *A copy of the Servlet 2.3 and JSP 1.2 specifications.* The specifications are the best source of information on this technology. Don't get scared; unlike the Java Language specs, these specs are readable and easy to understand. We have included these on the accompanying CD.
- *The JWebPlus exam simulator.* We've developed this exam simulator to help you judge your level of preparedness. It not only includes detailed explanations of the questions but also explains why a certain option is right or wrong. We've included on the CD an abbreviated version of this tool that contains three full-sized exams. You can buy the full version, which contains six full-sized exams, at `www.enthuware.com`.

Although these items are all you need to pass the exam, if you want to learn how to take advantage of the Servlet/JSP technology in real-life applications, we recommend the following books from Manning Publications:

*Web Development with JavaServer Pages, 2nd Edition*
by Duane K. Fields, Mark A. Kolb, and Shawn Bayern
ISBN: 193011012X

*JSP Tag Libraries*
by Gal Shachor, Adam Chace, and Magnus Rydin
ISBN: 193011009X

*Java Servlets by Example*
by Alan R. Williamson
ISBN: 188477766X

*JSTL in Action*
by Shawn Bayern
ISBN: 1930110529

*JDK 1.4 Tutorial*
by Gregory M. Travis
ISBN: 1930110456

# about this book

This book is built around the objectives that Sun has published for the SCWCD exam. If you know everything that is covered by the objectives, you will pass the exam. The chapters in the book examine each objective in detail and explain everything you need to understand about web component development.

## How this book is organized

This book has four parts:

| Part | Topic | Chapters |
|---|---|---|
| 1 | The basics of web component development | 1 through 3 |
| 2 | The Servlet technology | 4 through 10 |
| 3 | The JavaServer Pages technology | 11 through 16 |
| 4 | Design patterns and filters | 17 and 18 |

For those of you new to web component development, we've included one introductory chapter each on Servlets and JavaServer Pages. The objectives of chapters 1 and 2 are to make you comfortable with this technology. They won't make you an expert, but they'll teach you enough so that you can understand the rest of the book. If you already have experience with the Servlet and JavaServerPages technologies, you can skip these two chapters. Since in practice servlets are written for HTTP, we have also included a brief discussion of the HTTP protocol and the basics of web applications in chapter 3. You should read this chapter even if you know the HTTP protocol.

Chapters 4 through 17 cover the exam objectives. We have written one chapter for each group of objectives, except for objective section 8, which is covered in two chapters, 11 and 12. Some chapters start with basic concepts that do not necessarily correspond to exam objectives but are very important in order to understand the remaining sections. In the chapters, we illustrate the concepts with simple test programs. You should try to write and run the programs, and we encourage you to modify them and try out similar examples. From our experience, we've seen that people tend to understand and remember the concepts a lot better if they actually put them in code and see them in action.

Chapter 18 is a discussion of filters. Although knowledge of filters is not required for the SCWCD exam, we have included this information because filters are an important addition to Servlet Specification 2.3.

There are five appendices. Appendix A will help you set up Tomcat. Because some of the exam objectives require basic knowledge of XML, we've included a brief introduction to XML in appendix B. Appendix C contains a sample `web.xml` file that illustrates the use of various deployment descriptor tags. Appendix D contains the answers to each chapter's review questions. In appendix E, you will find the Quick Prep, a summary of key concepts and helpful tips that you can review as part of your last-minute exam preparations.

### How each chapter is organized

After the introductory chapters in part 1, each chapter begins with a list of the exam objectives that are discussed within it, along with the chapter sections in which each objective is addressed. In some of the chapters, the order of the objectives departs slightly from the original Sun numbering to better correspond to the way the topics within the chapters have been organized.

As you read through the chapters, you will encounter Quizlets about the material you have just read. Try to answer the Quizlet without looking at the answer; if you are correct, you can feel confident that you have understood the concepts.

At the end of each chapter, you will find review questions that will help you to evaluate your ability to answer the exam questions related to the objectives for the chapter. The answers to these questions are in appendix D.

### What's on the CD?

The CD that accompanies this book includes the JWebPlus exam simulator, which contains three practice exams that will help you prepare to take the real exam. It also includes a copy of Tomcat 4.0 that you can install to run the examples in the book, and to write your own test programs. Of course, all of the examples from the book are also on the CD, along with the latest Servlet 2.3 and JSP 1.2 specifications. In addition, you will find relevant RFCs and a JSP syntax card. And finally, the CD contains a fully searchable electronic version of this complete book.

### Code conventions

*Italic* typeface is used to introduce new terms.

`Courier` typeface is used to denote code samples, as well as elements and attributes, method names, classes, interfaces, and other identifiers.

**`Bold courier`** is used to denote important parts of the code samples.

Code annotations accompany many segments of code.

Line continuations are indented.

### *Source code*

Source code for all the programming examples in this book is available for download from the publisher's web site, `www.manning.com/deshmukh`. Any corrections to code will be updated on an ongoing basis.

### *Author Online*

Purchase of the *SCWCD Exam Study Kit* includes free access to a private web forum run by Manning Publications, where you can make comments about the book, ask technical questions, and receive help from the author and from other users. To access the forum and subscribe to it, point your web browser to `www.manning.com/deshmukh`. This page provides information on how to get on the forum once you are registered, what kind of help is available, and the rules of conduct on the forum.

Manning's commitment to our readers is to provide a venue where a meaningful dialogue between individual readers and between readers and the authors can take place. It is not a commitment to any specific amount of participation on the part of the authors, whose contribution to the AO remains voluntary (and unpaid). We suggest you try asking the authors some challenging questions lest their interest stray!

The Author Online forum and the archives of previous discussions will be accessible from the publisher's web site as long as the book is in print.

You can also reach the authors through their web site at `www.jdiscuss.com`, where they maintain forums for the discussion of Java topics, especially those related to the Sun exams. Additionally, the web site contains material that you will find useful in your preparation for the exam, such as information about books, tutorials, free and commercial practice exams, and study notes. The site will continue to be updated with exciting new resources as they become available.

# *taking the exam*

Exam code: 310 – 080
Cost: $150
Number of questions: 59 multiple-choice questions

The questions tell you the number of correct answers. You may also get questions that ask you to match options on the left-hand side with options on the right-hand side, or that ask you to drag and drop options to the correct place. In general, many exam takers have reported that questions on this test are easier than the ones on the Sun Certified Java Programmer's exam. The exam starts with a survey that asks you questions about your level and experience with Servlet/JSP technology, but these questions are not a part of the actual exam.

At the time of this writing, the duration of the test was 90 minutes. But Sun has changed the duration for the SCJP exam a couple of times, so they could change the duration of this test as well. Please verify it before you take the exam. You can get the latest information about the exam from `http://suned.sun.com`.

Here's how to register and what to expect:

1. First, purchase an exam voucher from your local Sun Educational Services office. In the United States, you can purchase an exam voucher by calling (800) 422-8020. If you reside outside of the United States, you should contact your local Sun Educational Services office. You'll be given a voucher number.
2. Tests are conducted by Prometric all across the world. You have to contact them to schedule the test. Please visit the Prometric web site at www.`2test.com` for information about testing centers. Before you schedule the test, check out the testing center where you plan to take the exam. Make sure you feel comfortable with the environment there. Believe us, you do not want to take the test at a noisy place. Once you finalize the center, you can schedule the test.
3. You should reach the testing center at least 15 minutes before the test, and don't forget to take two forms of ID. One of the IDs should have your photograph on it.
4. After you finish the test, the screen will tell you whether or not you passed. You will receive a printed copy of the detailed results.

5. Within a week, your results will be available at the "My Certification" web site at `www.galton.com/~sun/`.
6. Within a month or so, you'll get a welcome kit from Sun that contains a pin and the certification.

Best of luck!

# *about the authors*

HANUMANT DESHMUKH is the president and founder of Enthuware.com Pvt. Ltd. He also manages `www.jdiscuss.com`, a free site designed for Java certification aspirants. He has been working in the information technology industry for the past six years, mainly consulting for projects with the Distributed Object Oriented System using J2EE technologies. Hanumant also designs and develops the Java certification software for his company. The exam simulators from Enthuware.com, JQPlus (for SCJP) and JWebPlus (for SCWCD), are well known and respected in the Java community.

JIGNESH MALAVIA is a senior technical architect at SourceCode, Inc. in New York. For the past six years, he has been involved in the design and development of various types of systems, from language interpreters to business applications. Teaching is one of his passions, and he has taught courses on Java and web development, as well as C, C++, and Unix, at various locations, including the Narsee Monjee Institute of Management Science (NMIMS), Mumbai. He has been actively involved with Enthuware projects and currently provides online guidance to candidates preparing for Sun certification exams.

JACQUELYN CARTER is a technical writer who also has many years' experience providing information technology solutions for organizations in both the business and nonprofit worlds. Her recent projects include developing enterprise web sites and portals using the Java technology.

# *acknowledgments*

Many thanks to Dan Barthel, former acquisitions editor, for considering our proposal for a book on this subject and for introducing us to the publisher of Manning Publications, Marjan Bace. To Marjan, for giving us the opportunity to fulfill a long-cherished dream of writing a book. His confidence in us, in spite of delays, motivated us throughout the development of the book. We could not have hoped for a better publisher.

We are indebted to Michael Tsuji for getting us started with the chapters and for introducing us to the "little book." We could not have done this without his guidance.

No book gets published without the hard work of a lot of people. We are very grateful to…

All the reviewers of the manuscript: April Johnson, Dave O'Meara, Fei Ng, Francois Merle, Gaurav Mantro, Kavitha Borra, Muhammad Ashikuzzaman, Muharem Lubovac, Roopa Bagur, and Tom Aronson, for their corrections and suggestions. Special thanks to Francois Merle, who tech-proofed all the chapters and reviewed all the questions in the JWebPlus test engine.

The publishing team at Manning: Liz Welch for copyediting, Ted Kennedy for setting up the reviews, Syd Brown and Denis Dalinnik for typesetting the raw manuscript, Mary Piergies for managing the production process, Lianna Wlasiuk for guiding us in the initial stages, and Susan Capparelle for paying us on time! Also the terrific crew in the back office who printed the book and brought it to the market in record time.

Finally, our kudos to Jackie Carter. She took great care with the "presentation logic" throughout the book and put in an incredible amount of effort to format and polish every chapter. She made sure that the concepts were explained in a clear and professional manner. We cannot thank her enough for all the hard work she put in to help us shape a better book. We wish she had joined us at the start of the project.

### HANUMANT DESHMUKH

I am thankful to my family—Aai, Baba, Sudarshan—for providing moral support at every stage. To my friend, Jignesh, who agreed to co-author this book. It would not have been possible for me to pull this one off alone. Thanks, buddy! To my friends, Sachin and Paul, for managing Enthuware while Jignesh and I were busy with the book.

I am also very grateful to Chirag Pradhan, whose timely help in reviewing the chapters gave us some valuable breathing room.

### JIGNESH MALAVIA

My gratitude to my parents for their many blessings. To my wife, Rachana, for enriching my life and making me complete. To my sister Sonal and my brother Nilesh for being my most critical students. That is how I constantly improve my teaching skills.

I am also grateful to my employer, Harold Fernandes, for his guidance and support. And many, many thanks to Hanumant for trusting me with this assignment and being the "Front Controller" on this project.

# *about the cover illustration*

The figure on the cover of the *SCWCD Exam Study Kit* is a "Res Efendi o Primer Secretario di Estado," a Turkish Secretary of State. The illustration is taken from a Spanish compendium of regional dress customs first published in Madrid in 1799. The book's title page informs us:

> *Coleccion general de los Trages que usan actualmente todas las Nacionas del Mundo, desubierto dibujados y grabados con la mayor exactitud por R.M.V.A.R. Obra muy util y en special para los que tienen la del viajero universal.*

which we loosely translate as:

> *General Collection of Costumes currently used in the Nations of the Known World, designed and printed with great exactitude by R.M.V.A.R. This work is very useful especially for those who hold themselves to be universal travelers.*

Although nothing is known of the designers, engravers, and artists who colored this illustration by hand, the "exactitude" of their execution is evident in this drawing, The figure on the cover is a "Res Efendi," a Turkish government official whom the Madrid editor renders as "Primer Secretario di Estado." The Res Efendi is just one of a colorful variety of figures in this collection, which reminds us vividly of how culturally apart the world's towns and regions were just 200 years ago. Dress codes have changed since then and the diversity by region, so rich at the time, has faded away. It is now often hard to tell the inhabitant of one continent from another. Perhaps we have traded a cultural and visual diversity for a more varied personal life—certainly a more varied and interesting world of technology.

At a time when it can be hard to tell one computer book from another, Manning celebrates the inventiveness and initiative of the computer business with book covers based on the rich diversity of regional life of two centuries ago—brought back to life by the picture from this collection.

# PART 1

# *Getting started*

Part 1 is intended for readers who are new to web component development. We introduce you to the concepts you'll need to understand before you begin the chapters that focus on the exam objectives. Our topics here include the Servlet and JSP technologies, web applications, and the HTTP protocol.

CHAPTER 1

# Understanding Java servlets



## INTRODUCTION

In the second part of the book, we will take a close look at the exam objectives that pertain to servlets. If you are new to servlets, this chapter will provide an introduction to the technology.

## 1.1 WHAT IS A SERVLET?

As is apparent from its name, a servlet is a server-side entity. But what exactly does it mean? Is it a new design pattern for writing servers? Is it a new Java class? Or is it a new technology? The answer to all these questions is yes, albeit in different contexts. To understand any new concept, it is important to know the reasons behind its conception. So, let's start by having a look at the tasks a server needs to do.

### 1.1.1 Server responsibilities

Every server that provides services to remote clients has two main responsibilities. The first is to handle network connections; the second is to create a response to be sent back. The first task involves programming at the socket level, extracting information from request messages, and implementing client-server protocols, such as FTP and HTTP.

The second task, creating the response, varies from service to service. For example, in the case of FTP servers that serve file transfer requests, response creation is as simple as locating a file on the local machine. On the other hand, HTTP servers that host full-fledged web applications are required to be more sophisticated in the way they generate output. They have to create the response dynamically, which may involve complicated tasks, such as retrieving data from the database, applying business rules, and presenting the output in the formats desired by different clients.

One way to write a simple server that serves only static data would be to code everything in a single executable program. This single program would take care of all the different chores, such as managing the network, implementing protocols, locating data, and replying. However, for HTTP servers that serve syndicated data, we require a highly flexible and extensible design. Application logic keeps changing, clients need personalized views of information, and business partners need customized processing rules. We cannot write a single program that handles all these tasks. Furthermore, what if a new functionality has to be added? What if the data format changes? Modifying the source files (especially after the developer has left!) to add new code is surely the last thing we want to do.

Well, there is a better design for these kinds of servers: divide the code into two executable parts—one that handles the network and one that provides the application logic—and let the two executables have a standard interface between them. This kind of separation makes it possible to modify the code in the application logic without affecting the network module, as long as we follow the rules of the interface. Traditionally, people have implemented this design for HTTP servers using Common Gateway Interface (CGI). On one side of this interface is the main web server, and on the other side are the CGI scripts. The web server acts as the network communications module and manages the clients, while the CGI scripts act as data processing modules and deliver the output. They follow the rules of the "common gateway interface" to pass data between them.

### 1.1.2 Server extensions

Although CGI provides a modular design, it has several shortcomings. The main issue for high-traffic web sites is scalability. Each new request invocation involves the creation and destruction of new processes to run the CGI scripts. This is highly inefficient, especially if the scripts perform initialization routines, like connecting to a database. Moreover, they use file input/output (I/O) as a means of communication with the server, causing a significant increase in the overall response time.

A better way is to have the server support separate executable modules that can be loaded into its memory and initialized only once—when the server starts up. Each request can then be served by the already in-memory and ready-to-serve copy of the modules. Fortunately, most of the industrial-strength servers have been supporting such modules for a long time, and they have made the out-of-memory CGI scripts obsolete. These separate executable modules are known as *server extensions*. On platforms other than Java, server extensions are written using native-language APIs provided by the server vendors. For example, Netscape Server provides the Netscape Server Application Programming Interface (NSAPI), and Microsoft's Internet Information Server (IIS) provides the Internet Server Application Programming Interface (ISAPI). In Java, server extensions are written using the Servlet API,[1] and the server extension modules are called *servlets*.

## 1.2 WHAT IS A SERVLET CONTAINER?

A web server uses a separate module to load and run servlets. This specialized module, which is dedicated to the servlet management, is called a *servlet container*, or *servlet engine*.

### 1.2.1 The big picture

Figure 1.1 shows how different components fit into the big picture. HTML files are stored in the file system, servlets run within a servlet container, and business data is in the database.

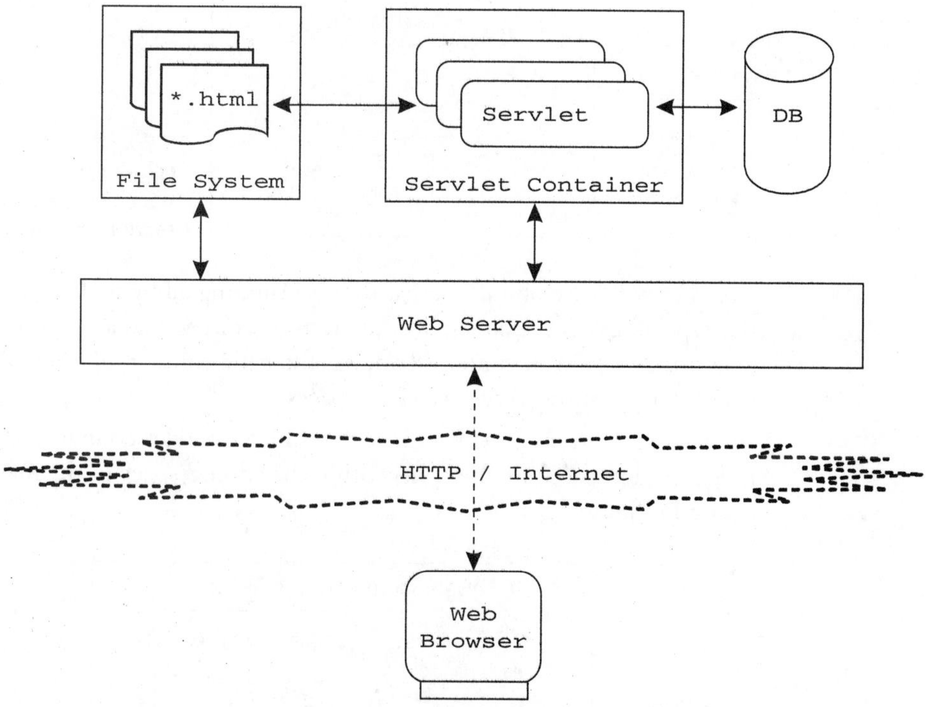


**Figure 1.1 The big picture: all the components of a web-based application.**

[1] An overview of the Servlet API is given in section 1.4. The details of the different elements of this API are explained in chapters 4 through 10.

The browser sends requests to the web server. If the target is an HTML file, the server handles it directly. If the target is a servlet, the server delegates the request to the servlet container, which in turn forwards it to the servlet. The servlet uses the file system and database to generate dynamic output.

### 1.2.2 Understanding servlet containers

Conceptually, a servlet container is a part of the web server, even though it may run in a separate process. In this respect, servlet containers are classified into the following three types:

- *Standalone.* Servlet containers of this type are typically Java-based web servers where the two modules—the main web server and the servlet container—are integral parts of a single program (figure 1.2).

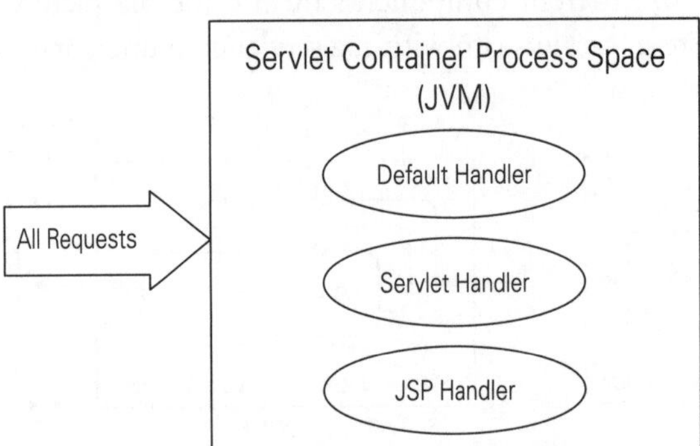


**Figure 1.2 A standalone servlet container.**

  Tomcat (we'll learn about Tomcat shortly) running all by itself is an example of this type of servlet container. We run Tomcat as we would any normal Java program inside a JVM. It contains handlers for static content, like HTML files, and handlers for running servlets and JSP pages.

- *In-process.* Here, the main web server and the servlet container are different programs, but the container runs within the address space of the main server as a plug-in (figure 1.3).

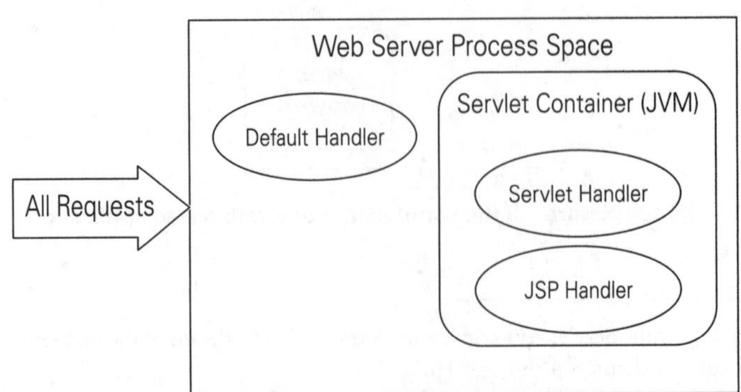


**Figure 1.3 An in-process servlet container.**

An example of this type is Tomcat running inside Apache Web Server. Apache loads a JVM that runs Tomcat. In this case, the web server handles the static content by itself, and Tomcat handles the servlets and JSP pages.

- *Out-of-process.* Like in-process servers, the main web server and the servlet container are different programs. However, with out-of-process, the web server runs in one process while the servlet container runs in a separate process (figure 1.4). To communicate with the servlet container, the web server uses a plug-in, which is usually provided by the servlet container vendor.

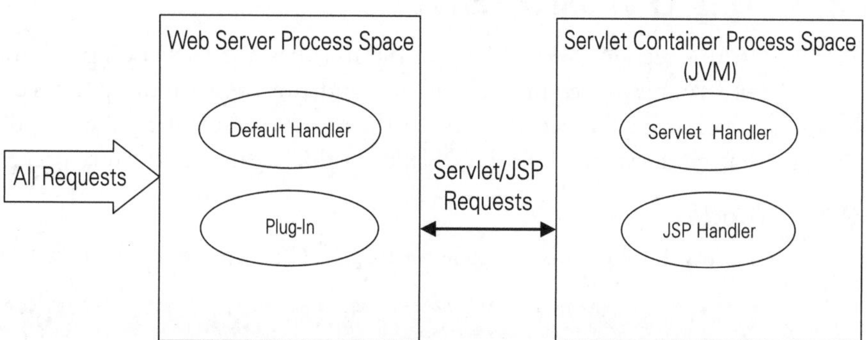


**Figure 1.4 An out-of-process servlet container.**

An example of this type is Tomcat running as a separate process configured to receive requests from Apache Web Server. Apache loads the `mod_jk` plug-in to communicate with Tomcat.

Each of these types has its advantages, limitations, and applicability. We will not discuss these details, since they are beyond the scope of this book.

Many servlet containers are available on the market—Tomcat (Apache), Resin (Caucho Technology), JRun (Macromedia), WebLogic (BEA), and WebSphere (IBM), just to name a few. Some of these, like WebLogic and WebSphere, are much more than just servlet containers. They also provide support for Enterprise JavaBeans (EJB), Java Message Service (JMS), and other J2EE technologies.

### 1.2.3 Using Tomcat

Tomcat is a servlet container developed under the Jakarta project at the Apache Software Foundation (ASF). You can get a wealth of information about Tomcat from `http://jakarta.apache.org`. We have decided to use Tomcat version 4.0.1 for the examples in this book because of the following reasons:

- It is free.
- It implements the latest Servlet 2.3 and JSP 1.2 specifications, which is what we need for the exam.

- It has the capability of running as a web server by itself (Standalone mode). There is no need for a separate web server.

We have given installation instructions for Tomcat in appendix A. In the discussions of the examples throughout the book, we have assumed that the Tomcat installation directory is `c:\jakarta-tomcat4.0.1`. Note that once you have installed Tomcat, you must set the `CATALINA_HOME`, `JAVA_HOME`, and `CLASSPATH` variables, as described in appendix A.

## 1.3 HELLO WORLD SERVLET

In this section, we will look at the four basic steps—coding, compiling, deploying, and running—required to develop and run the customary `Hello World` servlet,[2] which prints `Hello World!` in the browser window. By the way, do you know who started the trend of writing "Hello World!" as an introductory program?[3]

### 1.3.1 Code

Listing 1.1 contains the code for `HelloWorldServlet.java`:

**Listing 1.1 HelloWorldServlet.java**

```
import java.io.*;
import javax.servlet.*;
import javax.servlet.http.*;

public class HelloWorldServlet extends HttpServlet
{
   public void service(HttpServletRequest request,
                       HttpServletResponse response)
                     throws ServletException,
                            IOException
   {
      PrintWriter pw = response.getWriter();
      pw.println("<html>");
      pw.println("<head>");
      pw.println("</head>");
      pw.println("<body>");
      pw.println("<h3>Hello World!</h3>");
      pw.println("</body>");
      pw.println("</html>");
   }
}
```

2 The details of the code will become clear as we move through the chapters.

3 Kernighan and Ritchie, *The C Programming Language.*

### 1.3.2 Compilation

Note the import statements in listing 1.1. They import the classes from the `javax.servlet` and `javax.servlet.http` packages. In Tomcat, they are provided as part of the `servlet.jar` file, which is in the directory `c:\jakarta-tomcat4.0.1\common\lib\`. To compile the program in listing 1.1, include the JAR file in the classpath, as directed in appendix A. We will explain the details of these packages in section 1.4.

### 1.3.3 Deployment

Deployment is a two-step process. (We'll discuss the deployment structure in chapter 5.) First, we put the resources into the required directory. Then, we inform Tomcat about our servlet by editing the `web.xml` file:

1. Copy the `HelloWorldServlet.class` file to the directory

   ```
   c:\jakarta-tomcat4.0.1\webapps\chapter01\WEB-INF\classes
   ```

2. Create a text file named `web.xml` in the `c:\jakarta-tomcat4.0.1\webapps\chapter01\WEB-INF` directory. Write the following lines in the file:

```
<web-app>
   <servlet>
      <servlet-name>HelloWorldServlet</servlet-name>
      <servlet-class>HelloWorldServlet</servlet-class>
   </servlet>
</web-app>
```

You can also copy the `chapter01` directory directly from the accompanying CD to your `c:\jakarta-tomcat4.0.1\webapps` directory. This will provide all the files you need to run the example.

### 1.3.4 Execution

Start Tomcat (`c:\jakarta-tomcat4.0.1\bin\startup.bat`). Open a browser window and go to the URL `http://localhost:8080/chapter01/servlet/HelloWorldServlet`.

`Hello World!` should appear in the browser window.

## 1.4 THE RELATIONSHIP BETWEEN A SERVLET CONTAINER AND THE SERVLET API

Sun's Servlet specification provides a standard and a platform-independent framework for communication between servlets and their containers. This framework is made up of a set of Java interfaces and classes. These interfaces and classes are collectively called the *Servlet Application Programmer Interfaces*, or the *Servlet API*. Simply put, we develop servlets using this API, which is implemented by the servlet container (see figure 1.5). The Servlet API is all we as servlet developers need to know. Since all

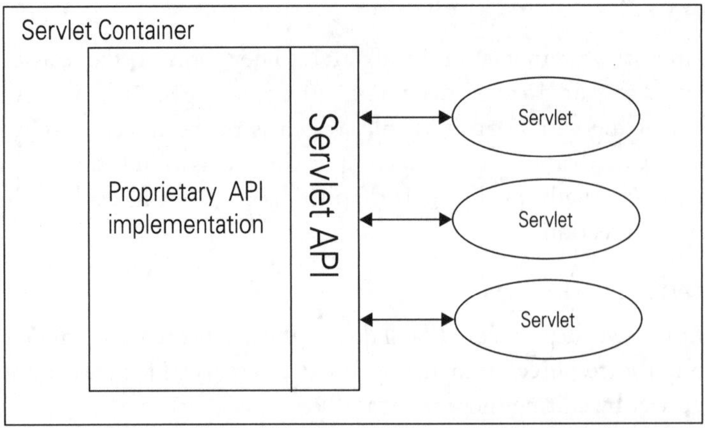


**Figure 1.5 Servlets interact with the servlet container through the Servlet API.**

the servlet containers must provide this API, the servlets are truly platform- and servlet container–independent. Essentially, understanding the rules of this API and the functionality that it provides is what servlet programming is all about!

The Servlet API is divided into two packages: `javax.servlet` and `javax.servlet.http`. We will discuss these packages in more detail as we progress through the book, but for now, let's take a quick look at them.

## 1.4.1 The javax.servlet package

This package contains the generic servlet interfaces and classes that are independent of any protocol.

### *The javax.servlet.Servlet interface*

This is the central interface in the Servlet API. Every servlet class must directly or indirectly implement this interface. It has five methods, as shown in table 1.1.

**Table 1.1 Methods of the javax.servlet.Servlet interface**

| Method | Description |
|---|---|
| init() | This method is called by the servlet container to indicate to the servlet that it must initialize itself and get ready for service. The container passes an object of type ServletConfig as a parameter. |
| service() | This method is called by the servlet container for each request from the client to allow the servlet to respond to the request. |
| destroy() | This method is called by the servlet container to indicate to the servlet that it must clean up itself, release any acquired resource, and get ready to go out of service. |

*continued on next page*

**Table 1.1 Methods of the javax.servlet.Servlet interface *(continued)***

| Method | Description |
|---|---|
| getServletConfig() | Returns information about the servlet, such as a parameter to the init() method. |
| getServletInfo() | The implementataion class must return information about the servlet, such as the author, the version, and copyright information. |

The `service()` method handles requests and creates responses. The servlet container automatically calls this method when it gets any request for this servlet. The complete signature of this method is:

```
public void service (ServletRequest, ServletResponse)
          throws ServletException,java.io.IOException;
```

### *The javax.servlet.GenericServlet class*

The `GenericServlet` class implements the `Servlet` interface. It is an abstract class that provides implementation for all the methods except the `service()` method of the `Servlet` interface. It also adds a few methods to support logging. We can extend this class and implement the `service()` method to write any kind of servlet.

### *The javax.servlet.ServletRequest interface*

The `ServletRequest` interface provides a generic view of the request that was sent by a client. It defines methods that extract information from the request.

### *The javax.servlet.ServletResponse interface*

The `ServletResponse` interface provides a generic way of sending responses. It defines methods that assist in sending a proper response to the client.

## 1.4.2 The javax.servlet.http package

This package provides the basic functionality required for HTTP servlets. Interfaces and classes in this package extend the corresponding interfaces and classes of the `javax.servlet` package to build support for the HTTP protocol.

### *The javax.servlet.http.HttpServlet class*

`HttpServlet` is an abstract class that extends `GenericServlet`. It adds a new `service()` method with this signature:

```
protected void service (HttpServletRequest, HttpServletResponse)
            throws ServletException, java.io.IOException;
```

In the `Hello World` example, we extended our servlet class from this class and we overrode the `service()` method.

#### *The javax.servlet.http.HttpServletRequest interface*

The `HttpServletRequest` interface extends `ServletRequest` and provides an HTTP-specific view of the request. It defines methods that extract information, such as HTTP headers and cookies, from the request.

#### *The javax.servlet.http.HttpServletResponse interface*

The `HttpServletResponse` interface extends `ServletResponse` and provides an HTTP-specific way of sending responses. It defines methods that assist in setting information, such as HTTP headers and cookies, into the response.

### 1.4.3 Advantages and disadvantages of the Servlet API

The advantages of the Servlet API are:

- *Flexibility.* Each time we need to add a new functionality to the server, all we have to do is write a new servlet specific to that set of requirements and plug it into the server, without modifying the server itself.
- *Separation of responsibilities.* The main server now only needs to worry about the network connections and communications part. The job of interpreting requests and creating appropriate responses is delegated to the servlets.
- *It's Java.* Java programmers don't need to learn a new scripting language. Also, they can use all the object-oriented features provided by Java.
- *Portability.* We can develop and test a servlet in one container and deploy it in another. Unlike proprietary solutions, the Servlet API is independent of web servers and servlet containers. We can "write once, run anywhere," as long as the containers support the standard Servlet API.

One obvious limitation, or rather restriction, of the Servlet API is one that is common to all kinds of frameworks: you have to stick to the rules set forth by the framework. This means we have to follow certain conventions to make the servlet container happy.

Another disadvantage involves the containers available in the market and not the Servlet API itself. Theoretically, using the API, you can write servlets for almost any kind of protocol, including FTP, SMTP, or even proprietary protocols. Nevertheless, it would not be fair to expect the servlet container providers to build support for all of them. As of now, the Servlet specification mandates support only for HTTP through the `javax.servlet.http` package.

## 1.5 *SUMMARY*

In this chapter, we learned about the basics of servlets and the servlet container, and how they provide extensions to a server's functionality. We also ran a sample `Hello World` servlet that displayed a line of text in the browser window. Finally, we looked at the Servlet API and its classes and interfaces.

Armed with this knowledge, we can now answer the question "What is a servlet?" from several different perspectives. Conceptually, a servlet is a piece of code that can be:

- Plugged into an existing server to extend the server functionality
- Used to generate the desired output dynamically

For a servlet container, a servlet is:

- A Java class like any other normal Java class
- A class that implements the `javax.servlet.Servlet` interface

For a web component developer, a servlet, or specifically an HTTP servlet, is a class that:

- Extends `javax.servlet.http.HttpServlet`
- Resides in a servlet container (such as Tomcat or JRun)
- Serves HTTP requests

CHAPTER 2

# *Understanding JavaServer Pages*



## INTRODUCTION

Part three of this book addresses the exam objectives that apply to JavaServer Pages. For those of you who are just learning about the JSP technology, this chapter will give you all the information you need to get started.

## 2.1 WHAT IS A JSP PAGE?

A JSP page is a web page that contains Java code along with the HTML tags. Like any other web page, a JSP page has a unique URL, which is used by the clients to access the page. When accessed by a client, the Java code within the page is executed on the server side, producing textual data. This data, which is surrounded by HTML tags, is sent as a normal HTML page to the client. Since the Java code embedded in a JSP page is processed on the server side, the client has no knowledge of the code. The code is replaced by the HTML generated by the Java code before the page is sent to the client. Before we discuss how to create JSP pages, let's discuss the need for such a technology.

### 2.1.1 Server-side includes

HTML is a markup language that specifies how to label different parts of data for visual presentation. The hyperlinks provide a way to jump from one piece of information to another. However, the content is already inside the HTML tags. The tags do not create it; they merely decorate it for presentation. HTML by itself produces static web pages, but today, it is necessary for most web sites to have dynamic content. To generate the content dynamically, we need something that can allow us to specify business logic and that can generate data in response to a request. The data can then be formatted using HTML.

A dynamic web page consists of markup language code as well as programming language code. Instead of serving the page as is to the clients, a server processes the programming language code, replaces the code with the data generated by the code, and then sends the page to the client. This methodology of embedding programming languages within HTML is called the *server-side include* and the programming language that is embedded within the HTML is called the *scripting language*. For example, Netscape's Server-Side JavaScript (SSJS) and Microsoft's Active Server Pages (ASP) are examples of server-side includes. They use JavaScript and VBScript, respectively, as the scripting languages. JavaServer Pages (JSP) is the name of the technology that provides a standard specification for combining Java as the scripting language with HTML. It forms the presentation layer of Sun's Java 2 Enterprise Edition (J2EE) architecture.

The JSP specification lists the syntax and describes the semantics of the various elements that make up a JSP page. These elements are called *JSP tags*. Thus, a JSP page is an HTML template made up of intermixed active JSP tags and passive HTML tags. At runtime, the template is used to generate a purely HTML page, which is sent to the client.

## 2.2 HELLO USER

To see the benefits of JSP, let's look at the following example. We have written it three times: first as an HTML page, then as a servlet, and finally as a JSP page. The purpose of the example is to greet the visitors to a web page with the word `Hello`.

### 2.2.1 The HTML code

Let's start with some simple HTML code, shown in listing 2.1.

**Listing 2.1 Hello.html**

```
<html>
<body>
<h3>Hello User</h3>
</body>
</html>
```

When accessed with the URL `http://localhost:8080/chapter02/Hello.html`, the code in listing 2.1 prints `Hello User`. However, since HTML is static, it cannot print the user's name. For example, printing either `Hello John` or `Hello Mary` (depending on the user's input) is not possible when using a pure HTML page. It will print the same two words—`Hello User`—regardless of the user.

### 2.2.2 The servlet code

To implement this example using a servlet, we will write the `service()` method shown in listing 2.2.

**Listing 2.2 HelloServlet.java**

```
public void service(HttpServletRequest request,
                    HttpServletResponse response)
            throws ServletException,
                   IOException
{
   //Get the user's name from request parameters
   String userName = request.getParameter("userName");

   PrintWriter pw = response.getWriter();
   pw.println("<html>");
   pw.println("<body>");
   pw.println("<h3>Hello " + userName + "</h3>");
   pw.println("</body>");
   pw.println("</html>");
}
```

When accessed with the URL `http://localhost:8080/chapter02/servlets/HelloServlet?userName=John`, the code in listing 2.2 prints `Hello John`. The user's name is passed to the servlet as part of the URL. The `service()` method sends it back to the browser as part of the generated HTML.

### 2.2.3 The JSP code

Listing 2.3 contains the JSP code that is equivalent to the previous servlet code.

**Listing 2.3 Hello.jsp**

```
<html>
<body>
<h3>Hello <%=request.getParameter("userName")%> </h3>
</body>
</html>
```

When accessed with the URL `http://localhost:8080/chapter02/Hello.jsp?userName=John`, the code in listing 2.3 prints `Hello John`. Again, the user's name is passed to the JSP page as part of the URL.

As you can see from this example, a JSP page contains standard HTML tags. Unlike servlets, it does not involve the explicit writing and compilation of a Java class by the page author. What gives it the power of dynamically generating the greeting is the small amount of JSP code enclosed within the characters `<%=` and `%>`.

## 2.3 SERVLET OR JSP?

Well, if servlets can do whatever JSP pages can, and vice versa, what is the difference between them? And if JSP pages are that easy to write, why bother learning about servlets?

You will recall from the first chapter that servlets are server extensions and provide extra functionality to the main server. This could include implementation of specialized services, such as authentication, authorization, database validation, and transaction management. Servlets act as controller components that control the business logic. They are developed by Java programmers with strong object-oriented programming skills.

On the other hand, JavaServer Pages are web pages. They are similar in structure to HTML pages at design time. Any web page designer who has some knowledge of JSP tags and the basics of Java can write JSP pages.

Web applications typically consist of a combination of servlets and JSP pages. A user-authentication process that accepts login and password information is a good example. The code that generates the HTML FORM, success and error messages, and so forth should be in a JSP page, while the code that accesses the database, validates the password, and authenticates the user should be in a servlet.

Keep these conventions in mind:

- JSP pages are meant for visual presentation.
- Business logic is deferred to servlets.

## 2.4 JSP ARCHITECTURE MODELS

The JSP tutorials from Sun describe two architectural approaches for building applications using the JSP and servlet technology. These approaches are called the JSP Model 1 and JSP Model 2 architectures. The difference between the two lies in the way they handle the requests.

### 2.4.1 The Model 1 architecture

In the Model 1 architecture, the target of every request is a JSP page. This page is completely responsible for doing all the tasks required for fulfilling the request. This includes authenticating the client, using JavaBeans to access the data, managing the state of the user, and so forth. This architecture is illustrated in figure 2.1.

As you can see in figure 2.1, there is no central component that controls the workflow of the application. This architecture is suitable for simple applications. However, it has some serious drawbacks that limit its usage for complex applications. First, it requires embedding business logic using big chunks of Java code into the JSP page. This creates a problem for the web page designers who are usually not comfortable

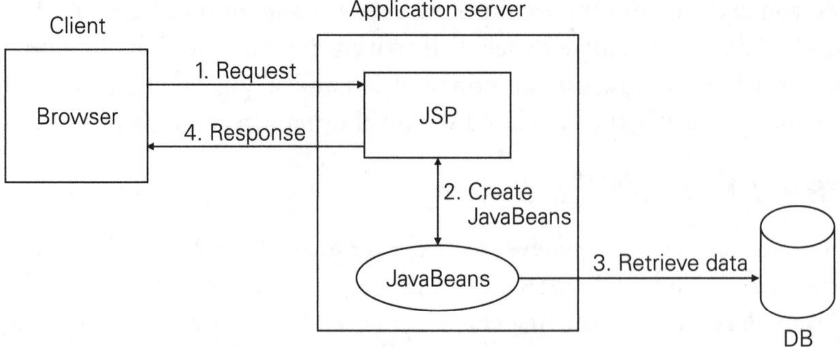


**Figure 2.1 The JSP Model 1 architecture.**

with the server-side programming. Second, this approach does not promote reusability of application components. For example, the code written in a JSP page for authenticating a user cannot be reused in other JSP pages.

### 2.4.2 The Model 2 architecture

This architecture follows the Model-View-Controller (MVC) design pattern (which we will discuss in chapter 17, "Design patterns."). In this architecture, the targets of all the requests are servlets that act as the controller for the application. They analyze the request and collect the data required to generate a response into JavaBeans objects, which act as the model for the application. Finally, the controller servlets dispatch the request to JSP pages. These pages use the data stored in the JavaBeans to generate a presentable response. Thus, the JSP pages form the view of the application. Figure 2.2 illustrates this architecture.

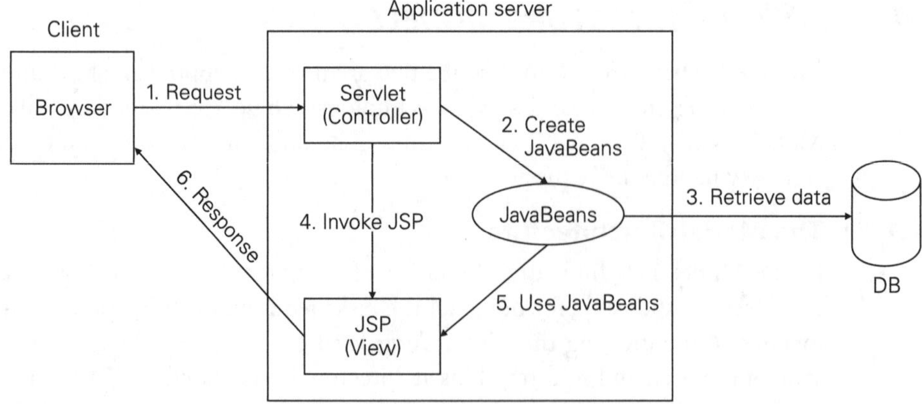


**Figure 2.2 The JSP Model 2 architecture.**

The biggest advantage of this model is the ease of maintenance that results from the separation of responsibilities. The Controller presents a single point of entry into the application, providing a cleaner means of implementing security and state management; these components can be reused as needed. Then, depending on the client's request, the Controller forwards the request to the appropriate presentation component, which in turn replies to the client. This helps the web page designers by letting them work only with the presentation of the data, since the JSP pages do not require any complex business logic. In this way, it satisfactorily solves the problems associated with the Model 1 architecture.

## 2.5 A NOTE ABOUT JSP SYNTAX

Since this book is specifically meant for the SCWCD exam, its chapters are designed according to the exam objectives specified by Sun. The JSP syntax elements are spread over multiple sections in the exam specification, and therefore, we have spread out the explanations of the elements over several chapters in the book. Table 2.1 contains all of the JSP elements and points out which of them are covered in the exam and which are not. It also documents in which exam objective sections these elements are addressed and where you can find explanations in this book.

**Table 2.1 JSP syntax elements**

| Elements | | Exam Objective Section/Subsection | Book Section |
|---|---|---|---|
| Directives | | 8.1 | 11.1.1 |
| | page | 8.4 | 11.3 |
| | include | 9.1 | 13.1 |
| | taglib | 11 and 12 | 15 and 16 |
| Declarations | | 8.1 | 11.1.2 and 12.1.1 |
| Scriptlets | | 8.1 | 11.1.3 and 12.1.1 |
| | Conditional | 8.7 | 12.1.2 |
| | Iteration | 8.7 | 12.1.2 |
| Expressions | | 8.1 | 11.1.4 and 12.1.3 |
| Actions | | | 11.1.5 |
| | jsp:include | 9.1 | 13.2.1 |
| | jsp:forward | 9.1 | 13.2.2 |
| | jsp:useBean | 10.1 | 14.2.1 |
| | jsp:setProperty | 10.1 | 14.2.2 |
| | jsp:getProperty | 10.1 | 14.2.3 |
| | jsp:plugin | NC | 11.1.5 |
| Comments | | NC | 11.1.6 |
| XML-based syntax | | 8.3 | 12.4 |

NC = Not covered on the exam

## 2.6 SUMMARY

In this chapter, we learned about the basics of JavaServer Pages technology and server-side includes. We briefly compared JSP pages to servlets and discussed when it is appropriate to use one or the other. We also discussed the two JSP architectural models and how they differ in their request-handling process.

CHAPTER 3

# *Web application and HTTP basics*



## INTRODUCTION

In the early years of the Internet, most web sites were constructed entirely of HTML pages. HTML pages are called *static web pages*, since they have all of their content embedded within them and they cannot be modified at execution time. As web technology became more sophisticated, web sites started to incorporate various techniques to create or modify the pages at the time of the user's visit to the site, often in response to the user's input. These are called *dynamic pages*. Today, web sites come in all kinds of styles, and most of them offer at least some type of dynamic features on their pages. The web technologies used to create these dynamic pages include plug-in web components, such as Java Applets or Microsoft ActiveX Controls; programs to build dynamic web pages, such as CGI programs or ASP pages; and n-tier web/distributed systems based on Java Servlets and JavaServer Pages.

## 3.1 WHAT IS A WEB APPLICATION?

An obvious but still accurate definition of a web application is that it is an application that is accessible from the web! A common example of a web application is a web site that provides free e-mail service. It offers all the features of an e-mail client such as Outlook Express; still, it is completely web based. A key benefit of web applications is the ease with which the users can access the applications. All a user needs is a web browser; there is nothing else to be installed on the user's machine. This increases the reach of the applications tremendously while alleviating versioning and upgrading issues.

A *web application* is built of *web components* that perform specific tasks and are able to expose their services over the Web. For example, the `HelloWorldServlet` that we developed in chapter 1 is a *web component*. Since it is complete in itself, it is also a *web application*. In real life, however, a web application consists of multiple servlets, JSP pages, HTML files, image files, and so forth. All of these components coordinate with one another and provide a complete set of services to users.

### 3.1.1 Active and passive resources

One way of categorizing web resources is that they are either *passive* or *active*. A resource is passive when it does not have any processing of its own; active objects have their own processing capabilities.

For example, when a browser sends a request for `www.myserver.com/myfile.html`, the web server at `myserver.com` looks for the `myfile.html` file, a passive resource, and returns it to the browser. Similarly, when a browser sends a request for `www.myserver.com/reportServlet`, the web server at `myserver.com` forwards the request to `reportServlet`, an active resource. The servlet generates the HTML text on the fly and gives it to the web server. The web server, in turn, forwards it to the browser. A passive resource is also called a static resource, since its contents do not change with requests.

A web application is usually a mixture of active and passive resources, but it is the presence of the active resources that make a web application nearly as interactive as normal applications. Active resources in a web application typically provide dynamic content to users and enable them to execute business logic via their browsers.

### 3.1.2 Web applications and the web application server

A web application resides in a web application server (or application server). The application server provides the web application with easy and managed access to the resources of the system. It also provides low-level services, such as the HTTP protocol implementation and database connection management. A servlet container is just a part of an application server. In addition to the servlet container, an application server may provide other J2EE components, such as an EJB container, a JNDI server, and a JMS server. You can find detailed information about J2EE and application servers at `http://java.sun.com/j2ee`. Examples of J2EE application servers include BEA Systems' WebLogic, IBM's WebSphere, and Sun's iPlanet.

A web application is described using a *deployment descriptor*. A deployment descriptor is an XML document named `web.xml`, and it contains the description of all the dynamic components of the web application. For example, this file has an entry for every servlets used in the web application. It also declares the security aspects of the application. An application server uses the deployment descriptor to initialize the components of the web application and to make them available to the clients.

## 3.2 UNDERSTANDING THE HTTP PROTOCOL

Simply put, the Hypertext Transfer Protocol is a request-response-based stateless protocol. A client sends an HTTP request for a resource and the server returns an HTTP response with the desired resource, as shown in figure 3.1.

A client opens a connection to the server and sends an HTTP request message. The client receives an HTTP response message sent by the server and closes the connection. It is stateless because once the server sends the response it forgets about the client. In other words, the response to a request does not depend on any previous requests that the client might have made. From the server's point of view, any request is the first request from the client.

In the case of the Internet, the web browser is an HTTP client, the web server is an HTTP server, and the resources are HTML files, image files, servlets, and so forth. Each resource is identified by a unique *Uniform Resource Identifier* (URI). You will frequently hear three terms used interchangeably: URI, URL, and URN. Although they are similar, they have subtle differences:

- *Uniform Resource Identifier.* A URI is a string that identifies any resource. Identifying the resource may not necessarily mean that we can retrieve it. URI is a superset of URL and URN.
- *Uniform Resource Locator.* URIs that specify common Internet protocols such as HTTP, FTP, and mailto are also called URLs. URL is an informal term and is not used in technical specifications.

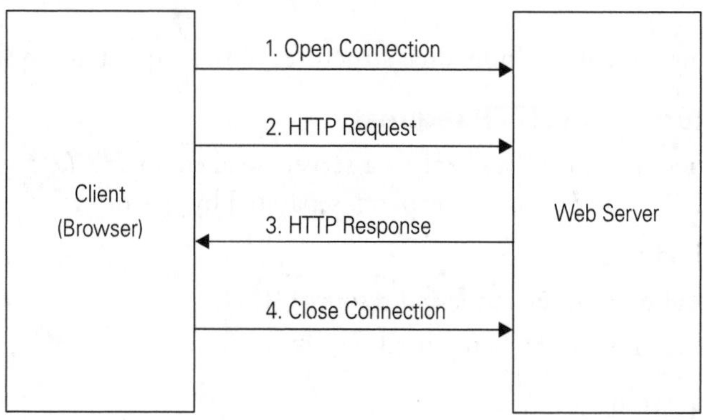


**Figure 3.1 HTTP is a request-response-based stateless protocol.**

- *Uniform Resource Name.* A URN is an identifier that uniquely identifies a resource but does not specify how to access the resource. URNs are standardized by official institutions to maintain the uniqueness of a resource.

Here are some examples:

- `files/sales/report.html` is a URI, because it identifies some resource. However, it is not a URL because it does not specify how to retrieve the resource. It is not a URN either, because it does not identify the resource uniquely.
- `http://www.manning.com/files/sales/report.html` is a URL because it also specifies how to retrieve the resource.
- `ISBN:1-930110-59-6` is a URN because it uniquely identifies this book, but it is not a URL because it does not indicate how to retrieve the book.

For more details on these terms, visit `www.w3c.org`.

### 3.2.1 HTTP basics

An HTTP message is any request from a client to a server, or any response from a server to a client.

The formats of the request and response messages are similar and are in plain English. Table 3.1 lists the parts of an HTTP message.

**Table 3.1 The parts of an HTTP message**

| Message part | Description |
|---|---|
| The initial line | Specifies the purpose of the request or response message |
| The header section | Specifies the meta-information, such as size, type, and encoding, about the content of the message |
| A blank line | |
| An optional message body | The main content of the request or response message |

All the lines end with `CRLF`—that is, ASCII values 13 (Carriage Return) and 10 (Line Feed).

Let us now look at the individual structures of the request and response messages.

### 3.2.2 The structure of an HTTP request

An HTTP message sent by a client to a server is called an *HTTP request.* The initial line for an HTTP request has three parts, separated by spaces:

- A method name
- The local path of the requested resource (URI)
- The version of HTTP being used

A typical request line is:

```
GET /reports/sales/index.html HTTP/1.0
```

Here, GET is the method name, `/report/sales/index.html` is the resource URI, and `HTTP/1.0` is the HTTP version of the request.

The method name specifies the action that the client is requesting the server to perform. HTTP 1.0 requests can have only one of the following three methods: GET, HEAD, or POST. HTTP 1.1 adds five more: PUT, OPTIONS, DELETE, TRACE, and CONNECT.

### GET

The HTTP GET method is used to retrieve a resource. It means, "*get* the resource identified by this URI." The resource is usually a passive resource. A GET request may be used for an active resource if there are few or no parameters to be passed. If parameters are required, they are passed by appending a query string to the URI. For example, figure 3.2 illustrates the initial request line for passing `john` as a `userid`.

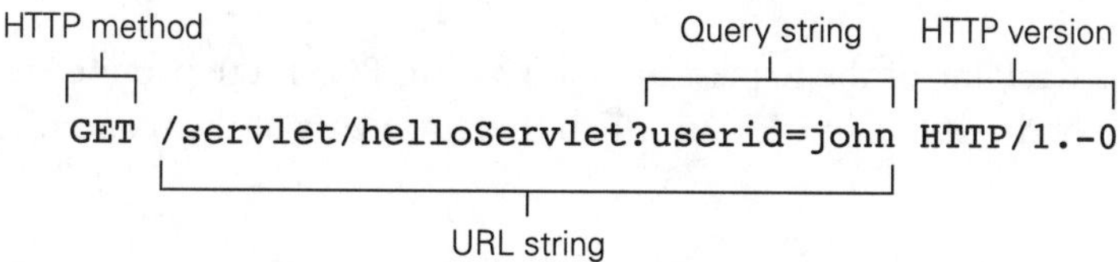


**Figure 3.2 An initial request line using GET and a query string.**

The part after the question mark is called a *query string*. It consists of parameter name-value pairs separated by an ampersand (&), as in:

```
name1=value1&name2=value2&…&nameM=valueM
```

In the example in figure 3.2, `userid` is the parameter name and `john` is the value.

### HEAD

An HTTP HEAD request is used to retrieve the meta-information about a resource. Therefore, the response for a HEAD request contains only the header. The structure of a HEAD request is exactly the same as that of a GET request.

HEAD is commonly used to check the time when the resource was last modified on the server before sending it to the client. A HEAD request can save a lot of bandwidth, especially if the resource is very big, since the actual resource would not have to be sent if the client already had the latest version.

### POST

A POST request is used to send data to the server in order to be processed. It means, "*post* the data to the active resource identified by this URI." The block of data is sent in the message body. Usually, to describe this message body, extra lines are present in the header, such as `Content-Type` and `Content-Length`.

HTML pages use POST to submit HTML FORM data. Figure 3.3 shows an example of an HTTP POST request generated by a typical form submission. The value of `Content-Type` is `application/x-www-form-urlencoded`, and the value of `Content-Length` is the length of the URL-encoded form data.

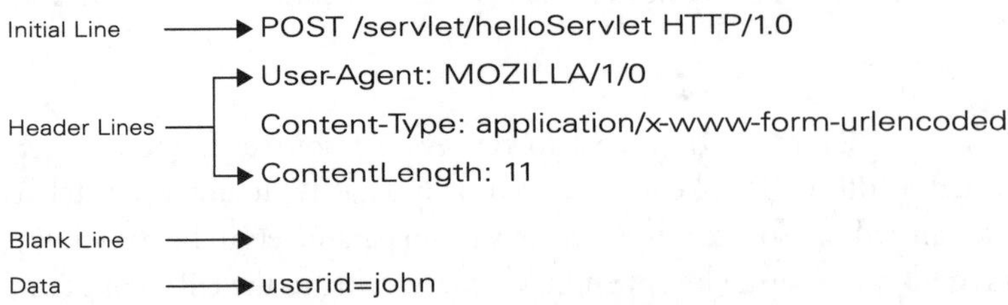


**Figure 3.3 A POST request as generated by a form submission.**

Observe the data line of the request in figure 3.3. In POST, the parameters are sent in the message body, unlike in GET, in which they are a part of the request URI.

### *PUT*

A PUT request is used to add a resource to the server. It means, "*put* the data sent in the message body and associate it with the given `Request-URI`." For example, when we PUT a local file named `sample.html` to the server `myhome.com` using the URI `http://www.myhome.com/files/example.html`, the file becomes a resource on that server and is associated with the URI `http://www.myhome.com/files/example.html`. The name of the file (`sample.html`) on the client machine is irrelevant on the server. This request is mainly used to publish files on the server.

**NOTE** There is a subtle difference between a POST and a PUT request. POST means we are sending some data to a resource for processing. On the other hand, a PUT request means we are sending some data that we want to be associated with a URI.

We will not describe the remaining four HTTP methods (OPTIONS, DELETE, TRACE, and CONNECT) because they are rarely used and are not mentioned in the exam objectives. If you want to learn more about them, please read the HTTP 1.1 specification at `www.w3.org/Protocols/rfc2068/rfc2068`. For your convenience, we have included this RFC on the CD that accompanies this book.

## 3.2.3 The structure of an HTTP response

An HTTP message sent by a server to a client is called an HTTP response. The initial line of an HTTP response is called the status line. It has three parts, separated by spaces: the HTTP version, a response status code that tells the result of the request, and an English phrase describing the status code. HTTP defines many status codes; common ones that you may have noticed are 200 and 404. Here are two examples of a status line that could be sent in the response:

```
HTTP/1.0 200 OK

HTTP/1.0 404 Not Found
```

When the browser receives a status code that implies a problem, it displays an appropriate message to the user. If some data is associated with the response, headers like `Content-Type` and `Content-Length` that describe the data may also be present.

A typical HTTP response looks like this:

```
HTTP/1.0 200 OK
Date: Tue, 01 Dec 2001 23:59:59 GMT
Content-Type: text/html
Content-Length: 52

<html>
<body>
   <h1>Hello, John!</h1>
</body>
</html>
```

## 3.3 SUMMARY

A web application is a collection of web components that perform specific tasks and allow the users to access business logic via their browsers.

In this chapter, we introduced the basic concepts of HTTP, the Hypertext Transfer Protocol. We examined the structure of the HTTP request, including GET, HEAD, POST, and PUT, as well as the structure of the HTTP response.

# PART 2

# *Servlets*

In the Java world, servlets are the cornerstone of web component technology. In this part of the book, we discuss aspects of the Servlet technology that you need to know, as specified by the exam objectives.

CHAPTER 4

# The Servlet model



## EXAM OBJECTIVES

**1.1** For each of the HTTP methods, GET, POST, and PUT, identify the corresponding method in the HttpServlet class. (Section 4.2)

**1.2** For each of the HTTP methods, GET, POST, and HEAD, identify triggers that might cause a browser to use the method, and identify benefits or functionality of the method. (Section 4.1)

**1.3** For each of the following operations, identify the interface and method name that should be used:

- Retrieve HTML form parameters from the request
- Retrieve a servlet initialization parameter
- Retrieve HTTP request header information
- Set an HTTP response header; set the content type of the response
- Acquire a text stream for the response
- Acquire a binary stream for the response
- Redirect an HTTP request to another URL

(Sections 4.3–4.6)

**1.4** Identify the interface and method to access values and resources and to set object attributes within the following three web scopes:

- Request
- Session
- Context

(Sections 4.6–4.8)

**1.5** Given a life-cycle method: init, service, or destroy, identify correct statements about its purpose or about how and when it is invoked. (Section 4.5)

**1.6** Use a RequestDispatcher to include or forward to a web resource. (Sections 4.6–4.8)

## INTRODUCTION

Java Servlet technology is commonly used to handle the business logic of a web application, although servlets may also contain presentation logic. We discussed the basics of Java servlets in chapter 1. In this chapter, we will take a closer look at the Servlet model.

The Servlet specification applies to any protocol, but in practice, most servlets are written for the HTTP protocol, which is why the SCWCD exam focuses on HTTP servlets. In this context, whenever we talk about *servlets*, we mean `HttpServlets`. Similarly, by *client* and *server*, we mean HTTP client and HTTP server, respectively.

This chapter is lengthy, and while it introduces many concepts about servlets, it will not provide in-depth discussions. Don't worry; at this point, we want you to get familiar with the servlet model without getting lost in the details. We will cover all of these concepts in detail in later chapters.

## 4.1 SENDING REQUESTS: WEB BROWSERS AND HTTP METHODS

As we discussed in chapter 3, the HTTP protocol consists of requests from the client to the server, and the responses from the server back to the client. Let's look at the request first. A web browser sends an HTTP request to a web server when any of the following events happen:

- A user clicks on a hyperlink displayed in an HTML page.
- A user fills out a form in an HTML page and submits it.
- A user enters a URL in the browser's address field and presses Enter.

Other events trigger a browser to send a request to a web server; for instance, a JavaScript function may call the `reload()` method on the current document. Ultimately, however, all such triggers boil down to one of the three events listed above, because such method calls are nothing but programmatic simulations of the user's actions.

By default, the browser uses the HTTP GET method in all of the above events. However, we can customize the browser's behavior to use different HTTP methods.

For example, the following HTML FORM forces the browser to use the HTTP POST method via the method attribute:

```
<FORM name='loginForm' method='POST' action='/loginServlet'>
<input type='text' name='userid'>
<input type='password' name='passwd'>
<input type='submit' name='loginButton' value='Login'>
</FORM>
```

**NOTE** If you do not specify the method attribute in a `<FORM>` tag, the browser uses GET by default. Conventionally, however, FORM is used to POST the data and so you have to explicitly specify `METHOD='POST'` in the `<FORM>` tag.

In the following section, we will look at other situations in which we might need to force the browser to use POST instead of GET.

### 4.1.1 Comparing HTTP methods

For the exam, you will be required to demonstrate that you understand both the benefits and functionality of these HTTP methods:

- GET
- POST
- HEAD

We have already seen their basic structure and meaning in chapter 3. Now we will look at the difference between their usages, and identify the situations in which one method is preferred over the other.

Table 4.1 compares the features of GET and POST.

**Table 4.1 Comparison of GET and POST methods**

| Feature | GET Method | POST Method |
|---|---|---|
| Target resource type | Active or passive. | Active. |
| Type of data | Text. | Text as well as Binary. |
| Amount of data | Maximum 255 chars. Although the HTTP protocol does not limit the length of the query string, some browsers and web servers may not be able to handle more than 255. | Unlimited. |
| Visibility | Data is part of the URL and is visible to the user in the URL field of the browser. | Data is not a part of the URL and is sent as the request message body. It is not visible to the user in the URL field of the browser. |
| Caching | Data can be cached in the browser's URL history. | Data is not cached in the browser's URL history. |

Based on table 4.1, we can make some generalizations about when to use each method.

Use GET:

- To retrieve an HTML file or an image file, because only the filename needs to be sent.

Use POST:

- To send a lot of data; for example, POST is well suited for an online survey, since the length of the query string may exceed 255 characters.
- To upload a file, because the file size may exceed 255 characters, and moreover, the file may be a binary file.
- To capture the username and password, because we want to prevent users from seeing the password as a part of the URL.

Recall from chapter 3 that HEAD is the same as GET except that for a HEAD request, the server returns only the response header and not the message body. This makes HEAD more efficient than GET in cases where we need only the response header. For example, a response header contains the modification timestamp, which can be used to determine the staleness of a resource.

In general, clicking on a hyperlink or using the browser's address field causes the browser to send a GET request. We can, of course, attach a JavaScript function, `onClick()`, to programmatically submit a form, thereby causing a POST request to be sent. However, that is not what we are concerned about for the purpose of the exam.

*Quizlet*

**Q:** A developer wants to upload a file from the browser to the server. The following is the HTML snippet from the HTML page that she wrote:

```
<FORM name='uploader' action='/saveServlet'
                      enctype='multipart/form-data' >
<input type='file' name='file'>
<input type='submit' name='uploadButton' value='Upload'>
</FORM>
```

What is wrong with this code snippet?

**A:** The contents of the file must be sent to the server using a POST request. However, the HTML FORM used in this code does not have any method attribute; therefore, a GET request will be sent. The developer must specify the `<FORM>` tag like this:

```
<FORM name='uploader' action='/saveServlet'
      enctype='multipart/form-data' method='POST'>
```

## 4.2 HANDLING HTTP REQUESTS IN AN HTTPSERVLET

In the previous section, we discussed three commonly used HTTP methods, their features and limitations, and the situations in which these methods are used. In this section, we will explore what happens when an HTTP request reaches an HTTP servlet.

For every HTTP method, there is a corresponding method in the `HttpServlet` class of type:

```
public void doXXX(HttpServletRequest, HttpServletResponse)
                        throws ServletException, IOException;
```

where do*XXX*() depends on the HTTP method, as shown in table 4.2.

**Table 4.2 HTTP methods and the corresponding servlet methods**

| HTTP Method | HttpServlet Method |
|---|---|
| GET | doGet() |
| HEAD | doHead() |
| POST | doPost() |
| PUT | doPut() |
| DELETE | doDelete() |
| OPTIONS | doOptions() |
| TRACE | doTrace() |

The `HttpServlet` class provides empty implementations for each of the do*XXX*() methods. We should override the do*XXX*() methods to implement our business logic.

### *Understanding the sequence of events in HttpServlet*

You may now wonder who calls the do*XXX*() methods. Here is the flow of control from the servlet container to the do*XXX*() methods of a servlet:

1. The servlet container calls the `service(ServletRequest, ServletResponse)` method of `HttpServlet`.
2. The `service(ServletRequest, ServletResponse)` method of `HttpServlet` calls the `service(HttpServletRequest, HttpServletResponse)` method of the same class. Observe that the service method is overloaded in the `HttpServlet` class.
3. The `service(HttpServletRequest, HttpServletResponse)` method of `HttpServlet` analyzes the request and finds out which HTTP method is being used. Depending on the HTTP method, it calls the corresponding do*XXX*() method of the servlet. For example, if the request uses the POST method, it calls the `doPost()` method of the servlet.

**NOTE** If you override the service methods in your servlet class, you will lose the functionality provided by the `HttpServlet` class, and the do*XXX*() methods will not be called automatically. In your implementation, you will have to determine the HTTP method used in the request, and then you will have to call the appropriate do*XXX*() method yourself.

All of the do*XXX*() methods take two parameters: an `HttpServletRequest` object and an `HttpServletResponse` object. We will learn about these objects in the following sections.

But first, here's a note about the Servlet API: Most of the important components of the Servlet API, including `HttpServletRequest` and `HttpServletResponse`, are interfaces. The servlet container provides the classes that implement these interfaces. So, whenever we say something like "an `HttpServletRequest` object," we mean "an object of a class that implements the `HttpServletRequest` interface." The name of the actual class is not significant and is, in fact, unknown to the developer.

*Quizlet*

**Q:** Which method of TestServlet will be called when a user clicks on the following URL?

```
<a href="/servlet/TestServlet" method="POST">Test URL</a>
```

**A:** The `method="POST"` attribute-value pair does not make sense in the `<a href>` tag. Clicking on a hyperlink always sends a GET request and thus, the `doGet()` method of the servlet will be called.

## 4.3 ANALYZING THE REQUEST

Both `ServletRequest` and its subclass, `HttpServletRequest`, allow us to analyze a request. They provide us with a view of the data sent by the browser. The data includes parameters, meta information, and a text or binary data stream.

`ServletRequest` provides methods that are relevant to any protocol, while `HttpServletRequest` extends `ServletRequest` and adds methods specific to HTTP. It is for this reason that the `ServletRequest` interface belongs to the `javax.servlet` package and the `HttpServletRequest` interface belongs to the `javax.servlet.http` package.

We always use the `HttpServletRequest` class, but it is important to know which methods are implemented in the `HttpServletRequest` class and which methods are inherited from the `ServletRequest` class.

### 4.3.1 Understanding ServletRequest

The primary use of `ServletRequest` is to retrieve the parameters sent by a client. Table 4.3 describes the methods provided to retrieve the parameters.

**Table 4.3 Methods provided by ServletRequest for retrieving client-sent parameters**

| Method | Description |
|---|---|
| String getParameter(String paramName) | This method returns just one of the values associated with the given parameter. |
| String[] getParameterValues(String paramName) | This method returns all the values associated with the parameter. For example, while doing a job search, you might have seen a "location" list box that allows you to select multiple states. In this case, the parameter "location" may have multiple values. |

*continued on next page*

Table 4.3 **Methods provided by ServletRequest for retrieving client-sent parameters** ***(continued)***

| Method | Description |
|---|---|
| Enumeration getParameterNames() | This method is useful when you don't know the names of the parameters. You can iterate through the Enumeration of Strings returned by this method and for each element you can call getParameter() or getParameterValues(). |

## 4.3.2 Understanding HttpServletRequest

The class that implements the `HttpServletRequest` interface implements all of the methods of `ServletRequest` in an HTTP-specific manner. It parses and interprets HTTP messages and provides the relevant information to the servlet.

Let's look at an example of how we can use these methods. Figure 4.1 shows an HTML page that allows a user to send two parameters to the server.

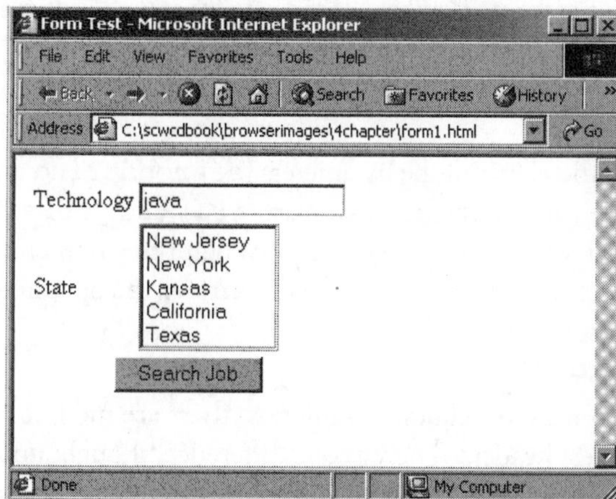


**Figure 4.1 An HTML page containing a FORM.**

Listing 4.1 is the HTML code for this page.

**Listing 4.1 HTML page snippet**

```
<form action="../servlet/TestServlet" method="POST">   <— Uses HTTP POST
Technology : <input type="text" name="searchstring" value="java">
<br><br>
State : <select name="state" size="5" multiple>   <— Allows selection of multiple values
   <option value="NJ">New Jersey</option>
   <option value="NY">New York</option>
   <option value="KS">Kansas</option>
   <option value="CA">California</option>
   <option value="TX">Texas</option>
</select>
<br><br>
<input type="submit" value="Search Job">
</form>
```

This FORM displays a text field, a list box, and a submit button. The action attribute of the FORM specifies that TestServlet should handle the request. Observe that the method attribute of the FORM is set to POST, and so the parameters will be sent to the server using an HTTP POST request.

Once the request is sent to the server, `TestServlet` is invoked. Listing 4.2 shows how `TestServlet`'s `doPost()` method retrieves the parameters that were sent by submitting the form (listing 4.1).

**Listing 4.2 Code for doPost to retrieve parameter values**

```
public void doPost(HttpServletRequest req,
                   HttpServletResponse res)
{
   String searchString = req.getParameter("searchstring");

   String[] stateList = req.getParameterValues("state");

   //use the values and generate appropriate response
}
```

Retrieves searchstring parameter value

Retrieves all the values selected in the state list

In the above code, we know the names of the parameters (`searchstring` and `state`) sent with the request, so we can use the `getParameter()` and `getParameterValues()` methods to retrieve the parameter values. When the parameter values are not known, we can use `getParameterNames()` to retrieve the parameter names.

### *Retrieving request headers*

Just as there are methods to retrieve request parameters, there are methods to retrieve names and values from request headers. There is one difference, though; unlike parameters, headers are specific to the HTTP protocol and so the methods that deal with the headers belong to `HttpServletRequest` and not to `ServletRequest`.

`HttpServletRequest` provides the methods shown in table 4.4 to help us retrieve the header information.

**Table 4.4 HttpServletRequest methods for managing request headers**

| Method | Description |
|---|---|
| String getHeader(String headerName) | This method returns just one of the values associated with the given header. |
| Enumeration getHeaderValues(String headerName) | This method returns all the values associated with the header as an Enumeration of String object. |
| Enumeration getHeaderNames() | This method is useful when you don't know the names of the headers. You can iterate through the enumeration returned by this method, and for each element you can call getHeader() or getHeaderValues(). |

Let's see how we can use the methods described in table 4.4. The `service()` method code shown in listing 4.3 prints out all the headers present in a request.

**Listing 4.3 Printing out all the headers on the console**

```
public void service(HttpServletRequest req,
                    HttpServletResponse res)
{
   Enumeration headers = req.getHeaderNames();   <-- Retrieves header names
   while (headers.hasMoreElements())
   {
      String header = (String) headers.nextElement();
      String value = req.getHeader(header);      <-- Retrieves header values
      System.out.println(header+" = "+value);
   }
}
```

There are other convenience methods in `ServletRequest` and in `HttpServletRequest` that we will not discuss here, since they are not required for the exam. To learn more about them, please refer to the Servlet API documentation.

*Quizlet*

**Q:** Which method would you use to retrieve the number of parameters present in a request?

**A:** Neither `ServletRequest` nor `HttpServletRequest` provides any method to retrieve the number of parameters directly. You'll have to use `ServletRequest.getParameterNames()`, which returns an Enumeration, and count the number of parameters yourself.

## 4.4 SENDING THE RESPONSE

The `HttpServletResponse` object is a servlet's gateway to send information back to the browser. It accepts the data that the servlet wants to send to the client and formats it into an HTTP message as per the HTTP specification.

`ServletResponse` provides methods that are relevant to any protocol, while `HttpServletResponse` extends `ServletResponse` and adds HTTP-specific methods. Not surprisingly, the `ServletResponse` interface belongs to the `javax.servlet` package and the `HttpServletResponse` interface belongs to the `javax.servlet.http` package.

### 4.4.1 Understanding ServletResponse

`ServletResponse` declares several generic methods, including `getWriter()`, `getOutputStream()`, `setContentType()`, and so forth. We will now discuss two methods that you need to understand for the purpose of the exam.

### *Using PrintWriter*

Let's first look at the `getWriter()` method of `ServletResponse`. This method returns an object of class `java.io.PrintWriter` that can be used to send character data to the client. PrintWriter is extensively used by servlets to generate HTML pages dynamically. Listing 4.4 demonstrates its use by sending the header information of a request to the browser.

**Listing 4.4 Writing HTML code dynamically**

```
import java.io.*;
import java.util.*;
import javax.servlet.*;
import javax.servlet.http.*;

public class ShowHeadersServlet extends HttpServlet
{
   public void doGet(HttpServletRequest req, HttpServletResponse res)
                        throws ServletException, IOException
   {
      PrintWriter pw = res.getWriter();   <-- Gets the PrintWriter object

      pw.println("<html>");
      pw.println("<head>");          Uses PrintWriter to write
      pw.println("</head>");         the HTML page
      pw.println("<body>");

      pw.println("<h3>Following are the headers that the
                       server received.</h3><p>");

      Enumeration headers = req.getHeaderNames();
      while(headers.hasMoreElements())
      {
         String header = (String) headers.nextElement();
         String value = req.getHeader(header);

         pw.println(header+" = "+value+"<br>");
      }
      pw.println("</body>");
      pw.println("</html>");
   }
}
```

In listing 4.4, we use the `getWriter()` method to retrieve the `PrintWriter` object. Since the header information is available only at runtime, we use the `getHeaderNames()` and `getHeader()` methods to retrieve that information, and then we write the values using the `PrintWriter` object to create the HTML tags dynamically.

### *Using ServletOutputStream*

If we want to send a binary file, for example a JAR file, to the client, we will need an OutputStream instead of a PrintWriter. `ServletResponse` provides the `getOutputStream()` method that returns an object of class `javax.servlet.ServletOutputStream`. In listing 4.5, we have changed the `doGet()` method of the previous example to send a JAR file to the browser.

**Listing 4.5 Sending a JAR file to the browser**

```
public void doGet(HttpServletRequest req,
                  HttpServletResponse res)
                  throws ServletException, IOException
{
   res.setContentType("application/jar");   <-- Sets the content type

   File f = new File("test.jar");
   byte[] bytearray = new byte[(int) f.length()];      Reads the file into
   FileInputStream is = new FileInputStream(f);        a byte array
   is.read(bytearray);

   OutputStream os = res.getOutputStream();   <-- Gets the OutputStream

   os.write(bytearray);   <-- Sends the bytes of the byte array to the browser

   os.flush();   <-- Flushes the data
}
```

In listing 4.5, we retrieve the OutputStream using the `getOutputStream()` method. We simply read the contents of a JAR file into a byte array and write the byte array to the OutputStream.

Observe that we are calling the `setContentType()` method before calling the `getOutputStream()` method. The `setContentType()` method allows us to specify the type of data we are sending in the response. We must call this method to set the content type of the response before retrieving the OutputStream. This method belongs to the `ServletResponse` interface and is declared as shown in table 4.5.

**Table 4.5 The method provided by ServletResponse for setting the content type of the response**

| Method | Description |
|---|---|
| public void setContentType(String type) | This method is used to set the content type of the response. The content type may include the type of character encoding used, for example, text/html; charset=ISO-8859-4. This method should be called before getting the OutputStream from the Servlet-Response. If this method is not called, the content type is assumed to be text/html. The following are some commonly used values for the content type: text/html, image/jpeg, video/quicktime, application/java, text/css, and text/javascript. |

You might have also noticed that in the line `File f = new File("test.jar");` we are hard-coding the filename to `test.jar`. This requires the file `test.jar` to be in the `bin` directory of Tomcat. We will come back to this later in section 4.7 to learn a better way of specifying the file.

**NOTE** An important point to note about the `getWriter()` and `getOutputStream()` methods is that you can call only one of them on an instance of `ServletResponse`. For example, if you have already called the `getWriter()` method on a `ServletResponse` object, you cannot call the `getOutputStream()` method on the same `ServletResponse` object. If you do, the `getOutputStream()` method will throw an `IllegalStateException`. You can call the same method multiple times, though.

### 4.4.2 Understanding HttpServletResponse

HttpServletResponse declares HTTP-specific methods such as `setHeader()`, `setStatus()`, `sendRedirect()`, and `sendError()`. In this section, we will learn how to use this interface.

#### *Setting the response headers*

We use headers to convey additional information about the response by setting name-value pairs. For example, we can use a header to tell the browser to reload the page it is displaying every 5 minutes, or to specify how long the browser can cache the page. As shown in table 4.6, the `HttpServletResponse` interface provides seven methods for header management.

**Table 4.6 HttpServletResponse methods for managing response headers**

| Method | Description |
|---|---|
| void setHeader(String name, String value) | Used to set the name-value pair for a header in the ServletRequest. |
| void setIntHeader(String name, int value) | Saves you from converting the int value to string. |
| void setDateHeader(String name, long millisecs) | Pretty much the same as above. |
| void addHeader / addIntHeader / addDateHeader | These methods can be used to associate multiple values with the same header. |
| boolean containsHeader(String name) | Returns a Boolean that tells you whether or not a header with this name is already set. |

Table 4.7 shows four important header names. Although on the exam you will not be asked questions based on header names and values, it is good to know some commonly used headers. For a complete list of header names-values, please refer to the HTTP specification.

**Table 4.7 Typical response header names and their uses**

| Header name | Description |
|---|---|
| Date | Specifies the current time at the server. |
| Expires | Specifies the time when the content can be considered stale. |
| Last-Modified | Specifies the time when the document was last modified. |
| Refresh | Tells the browser to reload the page. |

Another useful method related to headers is `addCookie(Cookie c)`. This method lets us set cookies in the response. We will learn about cookies in chapter 8, "Session management."

### *Redirecting the request*

After analyzing a request, a servlet may decide that it needs to redirect the browser to another resource. For example, a company web site may be able to provide only company news. For all other kind of news, it may redirect the browser to another web site. The `HttpServletResponse` class provides the `sendRedirect()` method exactly for this purpose, as shown here:

```
if("companynews".equals(request.getParameter("news_category")))
{
   //retrieve internal company news and generate
   //the page dynamically
}
else
{
   response.sendRedirect("http://www.cnn.com");
}
```

The above code checks the `news_category` parameter to decide whether it should generate a reply on its own or redirect the browser to cnn.com. When the browser receives the redirect message, it automatically goes to the given URL.

We should keep in mind a couple of important points about the `sendRedirect()` method. We cannot call this method if the response is committed—that is, if the response header has already been sent to the browser. If we do, the method will throw a `java.lang.IllegalStateException`. For example, the following code will generate an `IllegalStateException`:

```
public void doGet(HttpServletRequest req, HttpServletResponse res)
{
   PrintWriter pw = res.getPrintWriter();
   pw.println("<html><body>Hello World!</body></html>");
   pw.flush();                                  <— Sends the response
   res.sendRedirect("http://www.cnn.com");      <— Tries to redirect
}
```

In this code, we are forcing the servlet container to send the header and the generated text to the browser immediately by calling `pw.flush()`. The response is said to be *committed* at this point. Calling `sendRedirect()` after committing the response causes the servlet container to throw an `IllegalStateException`. Obviously, there is no point in writing to the response once the user has already received it!

**NOTE** Another important point to understand about `sendRedirect()` is that the browser goes to the second resource only after it receives the redirect message from the first resource. In that sense, `sendRedirect()` is not transparent to the browser. In other words, the servlet sends a message telling the browser to get the resource from elsewhere.

### Sending status codes for error conditions

HTTP defines status codes for common error conditions such as *Resource not found*, *Resource moved permanently*, and *Unauthorized access*. All such codes are defined in the `HttpServletResponse` interface as constants. `HttpServletResponse` also provides `sendError(int status_code)` and `sendError(int status_code, String message)` methods that send a status code to the client. For example, if a servlet finds out that the client should not have access to its output, it may call

```
response.sendError(HttpServletResponse.SC_UNAUTHORIZED);
```

When the browser receives this status code, it displays an appropriate message to the user.

For a complete list of status codes, please refer to the API documentation on `HttpServletResponse`.

*Quizlet*

**Q:** Which methods should you use to do the following?

1 Write HTML tags to the output.
2 Specify that the content of the response is a binary file.
3 Send a binary file to the browser.
4 Add a header to a response.
5 Redirect a browser to another resource.

**A:**
1 First, get the PrintWriter using `ServletResponse.getWriter()` and then call `PrintWriter.print("<html tags>");`
2 Use `ServletResponse.setContentType(String content-type);`
3 Use `ServletResponse.getOutputStream();` and then `OutputStream.write(bytes);`
4 Use `HttpServletResponse.setHeader("name", "value");`
5 Use `HttpServletResponse.sendRedirect(String url-string);`

## 4.5 SERVLET LIFE CYCLE

By now, it should be very clear that a servlet receives a request, processes it, and sends a response back using the do*XXX*() methods. There is, however, a little bit more to understand than just the do*XXX*() methods. Before a servlet can service the client requests, a servlet container must take certain steps in order to bring the servlet to a state in which it is ready to service the requests. The first step is loading and instantiating the servlet class; the servlet is now considered to be in the loaded state. The second step is initializing the servlet instance. Once the servlet is in the initialized state, the container can invoke its `service()` method whenever it receives a request from the client. There may be times when the container will call the `destroy()` method on the servlet instance to put it in the destroyed state. Finally, when the servlet container shuts down, it must unload the servlet instance. Figure 4.2 shows these servlet states and their transitions.

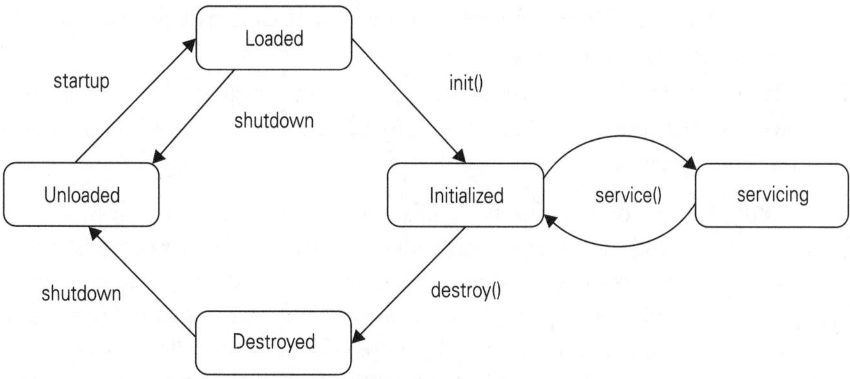


**Figure 4.2 Servlet state transition diagram.**

These states constitute the life cycle of a servlet. Let's take a closer look at them.

### 4.5.1 Loading and instantiating a servlet

When we start up a servlet container, it looks for a set of configuration files, also called the deployment descriptors, that describe all the web applications. Each web application has its own deployment descriptor file, `web.xml`, which includes an entry for each of the servlets it uses. An entry specifies the name of the servlet and a Java class name for the servlet. The servlet container creates an instance of the given servlet class using the method `Class.forName(className).newInstance()`. However, to do this the servlet class must have a public constructor with no arguments. Typically, we do not define any constructor in the servlet class. We let the Java compiler add the default constructor. At this time, the servlet is *loaded.*

### 4.5.2 Initializing a servlet

It is entirely possible that we will want to initialize the servlet with some data when it is instantiated. How can we do that if we do not define a constructor? Good question. It is exactly for this reason that once the container creates the servlet instance, it calls the `init(ServletConfig)` method on this newly created instance. The `ServletConfig` object contains all the initialization parameters that we specify in the deployment descriptor of the web application. We will see how these parameters can be specified in the `web.xml` file in section 4.6.2. The servlet is *initialized* after the `init()` method returns.

This process of initializing a servlet using the initialization parameters from the `ServletConfig` object is quite important in order to ensure the reusability of a servlet. For example, if we wanted to create a database connection in the servlet we would not want to hard-code the username/password and the database URL in the servlet. The `init()` method allows us to specify them in the deployment descriptor. The values in the deployment descriptor can be changed as needed without affecting the servlet code. When the servlet initializes, it can read the values in its `init()` method and make the connection.

It does not make sense to initialize an object repeatedly; therefore, the framework guarantees that the servlet container will call the `init()` method once and only once on a servlet instance.

> **NOTE** If you look up the API for the `GenericServlet` class, you will see that it has two `init()` methods: one with a parameter of type `ServletConfig` as required by the `Servlet` interface and one with no parameters. The no parameter `init()` method is a convenience method that you can override in your servlet class. If you override the `init(ServletConfig config)` method, you will have to include a call to `super.init(config)` in the method so that the `GenericServlet` can store a reference to the config object for future use. To save you from doing that, the GenericServlet's `init(ServletConfig)` method makes a call to the GenericServlet's no parameter `init()` method, which you can implement freely. To get the `ServletConfig` object in the no parameter `init()` method, you can call the `getServletConfig()` method implemented by the `GenericServlet` class.

#### *Preinitializing a servlet*

Usually, a servlet container does not initialize the servlets as soon as it starts up. It initializes a servlet when it receives a request for that servlet for the first time. This is called *lazy loading*. Although this process greatly improves the startup time of the servlet container, it has a drawback. If the servlet performs many tasks at the time of initialization, such as caching static data from a database on initialization, the client that sends the first request will have a poor response time. In many cases, this is unacceptable. The servlet specification defines the `<load-on-startup>` element, which can be specified in the deployment descriptor to make the servlet container load and initialize the servlet as soon as it starts up. This process of loading a servlet before any request comes in is called *preloading*, or *preinitializing*, a servlet.

### 4.5.3 Servicing client requests

After the servlet instance is properly initialized, it is ready to service client requests. When the servlet container receives requests for this servlet, it will dispatch them to the servlet instance by calling the `Servlet.service(ServletRequest, ServletResponse)` method.

### 4.5.4 Destroying a servlet

If the servlet container decides that it no longer needs a servlet instance, it calls the `destroy()` method on the servlet instance. In this method, the servlet should clean up the resources, such as database connections that it acquired in the `init()` method. Once this method is called, the servlet instance will be out of service and the container will never call the `service()` method on this instance. The servlet container cannot reuse this instance in any way. From this state, a servlet instance may only go to the unloaded state. Before calling the `destroy()` method, the servlet container waits for the remaining threads that are executing the servlet's `service()` method to finish.

A servlet container may destroy a servlet if it is running low on resources and no request has arrived for a servlet in a long time. Similarly, if the servlet container maintains a pool of servlet instances, it may create and destroy the instances from time to time as required. A servlet container may also destroy a servlet if it is shutting down.

### 4.5.5 Unloading a servlet

Once destroyed, the servlet instance may be garbage collected, in which case the servlet instance is said to be *unloaded*. If the servlet has been destroyed because the servlet container is shutting down, the servlet class will also be unloaded.

### 4.5.6 Servlet state transition from the servlet container's perspective

Figure 4.3 illustrates the relationship between the servlet container and the life-cycle phases of a servlet.

A servlet goes from the unloaded to the loaded state when a servlet container loads the servlet class and instantiates an object of the class. The servlet container initializes the servlet object by calling its `init()` method, thereby putting it in the initialized state.

The servlet stays in the initialized state until the servlet container decides to destroy the servlet. From the initialized state, the servlet enters the servicing state whenever the servlet container calls its `service()` method in order to process client requests.

The servlet enters the destroyed state when the servlet container calls its `destroy()` method. Finally, the servlet goes to the unloaded state when the servlet instance is garbage collected.

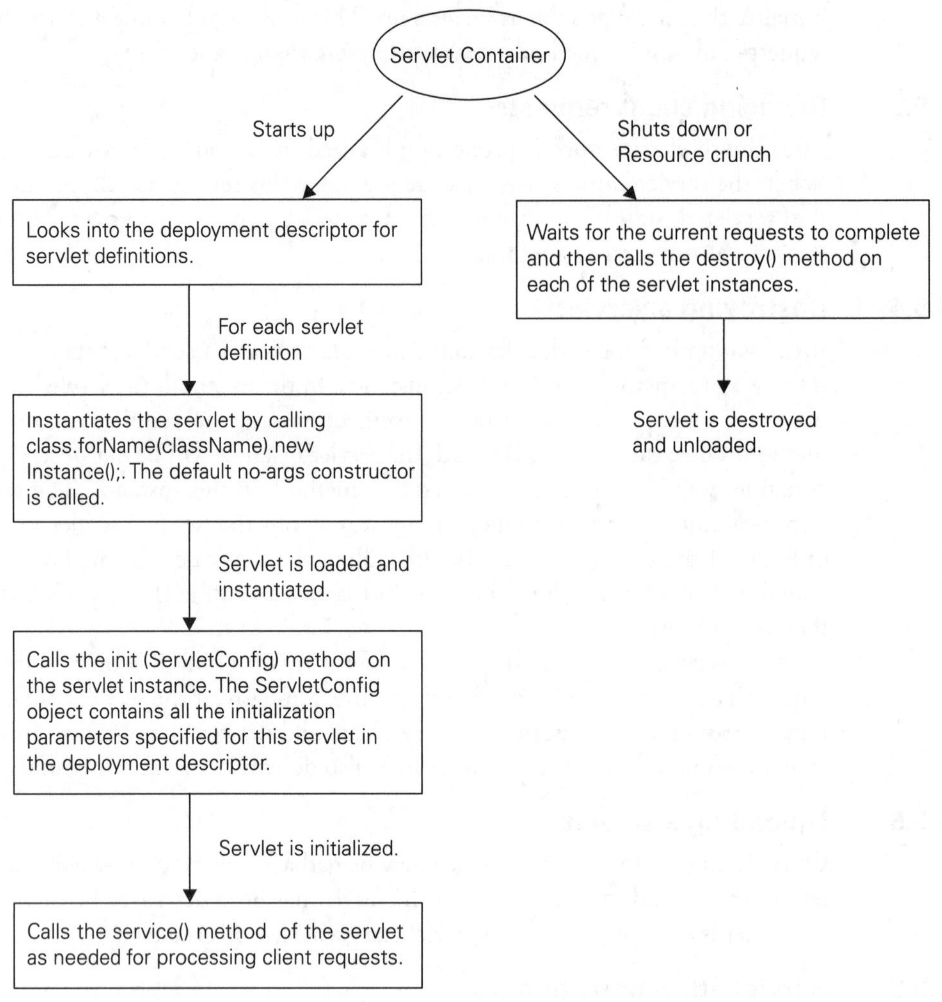


**Figure 4.3 The servlet life cycle from the servlet container's perspective.**

Table 4.8 summarizes all the servlet life-cycle methods.

**Table 4.8 Servlet life-cycle methods as defined in servlet interface**

| Method | Description |
|---|---|
| void init(ServletConfig) | The servlet container calls this method to initialize the servlet. |
| service(ServletRequest, ServletResponse) | The servlet container calls this method to service client requests. |
| void destroy() | The servlet container calls this method when it decides to unload the servlet. |

**NOTE** A servlet container calls the `init(ServletConfig)` method on a servlet object only once. However, it is possible that it will create multiple servlet objects of the same servlet class if:

- More than one `<servlet>` element is defined in the `web.xml` file having the same servlet class names. You can do this if you want to have multiple sets of initialization parameters. For example, you may want one instance to connect to one database and a second instance to connect to another database.
- The servlet implements the `SingleThreadModel` interface. In this case, the servlet container may instantiate multiple objects of the servlet to service requests concurrently. We will discuss this in detail in chapter 10, "Developing thread-safe servlets."

*Quizlet*

**Q:** Which method does the servlet container call on a servlet to initialize the servlet?

**A:** The `init(javax.servlet.ServletConfig)` method of the `javax.servlet.Servlet` interface. The `javax.servlet.GenericServlet` class implements this method.

## 4.6 SERVLETCONFIG: A CLOSER LOOK

We learned in the previous section that the servlet container passes a `ServletConfig` object in the `init(ServletConfig)` method of the servlet. In this section, we will look at the details of ServletConfig that you need to understand for the exam.

### 4.6.1 ServletConfig methods

The `ServletConfig` interface is defined in the `javax.servlet` package and is rather simple to use. It provides four methods, as shown in table 4.9.

**Table 4.9 ServletConfig methods for retrieving initialization parameters**

| Method | Description |
|---|---|
| String getInitParameter(String name) | Returns the value of the parameter or null if no such parameter is available. |
| Enumeration getInitParameterNames() | Returns an Enumeration of Strings for all the parameter names. |
| ServletContext getServletContext() | Returns the ServletContext for this servlet. |
| String getServletName() | Returns the servlet name as specified in the configuration file. |

Notice that `ServletConfig` provides methods only to retrieve parameters. You cannot add or set parameters to the `ServletConfig` object.

A servlet container takes the information specified about a servlet in the deployment descriptor and wraps it into a `ServletConfig` object. This information can then be retrieved by the servlet at the time of its initialization.

### 4.6.2 Example: a servlet and its deployment descriptor

To really understand the `ServletConfig` methods, you first need to understand how to specify the initialization parameters in the deployment descriptor. The `web.xml` file shown in listing 4.6 declares a servlet and specifies four initialization parameters for the servlet. Later, we will use these parameters in our servlet to make a connection to the database.

**Listing 4.6 The web.xml file specifying init parameters**

```
<?xml version="1.0" encoding="ISO-8859-1"?>

<!DOCTYPE web-app
    PUBLIC "-//Sun Microsystems, Inc.//DTD Web Application 2.2//EN"
    "http://java.sun.com/j2ee/dtds/web-app_2_2.dtd">

<web-app>

  <servlet>                                                  <-- Defines a servlet
    <servlet-name>TestServlet</servlet-name>
    <servlet-class>TestServlet</servlet-class>               Allows preloading
    <load-on-startup>1</load-on-startup>                     of the servlet
    <init-param>
       <param-name>driverclassname</param-name>
       <param-value>sun.jdbc.odbc.JdbcOdbcDriver</param-value>
    </init-param>
    <init-param>                                             Defines a parameter
       <param-name>dburl</param-name>                        and specifies its
       <param-value>jdbc:odbc:MySQLODBC</param-value>        name and value
    </init-param>
    <init-param>
       <param-name>username</param-name>
       <param-value>testuser</param-value>
    </init-param>
    <init-param>
       <param-name>password</param-name>
       <param-value>test</param-value>
    </init-param>
  </servlet>

</web-app>
```

We will discuss the complete structure of a deployment descriptor in chapter 5, but for now, just note that the above listing has one `<servlet>` element, which defines a servlet named `TestServlet`. The `<servlet>` element has four `<init-param>` elements, which define four parameters: `driverclassname`, `dburl`, `username`, and password. Notice the <load-on-startup> element, which ensures that this servlet will be loaded as soon as the container starts up.

Now we are ready to examine the ServletConfig methods in action. Listing 4.7 shows the complete code for the TestServlet servlet, which uses the initialization parameters we defined in the deployment descriptor (listing 4.6) to connect to a database.

**Listing 4.7 TestServlet.java; making use of init parameters**

```
import java.io.*;
import java.util.*;
import java.sql.*;
import javax.servlet.*;
import javax.servlet.http.*;

public class TestServlet extends HttpServlet
{
   Connection dbConnection;

   public void init()        <-- Creates connection in init()
   {
      System.out.println(getServletName()+" : Initializing...");

      ServletConfig config = getServletConfig();

      String driverClassName =
             config.getInitParameter("driverclassname");

      String dbURL = config.getInitParameter("dburl");
      String username = config.getInitParameter("username");
      String password = config.getInitParameter("password");
                                          Retrieves parameters
      //Load the driver class
      Class.forName(driverClassName);

      //get a database connection
      dbConnection =
          DriverManager.getConnection(dbURL,username,password);

      System.out.println("Initialized.");
   }

   public void service(HttpServletRequest req,
                       HttpServletResponse res)
            throws ServletException, java.io.IOException
   {
      //get the requested data from the database and
      //generate an HTML page.
   }

   public void destroy()   <-- Cleans up the resources
   {
      try
      {
```

```
            dbConnection.close();
         }
         catch(Exception e)
         {
            e.printStackTrace();
         }
      }
   }
```

The above servlet reads the initialization parameters specified in the deployment descriptor and makes a connection to the database in the `init()` method. It also uses the `getServletName()` method to print a debug statement on the console. The `getServletName()` method returns the name of the servlet as defined in the `<servlet-name>` element of the deployment descriptor. Observe the use of the `destroy()` method to close the connection.

## 4.7 SERVLETCONTEXT: A CLOSER LOOK

We can think of the `ServletContext` interface as a window for a servlet to view its environment. A servlet can use this interface to get information, such as initialization parameters for the web application or the servlet container's version. This interface also provides utility methods for retrieving the MIME type for a file, for retrieving shared resources (such as property files), for logging, and so forth. Every web application has one and only one `ServletContext`, and it is accessible to all the active resources of that application. It is also used by the servlets to share data with one another.

It is important to have a thorough understanding of `ServletContext`, since the exam contains many questions about this interface. This book is organized according to the exam objectives, and we will discuss the various `ServletContext` methods in different chapters as they apply to those objectives.

In this section, we will work with the `getResource()` and `getResourceAs-Stream()` methods. These methods are used by a servlet to access any resource without worrying about where the resource actually resides.

For a detailed description of these methods, you should refer to the API documentation. Table 4.10 provides a brief description of each.

**Table 4.10 ServletContext methods for retrieving a resource**

| Method | Description |
| --- | --- |
| java.net.URL getResource(String path) | This method returns a java.net.URL object for the resource that is mapped to the given path. Although the path should start with / it is not an absolute path. It is relative to the document root of this web application. For instance, if you pass a path to a JSP file, it will give you the unprocessed data, i.e., in this case, the JSP source code, when you read the contents. |

*continued on next page*

**Table 4.10 ServletContext methods for retrieving a resource *(continued)***

| Method | Description |
|---|---|
| java.io.InputStream getResourceAs-Stream(String path) | This is a shortcut method if you just want to get an Input-Stream out of the resource. It is equivalent to getRe-source(path).openStream(). |

If you recall from listing 4.5, in which we sent a JAR file to the browser, we had hard-coded the JAR filename in the line:

```
File f = new File("test.jar");
```

The code in listing 4.8 uses the `getResource()` method to specify the filename independently of the file system.

**Listing 4.8 Making use of ServletContext.getResource()**

```
public void service(HttpServletRequest req,
                    HttpServletResponse res)
            throws javax.servlet.ServletException,
                   java.io.IOException
  {

    res.setContentType("application/jar");

    OutputStream os = res.getOutputStream();

    //1K buffer
    byte[] bytearray = new byte[1024];

    ServletContext context = getServletContext();
    URL url = context.getResource("files/test.jar");   <-- Returns a URL object
                                                           to the file
    InputStream is = url.openStream();

    int bytesread = 0;
    while( (bytesread = is.read(bytearray) ) != -1 )
    {
       os.write(bytearray, 0, bytesread);
    }
    os.flush();
    is.close();
  }
```

In listing 4.8, we have specified a relative path to the file `test.jar`. This allows us to deploy this servlet anywhere without worrying about the absolute location of the file. As long as `test.jar` is available under the `<webappdirectory>\files` directory, it can be found.

Here are the limitations of the `getResource()` and `getResourceAs-Stream()` methods:

- You cannot pass a URL of any active resource—for example, a JSP page or servlet—to this method.
- If used improperly, this method can become a security hole; it can read all of the files that belong to this web application, including the files under the `WEB-INF` directory of this web application.

A servlet can, of course, access a resource directly by converting a relative path to an absolute path using the `getRealPath(String relativePath)` method of ServletContext. However, the problem with this approach is that it is not helpful when the resource is inside a JAR file. It is also useless when the servlet is running in a distributed environment where the resource may reside on a different machine. In such situations, the `getResource()` method comes handy.

## 4.8 BEYOND SERVLET BASICS

Until now, we have been discussing servlets from the point of view of just one servlet. But in the real world, having just one servlet to do all the tasks is not practical. Typically, we divide the business process into multiple tasks. For example, consider a grossly simplified business process of a bank. A user should be able to:

- Open an account
- View the account balance
- Make deposits
- Make withdrawals
- Close the account

Besides these activities, many other business rules need to be addressed as well; for example, a user should not be able to view or withdraw from anyone else's account.

We usually break up the whole business process into different tasks and have one servlet focus on one task. In the example described above, we can have a `LoginServlet` that allows a user to sign up and log in/log out, and an `AccountServlet` that allows users to view their account balance and deposit or withdraw money.

To implement the required functionality, the servlets will have to coordinate their processes and share the data. For example, if a user directly tries to access an account, `AccountServlet` should be able to determine the user's login status, and it should redirect the user to the login page if he is not logged in. On the other hand, once a user logs in, `LoginServlet` should be able to share the `userid` with `AccountServlet` so that `AccountServlet` can display the status of the account without asking for the `userid` again.

The Servlet API provides elegant ways to share data and to coordinate the servlet processes. We will discuss these ways in the following sections.

### 4.8.1 Sharing the data (attribute scopes)

Data is shared between the servlets using the rendezvous concept. One servlet puts the data in a well-known place, which acts as a container, and other servlets access the data from that place. These well-known containers are the `ServletRequest` object, the `HttpSession` object, and the `ServletContext` object. All three objects provide a `setAttribute(String name, Object value)` method (to put the data in the container) and an `Object getAttribute(String name)` method (to access the data).

Although data can be shared using any of these containers, there is a difference in the visibility of the data present in these containers. Simply put, objects shared using `ServletRequest` are accessible only for the life of a request, objects shared using `HttpSession` are accessible only while the client is active, and objects shared using `ServletContext` are accessible for the life of the web application. To understand this difference clearly, consider the following situations where we have different requirements for sharing the data:

- The banking application that we described earlier needs to provide credit reports for the users. So, we add a `ReporterServlet` which, given a social security number (SSN), can generate a credit report for any user. When a user asks for his credit report, `AccountServlet` should be able to retrieve the SSN and pass it on to `ReporterServlet`. In this case, `AccountServlet` should be able to share the SSN with `ReporterServlet` only for that request. Once the request is serviced, `ReporterServlet` should not be able to access the SSN anymore.
- As described before, `LoginServlet` should be able to share the `userid` with `AccountServlet`, but `AccountServlet` should be able to access only the `userid` for the user whose request it is servicing. Further, it should be able to access it for as long as the user is logged in.
- All three servlets—`LoginServlet`, `AccountServlet`, and `ReporterServlet`—need to access the same database, and so `driverclassname`, `dburl`, `dbusername`, and `dbpassword` should be shared with all the servlets all of the time.

The three containers that we mentioned before help us in these situations:

- If we put an object in a `javax.servlet.ServletRequest` object, it can be shared with anybody by passing this request object but only as long as the request object is valid. A request object is valid until the response is committed. We will see how to pass this request object around in section 4.8.2.
- If a servlet puts an object in a `javax.servlet.http.HttpSession` object, it can be accessed by any servlet anytime but only while the servlet is servicing a request for the same client who put the object into the session. We will learn about this in detail in chapter 8, "Session management."

- If a servlet puts an object in the `java.servlet.ServletContext` object, it can be accessed anytime by any servlet of the same web application. We will work with the ServletContext object in chapter 6, "The servlet container model."

All three interfaces provide the same set of three methods for setting and getting attributes, as shown in table 4.11.

**Table 4.11 The methods available in ServletRequest, HttpSession, and ServletContext for getting and setting attributes**

| Method | Description |
|---|---|
| Object getAttribute(String name) | This method returns the value mapped to this name or null if no such name exists. |
| Enumeration getAttributeNames() | This method returns an Enumeration of Strings for all the names that are available in this container. |
| void setAttribute(String name, Object value) | The method adds the given name-value pair to this container. If the name is already present, then the old value is removed. |

We will build a simple web application that uses these concepts in section 4.8.3.

### 4.8.2 Coordinating servlets using RequestDispatcher

Again, with respect to the banking application, if a user is not logged in, `AccountServlet` should forward the request to `LoginServlet`. Similarly, once a user enters her user ID/password, `LoginServlet` should forward the request to `AccountServlet`.

The Servlet API includes the `javax.servlet.RequestDispatcher` interface, which allows us to do this. It has the two methods shown in table 4.12.

**Table 4.12 Methods provided by RequestDispatcher for forwarding/including a request to/from another resource**

| Method | Description |
|---|---|
| void forward(ServletRequest request, ServletResponse response) | This method allows a servlet to process a request partially and then forwards the request to another servlet for generating the final response. It can also be used to forward a request from one active resource (a servlet or a JSP page) to another resource (servlet, JSP file, or HTML file) on the server. This method can be called only if the response is not committed; otherwise, it will throw an IllegalStateException. |
| void include(ServletRequest request, ServletResponse response) | This is pretty much the same as forward(), but in this case the request is not "forwarded" permanently. Instead, it is passed to the other resource temporarily so that the other resource can partially process the request, and then the forwarding servlet/JSP page can take over the request again and service it to completion. Because the request is not forwarded permanently, all changes to the headers or status code of the request made by the other resource are ignored. |

For both of the methods, the request and response objects that are passed to them should be the same as the ones received by the caller servlet.

**NOTE** An important difference between `RequestDispatcher.forward()` and `HttpServletRequest.sendRedirect()` (which we discussed in section 4.4) is that `RequestDispatcher.forward()` is completely handled on the server side while `HttpServletRequest.sendRedirect()` sends a redirect message to the browser. In that sense, `HttpServletRequest.forward()` is transparent to the browser while `HttpServletRequest.sendRedirect()` is not.

This sounds good, but how do we obtain a `RequestDispatcher` in the first place? Simple: both `javax.servlet.ServletContext` and `javax.servlet.ServletRequest` have the method shown in table 4.13.

**Table 4.13 The method in ServletContext and ServletRequest for getting a RequestDispatcher**

| Method | Description |
|---|---|
| public RequestDispatcher getRequestDispatcher(String path) | The path parameter is the path to the resource; for example, request.getRequestDispatcher("/servlet/AccountServlet"). It will not accept a path outside the current web application. |

Besides the `getRequestDispatcher()` method, the `ServletContext` interface also provides a `getNamedDispatcher()` method, which allows us to dispatch requests to a component by specifying its name (as given in the deployment descriptor) instead of a full URI path.

There is an important difference between the `getRequestDispatcher()` method of `ServletContext` and that of `ServletRequest`: you can pass a relative path to the `getRequestDispatcher()` method of `ServletRequest` but not to the `getRequestDispatcher()` method of `ServletContext`. For example, `request.getRequestDispatcher("../html/copyright.html")` is valid, and the `getRequestDispatcher()` method of `ServletRequest` will evaluate the path relative to the path of the request. For the `getRequestDispatcher()` method of `ServletContext`, the path parameter cannot be relative and must start with /. This makes sense because `ServletRequest` has a current request path to evaluate the relative path while `ServletContext` does not.

**NOTE** You cannot directly forward or include a request to a resource in another web application. To do this, you need to get a reference to the `ServletContext` of the other web application using `currentServletContext.getContext(uripath)`. Using this servlet context reference, you can retrieve an appropriate `RequestDispatcher` object as usual.

### 4.8.3 Putting it all together: A simple banking application

Let's build the banking application that we have been discussing, using two servlets:

- `LoginServlet`
- `AccountServlet`

#### *LoginServlet*

Listing 4.9 contains the code for `LoginServlet` that verifies the user ID and password and forwards the request to `AccountServlet`.

**Listing 4.9 LoginServlet.java for a simple banking web application**

```
package chapter4;

import java.io.*;
import java.util.*;
import javax.servlet.*;
import javax.servlet.http.*;

public class LoginServlet extends HttpServlet
{
   Hashtable users = new Hashtable();

   //This method will be called if somebody types the URL
   //for this servlet in the address field of the browser.
   public void doGet(HttpServletRequest req,
                     HttpServletResponse res)
   {
      doPost(req, res);
   }

   //This method retrieves the userid and password, verifies them,
   //and if valid, it forwards the request to AccountServlet.
   //Otherwise, it forwards the request to the login page.
   public void doPost(HttpServletRequest req,
                      HttpServletResponse res)
   {
      String userid = req.getParameter("userid");            // Retrieves the
      String password = req.getParameter("password");        // user ID/password

      if( userid != null && password != null &&
            password.equals(users.get(userid)) )
      {                                                  // Sets the userid
         req.setAttribute("userid", userid);             // in the request

         ServletContext ct = getServletContext();
         RequestDispatcher rd =
          ct.getRequestDispatcher("/servlet/AccountServlet");  // Gets the RequestDispatcher for AccountServlet

         rd.forward(req, res);      // Forwards the request to AccountServlet

         return;
      }
      else
```

```
        {
            RequestDispatcher rd =
             req.getRequestDispatcher("../login.html");   <-- Gets the RequestDispatcher for login.html
            rd.forward(req, res);
            return;
        }
    }

    //initialize some userids and passwords
    public void init()
    {
        users.put("ann", "aaa");
        users.put("john", "jjj");
        users.put("mark", "mmm");
    }
}
```

The logic of authenticating a user in the above servlet is simple. We initialize a Hashtable to store some user IDs and passwords. In the `doPost()` method, the servlet validates the credentials given by the user and forwards the request to either `AccountServlet` or to the login page.

Observe the use of an absolute path used in the creation of `RequestDispatcher` for `AccountServlet` and the use of a relative path in the creation of `RequestDispatcher` for the login page.

### *Login.html*

To access our application, a user will go to the login page. This page will allow the user to enter her user ID and password. Listing 4.10 contains the code for the login page.

**Listing 4.10 login.html for capturing the userid and password**

```
<!DOCTYPE HTML PUBLIC "-//W3C//DTD HTML 4.0 Transitional//EN">

<html>
<head>
     <title>SCWCD_Example_1_3</title>
</head>

<body>

<h3>Please enter your userid and password to see your account statement:</
h3><p>

<form action="servlet/LoginServlet" method="POST">   <-- Sends the data to LoginServlet using POST
Userid : <input type="text" name="userid"><br><br>
Password : <input type="password" name="password"><br><br>
<input type="submit" value="Show Statement">
</form>

</body>
</html>
```

### AccountServlet

Listing 4.11 contains the code for `AccountServlet`. Its job is to generate an HTML page that displays the user's account information.

**Listing 4.11 AccountServlet.java**

```
package chapter4;

import java.io.*;
import java.util.*;
import javax.servlet.*;
import javax.servlet.http.*;

public class AccountServlet extends HttpServlet
{
   Hashtable data = new Hashtable();

   //This method will be called if somebody types the URL
   //for this servlet in the address field of the browser.
   public void doGet(HttpServletRequest req, HttpServletResponse res)
          throws javax.servlet.ServletException, java.io.IOException
   {
      doPost(req, res);
   }

   public void doPost(HttpServletRequest req, HttpServletResponse res)
          throws javax.servlet.ServletException, java.io.IOException
   {

      String user ID = (String) req.getAttribute("user ID");   <-- Gets the userid set by LoginServlet

      if(user ID != null )
      {
         // Retrieve the data and generate the page dynamically.
         String[] records = (String[]) data.get(user ID);

         PrintWriter pw = res.getWriter();
         pw.println("<html>");
         pw.println("<head>");
         pw.println("</head>");
         pw.println("<body>");
         pw.println("<h3>Account Status for "+user ID+
            " at the start of previous three months...</h3><p>");
         for(int i=0; i<records.length; i++)
         {
            pw.println(records[i]+"<br>");
         }

         pw.println("</body>");
         pw.println("</html>");
      }
      else
      {
```

```java
            //No user ID. Send login.html to the user.
            //observe the use of relative path.
            RequestDispatcher rd =
             req.getRequestDispatcher("../login.html");   <-
           rd.forward(req, res);
        }

    }

    //initialize some data.
    public void init()
    {
        data.put("ann", new String[]{ "01/01/2002 : 1000.00",
                "01/02/2002 : 1300.00", "01/03/2002 : 900.00"} );
        data.put("john", new String[]{ "01/01/2002 : 4500.00",
                "01/02/2002 : 2100.00", "01/03/2002 : 2600.00"} );
        data.put("mark", new String[]{ "01/01/2002 : 7800.00",
                "01/02/2002 : 5200.00", "01/03/2002 : 1900.00"} );
    }
}
```

**Creates a request dispatcher using the relative path**

### *Running the application*

We have provided the above examples on the accompanying CD. Just copy the `chapter04` directory from the CD to the `webapps` directory of your Tomcat installation. For example, if you have installed Tomcat to `c:\jakarta-tomcat4.0.1`, copy the `chapter04` directory to `c:\jakarta-tomcat4.0.1\webapps`. Once you restart Tomcat, you can go to `http://localhost:8080/chapter04/login.html`.

You should observe the following:

- If you enter an invalid user ID/password, you get the login page.
- If you enter a valid user ID/password, you get the statement page.

You may also notice that the user needs to enter the user ID and password every time he tries to access `AccountServlet`. This is indeed annoying. There should be some way for `AccountServlet` to remember the user ID during the time in which it is interacting with the user. There is: that's where the concept of *session* comes into the picture. We will discuss session in detail in chapter 8.

## 4.9 SUMMARY

In this chapter, we discussed the basics of the Servlet Model. An `HttpServlet` has methods, which can be overridden, that correspond to the HTTP methods of the request. The `service(HttpServletRequest, HttpServletResponse)` method of `HttpServlet` is responsible for calling the appropriate method on the servlet depending on the request.

Using `HttpServletRequest` and `HttpServletResponse`, we learned how to create a dynamic response by analyzing the request. We also discussed the life-cycle phases of a servlet, including loading, initializing, destroying, and unloading the servlet. The `ServletRequest`, `HttpSession`, and `ServletContext` objects are the containers used to share data within the three scopes of a servlet: `request`, `session`, and `application`.

Finally, we developed a small web application, in which we shared data between two servlets and coordinated their execution.

You should now be ready to answer exam questions based on the HTTP methods GET, POST, and HEAD and the methods of a servlet that correspond to these HTTP methods. You should be able to answer the questions based on the servlet life cycle and the usage of servlets and related classes to retrieve request header information, form parameters, and text and binary streams. Finally, you should be able to answer questions based on attribute sharing using the `request`, `session`, and `context` scopes.

In the next chapter, we will take a closer look at the structure of a web application, the deployment descriptor, and the way in which a request is mapped to a servlet.

## 4.10 REVIEW QUESTIONS

1. Which method in the `HttpServlet` class services the HTTP POST request? (Select one)

   **a** `doPost(ServletRequest, ServletResponse)`
   **b** `doPOST(ServletRequest, ServletResponse)`
   **c** `servicePost(HttpServletRequest, HttpServletResponse)`
   **d** `doPost(HttpServletRequest, HttpServletResponse)`

2. Consider the following HTML page code:

```
<html><body>
<a href="/servlet/HelloServlet">POST</a>
</body></html>
```

   Which method of `HelloServlet` will be invoked when the hyperlink displayed by the above page is clicked? (Select one)

   **a** `doGet`
   **b** `doPost`
   **c** `doForm`
   **d** `doHref`
   **e** `serviceGet`

3. Consider the following code for the `doGet()` method:

```
public void doGet(HttpServletRequest req,
                  HttpServletResponse res)
{
   PrintWriter out = res.getWriter);
```

```
    out.println("<html><body>Hello</body></html>");

    //1

    if(req.getParameter("name") == null)
    {
       res.sendError(HttpServletResponse.SC_UNAUTHORIZED);
    }
}
```

Which of the following lines can be inserted at `//1` so that the above code does not throw any exception? (Select one)

- **a** `if ( ! res.isSent() )`
- **b** `if ( ! res.isCommitted() )`
- **c** `if ( ! res.isDone() )`
- **d** `if ( ! res.isFlushed() )`
- **e** `if ( ! res.flush() )`

4. Which of the following lines would initialize the `out` variable for sending a Microsoft Word file to the browser? (Select one)

- **a** `PrintWriter out = response.getServletOutput();`
- **b** `PrintWriter out = response.getPrintWriter();`
- **c** `OutputStream out = response.getWriter();`
- **d** `PrintWriter out = response.getOutputStream();`
- **e** `OutputStream out = response.getOutputStream();`
- **f** `ServletOutputStream out = response.getServletOutputStream();`

5. You need to send a GIF file to the browser. Which of the following lines should be called after (or before) a call to `response.getOutputStream()`? (Select one)

- **a** `response.setContentType("image/gif");` Before
- **b** `response.setContentType("image/gif");` After
- **c** `response.setDataType("image/gif");` Before
- **d** `response.setDataType("image/gif");` After
- **e** `response.setStreamType("image/gif");` Before
- **f** `response.setStreamType("image/gif");` After

6. Consider the following HTML page code:

```
<html><body>
<form name="data" action="/servlet/DataServlet" method="POST">
<input type="text" name="name">
<input type="submit" name="submit">
</form>
</body></html>
```

Identify the two methods that can be used to retrieve the value of the name parameter when the form is submitted.

**a** `getParameter("name");`
**b** `getParameterValue("name");`
**c** `getParameterValues("name");`
**d** `getParameters("name");`
**e** `getValue("name");`
**f** `getName();`

7. Which of the following methods would you use to retrieve header values from a request? (Select two)

**a** `getHeader()` of `ServletRequest`
**b** `getHeaderValues()` of `HttpServletRequest`
**c** `getHeaderValue()` of `ServletRequest`
**d** `getHeader()` of `HttpServletRequest`
**e** `getHeaders()` of `ServletRequest`
**f** `getHeaders()` of `HttpServletRequest`

8. Consider the following code:

```
public void doGet(HttpServletRequest req,
                  HttpServletResponse res)
                  throws IOException
{
   if(req.getParameter("switch") == null)
   {
      //1
   }
   else
   {
      //other code
   }
}
```

Which of the following lines can be inserted at `//1` so that the request is redirected to `collectinfo.html` page? (Select one)

**a** `req.sendRedirect("collectinfo.html");`
**b** `req.redirect("collectinfo.html");`
**c** `res.direct("collectinfo.html");`
**d** `res.sendRedirect("collectinfo.html");`
**e** `this.sendRedirect("collectinfo.html");`
**f** `this.send("collectinfo.html");`

9. Consider the following code:

```
public void doGet(HttpServletRequest req,
                  HttpServletResponse res)
{
   HttpSession session = req.getSession();
   ServletContext ctx = this.getServletContext();

   if(req.getParameter("userid") != null)
   {
      String userid = req.getParameter("userid");
      //1
   }
}
```

You want the `userid` parameter to be available only to the requests that come from the same user. Which of the following lines would you insert at `//1`? (Select one)

**a** `session.setAttribute("userid", userid);`
**b** `req.setAttribute("userid", userid);`
**c** `ctx.addAttribute("userid", userid);`
**d** `session.addAttribute("userid", userid);`
**e** `this.addParameter("userid", userid);`
**f** `this.setAttribute("userid", userid);`

10. Which of the following lines would you use to include the output of `DataServlet` into any other servlet? (Select one)

**a**
```
RequestDispatcher rd =
    request.getRequestDispatcher("/servlet/DataServlet");
rd.include(request, response);
```
**b**
```
RequestDispatcher rd =
    request.getRequestDispatcher("/servlet/DataServlet");
rd.include(response);
```
**c**
```
RequestDispatcher rd = request.getRequestDispatcher();
rd.include("/servlet/DataServlet", request, response);
```
**d**
```
RequestDispatcher rd = request.getRequestDispatcher();
rd.include("/servlet/DataServlet", response);
```
**e**
```
RequestDispatcher rd = request.getRequestDispatcher();
rd.include("/servlet/DataServlet");
```

CHAPTER 5

# Structure and deployment



## EXAM OBJECTIVES

**2.1** Identify the structure of a Web Application and Web Archive file, the name of the WebApp deployment descriptor, and the name of the directories where you place the following:

- The WebApp deployment descriptor
- The WebApp class files
- Any auxiliary JAR files

(Section 5.1)

**2.2** Match the name with a description of purpose or functionality, for each of the following deployment descriptor elements:

- Servlet instance
- Servlet name
- Servlet class
- Initialization parameters
- URL to named servlet mapping

(Section 5.2)

## INTRODUCTION

A web application consists of many resources, including servlets, JSP pages, utility classes, third-party JAR files, HTML files, and so forth. Managing so many resources can be a difficult task in itself; to complicate matters, the resources have dependencies. For example, a servlet may depend on third-party JAR files containing ready-made components, or a servlet may redirect a request to a JSP page. This requires the resources to learn the location of the other resources. Furthermore, a web application must be portable across different servlet containers.

Fortunately, to satisfy the above requirements, the Java Servlet Specification mandates that web applications be packaged in a standard way. In this chapter, we will discuss the way we package and deploy web applications.

## 5.1 DIRECTORY STRUCTURE OF A WEB APPLICATION

The resources of a web application are kept in a structured hierarchy of directories. The directory structure is well defined in terms of the placement of the resources and files. Figure 5.1 shows an imaginary web application named `helloapp`. To put the

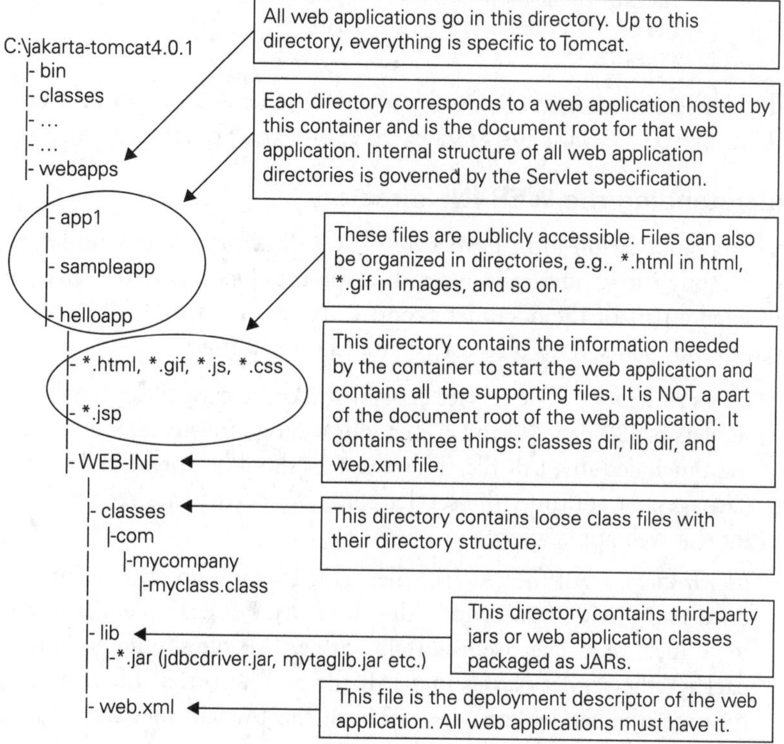


**Figure 5.1 The directory structure of a web application.**

structure in perspective, we've shown it in relationship to its location within the Tomcat directory structure.

The webapps directory under the Tomcat installation is the home directory of all the web applications that it hosts. In the directory structure shown in figure 5.1, the webapps directory contains the app1, sampleapp, and helloapp web applications. In the following sections, we will take a closer look at the directory structure of the helloapp web application.

### 5.1.1 Understanding the document root directory

In figure 5.1, the helloapp directory is the document root for the helloapp web application. A request for http://www.myserver.com/helloapp/index.html will refer to the index.html file in the helloapp directory. All publicly accessible files should go in this directory. It is very common to organize these files into multiple subdirectories. A typical root directory looks like this:

```
|-
|- helloapp
     |- html (contains all the HTML files)
     |- jsp (contains all the JSP files)
     |- images (contains all the GIFs, JPEGs, BMPs)
     |- javascripts (contains all *.js files)
     |- index.html (default HTML file)
     |- WEB-INF
```

In the above structure, an HTML file named hello.html can be accessed through the URL http://www.myserver.com/helloapp/html/hello.html.

### 5.1.2 Understanding the WEB-INF directory

Every web application must have a WEB-INF directory directly under its root directory. Although it is physically located inside the document root directory, it is not considered a part of the document root; i.e., files in the WEB-INF directory are not served to the clients. This directory contains three things:

- *classes directory.* The servlet class files and the class files needed to support the servlets or JSP pages of this web application go in this directory if they have not been included in a JAR file. The class files should be organized according to their packages. At runtime, the servlet container adds this directory to the classpath for this web application.
- *lib directory.* All the JAR/zip files used by the web application, including the third-party JAR/zip files, go in this directory. For example, if a servlet uses JDBC to connect to a database, the JDBC driver JAR file should go here. We can also package the servlet classes in a JAR file and keep that file in this directory. At runtime, the servlet container adds all the JAR/zip files from this directory to the classpath for this web application.

- `web.xml` *file (also known as the deployment descriptor).* This file is the heart of a web application, and every web application must have it. It contains the information needed by the servlet container in order to run the web application, such as servlet declarations and mappings, properties, authorization and security constraints, and so forth. We will learn more about this file in section 5.2.

*Quizlet*

**Q:** Your web application includes an applet packaged as a JAR file. Which directory would you keep the JAR file in?

**A:** Because an applet is only run on the client side, the applet JAR file should be accessible to the clients. This means that it may be kept anywhere in the document root of the application except in the `WEB-INF` directory and its subdirectories.

### 5.1.3 The web archive (WAR) file

Since a web application contains many files, it can be cumbersome to migrate the application from one environment to another—for instance, from development to production. To simplify the process, these files can be bundled into a single JAR file but with the extension `.war` instead of `.jar`. The extension `.war` stands for *web archive* and signifies that the file should be treated differently than a JAR file. For example, if we place a WAR file in Tomcat's `webapps` directory, Tomcat automatically extracts its contents to a directory under `webapps`. The name of the new directory is the same as the name of the WAR file without the extension.

In essence, a servlet container can install a WAR file as a web application without manual intervention.

Creating a WAR file is simple. For example, to create a WAR file for the `helloapp` web application, follow these steps:

1. From the DOS prompt (or from the `$` prompt), go to the `webapps` directory (`c:\jakarta-tomcat4.0.1\webapps`).
2. Jar the `helloapp` directory by using the jar utility:

```
c:\jakarta-tomcat4.0.1\webapps>jar -cvf helloapp.war helloapp
```

This will create a `helloapp.war` file in the `c:\jakarta-tomcat4.0.1\webapps` directory.

### 5.1.4 The default web application

Besides the web applications created by the users, a servlet container maintains a default web application. This application handles all requests that do not match any of the user-created web applications. It is similar to any other web application except that we can access its resources without specifying its name or context path. In Tomcat, the `webapps\ROOT` directory is set as the document root for the default web application.

A default web application allows you to deploy individual JSPs, servlets, and static content without pre-packaging them into a separate application. For example, if you want to test an individual JSP file named `test.jsp`, you can place it in the `ROOT` directory instead of creating a separate application. You can access it through the URL `http://localhost:8080/test.jsp`, and you can modify the deployment descriptor of this application to add your own components, such as servlets, as needed.

## 5.2 THE DEPLOYMENT DESCRIPTOR: AN OVERVIEW

The deployment descriptor (`web.xml`) of a web application describes the web application to the servlet container. As is evident from the extension of `web.xml`, it is an XML file. To ensure portability across the servlet containers, the DTD for this XML file is standardized by Sun. If you are new to XML technology, you should read the brief tutorial that we have provided in appendix B. It will help you to understand this section.

Table 5.1 shows the properties that can be defined in a deployment descriptor.

**Table 5.1 Properties defined in a deployment descriptor**

| Web Application Properties | Short Description | Discussed in: |
|---|---|---|
| Servlet Declarations | Used to specify servlet properties. | Chapters 4, 5 |
| Servlet Mappings | Used to specify URL to servlet mapping. | Chapter 5 |
| Application Lifecycle Listener classes | Used to specify listener classes for HttpSessionEvents and ServletContextAttributeEvent. | Chapter 6 |
| ServletContext Init Parameters | Used to specify initialization parameters for the web application. | Chapter 6 |
| Error Pages | Used to specify error pages for error conditions. | Chapter 7 |
| Session Configuration | Used to specify session timeout. | Chapter 8 |
| Security Constraints | Used to specify security requirements of the web application. | Chapter 9 |
| Tag libraries | Used to specify the tag libraries required by JSP pages. | Chapter 15 |
| Welcome File list | Used to specify the welcome files for the web application. | Not needed for the exam |
| Filter Definitions and Filter Mappings | Used to specify the filter. | Chapter 18—not needed for the exam |
| MIME Type Mappings | Used to specify MIME types for common file extensions. | Not needed for the exam |
| JNDI names | Used to specify JNDI names of the EJBs. | Not needed for the exam |

We discuss eight of these properties throughout the book as they apply to the exam objectives. In this section, we will look at the general structure of the deployment descriptor, and we will learn how to define servlets and servlet mappings in a deployment descriptor.

### 5.2.1 Example: A simple deployment descriptor

Listing 5.1 shows the general structure of a simple deployment descriptor.

**Listing 5.1 Simple deployment descriptor**

```
<?xml version="1.0" encoding="ISO-8859-1">          <- Declares the XML version and
                                                       character set used in this file
<!DOCTYPE web-app PUBLIC
 "-//Sun Microsystems, Inc.//DTD Web Application 2.3//EN"
 "http://java.sun.com/j2ee/dtds/web-app_2_3.dtd">     <- Declares the DTD
                                                         for this file
<web-app>
   <display-name>Test Webapp</display-name>

      <context-param>
         <param-name>author</param-name>              Specifies a parameter for this
         <param-value>john@abc.com</param-value>      web application
      </context-param>

   <servlet>                                 <- Specifies a servlet
      <servlet-name>test</servlet-name>
      <servlet-class>com.abc.TestServlet</servlet-class>
      <init-param>                            <- Specifies a parameter
         <param-name>greeting</param-name>       for this servlet
         <param-value>Good Morning</param-value>
      </init-param>
   </servlet>

   <servlet-mapping>
      <servlet-name>test</servlet-name>        Maps /test/*
      <url-pattern>/test/*</url-pattern>       to test servlet
   </servlet-mapping>

   <mime-mapping>
      <extension>zip</extension>
      <mime-type>application/zip</mime-type>
   </mime-mapping>

</web-app>
```

A `web.xml` file, like all XML files, starts with the line `<?xml version="1.0" encoding="ISO-8859-1">`, which specifies the version of XML and the character set it is using. Next, it must have a `DOCTYPE` declaration, which specifies the DTD for the file. In the case of a `web.xml` file that follows version 2.3 of the servlet specification, we must use

```
<!DOCTYPE web-app PUBLIC "-//Sun Microsystems, Inc.//DTD Web Application
2.3//EN" "http://java.sun.com/j2ee/dtds/web-app_2_3.dtd">
```

The rest of the content must go under the `<web-app>` element, which is the root of this XML file.

Now let's look at the servlet-specific elements of the deployment descriptor that are required by the exam.

### 5.2.2 Using the <servlet> element

Each <servlet> element under <web-app> defines a servlet for that web application. The following is the definition of the <servlet> element as given by the DTD for web.xml:

```
<!ELEMENT servlet (icon?, servlet-name, display-name?,
description?, (servlet-class|jsp-file), init-param*,
load-on-startup?, security-role-ref*)>
```

The code that follows demonstrates a typical use of the <servlet> element within a deployment descriptor:

```
<servlet>

   <servlet-name>us-sales</servlet-name>   <-- The servlet name

   <servlet-class>com.xyz.SalesServlet</servlet-class>   <-- The servlet class

   <init-param>
      <param-name>region</param-name>
      <param-value>USA</param-value>
   </init-param>
                                           The servlet parameters
   <init-param>
      <param-name>limit</param-name>
      <param-value>200</param-value>
   <init-param>

</servlet>
```

The servlet container instantiates the class of the servlet and associates it with the given servlet name. Every parameter should be specified using the <init-param> element. The above servlet definition tells the servlet container to create a servlet named us-sales using the class com.xyz.SalesServlet. The container passes region and limit as the initialization parameters through the ServletConfig object.

#### *servlet-name*

This element defines the name for the servlet. Clients use this name to access the servlet. For example, the servlet defined above can be accessed through the URL http://www.myserver.com/servlet/us-sales. This name is also used to define the URL to the servlet mapping for the servlet. This element is mandatory, and the name should be unique across the deployment descriptor. We can retrieve the name of a servlet by using the ServletConfig.getServletName() method.

#### *servlet-class*

This element specifies the Java class name that should be used by the servlet container to instantiate this servlet. In the above example, the servlet container will use the com.xyz.SalesServlet class. This element is mandatory. This class, as well as all the classes that it depends on, should be available in the classpath for this web application. Remember that the classes directory and JAR files in the lib directory inside WEB-INF are automatically added to the classpath by the servlet container, so there is no need to set your classpath if you put the classes in either of these two places.

### *init-param*

This element is used to pass initialization parameters to the servlet. We can have any number of <init-param> elements in the <servlet> element. Each <init-param> element must have one and only one set of <param-name> and <param-value> subelements. <param-name> defines the name of the parameter and must be unique across the servlet element. <param-value> defines the value for that parameter. A servlet can retrieve the initialization parameters using the method ServletConfig.getInitParameter("paramname").

Notice the name us-sales given to the above servlet. You can define another servlet named euro-sales with the same servlet class and set the value of the region parameter to europe. In such cases, multiple instances of the servlet class will be created, one for each name.

*Quizlet*

**Q:** How can you associate an array of values for an initialization parameter of a servlet?

**A:** You can't; at least not directly! The deployment descriptor does not allow you to specify multiple parameters with the same name. So you have to do something like this:

```
<init-param>
   <param-name>countries</param-name>
   <param-value>Australia, Brazil, India, UK, US</param-value>
<init-param>
```

You would then have to parse the param-value string in the servlet and interpret the multiple values listed in the string.

### 5.2.3 Using the <servlet-mapping> element

Simply put, servlet mappings specify which URL patterns should be handled by which servlet. The servlet container uses these mappings to invoke the appropriate servlets depending on the actual URL. Here is the definition of the <servlet-mapping> element:

```
<!ELEMENT servlet-mapping (servlet-name, url-pattern)>
```

In the above definition, servlet-name should be the name of one of the servlets defined using the <servlet> element, and url-pattern can be any string that we want to associate with this servlet.

The following are examples of using the <servlet-mapping> element in a deployment descriptor:

```
<servlet-mapping>
   <servlet-name>accountServlet</servlet-name>
   <url-pattern>/account/*</url-pattern>
</servlet-mapping>

<servlet-mapping>
   <servlet-name>accountServlet</servlet-name>
   <url-pattern>/myaccount/*</url-pattern>
</servlet-mapping>
```

In these mappings, we are associating /account and /myaccount URL patterns to accountServlet. Whenever the container receives a request URL that starts with <webapp name>/account or <webapp name>/myaccount, it will send that request to accountServlet.

A servlet container interprets the url-pattern according to the following rules:

- A string beginning with a / and ending with the /* characters is used for determining a *servlet path* mapping. We will discuss servlet paths in section 5.2.4.
- A string beginning with a *. prefix is used to map the request to a servlet that handles the extension specified in the string. For example, the following mapping will direct all the requests ending with .pdf to pdfGeneratorServlet:

```
<servlet-mapping>
   <servlet-name>pdfGeneratorServlet</servlet-name>
   <url-pattern>*.pdf</url-pattern>
</servlet-mapping>
```

- All other strings are used as exact matches only. For example, the following mapping will direct http://www.mycompany.com/report to reportServlet. However, it will not direct http://www.mycompany.com/report/sales to reportServlet.

```
<servlet-mapping>
   <servlet-name>reportServlet</servlet-name>
   <url-pattern>report</url-pattern>
</servlet-mapping>
```

- A string containing only the / character indicates that servlet specified by the mapping becomes the default servlet of the application. In this case, the servlet path is the request URI minus the context path and the path info is null. We will discuss context path and path info in the next section.

### 5.2.4 Mapping a URL to a servlet

In the previous section, we learned how to specify the servlet mappings in the deployment descriptor of a web application. Now let's look at how the container uses these mappings to route a request to the appropriate servlet. Routing a request to a servlet is a two-step process. First, the servlet container identifies the web application that the request belongs to, and then it finds an appropriate servlet of that web application to handle the request.

Both steps require the servlet container to break up the request URI into three parts: the context path, the servlet path, and the path info. Figure 5.2 shows these three components of a URL.

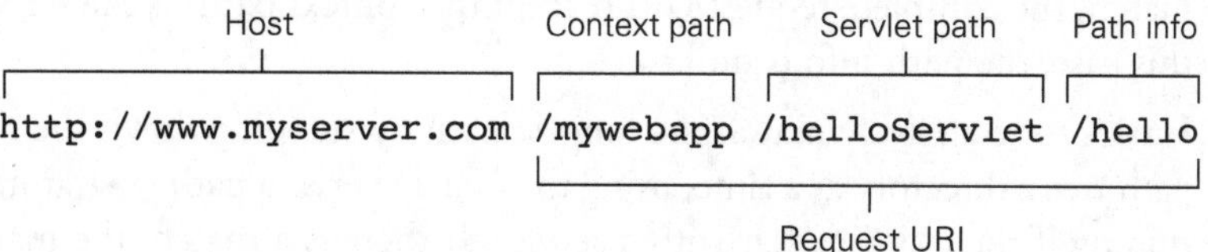


**Figure 5.2 The context path, servlet path, and path info.**

Let's take a look at each component:

- *Context path.* The servlet container tries to match the longest possible part of the request URI, starting from the beginning, with the available web application names. This part is called the *context path*. For example, if the request URI is `/autobank/accountServlet/personal`, then `/autobank` is the context path (assuming that a web application named `autobank` exists within the servlet container). If there is no match, the context path is empty; in this case, it associates the request with the default web application.
- *Servlet path.* After taking out the context path, the servlet container tries to match the longest possible part of the remaining URI with the servlet mappings defined for the web application that was specified as the context path. This part is called the *servlet path*. For example, if the request URI is `/autobank/accountServlet/personal`, then `/accountServlet` is the servlet path (assuming that a servlet named `accountServlet` is defined in the `autobank` web application). If it is unable to find any match, it returns an error page. We will see how the servlet container determines this path shortly.
- *Path info.* Anything that remains after determining the servlet path is called *path info*. For example, if the request URI is `/autobank/accountServlet/personal`, `/personal` is the path info.

**NOTE** Remember the following three points:

- Request URI = context path + servlet path + path info.
- Context paths and servlet paths start with a / but do not end with it.
- `HttpServletRequest` provides three methods—`getContextPath()`, `getServletPath()` and `getPathInfo()`—to retrieve the context path, the servlet path, and the path info, respectively, associated with a request.

### *Identifying the servlet path*

To match a request URI with a servlet, the servlet container follows a simple algorithm. Once it identifies the context path, if any, it evaluates the remaining part of the request URI with the servlet mappings specified in the deployment descriptor, in the following order. If it finds a match at any step, it does not take the next step.

1 The container tries to match the request URI to a servlet mapping. If it finds a match, the complete request URI (except the context path) is the servlet path. In this case, the path info is null.

2 It tries to recursively match the longest path by stepping down the request URI path tree a directory at a time, using the / character as a path separator, and determining if there is a match with a servlet. If there is a match, the matching part of the request URI is the servlet path and the remaining part is the path info.

3 If the last node of the request URI contains an extension (`.jsp`, for example), the servlet container tries to match it to a servlet that handles requests for the specified extension. In this case, the complete request URI is the servlet path and the path info is null.

4 If the container is still unable to find a match, it will forward the request to the default servlet. If there is no default servlet, it will send an error message indicating the servlet was not found.

Understanding the above process is very important for the exam, because you will be asked to map a given request URI to a servlet. Although the process looks complicated, it is actually not. The following detailed example will help you to understand this process. We will assume that the following servlet mappings are defined for the `colorapp` web application in `web.xml`:

```
<servlet-mapping>
   <servlet-name>RedServlet</servlet-name>
   <url-pattern>/red/*</url-pattern>
</servlet-mapping>

<servlet-mapping>
   <servlet-name>RedServlet</servlet-name>
   <url-pattern>/red/red/*</url-pattern>
</servlet-mapping>

<servlet-mapping>
   <servlet-name>RedBlueServlet</servlet-name>
   <url-pattern>/red/blue/*</url-pattern>
</servlet-mapping>

<servlet-mapping>
   <servlet-name>BlueServlet</servlet-name>
   <url-pattern>/blue/</url-pattern>
</servlet-mapping>

<servlet-mapping>
   <servlet-name>GreenServlet</servlet-name>
   <url-pattern>/green</url-pattern>
</servlet-mapping>
```

```
<servlet-mapping>
   <servlet-name>ColorServlet</servlet-name>
   <url-pattern>*.col</url-pattern>
</servlet-mapping>
```

Table 5.2 shows the separation of request URIs into servlet path and path info. For simplicity, we have kept the context path as `colorapp` for all the examples. The table also shows the servlets used for handling the requests.

**Table 5.2 Mapping a request URI to a servlet**

| Request URI | Servlet Used | Servlet Path | Path Info | Comments |
|---|---|---|---|---|
| /colorapp/red | RedServlet | /red | null | See Step 1. |
| /colorapp/red/ | RedServlet | /red | / | See Step 2. |
| /colorapp/red/aaa | RedServlet | /red | /aaa | See Step 2. |
| /colorapp/red/blue/aa | RedBlueServlet | /red/blue | /aa | See Step 2. |
| /colorapp/red/red/aaa | RedServlet | /red/red | /aaa | Longest matching URL mapping is chosen. So, servlet path is /red/red instead of /red. See Step 2. |
| /colorapp/aa.col | ColorServlet | /aa.col | null | *.col is mapped to ColorServlet. See Step 3. |
| /colorapp/hello/aa.col | ColorServlet | /hello/aa.col | null | /hello/aa.col matches with *.col, so the servlet path is /hello/aa.col and the path info is null. See Step 3. |
| /colorapp/red/aa.col | RedServlet | /red | /aa.col | RedServlet is chosen because there is a path (/red) matching with a url-mapping (/red/*). Extension mapping (*.col) is considered only if there is no match for path. See Step 2. |
| /colorapp/blue | NONE (Error message) | | | The url-pattern for BlueServlet is /blue/. Note the trailing /. |
| /colorapp/hello/blue/ | NONE (Error message) | | | /hello/blue does not start with /blue. |
| /colorapp/blue/mydir | NONE (Error message) | | | There is no * in the mapping for BlueServlet. |
| /colorapp/blue/dir/aa.col | ColorServlet | /blue/dir/aa.col | null | There is no mapping for blue/*, so extension mapping *.col is considered. See Step 3. |
| /colorapp/green | GreenServlet | /green | null | See Step 1. |

*Quizlet*

**Q:** In the above example, which servlet will handle the request with a request URI of /colorapp/blue/cool.col?

**A:** The only URI pattern that applies to BlueServlet is /blue/. In this case, our URI is /blue/cool.col, which does not match /blue/. However, it matches *.col, which maps to the ColorServlet. Therefore, ColorServlet will handle this request.

## 5.3 SUMMARY

We began the chapter with a look at the directory structure of a web application. The Java Servlet Specification mandates the way we package all the components, files, and other resources to ensure portability and ease of deployment. Every web application must have a deployment descriptor, named web.xml, which contains the information about the web application that the servlet container needs, such as servlet declarations and mappings, properties, authorization and security constraints, and so forth. We discussed the contents of the deployment descriptor and the manner in which it defines servlets and their initialization parameters. Finally, we looked at the way the servlet container uses the servlet mappings of the deployment descriptor to map a request URI to a servlet.

At this point, you should be able to answer the questions about the structure of a web application and the elements of the deployment descriptor and their uses. You should also be able to determine the servlet used for processing a request by looking at the servlet-mapping elements and the request URI.

In the next chapter, we will discuss how the components of a web application interact with the servlet container through the ServletContext of the web application.

## 5.4 REVIEW QUESTIONS

1. Which element is used to specify useful information about an initialization parameter of a servlet in the deployment descriptor? (Select one)

   **a** param-description

   **b** description

   **c** info

   **d** param-info

   **e** init-param-info

2. Which of the following deployment descriptor snippets correctly associates a servlet implemented by a class named com.abc.SalesServlet with the name SalesServlet? (Select one)

   **a**
```
<servlet>
    <servlet-class>com.abc.SalesServlet</servlet-class>
    <servlet-name>SalesServlet</servlet-name>
</servlet>
```

**b**
```
<servlet>
    <servlet-name>SalesServlet</servlet-name>
    <servlet-package>com.abc.SalesServlet</servlet-package>
</servlet>
```

**c**
```
<servlet>
    <servlet-name>SalesServlet</servlet-name>
    <servlet-class>com.abc.SalesServlet</servlet-class>
</servlet>
```

**d**
```
<servlet name="SalesServlet" class="com.abc.SalesServlet">
    <servlet>
    <servlet-class name="SalesServlet">
      com.abc.SalesServlet
    </servlet-class>
</servlet>
```

**e**
```
<servlet>
    <servlet-name class="com.abc.SalesServlet">
      SalesServlet
    </servlet-name>
</servlet>
```

3. A web application is located in a directory named `sales`. Where should its deployment descriptor be located? (Select one)

   **a** `sales`

   **b** `sales/deployment`

   **c** `sales/WEB`

   **d** `sales/WEB-INF`

   **e** `WEB-INF/sales`

   **f** `WEB-INF`

   **g** `WEB/sales`

4. What file is the deployment descriptor of a web application named `BankApp` stored in? (Select one)

   **a** `BankApp.xml`

   **b** `bankapp.xml`

   **c** `server.xml`

   **d** `deployment.xml`

   **e** `WebApp.xml`

   **f** `web.xml`

5. Your servlet class depends on a utility class named `com.abc.TaxUtil`. Where would you keep the `TaxUtil.class` file? (Select one)

   **a** `WEB-INF`

   **b** `WEB-INF/classes`

   **c** `WEB-INF/lib`

   **d** `WEB-INF/jars`

   **e** `WEB-INF/classes/com/abc`

6. Your web application, named `simpletax`, depends on a third-party JAR file named `taxpackage.jar`. Where would you keep this file? (Select one)

   **a** `simpletax`

   **b** `simpletax/WEB-INF`

   **c** `simpletax/WEB-INF/classes`

   **d** `simpletax/WEB-INF/lib`

   **e** `simpletax/WEB-INF/jars`

   **f** `simpletax/WEB-INF/thirdparty`

7. Which of the following deployment descriptor elements is used to specify the initialization parameters for a servlet named `TestServlet`? (Select one)

   **a** No element is needed because initialization parameters are specified as attributes of the `<servlet>` element.

   **b** `<servlet-param>`

   **c** `<param>`

   **d** `<initialization-param>`

   **e** `<init-parameter>`

   **f** `<init-param>`

8. Assume that the following servlet mapping is defined in the deployment descriptor of a web application:

```
<servlet-mapping>
   <servlet-name>TestServlet</servlet-name>
   <url-pattern>*.asp</url-pattern>
</servlet-mapping>
```

   Which of the following requests will not be serviced by `TestServlet`? (Select one)

   **a** `/hello.asp`

   **b** `/gui/hello.asp`

   **c** `/gui/hello.asp/bye.asp`

   **d** `/gui/*.asp`

   **e** `/gui/sales/hello.asp`

   **f** `/gui/asp`

CHAPTER 6

# The servlet container model



## EXAM OBJECTIVES

**3.1** Identify the uses for and the interfaces (or classes) and methods to achieve the following features:

- Servlet context init parameters
- Servlet context listener
- Servlet context attribute listener
- Session attribute listeners

(Sections 6.1–6.2)

**3.2** Identify the WebApp deployment descriptor element name that declares the following features:

- Servlet context init parameters
- Servlet context listener
- Servlet context attribute listener
- Session attribute listeners

(Section 6.3)

**3.3** Distinguish the behavior of the following in a distributable environment:

- Servlet context init parameters
- Servlet context listener
- Servlet context attribute listener
- Session attribute listeners

(Section 6.4)

### INTRODUCTION

Within a web application, all of the servlets share the same environment. The servlet container exposes the environment to the servlets through the `javax.servlet.ServletContext` interface. The Servlet API also defines interfaces that allow the servlets and the servlet container to interact with each other. In this chapter, we will learn about these interfaces, and we will see how to configure the environment using the deployment descriptor. We will also examine the behavior of the servlets and the servlet container in a distributed environment.

## 6.1 INITIALIZING SERVLETCONTEXT

Every web application has exactly one instance of `javax.servlet.ServletContext` (assuming that the servlet container is not distributed across multiple JVMs). The context is initialized at the time that the web application is loaded. Just as we have initialization parameters for a servlet, we have initialization parameters for a servlet context. These parameters are defined in the deployment descriptor of the web application. The servlets of a web application can retrieve these initialization parameters using the methods of the `ServletContext` interface, shown in table 6.1.

**Table 6.1 ServletContext methods for retrieving the initialization parameters**

| Method | Description |
|---|---|
| String getInitParameter(String name) | Returns a String containing the value of the parameter, or null if the parameter does not exist. |
| java.util.Enumeration getInitParameterNames() | Returns an Enumeration of the names of the context's initialization parameters. |

The servlet context initialization parameters are used to specify application-wide information, such as the developer's contact information and the database connection information. Of course, before we can use these methods we must get a reference to `ServletContext`. The following code snippet from the `init()` method of a servlet demonstrates this:

```
public void init()
{
   ServletContext context =
                  getServletConfig().getServletContext();   <- Uses ServletConfig to get ServletContext
```

```
    //ServletContext context =
                   getServletContext();
    String dburl = context.getInitParameter("dburl");
    //use the dburl to create database connections
}
```

Uses GenericServlet.getServletContext

The `ServletContext` object is contained in the `ServletConfig` object. The above code uses the `getServletContext()` method of `ServletConfig` to get the `ServletContext`. You can also use the `getServletContext()` method of the `GenericServlet` class. `GenericServlet` provides this method since it implements the `ServletConfig` interface.

**NOTE** There is a difference between servlet context initialization parameters and servlet initialization parameters. Servlet context parameters belong to the web application and are accessible to all servlets and JSP pages of that web application. On the other hand, servlet initialization parameters belong to the servlet for which they are defined, and cannot be accessed by any other component of the web application.

*Quizlet*

**Q:** Which method would you use to add an initialization parameter to `ServletContext`?

**A:** Initialization parameters are specified in the deployment descriptor and cannot be added programmatically. You can add an attribute to `ServletContext` by using the `setAttribute()` method, though.

## 6.2 UNDERSTANDING APPLICATION EVENTS AND LISTENERS

We saw in the previous section that the servlet container creates a context for each web application at the time that it is loaded. The creation of the servlet context is an *event*. Similarly, the destruction of the servlet context at the time of shutdown is another event.

Many times, it is useful to know of such events so that, as developers, we can take necessary actions. For example, we can log an entry in the log file when the context is created, or we can page the support people when the context is destroyed. The Servlet Specification 2.3 defines *listener interfaces* as a way to receive notifications when important events related to a web application occur. To receive a notification, we first need to write a class that implements the corresponding listener interface, and then specify the class name in the deployment descriptor. The servlet container will then call the appropriate methods on objects of this class when the events occur. In the following sections, we will look at three listener interfaces and their corresponding event classes:

- ServletContextListener and ServletContextEvent
- ServletContextAttributeListener and ServletContextAttributeEvent
- HttpSessionAttributeListener and HttpSessionBindingEvent

All three listener interfaces extend java.util.EventListener. You are required to know the semantics of these interfaces for the exam. In section 6.3, we will see how to configure the classes that implement these interfaces in the deployment descriptor.

### 6.2.1 javax.servlet.ServletContextListener

This interface allows a developer to know when a servlet context is initialized or destroyed. For example, we might want to create a database connection as soon as the context is initialized and close it when the context is destroyed.

Table 6.2 shows the two methods of the ServletContextListener interface.

**Table 6.2 ServletContextListener methods**

| Method | Description |
|---|---|
| void contextDestroyed(ServletContextEvent sce) | This method is called when the context is destroyed. |
| void contextInitialized(ServletContextEvent sce) | This method is called when the context is initialized. |

Implementing the interface is rather trivial. Listing 6.1 shows how we can write a class that implements the interface in order to use these notifications to open and close a database connection.

**Listing 6.1 Implementing ServletContextListener to create a database connection**

```
package com.abcinc;

import javax.servlet.*;
import java.sql.*;

public class MyServletContextListener implements
                                      ServletContextListener
{
   public void contextInitialized(ServletContextEvent sce)
   {
      try
      {
         Connection c = //create connection to database;
         sce.getServletContext().setAttribute("connection", c);
      }catch(Exception e) { }
   }

   public void contextDestroyed(ServletContextEvent sce)
   {
```

```
        try
        {
            Connection c = (Connection)
            sce.getServletContext().getAttribute("connection");
            c.close();
        }catch(Exception e) { }
    }
}
```

In listing 6.1, we create a database connection in the `contextInitialized()` method and store it in `ServletContext`. Since `ServletContext` is accessible to all of the servlets of the web application, the database connection is also available to them. The `contextDestroyed()` method will be called when the servlet container takes the web application out of service and is thus an ideal place to close the database connection.

Notice the use of the `ServletContextEvent` object that is passed in the `contextInitialized()` and `contextDestroyed()` methods. We use this object to retrieve a reference to the `ServletContext` object of the web application `ServletContextEvent` extends `java.util.EventObject`.

### 6.2.2 javax.servlet.ServletContextAttributeListener

The `ServletContextAttributeListener` interface is used to receive notifications about the changes to the attribute list of a servlet context. It has three methods, as shown in table 6.3.

**Table 6.3 ServletContextAttributeListener methods**

| Method | Description |
|---|---|
| void attributeAdded(ServletContextAttributeEvent scae) | This method is called when a new attribute is added to the servlet context. |
| void attributeRemoved(ServletContextAttributeEvent scae) | This method is called when an existing attribute is removed from the servlet context. |
| void attributeReplaced(ServletContextAttributeEvent scae) | This method is called when an attribute of the servlet context is replaced. |

This interface is implemented in the same way that `ServletContextListener` is implemented in listing 6.1. We write a class that implements the interface and specify the name of the class in the deployment descriptor. The servlet container will call its methods automatically when relevant events occur.

An object of type `ServletContextAttributeEvent` is passed to the methods of this interface. The `ServletContextAttributeEvent` class extends from the `ServletContextEvent` class and provides the name and value of the attribute that is added to, removed from, or replaced in the servlet context.

### 6.2.3 javax.servlet.http.HttpSessionAttributeListener

As we discussed in chapter 4, "The Servlet model," we use the `HttpSession` object to share data among the servlets by setting attributes into the session. The `HttpSessionAttributeListener` interface allows a developer to receive notifications whenever changes occur to the attribute list of the `HttpSession` object. These changes include adding a new attribute, removing an existing attribute, and replacing an existing attribute. This interface declares three methods, as shown in table 6.4.

**Table 6.4 HttpSessionAttributeListener methods**

| Method | Description |
|---|---|
| void attributeAdded(HttpSessionBindingEvent se) | This method is called when an attribute is added to a session. |
| void attributeRemoved(HttpSessionBindingEvent se) | This method is called when an attribute is removed from a session. |
| void attributeReplaced(HttpSessionBindingEvent se) | This method is called when an attribute is replaced in a session. |

As we mentioned earlier, we need to specify the class that implements this interface in the deployment descriptor in order to receive the notifications. An object of type `HttpSessionBindingEvent` is passed to the methods of this interface. The `HttpSessionBindingEvent` class extends from the `HttpSessionEvent` class and provides the name and value of the attribute that is added to or removed or replaced from the session.

**NOTE** There is a discrepancy in the name of `ServletContextAttributeListener`. The Servlet Specification 2.3 says `ServletContextAttributesListener` while the API says `ServletContextAttributeListener`. A similar discrepancy is present in the name of the `HttpSessionAttributeListener` as well. In this book, we have assumed that the correct names are `ServletContextAttributeListener` and `HttpSessionAttributeListener`.

*Quizlet*

**Q:** Which application event listeners are notified when a web application starts up?

**A:** When the application starts up, the servlet context of the application is created. Therefore, only `ServletContextListeners` are notified.

## 6.3 CONFIGURING A WEB APPLICATION

We can configure the properties of a web application context by using the deployment descriptor. The following is the definition of the `<web-app>` element with the related subelements highlighted. You don't have to memorize this definition, but we have provided it here, since it is helpful to see all the elements in one place.

```
<!ELEMENT web-app (icon?, display-name?, description?, distributable?, context-param*, filter*, filter-mapping*, listener*, servlet*, servlet-mapping*, session-config?, mime-mapping*, welcome-file-list?, error-page*, taglib*, resource-env-ref*, resource-ref*, security-constraint*, login-config?, security-role*, env-entry*, ejb-ref*, ejb-local-ref*)>
```

The properties of the web application are accessible through ServletContext. Since the properties apply to all of the components of a web application, it is logical that the elements used to configure the properties come directly under the <web-app> element. Let's look at these elements briefly:

- *display-name.* Defines a short name that can be used by development tools, such as IDEs.
- *description.* Defines the usage and any important information that the developer might want to convey to the deployer.
- *distributable.* Indicates that the application can be distributed across multiple JVMs.
- *context-param.* Specifies initialization parameters for the web application. It contains a <param-name>, a <param-value>, and an optional <description> element. In section 6.1, we saw how the ServletContext initialization parameters can be used to create a database connection. The following lines specify a dburl parameter used by a servlet:

```
<context-param>
   <param-name>dburl</param-name>
   <param-value>jdbc:odbc:MySQLODBC</param-value>
</context-param>
```

- We can have as many <context-param> elements as we need.
- *listener.* Specifies the classes that listen for the application events that we discussed in section 6.2. It contains one and only one listener-class element that specifies the fully qualified class name of the class that implements the listener interface. The following lines show how we can configure two classes that implement the ServletContextListener and ServletContextAttributeListener interfaces:

```
<listener>
   <listener-class>
      com.abcinc.MyServletContextListener
</listener-class>
</listener>

<listener>
   <listener-class>
      com.abcinc.MyServletContextAttributeListener
   </listener-class>
</listener>
```

Observe that we did not specify which class should be used for which event; that is because the servlet container will figure it out on its own. It instantiates the specified class and checks all the interfaces that the class implements. For each relevant interface, it adds the instance to its list of respective listeners. The container delivers the events to the listeners in the order the classes are specified in the deployment descriptor. These classes should, of course, be present in the classpath of the web application. You can either keep them in the `WEB-INF\classes` directory or package them in a JAR file with other servlet classes.

**NOTE** You can also implement multiple listener interfaces in the same class and configure just this class to receive the various notifications through the methods of the respective interfaces. In this case, you will need only one `<listener>` element in the deployment descriptor. The servlet container will create only one instance of this class and will send all the notifications to this instance.

*Quizlet*

**Q:** You have written a class named `MySessionAttributeListener` to listen for `HttpSessionBindingEvents`. How will you configure this class in the deployment descriptor?

**A:** By adding a `<listener>` element in the deployment descriptor as shown here:

```
<web-app>
   ...
   <listener>
     <listener-class>MySessionAttributeListener</listener-class>
   </listener>
   ...
</web-app>
```

## 6.4 WEB APPLICATIONS IN A DISTRIBUTED ENVIRONMENT

An industrial-strength web application is expected to service thousands of simultaneous users with high reliability. It is common to distribute the applications across multiple server machines that are configured to work as a cluster. Server applications, such as the web server and the servlet container, are spread over these machines and thus work in a distributed mode. For example, one logical servlet container may actually run on multiple JVMs on multiple machines. Distributing an application has the following advantages:

- *Fail-over support.* If a server machine breaks down due to some reason, another server machine can take over transparently to the users.
- *Load balancing.* Requests are assigned to the least busy server of the cluster to be serviced.

Distributing an application is not an easy task, though. Configuring the machines and the servers to work in a cluster is quite complicated. Moreover, the servlets should be written while keeping in mind the constraints posed by a distributed environment. More often than not, it is easier to upgrade the machine than to distribute the application across multiple machines. However, certain requirements, like failover support, can only be met by clustering.

To develop web applications for a distributed environment, we need to understand that many assumptions we take for granted no longer are true. For example, we cannot assume that there is only one instance of a servlet; there may be multiple instances of a servlet running under different JVMs, and so we cannot use static or instance members to share data. We cannot directly use the local file system—the absolute path of the files may be different on different machines. We also have to keep the application state in a database instead of the `ServletContext`, because there will be different `ServletContexts` on different machines.

The Java Servlet Specification helps us by guaranteeing the behavior of some of the important aspects and features of a servlet container in a distributed environment.

### 6.4.1 Behavior of a ServletContext

Each web application has one and only one `ServletContext` instance on each JVM. The `ServletContext` for the default web application, however, exists on only one JVM—that is, it is not distributed.

On the exam, you will find questions based on the following points regarding the behavior of a `ServletContext` in a distributed environment:

- `ServletContext` attributes set on one JVM are not visible on another JVM. We must use the database or the session to share the information.
- A Servlet container is not required to propagate `ServletContextEvents` and `ServletContextAttributeEvents` to different JVMs. This means that changes to the `ServletContext` in one JVM may not trigger a method call on a `ServletContextListener` or a `ServletContextAttributeListener` in another JVM.
- `ServletContext` initialization parameters are available in all of the JVMs. Recall that `ServletContext` initialization parameters are specified in the deployment descriptor.

*Quizlet*

**Q:** Your web application uses a `ServletContextListener` to page support personnel whenever it goes down. What would be the impact on this functionality if the web application were deployed in a distributed environment?

**A:** There will be no impact on this functionality. Because an instance of `ServletContext` will be created on all the servers, the support personnel will be paged whenever any instance is destroyed.

**Q:** You maintain a list of users who are logged into the system in `ServletContext`. You print the list of these users upon request. How would this functionality be affected if your web application were deployed in a distributed environment?

**A:** This functionality will not work properly in a distributed environment. Remember that each server machine will have a separate instance of `ServletContext`. Therefore, a `ServletContext` will only know of the users who logged in through the server machine on which it resides. Obviously, a request to print the list of users will show only a partial list of the users.

### 6.4.2 Behavior of an HttpSession

In a distributed environment, the semantics of an `HttpSession` are a little different than those of a `ServletContext`. The specification mandates that requests belonging to a session must be serviced by only one JVM at a time. However, the container may migrate the session to another JVM for load balancing or fail-over.

You should remember the following points regarding the behavior of an `HttpSession` in a distributed environment:

- An `HttpSession` can reside on only one JVM at a time.
- A servlet container is not required to propagate `HttpSessionEvents` to different JVMs.
- Attributes of a session that implement the `java.io.Serializable` interface are migrated appropriately when the session migrates. This does not mean that if the attributes implement the `readObject()` and `writeObject()` methods, they will definitely be called.
- A container notifies all of the session attributes that implement the `HttpSessionActivationListener` interface when it migrates the session.
- A container may throw an `IllegalArgumentException` in the `setAttribute()` method of `HttpSession` if the attribute is not `Serializable`.

## 6.5 *SUMMARY*

The servlets of a web application share the application's environment through the methods of the `ServletContext` object. When a web application is loaded, `ServletContext` is initialized using the parameters that have been defined in the deployment descriptor. In this chapter, we learned how to use the initialization parameters of `ServletContext`.

Listener interfaces are implemented in order to receive notifications of certain events in a web application. We discussed the uses of `ServletContextListener`, `ServletContextAttributeListener`, and `HttpSessionAttributeListener` and their configuration in the deployment descriptor.

A web application can be distributed across multiple servers to improve performance and reliability. We discussed the ways that ServletContext and HttpSession function in a distributed environment.

You should now be able to answer the questions about servlet context initialization parameters, the application event listener classes, and the behavior of ServletContext and HttpSession in a distributed environment.

In the next chapter, we will discuss how to handle exceptions and error conditions occurring in a web application.

## 6.6 REVIEW QUESTIONS

1. Which of the following methods will be invoked when a ServletContext is destroyed? (Select one)

   **a** contextDestroyed() of javax.servlet.ServletContextListener
   **b** contextDestroyed() of javax.servlet.HttpServletContextListener
   **c** contextDestroyed() of javax.servlet.http.ServletContextListener
   **d** contextDestroyed() of javax.servlet.http.HttpServletContextListener

2. Which of the following methods will be invoked when a ServletContext is created? (Select one)

   **a** contextInstantiated() of javax.servlet.ServletContextListener
   **b** contextInitialized() of javax.servlet.ServletContextListener
   **c** contextInited() of javax.servlet.ServletContextListener
   **d** contextCreated() of javax.servlet.ServletContextListener

3. Consider the following class:

```
import javax.servlet.*;
public class MyListener implements ServletContextAttributeListener
{
   public void attributeAdded(ServletContextAttributeEvent scab)
   {
      System.out.println("attribute added");
   }

   public void attributeRemoved(ServletContextAttributeEvent scab)
   {
      System.out.println("attribute removed");
   }
}
```

   Which of the following statements about the above class is correct? (Select one)

   **a** This class will compile as is.
   **b** This class will compile only if the attributeReplaced() method is added to it.
   **c** This class will compile only if the attributeUpdated() method is added to it.
   **d** This class will compile only if the attributeChanged() method is added to it.

4. Which method is used to retrieve an attribute from a `ServletContext`? (Select one)

   **a** `String getAttribute(int index)`
   **b** `String getObject(int index)`
   **c** `Object getAttribute(int index)`
   **d** `Object getObject(int index)`
   **e** `Object getAttribute(String name)`
   **f** `String getAttribute(String name)`
   **g** `String getObject(String name)`

5. Which method is used to retrieve an initialization parameter from a `ServletContext`? (Select one)

   **a** `Object getInitParameter(int index)`
   **b** `Object getParameter(int index)`
   **c** `Object getInitParameter(String name)`
   **d** `String getInitParameter(String name)`
   **e** `String getParameter(String name)`

6. Which deployment descriptor element is used to specify a `ServletContextListener`? (Select one)

   **a** `<context-listener>`
   **b** `<listener>`
   **c** `<servlet-context-listener>`
   **d** `<servletcontextlistener>`
   **e** `<servletcontext-listener>`

7. Which of the following `web.xml` snippets correctly specify an initialization parameter for a servlet context? (Select one)

   **a**
```
<context-param>
    <name>country</name>
    <value>USA</value>
<context-param>
```

   **b**
```
<context-param>
    <param name="country" value="USA" />
<context-param>
```

   **c**
```
<context>
    <param name="country" value="USA" />
<context>
```

   **d**
```
<context-param>
    <param-name>country</param-name>
    <param-value>USA</param-value>
<context-param>
```

8. Which of the following is not a requirement of a distributable web application? (Select one)

**a** It cannot depend on the notification events generated due to changes in the `ServletContext` attribute list.

**b** It cannot depend on the notification events generated due to changes in the session attribute list.

**c** It cannot depend on the notification events generated when a session is activated or passivated.

**d** It cannot depend on the notification events generated when `ServletContext` is created or destroyed.

**e** It cannot depend on the notification events generated when a session is created or destroyed.

9. Which of the following is a requirement of a distributable web application? (Select one)

**a** It cannot depend on `ServletContext` for sharing information.

**b** It cannot depend on the `sendRedirect()` method.

**c** It cannot depend on the `include()` and `forward()` methods of the `RequestDispatcher` class.

**d** It cannot depend on cookies for session management.

CHAPTER 7

# Handling server-side exceptions



## EXAM OBJECTIVES

**4.1** For each of the following cases, identify correctly constructed code for handling business logic exceptions, and match that code with correct statements about the code's behavior:

- Return an HTTP error using the sendError response method.
- Return an HTTP error using the setStatus method.

(Section 7.1)

**4.2** Given a set of business logic exceptions, identify the following:

- The configuration that the deployment descriptor uses to handle each exception.
- How to use a RequestDispatcher to forward the request to an error page.
- Specify the handling declaratively in the deployment descriptor.

(Sections 7.2–7.3)

**4.3** Identify the method used for the following:

- Write a message to the WebApp log.
- Write a message and an exception to the WebApp log.

(Section 7.4)

## INTRODUCTION

Like any Java program, a servlet may encounter exceptions while it is executing the normal flow of the statements. For example, a network problem may cause an `SQLException` to be thrown while executing a query, or a corrupted file may cause an `IOException` to be thrown while it is being read. If not handled properly, these exceptions will fall through to the servlet container, and the servlet container will generate the famous "Internal Server Error" page showing a long stack trace. This behavior is usually not acceptable in production environments for obvious reasons.

Besides standard exceptions, a web application may also define classes for business logic exceptions. For example, a banking application may define a set of business logic exceptions, such as `InsufficientFundsException` or `InvalidTransactionException`, that represent common error conditions. We need to extract the error messages contained in these exceptions and present them to the user.

In this chapter, we will learn how to handle such exceptions and how to generate a presentable response in such situations.

## 7.1 HANDLING EXCEPTIONS PROGRAMMATICALLY

A simple solution to handle all kinds of exceptions that may occur in a servlet is to wrap the servlet code in a `try` block and, in case of any exceptions, programmatically send an error message to the browser from the `catch` block. Listing 7.1 illustrates this approach.

**Listing 7.1 Using the sendError method**

```
import javax.servlet.*;
import javax.servlet.http.*;
import java.sql.*;
import java.util.*;

public class ItemServlet extends HttpServlet
{
   Connection connection;

   public void init()
   {
      //initialize connection
   }

   public void doGet(HttpServletRequest req,
                               HttpServletResponse res)
   {
      String category = req.getParameter("category");
```

```
        Vector items = new Vector();
        try
        {
            Statement stmt = connection.createStatement();
            ResultSet rs = stmt.executeQuery(
            "select * from ITEM where CATEGORY=' "+category+"'"
                                           );
            while(rs.next())
            {
                items.addElement(rs.getString("name"));
            }
            //generate HTML page using items.
        }
        catch(SQLException e)
        {
            //send an error message to the browser.
            res.sendError(
                    HttpServletResponse.SC_INTERNAL_SERVER_ERROR,
                        "There was some problem with the database. \
                            Please report it to the webmaster. ");
        }
    }
}
```

In listing 7.1, any `SQLException` thrown by the database access code in the `try` block is caught by the `catch` block. We then call the `sendError()` method on the response object and pass the error code and the error message as parameters. This method will cause the servlet container to send an error page to the browser containing these values.

The `javax.servlet.http.HttpServletResponse` interface provides two flavors of the `sendError()` method, as shown in table 7.1.

**Table 7.1 HttpServletResponse methods for sending an error message to the client**

| Method | Description |
|---|---|
| void sendError(int sc) | Sends the status code to the client and clears the response buffer |
| void sendError(int sc, String msg) | Sends the status code as well as the message to the client and clears the response buffer |

The semantics of both methods are the same. They trigger the servlet container to generate and send an appropriate HTML page showing the status code to the client. In the second method, a message is also included.

Both methods throw a `java.lang.IllegalStateException` if the response is already committed. Similarly, after calling these methods, the response should be assumed to be committed, and no other data should be written to the output stream.

HttpServletResponse also provides a setStatus() method, shown in table 7.2, which may be used to set the status code of an HTTP response message.

**Table 7.2 The setStatus() method of HttpServletResponse**

| Method | Description |
|---|---|
| void setStatus(int sc) | Sets the status code for the response |

This method is similar to the sendError() methods in the sense that we may use it to set the status codes representing errors in the response. However, an important point about the setStatus() method is that, unlike the sendError() methods, it does not trigger the container to generate an error page. It just sends the status code to the browser, which is displayed by the browser as per its settings. For this reason, it should be used only for setting non-error status codes, such as SC_OK.

**NOTE** The method setStatus(int sc, String message) of HttpServletResponse is deprecated.

### 7.1.1 Handling business logic exceptions

Handling business logic exceptions is no different than handling standard exceptions, such as java.sql.SQLException. Listing 7.2 contains a partial listing of an imaginary AccountServlet.

**Listing 7.2 Handling business logic exceptions**

```
import javax.servlet.*;
import javax.servlet.http.*;
import java.util.*;

public class AccountServlet extends HttpServlet
{
   private double debit(String accountid, double amount)
                  throws InsufficientFundsException
   {
       double currentBalance = getBalance(accountId);
       if(currentBalance < amount)
          throw new InsufficientFundsException(currentBalance, amount);
       else
       {
          setNewBalance(accountId, currentBalance - amount);
          return currentBalance - amount;
       }
   }

   public void doPost(HttpServletRequest req,
                      HttpServletResponse res)
   {
      String command = req.getParameter("command");
      if("debit".equals(command))
```

```
        {
            try
            {
                double amount =
                        Double.parseDouble(req.getParameter("amount"));
                String accountId =
                        req.getSession().getAttribute("accountId");
                double newBalance = debit(accountId, amount);

                //generate HTML page showing new balance.
            }
            catch(InsufficientFundsException e)
            {
                String message = e.getMessage();
                //send an error message to the browser.
                res.sendError(
                        HttpServletResponse.SC_INTERNAL_SERVER_ERROR,
                        message);
            }
        }
        else
        {
            //do something else
        }

    }
}
```

This servlet uses the `debit()` method to debit an amount specified by the user in a `try` block. If the account does not have enough funds, this method throws an `InsufficientFundsException`, which is a custom business exception. We handle this exception in the `catch` block so that it is not propagated to the container. We then get the message from the business exception object and send the message to the user using the `HttpServletResponse.sendError()` method. The code for `InsufficientFundsException` may be as simple as the following:

```
public class InsufficientFundsException extends Exception
{
    public double amtIntheAcc, amtTobeWithdrawn;
    public InsufficientFundsException(
            double pAmtIntheAcc, double pAmtTobeWithdrawn)
    {
        super("Your account has only "+ amtIntheAcc
                + " dollars. You cannot withdraw "
                + amtTobeWithdrawn +" dollars.");
        amtIntheAcc = pAmtIntheAcc;
        amtTobeWithdrawn = pAmtTobeWithdrawn;
    }
}
```

## 7.2 HANDLING EXCEPTIONS DECLARATIVELY

Instead of handling the exceptions in our code and then calling `sendError()`, we can define error pages in the deployment descriptor and leave the rest to the container. The idea is to specify the mapping of exception classes and error codes to the resources that can generate appropriate responses. When it starts up the web application, the servlet container assembles these mappings from the deployment descriptor into a map that it will use to display the proper error pages in response to exceptions and errors. At runtime, when an uncaught exception occurs, the servlet container looks up this map and invokes the associated resource. For example, if we map `java.sql.SQLException` with `SQLExceptionHandlerServlet`, the servlet container will invoke `SQLExceptionHandlerServlet` whenever a `SQLException` is left unhandled.

The `error-page` element is used to specify this mapping. This element is defined as follows:

```
<!ELEMENT error-page ((error-code | exception-type), location)>
```

This element comes directly under the `<web-app>` element; it associates an exception type or an error code with a resource. Each `<error-page>` element describes one mapping:

- *error-code.* Specifies the HTTP error code (such as `404`) for an error-page mapping. It must be unique across all the error-page mappings.
- *exception-type.* Specifies the full exception class name for an error-page mapping. It must be unique across all the error-page mappings.
- *location.* Specifies the resource for an error-page mapping. The value must start with a /.

Let's take a closer look at the way we handle exceptions using the declarative approach.

### 7.2.1 Using declarative exception handling

You may have observed that the do*XXX*() methods of the `Servlet` interface declare `ServletException` and `IOException` in their `throws` clauses. An important implication of this is that we cannot throw any exception other than these two, or the `RuntimeException` or their subclasses. So how do we throw exceptions like `SQLException` or any custom non-runtime exceptions? Well, we do not throw them directly; we catch the exceptions in our code, wrap them in a `ServletException`, and then rethrow the `ServletException`. The wrapped exception is called the *root exception*, or *root cause*. When the servlet container receives an exception, it tries to find a matching resource. If it is unable to find one and if the exception is a `ServletException`, the container uses the `ServletException.getRootCause()` method to extract the wrapped exception and tries to find a match for it.

Another way to throw custom exceptions is to extend the custom exceptions from `RuntimeException`, `ServletException`, or `IOException`. We can throw such exceptions without wrapping them in a `ServletException` because they do not break the `throws` clauses of the do*XXX*() methods. The servlet container uses these exceptions directly for finding an error-page mapping.

Listing 7.3 shows the modified version of the code we saw earlier and illustrates the use of declarative exception handling.

**Listing 7.3 Declarative error handling**

```
//code for doGet of ItemServlet
public void doGet(HttpServletRequest req,
                              HttpServletResponse res)

{
   String category = req.getParameter("category");
   if( !loggedIn(req) )
   {
      //Set the status code to 403 if the user is not logged in.
      //we may also use setStatus().
      res.sendError(res.SC_FORBIDDEN);
      return;
   }
   Vector items = new Vector();
   try
   {
      Statement stmt = connection.createStatement();
      ResultSet rs = stmt.executeQuery(
      "select * from ITEM where CATEGORY=' "+category+"' "
                                 );

      while(rs.next())
      {
         items.addElement(rs.getString("name"));
      }
   }
   catch(SQLException e)
   {
      //wrap the exception in a ServletException and rethrow
      throw new ServletException("Wrapped SQLException", e);
   }
}
```

In listing 7.3, we set the status code of the response to `SC_FORBIDDEN` if the user is not logged in. In this case, before sending the response to the browser, the servlet container will look through all the `<error-page>` elements and try to find an error page that is mapped to the status code (here, `403`). If the container finds an error page, it will use that page to generate a response; otherwise, it will send a default error page.

Similarly, if the servlet throws a ServletException, the servlet container will extract the root cause (here, SQLException). The servlet container will then look through all the <error-page> elements and try to find an error page that is mapped to the SQLException exception type.

The following code snippet contains the relevant portion of web.xml showing the error-page mapping:

```
<web-app>

   <servlet>
      <servlet-name>ItemServlet</servlet-name>
      <servlet-class>ItemServlet</servlet-class>
    </servlet>

    <error-page>
       <error-code>403</error-code>        <-- Specifies error page for SC_FORBIDDEN
       <location>/errorpages/securityerror.html</location>
    </error-page>

    <error-page>
       <exception-type>java.sql.SQLException</exception-type>   <-- Specifies error page for SQLException
       <location>/errorpages/sqlerror.html</location>
    </error-page>

</web-app>
```

**NOTE** If you specify ServletException in the error-page mapping, the servlet container will not try to match the exception wrapped inside Servlet-Exception.

### 7.2.2 Using servlets and JSP pages as exception handlers

In the previous example, we have configured HTML pages as the exception handlers. However, since they are static, HTML pages cannot analyze the exception or provide any detailed information about the error to the user. This problem can be easily solved by using either servlets or JSP pages as the exception handlers. The following web.xml snippet maps the error code 403 and the SQLException to MyErrorHandler-Servlet:

```
<error-page>
   <error-code>403</error-code>        <-- Specifies error page for SC_FORBIDDEN
   <location>/servlet/MyErrorHandlerServlet</location>
</error-page>

<error-page>
   <exception-type>java.sql.SQLException</exception-type>   <-- Specifies error page for SQLException
   <location>/servlet/MyErrorHandlerServlet</location>
</error-page>
```

The above mapping is the same as the previous one except that, in this case, we have specified servlets instead of HTML files to generate error pages.

To help the error handler servlet (or a JSP page) analyze the problem and generate a detailed response, the servlet container sets certain attributes in the request before dispatching it to the error page. See table 7.3 for an explanation. The attribute names are self-explanatory.

**Table 7.3 Attributes available to an error handler**

| Attribute Name | Attribute Type | Description |
|---|---|---|
| javax.servlet.error.status_code | java.lang.Integer | Contains the status_code value passed in the setStatus() or sendError() methods |
| javax.servlet.error.exception_type | java.lang.Class | Contains the Class object for the uncaught exception |
| javax.servlet.error.message | java.lang.String | Contains the message passed in the sendError() method or the message contained in the uncaught exception |
| javax.servlet.error.exception | java.lang.Throwable | Contains the uncaught exception that invokes the error page |
| javax.servlet.error.request_uri | java.lang.String | The current request URI |
| javax.servlet.error.servlet_name | java.lang.String | Contains the name of the servlet that caused the error page to be invoked |

Listing 7.4 shows the `service()` method of `MyErrorHandlerServlet` that uses these attributes to generate a page containing useful error messages.

**Listing 7.4 The service() method of MyErrorHandlerServlet**

```
public void service(HttpServletRequest req,
                    HttpServletResponse res)
{

   PrintWriter pw = res.getWriter();
   pw.println("<html>");
   pw.println("<head>");
   pw.println("</head>");
   pw.println("<body>");

   String code = "" +
           req.getAttribute("javax.servlet.error.status_code");

   if("403".equals(code) )
   {
      pw.println("<h3>Sorry, you do not have
                               appropriate rights!</h3><p>");
      pw.println("<h3>Please log into the system to
                              access this feature.</h3><p>");
```

```
    }
    else
    {
       pw.println("<h3>Sorry, we are unable to
                                  process your request.</h3><p>");
       pw.println("Please report this URL to
                                 webmaster@xyz.com : " +
           req.getAttribute("javax.servlet.error.request_uri"));
    }
    pw.println("</body>");
    pw.println("</html>");
}
```

The above servlet generates a customized HTML page depending on the error code.

If this servlet is invoked as a result of an uncaught exception instead of an error code, it can use the `javax.servlet.error.exception` attribute to retrieve the detailed exception message:

```
Object exception =
           req.getAttribute("javax.servlet.error.exception");
if(exception != null && exception instanceof ServletException)
{
   Throwable actualexception =
      (Throwable) ((ServletException) exception).getRootCause();

  pw.println("The servlet encountered the following problem
                        while processing your request:<br>");
   pw.println(actualexception.getMessage());
}
```

The `javax.servlet.error.exception` attribute is a recent addition to the list of attributes that may be set in the request for the error handler. This makes `javax.servlet.error.exception_type` and `javax.servlet.error.message` redundant because values for these attributes can be easily retrieved from the `exception` object, as shown in the above code. These attributes are kept only for backward compatibility.

**NOTE** If an error handler is invoked as a result of either the `setStatus()` or the `sendError()` method, `javax.servlet.error.exception` and `javax.servlet.error.exception_type` are set to null. Similarly, if an error handler is invoked as a result of an exception, `javax.servlet.error.code` is set to null.

As you can see, handling exceptions by using servlets can take some effort. We will see in chapter 11 how JSP pages make this task easier.

*Quizlet*

**Q:** In section 7.2.1, we discussed an imaginary account servlet that handles `InsufficientFundsException` programmatically. How will you implement the servlet using declarative exception handling?

**A:** Step 1: Extend the `InsufficientFundsException` from `Runtime-Exception` and let it be thrown outside the servlet, as shown here:

```
public void doPost(HttpServletRequest req,
                   HttpServletResponse res)
{
   String command = req.getParameter("command");
   if("debit".equals(command))
   {
      double amount =
           Double.parseDouble(req.getParameter("amount"));
      String accountId =
           req.getSession().getAttribute("accountId");

      //do not handle the exception thrown by debit()
      double newBalance = debit(accountId, amount);

      //generate HTML page showing new balance.
   }
   else
   {
      //do something else
   }

}
```

Step 2: Define the mapping of this exception to an error page in the `web.xml` file:

```
<error-page>
   <exception-type>InsufficientFundsException</exception-type>
   <location>/servlet/BusinessLogicExceptionHandlerSerlvet</
      location>
</error-page>
```

Step 3: Implement the exception handler to generate an appropriate message. The following is a sample implementation of the `service()` method of the exception handler servlet:

```
public void service(HttpServletRequest req,
                    HttpServletResponse res)
{

   PrintWriter pw = res.getWriter();
   pw.println("<html><head></head><body>");

   Throwable exception = (Throwable)
      req.getAttribute("javax.servlet.error.exception");
```

```
        if(exception instanceof InsufficientFundsException)
        {
           pw.println("<h3>Sorry, you do not have
                        enough funds in your account!</h3><p>");
           pw.println("<h4>Current balance :"+
           ((InsufficientFundsException) exception).amtInAcc+
                                             "</h4><p>");
           pw.println("<h4>Amount :"+
          ((InsufficientFundsException) exception).amtTobeWithdrawn +
                                             "</h4><p>");
        }
        else
        {
           //do something else
        }
        pw.println("</body></html>");
    }
```

## 7.3 USING REQUESTDISPATCHER TO HANDLE EXCEPTIONS

Recall that we use a `RequestDispatcher` to include or forward a request to another resource. We can also use it to forward a request to an error page. The following code for the `doPost()` method illustrates this approach:

```
public void doPost(HttpServletRequest req,
                   HttpServletResponse res)
{
   String command = req.getParameter("command");
   if("debit".equals(command))
   {
      double amount =
        Double.parseDouble(req.getParameter("amount"));
      String accountId =
        req.getSession().getAttribute("accountId");

      try
      {
         double newBalance = debit(accountId, amount);
      }
      catch(InsufficientFundsException isfe)
      {
         req.setAttribute("javax.servlet.error.exception", isfe);
         req.setAttribute("javax.servlet.error.request_uri",
                          req.getRequestURI());
         req.setAttribute("javax.servlet.error.servlet_name",
                          req.getServletName());

         RequestDispatcher rd = req.getRequestDispatcher(
                 "/servlet/BusinessLogicExceptionHandlerSerlvet");
         rd.forward(req, res);
```

```
            return;
        }

        //generate HTML page showing new balance.
    }
    else
    {
        //do something else
    }
}
```

In this example, we catch the business logic exception in the `catch` block. We then set appropriate attributes in the request and forward the request to a servlet.

Please note that we are using this example merely to illustrate the way that we can use a `RequestDispatcher` to forward a request to an exception handler in case of an exception. We would not normally use this approach because it requires us to hard-code the name of the error handler in the servlet code. In the future, if we wanted to change the error handler page, we would have to modify the servlet code.

### 7.3.1 Handling exceptions thrown by RequestDispatcher

As we discussed in chapter 4, we use the `include()` or `forward()` methods of the `RequestDispatcher` to include or forward a request to another resource. What will happen if that resource—for instance, a servlet—throws an exception? In such cases, the call to `include()` or `forward()` ends with an exception. The specification lays out the following rules for handling such exceptions:

1. If the exception thrown by the included or forwarded resource is a `RuntimeException`, a `ServletException`, or an `IOException`, it is thrown as is by the `include()` or `forward()` method.
2. Otherwise, the exception is wrapped in a `ServletException` as the `rootCause`, and the `ServletException` is thrown by the `include()` or `forward()` method.

These rules ensure that the caller servlet gets a chance to handle the exceptions generated by the included or forwarded resource, as shown by the following code for the `doGet()` method of a servlet:

```
public void doGet(HttpServletRequest req,
                  HttpServletResponse res)
                  throws ServletException, IOException
{
   try
   {
      RequestDispatcher rd =
        req.getRequestDispatcher("/servlet/someServlet");
      return;
   }
   catch(RuntimeException re)
   {
```

```
            //take actions as per business logic

            //and/or rethrow the exception
            throw re;
        }
        catch(IOException ie)
        {
            //take actions as per business logic

            //and/or rethrow the exception
            throw ie;
        }
        catch(ServletException se)
        {
            //extract the actual exception.
            Throwable t = se.getRootCause();

            //take actions as per business logic

            //and/or rethrow the exception
            throw se;
        }
    }
```

## 7.4 LOGGING

Usually, we use `System.out` to print messages and debug information on the console. Although this approach is very convenient, we should not use it in a production environment—a servlet container usually runs as a background process, and we cannot assume the availability of the standard output stream. Moreover, messages printed by all the web applications go to the same standard output, which makes their analysis very difficult.

The servlet API provides basic support for logging through `javax.servlet.ServletContext` and `javax.servlet.GenericServlet`. Table 7.4 shows the two logging methods provided by both `GenericServlet` and `ServletContext`.

**Table 7.4 GenericServlet and ServletContext logging methods**

| Method | Description |
|---|---|
| void log(java.lang.String msg) | Writes the given message to the log file |
| void log(java.lang.String message, java.lang.Throwable t) | Writes the given message and a stack trace for the given Throwable object to the log file |

The actual file used to log the messages depends on the servlet container. Most of the containers allow us to configure different files for different web applications. Tomcat keeps this information in the `conf/server.xml` file.

The only difference between the `log()` methods provided by `GenericServlet` and those provided by `ServletContext` is that the `GenericServlet` methods prepend the servlet name to the message while the `ServletContext` methods do not.

The following doGet() method code for a servlet uses GenericServlet's log() method to log an exception:

```
public void doGet(HttpServletRequest req,
                  HttpServletResponse res)
{
   try
   {
      //business logic here
   }
   catch(SQLException e)
   {
      //log the exception
      log("Exception in servlet", e);

      //wrap the exception in a ServletException and rethrow
      throw new ServletException("Wrapped Exception", e);
   }
}
```

If the above code generates an exception, it will write the stack trace associated with the exception in the log file. The following is the sample text written to the log file <tomcat-root>/logs/localhost_log.2001-12-28.txt:

```
2001-12-28 21:48:50 TestServlet: Exception in servlet
java.sql.SQLException: sql exception
   at cgscwcd.chapter7.TestServlet.doGet(TestServlet.java:46)
   at javax.servlet.http.HttpServlet.service(HttpServlet.java:740)
   at javax.servlet.http.HttpServlet.service(HttpServlet.java:853)
   at org.apache.catalina.servlets.InvokerServlet.serveRequest(
      InvokerServlet.java:446)
   at org.apache.catalina.servlets.InvokerServlet.doGet(
      InvokerServlet.java:180)
...
...
```

## 7.5 SUMMARY

Exception handling is an important part of writing servlets. In this chapter, we learned that displaying informative error pages instead of just dumping the stack trace is not very difficult. The Servlet specification allows us to handle exceptions either programmatically or declaratively. To handle exceptions programmatically, we wrap the code in a try-catch block and use the sendError() method to send a message to the browser when the exceptions are caught. To handle exceptions declaratively, we define error pages and map them to exception classes and error codes in the deployment descriptor, and the servlet container automatically invokes the appropriate resource in response to exceptions and errors.

Exception handler pages can be static HTML pages, or if we want them to provide detailed information about the error, we can use servlets or JSP pages as the exception handlers.

Often in an application, we will want to log informational and error messages, and monitor the status of the application. We discussed how to do this using the `log()` methods provided by `GenericServlet` and `ServletContext`.

You should now be ready to answer questions based on the `sendError()` and `setStatus()` methods of `ServletResponse`. You should know how to configure error pages in the deployment descriptor for handling exceptions and error codes. In addition, you should be able to answer questions based on the logging methods of `GenericServlet` and `ServletContext`.

In the next chapter, we will learn how to develop stateful web applications using sessions.

## 7.6 REVIEW QUESTIONS

1. Your servlet encounters an exception while processing a request. Which method would you use to send an error response to the browser? (Select two)

   **a** `sendError(int errorCode)` of `HttpServlet`
   **b** `sendError(int errorCode)` of `HttpServletRequest`
   **c** `sendError(int errorCode)` of `HttpServletResponse`
   **d** `sendError(String errorMsg)` of `HttpServletRequest`
   **e** `sendError(int errorCode, String errorMsg)` of `HttpServletResponse`

2. Consider the following `doPost()` method of a servlet:

```
public void doPost (HttpServletRequest request,
                    HttpServletResponse response)
                    throws ServletException, IOException
{
   System.out.println("Inside doPost");
   PrintWriter out = response.getWriter();
   out.println("Hello, ");
   out.flush();
   String name = getNameFromDBSomeHow();
   if(name == null)
   {
      response.sendError(HttpServletResponse.SC_NOT_FOUND,
                         "Unable to get name.");
   }
   out.println(name);
}
```

   Assuming that `getNameFromDBSomeHow()` returns null, which of the following statements regarding this code are correct? (Select one)

   **a** It will throw an `InvalidStateException` while serving a request.
   **b** It will throw a `ServletException` while serving a request.
   **c** It will throw a `NullPointerException` while serving a request.
   **d** It will throw an `IllegalStateException` while serving a request.
   **e** It will not throw an exception.

3. You want to send a status message of HttpServletResponse.SC_OK after successfully processing a request. Which of the following methods would you use? (Select one)

   **a** HttpServletResponse.setStatus(HttpServletResponse.SC_OK)

   **b** HttpServletResponse.setStatusCode(HttpServletResponse.SC_OK)

   **c** HttpServletResponse.sendStatus(HttpServletResponse.SC_OK)

   **d** HttpServletResponse.sendStatusCode(HttpServletResponse.SC_OK)

   **e** HttpServletRequest.sendStatus(HttpServletResponse.SC_OK)

   **f** HttpServletRequest.setStatus(HttpServletResponse.SC_OK)

4. Which deployment descriptor element contains the <exception-type> element? (Select one)

   **a** <error>

   **b** <error-mapping>

   **c** <error-page>

   **d** <exception-mapping>

   **e** <exception-page>

5. Your servlet may throw a business logic exception named AccountFrozen-Exception that extends from RuntimeException. Which of the following web.xml snippets correctly maps this exception to accounterror.html so that whenever the servlet throws this exception, accounterror.html is displayed? (Select one)

   **a**
```
<error-page>
    <exception-type>AccountFrozenException</exception-type>
    <page>accounterror.html</page>
</error-page>
```

   **b**
```
<error>
    <exception-type>AccountFrozenException</exception-type>
    <location>accounterror.html</location>
</error>
```

   **c**
```
<error-page>
    <exception>AccountFrozenException</exception>
    <location>accounterror.html</location>
</error-page>
```

   **d**
```
<error-page>
    <exception-type>AccountFrozenException</exception-type>
    <location>accounterror.html</location>
</error-page>
```

   **e**
```
<error-page>
    <exception-type>AccountFrozenException</exception-type>
    <page>accounterror.html</page>
</error-page>
```

6. Which of the following is true about the business logic exceptions thrown by a servlet? (Select one)

   **a** Error-page mapping can be specified only for exceptions that extend from `ServletException`.

   **b** Error-page mapping can be specified only for exceptions that extend from `ServletException` or `IOException`.

   **c** Error-page mapping can be specified only for exceptions that extend from `RuntimeException`.

   **d** Error-page mapping can be specified for any exception.

7. Instead of displaying the standard `HTTP 404 - NOT FOUND` message for all bad requests to a web application, you want to display a customized page. Which of the following is the correct way to do this? (Select one)

   **a** You have to check the servlet container documentation and change the default error message file.

   **b** You have to change your servlets to redirect the responses to your customized error message file.

   **c** You have to specify the mapping of the error-code (404) and the customized error page in `web.xml`.

   **d** You cannot do it in a standard way.

8. Consider the following servlet code:

```
public class LogTestServlet extends HttpServlet
{
   public void service(HttpServletRequest req,
                       HttpServletResponse res)
                       throws ServletException, IOException
   {
      String logMsg = "LogTestServlet.service():Probe message";
      //1
   }
}
```

   Which of the following statements can be inserted at `//1` so that `logMsg` may be entered into the servlet log file? (Select three)

   **a** `log(logMsg);`

   **b** `req(logMsg);`

   **c** `getServletConfig().log(logMsg);`

   **d** `getServletContext().log(logMsg);`

   **e** `getServletConfig().getServletContext().log(logMsg);`

   **f** `res.log(logMsg);`

   **g** `req.getSession().log(logMsg);`

9. Consider the following code for the `doGet()` method of a servlet:

```
public void doGet(HttpServletRequest req, HttpServletResponse res)
            throws ServletException, IOException
{
   String userId = null;
   try
   {
      userId = loginUser(req);
   }
   catch(Exception e)
   {
      // 1:  log "Unknown User" and the exception to the log file.
   }
   if(userId != null)
   {
      //do something.
   }
}
```

Which of the following statements can be inserted at `//1` to write a message as well as the exception stack trace to the log file? (Select one)

**a** `req.log(e, "Unknown User");`

**b** `this.log(e, "Unknown User")`

**c** `this.getServletContext().log("Unknown User", e);`

**d** `this.getServletContext().log(e, "Unknown User");`

**e** The stack trace of the exception cannot be logged using any of the `log()` methods.

CHAPTER 8

# Session management



## EXAM OBJECTIVES

**5.1** Identify the interface and method for each of the following:

- Retrieve a session object across multiple requests to the same or different servlets within the same WebApp
- Store objects into a session object
- Retrieve objects from a session object
- Respond to the event when a particular object is added to a session
- Respond to the event when a session is created and destroyed
- Expunge a session object

(Section 8.1)

**5.2** Given a scenario, state whether a session object will be invalidated. (Section 8.2)

**5.3** Given that URL-rewriting must be used for session management, identify the design requirement on session-related HTML pages. (Section 8.3)

## INTRODUCTION

Since a web application is normally interacting with more than one user at the same time, it needs to remember each user and his history of transactions. The session provides this continuity by tracking the interaction between a user and the web application. To do well on the exam, you must know how to create and manage a session and how to associate it with its specific user.

In this chapter, we will discuss the session object, three of the session-related listener interfaces (we introduced the fourth session-related listener interface in chapter 6, "The servlet container model"), and the session timeout. We will also learn how to track the sessions using cookies and URL rewriting.

## 8.1 UNDERSTANDING STATE AND SESSIONS

The ability of a protocol to remember the user and her requests is called its *state.* From this perspective, protocols are divided into two types: stateful and stateless. In chapter 3, we observed that HTTP is a stateless protocol; each request to a web server and its corresponding response is handled as one isolated transaction.

Since all of the requests are independent and unrelated, the HTTP server has no way to determine whether a series of requests came from the same client or from different clients. This means that the server cannot maintain the state of the client between multiple requests; in other words, the server cannot remember the client.

In some cases, there may be no need to remember the client. For example, an online library catalog does not need to maintain the state of the client. While stateless HTTP may work well for this type of simple web browsing, the interaction between a client and a server in a web application needs to be stateful. A classic example is a shopping cart application. A user may add items and remove items from his shopping cart many times. At any time during the process, the server should be able to display the list of items in the cart and calculate their total cost. In order to do this, the server must track all of the requests and associate them with the user. We use a session to do this and turn stateless HTTP pages into a stateful Web application.

A session is an uninterrupted series of request-response interactions between a client and a server. For each request that is a part of this session, the server is able to identify the request as coming from the same client. A session starts when an unknown client sends the first request to the web application server. It ends when either the client explicitly ends the session or the server does not receive any requests from the client within a predefined time limit. When the session ends, the server conveniently forgets the client as well as all the requests that the client may have made.

It should be made clear at this point that the first request from the client to the web application server may not be the very first interaction between that client and the server. By *first request,* we mean the request that requires a session to be created. We call it the first request because this is the request when the numbering of the requests starts (logically) and this is the request from which the server starts remembering the client. For example, a server can allow a user to browse a catalog of items without creating a session. However, as soon as the user logs in or adds an item to the shopping cart, it is clear that a session must be started.

So, how does a server establish and maintain a session with a client if HTTP does not provide any way to remember the client? There is only one way:

- When the server receives the first request from a client, the server initiates a session and assigns the session a unique identifier.
- The client must include this unique identifier with each subsequent request. The server inspects the identifier and associates the request with the corresponding session.

You may wonder why a server can't just look at the IP address of a request to identify a user. Many users access the Internet through a proxy server, in which case the server gets the IP address of the proxy server and not of the actual user, which makes the IP address non-unique for the set of users using that proxy server. For this reason, the server generates a unique identifier instead of relying on the IP address. This identifier is called a *session ID*, and the server uses this ID to associate the client's requests in a session. The exam requires you to understand the two most commonly used approaches for implementing session support: cookies and URL rewriting. We will discuss both of these approaches later in this chapter, in section 8.4.

In the following sections, we will see how the Servlet API helps us in implementing stateful web applications.

## 8.2 USING HTTPSESSION

The Servlet API abstracts the concept of session through the `javax.servlet.http.HttpSession` interface. This interface is implemented by the servlet container and provides a simple way to track the user's session.

A servlet container creates a new `HttpSession` object when it starts a session for a client. In addition to representing the session, this object acts as the data store for the information related to that session. In short, it provides a way to store data into memory and then retrieve it when the same user comes back later. Servlets can use this object to maintain the state of the session. As you'll recall, we discussed sharing data within the session scope using the `HttpSession` object in chapter 4, "The Servlet model."

To put this in perspective, let's go back to the shopping cart example. The servlet container creates an `HttpSession` object for a user when the user logs in. The servlet implementing the shopping cart application uses this object to maintain the list of items selected by the user. The servlet updates this list as the user adds or removes the items from his cart. Anytime the user wants to check out, the servlet retrieves the list of items from the session and calculates the total cost. Once the payment is made, the servlet closes the session; if the user sends another request, a new session is started.

Obviously, the servlet container creates as many `HttpSession` objects as there are sessions. In other words, there is an `HttpSession` object corresponding to each session (or user). However, we need not worry about associating the HttpSession objects with the users. The servlet container does that for us and, upon request, automatically returns the appropriate session object.

### 8.2.1 Working with an HttpSession

Using HttpSession is usually a three-step process:

1. Retrieve the session associated with the request.
2. Add or remove name-value pairs of attributes from the session.
3. Close or invalidate the session if required.

Often the client offers no indication that it is ending the session. For example, a user may browse away to another site and may not return for a long time. In this case, the server will never know whether the user has ended her session or not. To help us in such situations, the servlet container automatically closes the session after a certain period of inactivity. The period is, of course, configurable through the deployment descriptor and is known as the *session timeout* period. We will learn more about it in section 8.3.

Listing 8.1 contains the doPost() method of an imaginary ShoppingCartServlet. This listing illustrates a common use of HttpSession.

**Listing 8.1 Using HttpSession methods**

```
//code for the doPost() method of ShoppingCartServlet
public void doPost(HttpServletRequest req,
                                   HttpServletResponse res)
{

   HttpSession session = req.getSession(true);   <— Retrieves the session
   List listOfItems =
         (List) session.getAttribute("listofitems");   <— Retrieves an attribute
   if(listOfItems == null)                                from the session
   {
      listOfItems = new Vector();
      session.setAttribute("listofitems", listOfItems);   <— Sets an attribute
   }                                                          in the session
   String itemcode = req.getParameter("itemcode");
   String command = req.getParameter("command");
      if("additem".equals(command) )
   {
      listOfItems.add(itemcode);
   }
   else if("removeitem".equals(command) )
   {
      listOfItems.remove(itemcode);
   }
}
```

In listing 8.1, we first get a reference to the `HttpSession` object using `req.getSession(true)`. This will create a new session if a session does not already exist for the user. The `HttpServletRequest` interface provides two methods to retrieve the session, as shown in table 8.1.

**Table 8.1 HttpServletRequest methods for retrieving the session**

| Method | Description |
|---|---|
| HttpSession getSession(boolean create) | This method returns the current HttpSession associated with this request, or if there is no current session and the create parameter is true, then it returns a new session. |
| HttpSession getSession() | This method is equivalent to calling getSession(true). |

Notice that we have not written any code to identify the user. We just call the `getSession()` method and assume that it will return the same `HttpSession` object each time we process a request from a specific user. It is the job of the implementation of the `getSession()` method to analyze the request and find the right `HttpSession` object associated with the request. We have used `getSession(true)` just to emphasize that we want to create a new session if it does not exist, although `getSession()` would have the same effect. A session will not be available for the first request sent by a user. In that case, the user is a new client and a new session will be created for her.

After retrieving the session, we get the list of items from the session. We use the `HttpSession` methods shown in table 8.2 to set and get the `listofitems` attribute that stores the item codes in the session. If this is a new session, or if this is the first time the user is adding an item, the `session.getAttribute()` will return null, in which case we create a new list object and add it to the session. Then, based on the `command` and the `itemCode` request parameters, we either add or remove the item from the list.

**Table 8.2 HttpSession methods for setting/getting attributes**

| Method | Description |
|---|---|
| void setAttribute(String name, Object value) | This method adds the passed object to the session, using the name specified. |
| Object getAttribute(String name) | This method returns the object bound with the specified name in this session, or null if no object is bound under the name. |

*Quizlet*

**Q:** Listing 8.1 shows the `doPost()` method of `ShoppingCartServlet`. As you can see, this servlet only maintains the list of item codes. However, once a user has finished selecting the items, he needs to complete the process by "checking out." Is it possible to implement this functionality using a different servlet instead of adding the functionality to `ShoppingCartServlet`? Can you retrieve the `listofitems` attribute associated with a user from another servlet?

**A:** Definitely. An `HttpSession` object associated with a user is accessible from all of the components of a web application (servlets and JSP pages) during the time that the components are serving a request from that user. In this case, we can have a hyperlink named *Check Out* on our page that refers to a different servlet named `CheckOutServlet`. This servlet can access the session information and retrieve the `listofitems` attribute, as shown here:

```
//code for the doGet() method of CheckOutServlet
public void doGet(HttpServletRequest req,
                                          HttpServletResponse res)
{
   HttpSession session = req.getSession();

   Vector listOfItems =
         (Vector) session.getAttribute("listofitems");

   //process the listOfItems.
}
```

As we mentioned earlier, the `HttpServletRequest.getSession()` method will return the correct session object for a specific user.

### 8.2.2 Handling session events with listener interfaces

As we saw in chapter 6, listener interfaces are a way to receive notifications when important events occur in a web application. To receive notification of an event, we need to write a class that implements the corresponding listener interface. The servlet container then calls the appropriate methods on the objects of this class when the events occur.

The Servlet API defines four listeners and two events related to the session in the `javax.servlet.http` package:

- `HttpSessionAttributeListener` and `HttpSessionBindingEvent`
- `HttpSessionBindingListener` and `HttpSessionBindingEvent`
- `HttpSessionListener` and `HttpSessionEvent`
- `HttpSessionActivationListener` and `HttpSessionEvent`.

All four listener interfaces extend `java.util.EventListener`. `HttpSessionEvent` extends `java.util.EventObject` and `HttpSessionBindingEvent` extends `HttpSessionEvent`.

### *HttpSessionAttributeListener*

The `HttpSessionAttributeListener` interface allows a developer to receive notifications whenever attributes are added to, removed from, or replaced in the attribute list of any of the `HttpSession` objects of the web application. We specify the class that implements this interface in the deployment descriptor. We discuss this listener (`javax.servlet.http.HttpSessionAttributeListener`) in detail in chapter 6. Now let's look at the three other listeners.

### *HttpSessionBindingListener*

The `HttpSessionBindingListener` interface is implemented by the classes whose objects need to receive notifications whenever they are added to or removed from a session. We do not have to inform the container about such objects explicitly via the deployment descriptor. Whenever an object is added to or removed from any session, the container introspects the interfaces implemented by that object. If the object implements the `HttpSessionBindingListener` interface, the container calls the corresponding notification methods shown in table 8.3.

**Table 8.3 HttpSessionBindingListener methods for receiving notification of a change in the attribute list of HttpSession**

| Method | Description |
|---|---|
| void valueBound(HttpSessionBindingEvent event) | Notifies the object that it is being bound to a session |
| void valueUnbound(HttpSessionBindingEvent event) | Notifies the object that it is being unbound from a session |

The servlet container calls the interface methods even if the session is explicitly invalidated or has timed out. Listing 8.2 illustrates the use of this interface to log `HttpSessionBindingEvents`.

**Listing 8.2 Implementing HttpSessionBindingListener**

```
import javax.servlet.*;
import javax.servlet.http.*;

//An entry will be added to the log file whenever objects of
//this class are added to or removed from a session.
public class CustomAttribute implements
                                HttpSessionBindingListener
{
   public Object theValue;

   public void valueBound(HttpSessionBindingEvent e)
   {
      HttpSession session = e.getSession();                      <-- Retrieves the
      session.getServletContext().log("CustomAttribute "+           session associated
                    theValue+"bound to a session");                  with this event
   }
```

```
    public void valueUnbound(HttpSessionBindingEvent e)
    {
        HttpSession session = e.getSession();
        session.getServletContext().log("CustomAttribute "+
                     theValue+" unbound from a session.");
    }
}
```

In this example, we retrieve the session object from `HttpSessionBindingEvent`. From the session object, we retrieve the `ServletContext` object and log the messages using the `ServletContext.log()` method.

You may wonder what the difference is between `HttpSessionAttributeListener` and `HttpSessionBindingListener`, since both are used for listening to changes in the attribute list of a session. The difference is that `HttpSessionAttributeListener` is configured in the deployment descriptor and the container creates only one instance of the specified class. `HttpSessionBindingEvents` generated from all the sessions are sent to this object. On the other hand, `HttpSessionBindingListener` is not configured in the deployment descriptor. The servlet container calls methods on an object implementing this interface only if that object is added to or removed from a session. While the `HttpSessionAttributeListener` interface is used to track the activity of all the sessions on an application level, the `HttpSessionBindingListener` interface is used to take actions when certain kinds of objects are added to or removed from a session.

### *HttpSessionListener*

The `HttpSessionListener` interface is used to receive notifications when a session is created or destroyed. The listener class implementing this interface must be configured in the deployment descriptor. It has the methods shown in table 8.4.

**Table 8.4 HttpSessionListener methods for receiving notification when a session is created or destroyed**

| Method | Description |
|---|---|
| void sessionCreated(HttpSessionEvent se) | This method is called when a session is created. |
| void sessionDestroyed(HttpSessionEvent se) | This method is called when a session is destroyed. |

This interface can be used to monitor the number of active sessions, as demonstrated in the implementation of the `HttpSessionListener` interface in listing 8.3.

**Listing 8.3 Counting the number of sessions**

```
import javax.servlet.http.*;

public class SessionCounter implements HttpSessionListener
{
    private static int activeSessions = 0;
```

```
    public void sessionCreated(HttpSessionEvent evt)
    {
        activeSessions++;
        System.out.println("No. of active sessions on:"+
                new java.util.Date()+" : "+activeSessions);
    }

    public void sessionDestroyed (HttpSessionEvent evt)
    {
        activeSessions--;
    }
}
```

In listing 8.3, we increment the session count when a new session is created in the `sessionCreated()` method and decrement the session count when any session is invalidated in the `sessionDestroyed()` method.

At first, it appears that this interface also might be very useful to clean up a user's transient data from the database when that user's session ends. For example, as soon as a user logs in, we can set the user ID in the session. When the user logs out or when the session times out, we can use the `sessionDestroyed()` method to clean up the database, as shown in listing 8.4.

**Listing 8.4 Incorrect use of HttpSessionListener**

```
import javax.servlet.*;
import javax.servlet.http.*;

public class BadSessionListener implements
                                HttpSessionListener
{
    public void sessionCreated(HttpSessionEvent e)
    {
        //can't do much here as the session is just created and
        //does not contain anything yet, except the sessionid
        System.out.log("Session created: "+
                      e.getSession().getSessionId());
    }

    public void sessionDestoyed(HttpSessionEvent e)
    {
       HttpSession session = e.getSession();
        String userid = (String) session.getAttribute("userid");   <-- Will not work!
        //delete user's transient data from the database
        //using the userid.
    }
}
```

In listing 8.4, the line `session.getAttribute("userid");` will not work because the servlet container calls the `sessionDestroyed()` method after the session is invalidated. Therefore, a call to `getAttribute()` will throw an `IllegalStateException`.

So, how do we solve our problem of cleaning up the database when a session is invalidated? The solution is a little cumbersome. We will create a class that wraps the user ID and implements the `HttpSessionBindingListener` interface. When the user logs in, for instance through a `LoginServlet`, instead of setting the user ID directly in the session, we will set this wrapper in the session. The servlet container will call `valueUnbound()` on the wrapper as soon as the session is invalidated. We will use this method to clean up the database. Listing 8.5 illustrates the process.

**Listing 8.5 Cleaning up the database using HttpSessionBindingListener**

```
import javax.servlet.*;
import javax.servlet.http.*;
public class UseridWrapper implements HttpSessionBindingListener
{
   public String userid = "default";
   public UseridWrapper(String id)
   {
      this.userid = id;
   }
   public void valueBound(HttpSessionBindingEvent e)
   {
      //insert transient user data into the database
   }
   public void valueUnbound(HttpSessionBindingEvent e)
   {
      //remove transient user data from the database
   }
}
```

The following code for the `doPost()` method of `LoginServlet` shows the use of the `UseridWrapper` class:

```
//code for doPost() of LoginServlet
public void doPost(HttpServletRequest req, HttpServletResponse res)
{
   String userid = req.getParameter("userid");
   String password = req.getParameter("password");
   boolean valid = //validate the userid/password.
   if(valid)
   {
      UseridWrapper useridwrapper = new UseridWrapper(userid);
      req.getSession().setAttribute("useridwrapper", useridwrapper);
   }
   else
```

**Sets the UseridWrapper object in the session**

```
    {
        //forward the user to the login page.
    }
    ...
    ...
}
```

#### *HttpSessionActivationListener*

This interface is used by the session attributes to receive notifications when a session is being migrated across the JVMs in a distributed environment. This interface declares two methods, as shown in table 8.5.

**Table 8.5 HttpSessionActivationListener methods for receiving activation/passivation notification in a distributed environment**

| Method | Description |
|---|---|
| void sessionDidActivate(HttpSessionEvent se) | This method is called just after the session is activated. |
| void sessionWillPassivate(HttpSessionEvent se) | This method is called when the session is about to be passivated. |

We will not discuss this interface in detail since it is rarely used and is not required for the exam.

*Quizlet*

**Q:** Which interface would you use to achieve the following?

1 You want to listen to the `HttpSessionBindingEvents` but none of your session attributes implement the `HttpSessionBindingListener` interface.

2 You want to monitor the average time users are logged into your web application.

**A:** 1 Use `HttpSessionAttributeListener`. Remember, you will have to configure it in the deployment descriptor.

2 Use `HttpSessionListener`. You can use the `sessionCreated()` and `sessionDestroyed()` methods to calculate how long a user has been logged in.

### 8.2.3 Expunging a session

We observed at the beginning of this chapter that a session is automatically terminated when the user remains inactive for a specified period of time. In some cases, we may also want to end the session programmatically. For instance, in our shopping cart example, we would want to end the session after the payment process is complete so that if the user sends another request, a new session is started with no items in the shopping cart. `HttpSession` provides the method shown in table 8.6 for invalidating a session.

**Table 8.6 HttpSession method for expunging a session**

| Method | Description |
|---|---|
| void invalidate() | This method invalidates this session and then unbinds any objects bound to it. This means that the valueUnbound() method will be called on all of its attributes that implement HttpSessionBindingListener. It throws an IllegalStateException if the session is already invalidated. |

Listing 8.6 shows LogoutServlet's doGet() method. It uses the invalidate() method to expunge a session.

**Listing 8.6 Using HttpSession.invalidate() to expunge a session**

```
//code for doGet() of LogoutServlet
//This method will be invoked if a user clicks on
//a "Logout" button or hyperlink.
public void doGet(HttpServletRequest req,
                               HttpServletResponse res)
{
   ...
      req.getSession().invalidate();   <— Expunges the session
      //forward the user to the main page.
   ...
}
```

## 8.3 UNDERSTANDING SESSION TIMEOUT

Since the HTTP protocol does not provide any signal for the termination of the session to the server, if the user does not click on some kind of a logout button or hyperlink, the only way to determine whether a client is active or not is to observe the inactivity period. If a user does not perform any action for a certain period of time, the server assumes the user to be inactive and invalidates the session. The web.xml in listing 8.7 shows the configuration of the timeout period of a session.

**Listing 8.7 Configuring session timeout in web.xml**

```
<web-app>
...
<session-config>
  <session-timeout>30</session-timeout>      <— Sets timeout
</session-config>                               to 30 minutes
...
<web-app>
```

The <session-timeout> element contains the timeout in minutes. A value of 0 or less means that the session will never expire. The HttpSession interface provides the two methods shown in table 8.7 for getting and setting the timeout value of a session.

Table 8.7 **HttpSession methods for getting/setting the timeout value of a session**

| Method | Description |
|---|---|
| void setMaxInactiveInterval(int seconds) | This method specifies the number of seconds between client requests before the servlet container will invalidate this session. A negative value means that the session will never expire. |
| int getMaxInactiveInterval() | This method returns the maximum time interval, in seconds, that the servlet container will keep this session open between client accesses. |

It is important to note that `setMaxInactiveInterval()` affects only the session on which it is called. Other sessions will still have the same timeout period as specified in the deployment descriptor.

**NOTE** There are two inconsistencies in the way the `session-timeout` tag of the deployment descriptor and the `setMaxInactiveInterval()` method of `HttpSession` work:

1. The `session-timeout` value is specified in minutes, while the `setMaxInactiveInterval()` method accepts seconds.
2. A `session-timeout` value of 0 or less means that the session will never expire, while if we want to specify that a session will never expire using the `setMaxInactiveInterval()` method, a negative value (not 0) is required.

## 8.4 IMPLEMENTING SESSION SUPPORT

We have seen how storing attributes in the session object enables us to maintain the state of the application. In this section, we will see how a servlet container associates incoming requests with an appropriate `HttpSession` object. As we observed at the beginning of this chapter, the way we provide support for HTTP sessions is to identify each client with a unique ID, which is called a session ID, and force the client to send that ID to the server with each request. Let's go over in detail the steps that a client and a server must take to track a session:

1. A new client sends a request to a server. Since this is the first request, it does not contain any session ID.
2. The server creates a session and assigns it a new session ID. At this time, the session is said to be in the *new* state. We can use `session.isNew()` to determine if the session is in this state or not. The server then sends the ID back to the client with the response.
3. The client gets the session ID and saves it for future requests. This is the first time the client is aware of the existence of a session on the server.
4. The client sends another request, and this time, it sends the session ID with the request.

5 The server receives the request and observes the session ID. It immediately associates the request with the session that it had created earlier. At this time, the client is said to have *joined* the session, which means the session is no longer in the new state. Therefore, a call to `session.isNew()` will return false.

Steps 3–5 keep repeating for the life of the session. If the client does not send any requests for a length of time that exceeds the session timeout, the server invalidates the session. Once the session is invalidated, either programmatically or because it has timed out, it cannot be resurrected even if the client sends the same session ID again. After that, as far as the server is concerned, the next request from the client is considered to be the first request (as in step 1) that cannot be associated with an existing session. The server will create a new session for the client and will assign it a new ID (as in step 2).

In the following section, we look at two techniques—cookies and URL rewriting—that a servlet container uses to implement the steps described above to provide session support.

### 8.4.1 Supporting sessions using cookies

In this technique, to manage the sending and receiving of session IDs, the servlet container uses HTTP headers. As we saw in chapter 3, all HTTP messages—requests as well as responses—contain header lines. While sending a response, a servlet container adds a special header line containing the session ID. The container adds this header line transparently to the servlet developer. The client, which is usually a browser, receives the response, extracts the special header line, and stores it on the local machine. The browser does this transparently to the user. While sending another request, the client automatically adds a header line containing the stored session ID.

The header line that is stored by the browser on the user's machine is called a *cookie*. If you recall the discussion about HTTP headers, a header line is just a name-value pair. Not surprisingly, the header name used for sending a cookie is *cookie*. A sample HTTP request containing a cookie looks like this:

```
POST /servlet/testServlet HTTP/1.0
User-Agent= MOZILLA/1.0
cookie=JSESSIONID=61C4F23524521390E70993E5120263C6
Content-Type: application/x-www.formurlencoded

userid=john
```

**Header line for the cookie** (annotation pointing to the cookie line)

The value of the cookie header shown above is:

```
JSESSIONID=61C4F23524521390E70993E5120263C6
```

This technique was developed by Netscape and was adopted by all other browsers. Back in the early days of the Internet, cookies were only used to keep the session ID. But later on, companies started using cookies to store a lot of other information, such as user IDs, preferences, and so forth. They also started using cookies to track the browsing patterns of the users. Since the cookie management happens behind the scenes, very soon cookies became known as a potential security hazard, and many users started disliking them. Although most users still enable cookies in their browsers, some corporate houses now disable them. When cookies are disabled, the browser ignores any cookie header lines that are present in the HTTP responses, and consequently does not send any cookie header lines in the requests.

For some web sites, session support is extremely important, and so they cannot rely solely on cookies. In such cases, we need to use another technique that will work even if the users disable cookies. We examine this technique in the next section.

### 8.4.2 Supporting sessions using URL rewriting

In the absence of cookie support, we can attach the session ID to all of the URLs that are within an HTML page that is being sent as a response to the client. That way, when the user clicks on one of the URLs, the session ID is automatically sent back to the server as a part of the request line itself, instead of as a header line.

To better understand this, consider the following HTML page code returned by an imaginary servlet named `HomeServlet`:

```
<html>
<head></head>

<body>
A test page showing two URLs:<br>
<a href="/servlet/ReportServlet">First URL</a><br>
<a href="/servlet/AccountServlet">Second URL</a><br>
</body>
</html>
```

The above HTML page is a normal HTML page without any special code. However, if the cookies are disabled, the session ID will not be sent when the user clicks on the hyperlink displayed by this page. Now, let's see the same HTML code but with the URLs rewritten to include the session ID:

```
<html>
<head></head>
<body>
A test page showing two URLs:<br>
<a href=
"/servlet/ReportServlet;JSESSIONID=C084B32241B2F8F060230440C0158114">
  View Report</a><br>
<a href=
  "/servlet/AccountServlet;JSESSIONID=C084B32241B2F8F060230440C0158114">
  View Account</a><br>
</body>
</html>
```

When the user clicks on the URLs displayed by the above page, the session ID will be sent as a part of the request line. We do not need cookies to do this. Although it is quite easy to attach the session ID with all the URLs, unlike cookies, it is not transparent to the servlet developer. The `HttpServletResponse` interface provides two methods for this purpose, as shown in table 8.8.

**Table 8.8 HttpServletResponse methods for appending session IDs to the URLs**

| Method | Description |
|---|---|
| String encodeURL(String url) | This method returns the URL with the session ID attached. It is used for normal URLs emitted by a servlet. |
| String encodeRedirectURL(String url) | This method returns the URL with the session ID attached. It is used for encoding a URL that is to be used for the HttpServletResponse.sendRedirect() method. |

Both methods first check to see if attaching the session ID is necessary. If the request contains a cookie header line, then cookies are enabled and we do not need to rewrite the URL. In this case, the URL is returned without the session ID attached to it.

> **NOTE** Observe that `JSESSIONID` is appended to the URL using a `;` and not a `?`. This is because `JSESSIONID` is a part of the path info of the request URI. It is not a request parameter and thus cannot be retrieved using the `getParameter("JSESSIONID")` method of `ServletRequest`.

Listing 8.8 illustrates how these methods can be used. `HomeServlet` generates the HTML page shown above.

**Listing 8.8 Using URL rewriting to implement session support**

```
import javax.servlet.*;
import javax.servlet.http.*;

public class HomeServlet extends HttpServlet
{
   public void doGet(HttpServletRequest req,
                                    HttpServletResponse res)
   {
      HttpSession s = req.getSession();    <— Gets the session
      PrintWriter pw = res.getWriter();
      pw.println("<html>");
      pw.println("<head></head>");

      pw.println("<body>");
      pw.println("A test page showing two URLs:<br>");
      pw.println("<a href=\""
                  + res.encodeURL("/servlet/ReportServlet")
                  + "\">View Report</a><br>");
      pw.println("<a href=\""
                  + res.encodeURL("/servlet/AccountServlet")
                  +"\">View Account</a><br>");
      pw.println("</body>");
      pw.println("</html>");
   }
}
```

Appends the session ID

Observe that the process of retrieving the session in the servlet remains the same. We can still safely call the `getSession()` methods to retrieve the session. The servlet container transparently parses the session ID attached to the requested URL and returns the appropriate session object.

In general, URL rewriting is a very robust way to support sessions. We should use this approach whenever we are uncertain about cookie support. However, it is important to keep the following points in mind:

- We should encode all the URLs, including all the hyperlinks and action attributes of the forms, in all the pages of the application.
- All the pages of the application should be dynamic. Because different users will have different session IDs, there is no way to attach proper session IDs to the URLs present in static HTML pages.
- All the static HTML pages must be run through a servlet, which would rewrite the URLs while sending the pages to the client. Obviously, this can be a serious performance bottleneck.

*Quizlet*

**Q:** You have developed your web application assuming that your clients support cookies. However, after deploying the application, you realize that most of your clients have disabled cookies. What will be the impact on your application? How can you fix it?

**A:** The impact will be drastic. The application will not be able to maintain the user's state. The servlet container will create a new session for each request from each user. The only way to fix this problem is to modify your servlet code to incorporate URL rewriting.

## 8.5 SUMMARY

A web application needs to impose state upon the inherently stateless HTTP protocol in order to keep track of a client's interactions with the server. This is done through session management using the `HttpSession` object. A session is a complete series of interactions between a client and the server; during a session, the server "remembers" the client and associates all the requests from that client with the client's unique session object.

We use listener interfaces to receive notifications when important events take place in the session and to initiate appropriate actions. These events include changes to the session attribute list and creating and destroying the session.

The server implements a session by assigning a unique identifier to it. Using either cookies or URL rewriting, this session ID is sent to the client in the response and returned to the server with each subsequent request. The session ends either when it times out or when the session is invalidated. The "session timeout" period is configurable through the deployment descriptor. This affects the timeout period of all the sessions. To change the timeout of a specific session, we can use `HttpSession.setMaxInactiveInterval(int seconds)` method.

At this point, you should be able to answer exam questions based on the semantics of `HttpSession` and the interfaces that are used to listen for changes in an `HttpSession`. You should also be able to answer questions based on session management using cookies and URL rewriting.

In the next chapter, we will look at another topic that is important from the perspective of the exam: security.

## 8.6 REVIEW QUESTIONS

1. Which of the following interfaces or classes is used to retrieve the session associated with a user? (Select one)

   **a** `GenericServlet`
   **b** `ServletConfig`
   **c** `ServletContext`
   **d** `HttpServlet`
   **e** `HttpServletRequest`
   **f** `HttpServletResponse`

2. Which of the following code snippets, when inserted in the `doGet()` method, will correctly count the number of GET requests made by a user? (Select one)

   **a**
   ```
   HttpSession session = request.getSession();
   int count = session.getAttribute("count");
   session.setAttribute("count", count++);
   ```
   **b**
   ```
   HttpSession session = request.getSession();
   int count = (int) session.getAttribute("count");
   session.setAttribute("count", count++);
   ```
   **c**
   ```
   HttpSession session = request.getSession();
   int count = ((Integer) session.getAttribute("count")).intValue();
   session.setAttribute("count", count++);
   ```
   **d**
   ```
   HttpSession session = request.getSession();
   int count = ((Integer) session.getAttribute("count")).intValue();
   session.setAttribute("count", new Integer(count++));
   ```

3. Which of the following methods will be invoked on a session attribute that implements `HttpSessionBindingListener` when the session is invalidated? (Select one)

   **a** `sessionDestroyed`
   **b** `valueUnbound`
   **c** `attributeRemoved`
   **d** `sessionInvalidated`

4. Which of the following methods will be invoked on a session attribute that implements appropriate interfaces when the session is invalidated? (Select one)

   **a** `sessionDestroyed` of `HttpSessionListener`

   **b** `attributeRemoved` of `HttpSessionAttributeListener`

   **c** `valueUnbound` of `HttpSessionBindingListener`

   **d** `sessionWillPassivate` of `HttpSessionActivationListener`

5. Which of the following methods will expunge a session object? (Select one)

   **a** `session.invalidate();`

   **b** `session.expunge();`

   **c** `session.destroy();`

   **d** `session.end();`

   **e** `session.close();`

6. Which of the following method calls will ensure that a session will never be expunged by the servlet container? (Select one)

   **a** `session.setTimeout(0);`

   **b** `session.setTimeout(-1);`

   **c** `session.setTimeout(Integer.MAX_VALUE);`

   **d** `session.setTimeout(Integer.MIN_VALUE);`

   **e** None of these

7. How can you make sure that none of the sessions associated with a web application will ever be expunged by the servlet container? (Select one)

   **a** `session.setMaxInactiveInterval(-1);`

   **b** Set the session timeout in the deployment descriptor to `-1`.

   **c** Set the session timeout in the deployment descriptor to `0` or `-1`.

   **d** Set the session timeout in the deployment descriptor to `65535`.

   **e** You have to change the timeout value of all the sessions explicitly as soon as they are created.

8. In which of the following situations will a session be invalidated? (Select two)

   **a** No request is received from the client for longer than the session timeout period.

   **b** The client sends a `KILL_SESSION` request.

   **c** The servlet container decides to invalidate a session due to overload.

   **d** The servlet explicitly invalidates the session.

   **e** A user closes the active browser window.

   **f** A user closes all of the browser windows.

9. Which method is required for using the URL rewriting mechanism of implementing session support? (Select one)

   **a** `HttpServletRequest.encodeURL()`

   **b** `HttpServletRequest.rewriteURL()`

   **c** `HttpServletResponse.encodeURL()`

   **d** `HttpServletResponse.rewriteURL()`

10. The users of your web application do not accept cookies. Which of the following statements are correct? (Select one)

   **a** You cannot maintain client state.

   **b** URLs displayed by static HTML pages may not work properly.

   **c** You cannot use URL rewriting.

   **d** You cannot set session timeout explicitly.

CHAPTER 9

# Developing secure web applications



## EXAM OBJECTIVES

**6.1** Identify correct descriptions or statements about the security issues:

- Authentication, authorization
- Data integrity
- Auditing
- Malicious code
- Web site attacks

(Section 9.1)

**6.2** Identify the deployment descriptor element names, and their structure, that declare the following:

- A security constraint
- A Web resource

- The login configuration
- A security role

  (Section 9.3)

**6.3** Given an authentication type: BASIC, DIGEST, FORM, and CLIENT-CERT, identify the correct definition of its mechanism. (Section 9.2)

## INTRODUCTION

The utilization of the Internet as an essential business tool continues to grow, as more and more companies are web-enabling their operations. It is increasingly common for all types of business dealings to take place over the Internet. Currently, millions of people transmit personal information over the Internet as they shop at online stores. Many business transactions, such as banking, stock trading, and so forth, are conducted online each day. To support these applications, we need a robust security mechanism in place. It is not an overstatement to say that e-commerce is not possible without security.

In this chapter, we will learn about the various techniques that are used to make a web application secure.

# 9.1 BASIC CONCEPTS

The importance of web security will continue to increase as companies and individuals alike are paying more attention to ensuring that their resources are protected and their interactions are private. The Servlet specification provides methods and guidelines for implementing security in web applications, but before we go into the details of implementing those security features, let's look at some terms you need to know for the exam.

### 9.1.1 Authentication

The first fundamental requirement of security is to authenticate the user. *Authentication* is the process of identifying a person—or even a system, such as an application—and validating their credentials. It means verifying that the user is who she (or it) claims to be. For example, a traveler must show a driver's license or other photo ID before boarding a flight. This ID authenticates the traveler; it provides his credentials. In the Internet world, the basic credentials that authenticate a user are typically a username and a password.

### 9.1.2 Authorization

Once the user has been authenticated, she must be authorized. *Authorization* is the process of determining whether a user is permitted to access a particular resource that she has requested. For example, you will not be permitted to access a bank account that does not belong to you, even if you are a member of the bank. In short, you are not *authorized* to access anyone else's account. Authorization is usually enforced by maintaining an *access control list (ACL)*; this list specifies the users and the types of access they have to resources.

### 9.1.3 Data integrity

Data integrity is the process of ensuring that the data is not tampered with while in transit from the sender to the receiver. For example, if you send a request to transfer $1000 from your account to another account, the bank should get a transfer request for $1000 and not $10,000. Data integrity is usually ensured by sending a hashcode or signature of the data along with the data. At the receiving end, the data and its hashcode are verified.

### 9.1.4 Confidentiality or data privacy

*Confidentiality* is the process of ensuring that no one except the intended user is able to access sensitive information. For example, sometimes when you send your user ID/password to log onto a web site, the information travels in plain text across the Internet. It is possible for hackers to access this information by sniffing the HTTP packets. In this case, the data is not confidential. Confidentiality is usually ensured by encrypting the information so that only the intended user can decrypt it. Today, most web sites use the HTTPS protocol to encrypt messages so that even if a hacker sniffs the data, he will not be able to decrypt it and hence cannot use it.

The difference between authorization and confidentiality is in the way the information is protected. Authorization prevents the information from reaching unintended parties in the first place, while confidentiality ensures that even if the information falls into the wrong hands, it remains unusable.

### 9.1.5 Auditing

*Auditing* is the process of recording security-related events taking place in the system in order to be able to hold users accountable for their actions. Auditing can help determine the cause of a breach, and is usually accomplished by maintaining the log files generated by the application.

### 9.1.6 Malicious code

A piece of code that is meant to cause harm to computer systems is called *malicious code*. This includes viruses, worms, and Trojan horses. Besides the threat from the outside, sometimes in-house developers leave a back door open into the software that they write, which provides a potential opportunity for misuse. Although we cannot prevent unknown programmers from writing malicious code, companies can definitely prevent malicious code from being written in-house by conducting peer-to-peer code reviews.

### 9.1.7 Web site attacks

Anything that is deemed valuable is a potential target for attacks and should be protected. Web sites are no exception. Their value lies in the information they contain or the services they provide to legitimate users. A web site may be attacked by different people for different reasons. For example, a hacker may attack for pleasure, a terminated employee may attack for revenge, or a professional thief may attack for the purpose of stealing credit card numbers.

Broadly, there are three types of web site attacks:

- *Secrecy attacks.* Attempts to steal confidential information by sniffing the communications between two machines. Encrypting the data being transmitted can prevent such attacks. For example, it is a universal standard that financial institutions use HTTPS in online banking, stock trading, and so forth.
- *Integrity attacks.* Attempts to alter information in transit with malicious intent. If these attempts succeed, it will compromise the data integrity. IP spoofing is one of the common techniques used in integrity attacks. In this technique, the intruder sends messages to a server with an IP address indicating that the message is coming from a trusted machine. The server is thus fooled into giving access to the intruder. Such attacks can be prevented by using strong authentication techniques, such as public-key cryptography.
- *Denial-of-service attacks (or availability attacks).* Attempts to flood a system with fake requests so that the system remains unavailable for legitimate requests. Creating network congestion by sending spurious data packets also comes under this category. Such attacks can be prevented by using firewalls that block network traffic on unintended ports.

*Quizlet*

**Q:** The process of showing your ID card to the security guard before entering a building is known as what?

**A:** *Authentication* as well as *authorization.* When you show the ID card, the security guard makes sure that you are indeed who you claim to be, possibly by looking at you and then the photograph on the ID card. This is *authentication.* Next, the guard makes sure you are allowed to go into the building, probably by verifying that your name appears on a list of approved individuals. This is *authorization.*

## 9.2 UNDERSTANDING AUTHENTICATION MECHANISMS

Now that you understand the basic terms regarding security in web applications, let's take a closer look at how authentication is implemented in Java servlets. The Servlet specification defines four mechanisms to authenticate users:

- HTTP Basic authentication
- HTTP Digest authentication
- HTTPS Client authentication
- HTTP FORM-based authentication

For the purpose of the exam, you will need to understand the basic features of each of these authentication mechanisms. They are all based on the *username/password* mechanism, in which the server maintains a list of all the usernames and passwords as well as a list of resources that have to be protected.

### 9.2.1 HTTP Basic authentication

HTTP Basic authentication, which is defined in the HTTP 1.0 specification, is the simplest and most commonly used mechanism to protect resources. When a browser requests any of the protected resources, the server asks for a username/password. If the user enters a valid username/password, the server sends the resource. Let's take a closer look at the sequence of the events:

1. A browser sends a request for a protected resource. At this time, the browser does not know that the resource is protected, so it sends a normal HTTP request. For example:

```
GET /servlet/SalesServlet HTTP/1.0
```

2. The server observes that the resource is protected, and so instead of sending the resource, it sends a `401 Unauthorized` message back to the client. In the message, it also includes a header that tells the browser that the Basic authentication is needed to access the resource. The header also specifies the context in which the authentication would be valid. This context is called *realm*. It helps organize the access control lists on the server into different categories and, at the same time, tells users which user ID/password to use if they are allowed access in different realms. The following is a sample response sent by a server:

```
HTTP/1.0 401 Unauthorized
Server: Tomcat/4.0.1
WWW-Authenticate: Basic realm="sales"      <-- Specifies authentication type and realm
Content-Length=500
Content-Type=text/html

<html>
…detailed message
</html>
```

In the above response message, the `WWW-Authenticate` header specifies `Basic` and `sales` as the authentication type and the realm, respectively.

3. Upon receiving the above response, the browser opens a dialog box prompting for a username and password (see figure 9.1).

4. Once the user enters the username and password, the browser resends the request and passes the values in a header named `Authorization`:

```
GET /servlet/SalesServlet HTTP/1.0
Authorization: Basic am9objpqamo=      <-- Sends the Base64 encoded value
```

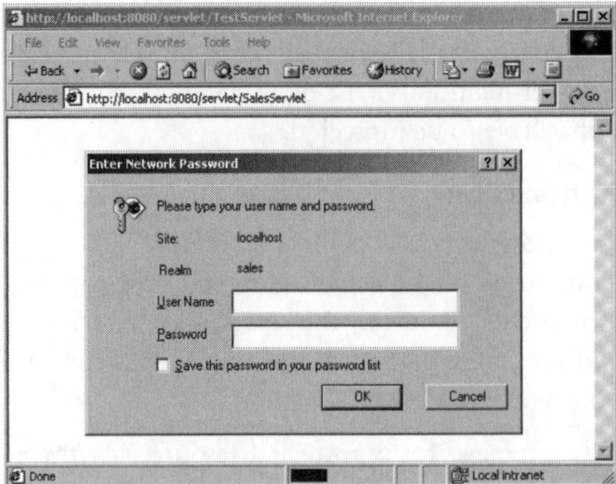


**Figure 9.1**
**HTTP Basic authentication.**

The above request header includes the Base64 encoded value of the `username:password` string. The string, `am9objpqamo=`, is the encoded form of `john:jjj`.

5 When the server receives the request, it validates the username and the password. If they are valid, it sends the resource; otherwise, it sends the same `401 Unauthorized` message again.

6 The browser displays the resource (or displays the username/password dialog box again).

### Advantages

The advantages of HTTP Basic authentication are:

- It is very easy to set up.
- All browsers support it.

### Disadvantages

The disadvantages of HTTP Basic authentication are:

- It is not secure because the username/password are not encrypted.
- You cannot customize the look and feel of the dialog box.

**NOTE** Base64 encoding is not an encryption method. Sun provides `sun.misc.Base64Encoder` and `sun.misc.Base64Decoder` classes that can encode and decode any string using this method. For more information, please refer to RFC 1521.

We will see how to use HTTP Basic authentication in section 9.2.5.

### 9.2.2 HTTP Digest authentication

The HTTP Digest authentication is the same as Basic except that in this case, the password[1] is sent in an encrypted format. This makes it more secure.

#### *Advantages*

The advantage of HTTP Digest authentication is:

- It is more secure than Basic authentication.

#### *Disadvantages*

The disadvantages of HTTP Digest authentication are:

- It is supported only by Microsoft Internet Explorer 5.
- It is not supported by many servlet containers since the specification does not mandate it.

### 9.2.3 HTTPS Client authentication

HTTPS is HTTP over SSL (Secure Socket Layer). SSL is a protocol developed by Netscape to ensure the privacy of sensitive data transmitted over the Internet. In this mechanism, authentication is performed when the SSL connection is established between the browser and the server. All the data is transmitted in the encrypted form using public-key cryptography, which is handled by the browser and the servlet container in a manner that is transparent to the servlet developers. The exam doesn't require you to know the details of this mechanism.

#### *Advantages*

The advantages of HTTPS Client authentication are:

- It is the most secure of the four types.
- All the commonly used browsers support it.

#### *Disadvantages*

The disadvantages of HTTPS Client authentication are:

- It requires a certificate from a certification authority, such as VeriSign.
- It is costly to implement and maintain.

### 9.2.4 FORM-based authentication

This mechanism is similar to Basic authentication. However, instead of using the browser's pop-up dialog box, it uses an HTML FORM to capture the username and password. Developers must create the HTML page containing the FORM, which

[1] Actually, instead of the password, an MD5 digest of the password is sent. Please refer to RFC 1321 for more information.

allows them to customize its look and feel. The only requirement of the FORM is that its action attribute should be `j_security_check` and it must have two fields: `j_username` and `j_password`. Everything else is customizable.

### *Advantages*

The advantages of FORM-based authentication are:

- It is very easy to set up.
- All the browsers support it.
- You can customize the look and feel of the login screen.

### *Disadvantages*

The disadvantages of FORM-based authentication are:

- It is not secure, since the username/password are not encrypted.
- It should be used only when a session is maintained using cookies or HTTPS.

We will see how to use FORM-based authentication in the next section.

## 9.2.5 Defining authentication mechanisms for web applications

To ensure portability and ease of configuration at the deployment location, the authentication mechanism is defined in the deployment descriptor (`web.xml`) of the web application. However, before specifying which users should be authenticated, we have to configure their usernames and passwords. This step depends on the servlet container vendor. For Tomcat, it is quite easy.

### *Configuring users in Tomcat*

Tomcat defines all the users in `<tomcat-root>\conf\tomcat-users.xml`. The following code snippet shows the default contents of this file:

```
<tomcat-users>
  <user name="tomcat" password="tomcat" roles="tomcat" />
  <user name="role1"  password="tomcat" roles="role1"  />
  <user name="both"   password="tomcat" roles="tomcat,role1" />
</tomcat-users>
```

This code defines three usernames: `tomcat`, `role1`, and `both`. The password is `tomcat` for all users.

An interesting piece of information in this file is the `roles` attribute. This attribute specifies the roles that the user plays. Permissions are assigned to roles instead of actual users. The concept of *role* comes straight from the real world; for example, a company may permit only a sales manager to access the sales data. It does not matter *who* the sales manager is. In fact, the sales manager may change over time. At any time, the sales manager is actually a user playing the sales manager role. Assigning permissions to roles instead of users gives us the flexibility to transfer permissions easily.

Let us add three more entries to the tomcat-users.xml file:

```
<tomcat-users>
  <user name="tomcat" password="tomcat" roles="tomcat" />
  <user name="role1"  password="tomcat" roles="role1"  />
  <user name="both"   password="tomcat" roles="tomcat,role1" />

  <user name="john"   password="jjj" roles="employee" />
  <user name="mary"   password="mmm" roles="employee" />
  <user name="bob"   password="bbb" roles="employee, supervisor" />
</tomcat-users>
```

We have added john and mary as employees and bob as a supervisor. Because a supervisor is also an employee, we have specified both roles for bob. We will employ these usernames later in the chapter.

### Specifying the authentication mechanism

The authentication mechanism is specified in the deployment descriptor of the web application using the <login-config> element. The Servlet specification defines the <login-config> element as follows:

```
<!ELEMENT login-config (auth-method?, realm-name?, form-login-config?)>
```

Let's look at the subelements:

- <auth-method>. Specifies which of the four authentication methods should be used to validate the user: BASIC, DIGEST, CLIENT-CERT, or FORM.
- <realm-name>. Specifies the realm name to be used in HTTP Basic authorization only.
- <form-login-config>. Specifies the login page URL and the error page URL. This element is used only if auth-method is FORM; otherwise, it is ignored.

The following is a web.xml code snippet that shows an authentication mechanism configuration:

```
<web-app>
 ...
 <login-config>
   <auth-method>BASIC</auth-method>
   <realm-name>sales</realm-name>
 </login-config>
 ...
<web-app>
```

The above code uses the Basic mechanism to authenticate users. If we wanted to use the FORM mechanism, we'd need to write two HTML pages: one for capturing the username and password, and another to display an error message if the login fails. Finally, we'd need to specify these HTML files in the <form-login-config> element, as shown here:

```
<web-app>
 ...
 <login-config>
   <auth-method>FORM</auth-method>
   <!--realm-name not required for FORM based authentication -->
   <form-login-config>
     <form-login-page>/formlogin.html</form-login-page>
     <form-error-page>/formerror.html</form-error-page>
   </form-login-config>
 </login-config>
 ...
<web-app>
```

The `formlogin.html` file can be as simple as the following:

```
<html>
<body>
<h4>Please login:</h4>
   <form method="POST" action="j_security_check">
      <input type="text" name="j_username">
      <input type="password" name="j_password">
      <input type="submit" value="OK">
   </form>
</body>
</html>
```

The `formerror.html` file is even simpler:

```
<html>
<body>
   <h4>Sorry, your username and password do not match.</h4>
</body>
</html>
```

Observe that for the FORM method, we do not have to write any servlet to process the form. The action `j_security_check` triggers the servlet container to do the processing itself.

## 9.3 SECURING WEB APPLICATIONS DECLARATIVELY

It is very common for a web application to be developed by one group of individuals and then deployed by a very different group of people at another location. For example, many companies sell web applications as ready-made solutions for business needs. This means that the developer should be able to easily convey the security requirements of the application to the deployer. The deployer should also be able to customize certain aspects of the application's security without modifying the code. The servlet framework allows us to specify the detailed security requirements of the application in the deployment descriptor. This is called *declarative security.*

By default, all of the resources of a web application are accessible to everybody. To restrict access to the resources, we need to identify three things:

- *Web resource collection.* Identifies the resources of the application—that is, HTML files, servlets, and so forth—that must be protected from public access. A user must have appropriate authorization to access resources identified under a web resource collection.
- *Authorization constraint.* Identifies the roles that a user can be assigned. Instead of specifying permissions for individual users, permissions are assigned to roles. As discussed earlier, this reduces a tight coupling of permissions and the actual users. For example, an `AdminServlet` may be accessible to any user who is in the administrator role. At deployment time, any of the actual users may be configured as the administrator.
- *User data constraint.* Specifies the way the data must be transmitted between the sender and the receiver. In other words, this constraint specifies the transport layer requirement of the application. It formulates the policies for maintaining data integrity and confidentiality. For example, an application may require the use of HTTPS as a means of communication instead of plain HTTP.

We can configure all three of these items in the deployment descriptor of the web application by using the element `<security-constraint>`. This element, which falls directly under the `<web-app>` element of `web.xml`, is defined as follows:

```
<!ELEMENT security-constraint (display-name?, web-resource-collection+,
auth-constraint?, user-data-constraint?)>
```

Let's look at the subelements one by one.

### 9.3.1 display-name

This is an optional element. It specifies a name for the security constraint that is easily identifiable.

### 9.3.2 web-resource-collection

As the name suggests, `web-resource-collection` specifies a collection of resources to which this security constraint applies. We can define one or more web resource collections in the `<security-constraint>` element. It is defined as follows:

```
<!ELEMENT web-resource-collection (web-resource-name, description?,
                                   url-pattern*, http-method*)>
```

- `web-resource-name`. Specifies the name of the resource.
- `description`. Provides a description of the resource.
- `url-pattern`. Specifies the URL pattern through which the resource will be accessed. We can specify multiple URL patterns to group multiple resources together. Recall from chapter 5, "Structure and deployment," that `<url-pattern>` is also used to specify the URL-to-servlet mapping.

- `http-method`. Provides a finer control over HTTP requests. This element specifies the HTTP methods to which this constraint will be applied. For example, we can use `http-method` to restrict POST requests only to authorized users while allowing GET requests for all the users.

Let's look at a sample web resource collection:

```
<web-app>
  ...
 <security-constraint>
   <web-resource-collection>      <-- Defines a web resource collection
    <web-resource-name>reports</web-resource-name>

      <url-pattern>/servlet/SalesReportServlet/*</url-pattern>
      <url-pattern>/servlet/FinanceReportServlet/*</url-pattern>
      <url-pattern>/servlet/HRReportServlet/*</url-pattern>

      <http-method>GET</http-method>
      <http-method>POST</http-method>
   </web-resource-collection>
      ...
 </security-constraint>
  ...
</web-app>
```

In this collection, we specify three servlets to which we want to apply the security constraint. We have defined only GET and POST in the `<http-method>` section. This means that only these methods will have a restricted access; all other requests to these servlets will be open to all users.

If no `<http-method>` element is present, then the constraint applies to all of the HTTP methods.

### 9.3.3 auth-constraint

This element specifies the roles that can access the resources specified in the `web-resource-collection` section. It is defined as follows:

```
<!ELEMENT auth-constraint (description?, role-name*)>
```

- `description`. Describes the constraint.
- `role-name`. Specifies the role that can access the resources. It can be `*` (which means all the roles defined in the web application), or it must be a name that is defined in the `<security-role>` element of the deployment descriptor.

Here's an example:

```
<web-app>
  ...
  <security-role>
     <role-name>manager</role-name>
     <role-name>director</role-name>
     <role-name>employee</role-name>
  </security-role>
```

```
    ...
    <security-constraint>
       ...
       <auth-constraint>
          <description>accessible to all managers and
                       directors</description>
          <role-name>manager</role-name>
          <role-name>director/role-name>
       </auth-constraint>
       ...
    </security-constraint>
    ...
</web-app>
```

This example specifies that the security constraint applies to all the users who are in the role of `manager` or `director`.

### 9.3.4 user-data-constraint

This element specifies how the data should be communicated between the client and the server. It is defined as follows:

```
<!ELEMENT user-data-constraint (description?, transport-guarantee)>
```

- `description`. Describes the constraint.
- `transport-guarantee`. Contains one of three values: `NONE`, `INTEGRAL`, or `CONFIDENTIAL`. `NONE` implies that the application does not need any guarantee about the integrity or confidentiality of the data transmitted, while `INTEGRAL` and `CONFIDENTIAL` imply that the application requires the data transmission to have data integrity and confidentiality, respectively. Usually, plain `HTTP` is used when `transport-guarantee` is set to `NONE`, and `HTTPS` is used when `transport-guarantee` is set to `INTEGRAL` or `CONFIDENTIAL`.

Here is an example of `user-data-constraint`:

```
<web-app>
   ...
   <security-constraint>
      ...
      <user-data-constraint>
         <description>requires the data transmission
                   to be integral</description>
         <transport-guarantee>INTEGRAL</transport-guarantee>
      </user-data-constraint>
      ...
   </security-constraint>
   ...
</web-app>
```

### 9.3.5 Putting it all together

Now, let's build a simple web application containing just one servlet but with all of the bells and whistles for its security.

### *The deployment descriptor*

As we explained earlier, all of the security requirements of a web application can be specified in the deployment descriptor, as illustrated in listing 9.1.

**Listing 9.1 web.xml showing declarative security configuration**

```
<?xml version="1.0" encoding="ISO-8859-1"?>

<!DOCTYPE web-app
    PUBLIC "-//Sun Microsystems, Inc.//DTD Web Application 2.3//EN"
    "http://java.sun.com/dtd/web-app_2_3.dtd">
<web-app>

 <servlet>     <-- Defines a servlet
  <servlet-name>SecureServlet</servlet-name>
  <servlet-class>SecureServlet</servlet-class>
 </servlet>

                                             Defines the security
 <security-constraint>                  <--  constraint for the servlet

   <web-resource-collection>
      <web-resource-name>declarative security test</web-resource-name>
      <url-pattern>/servlet/SecureServlet</url-pattern>
      <http-method>POST</http-method>
   </web-resource-collection>

   <auth-constraint>
      <role-name>supervisor</role-name>
   </auth-constraint>

   <user-data-constraint>
      <transport-guarantee>NONE</transport-guarantee>
   </user-data-constraint>

 </security-constraint>
                                         Defines the authentication
 <login-config>                     <--  mechanism
   <auth-method>FORM</auth-method>


   <form-login-config>
     <form-login-page>/formlogin.html</form-login-page>
     <form-error-page>/formerror.html</form-error-page>
   </form-login-config>
 </login-config>
                                    Defines the
 <security-role>               <--  security role
   <role-name>supervisor</role-name>
 </security-role>

</web-app>
```

The `web.xml` file for our web application (listing 9.1) is straightforward. It defines a servlet followed by a security constraint for the servlet.

The resource to be protected is identified by the `<url-pattern>` element of `<web-resource-collection>`. Observe that in the `<web-resource-collection>` section we have specified only the POST method; this means that this security constraint applies only to the POST requests. All other HTTP methods are accessible to all the users. We could say that the word `resource` in `web-resource-collection` is a misnomer. With respect to a `web-resource-collection`, a resource is not just a servlet or a JSP page—it is an HTTP method sent to that servlet. In listing 9.1, the resource to which we are applying the constraint is the POST method sent to `SecureServlet`.

The `auth-constraint` section specifies that this resource should only be accessible to supervisors. The `role-name` that we use here must be defined in the `security-role` section.

The `transport-guarantee` is `NONE`, implying that HTTP will be used as the communication protocol.

The `<login-config>` section is exactly as we discussed in section 9.2.5. We can use either `BASIC` or `FORM` as the authentication mechanism.

### The SecureServlet

Listing 9.2 contains the code for the `SecureServlet`, which was specified in the `<servlet-name>` element in the deployment descriptor in listing 9.1.

**Listing 9.2 Code for SecureServlet**

```
import javax.servlet.*;
import javax.servlet.http.*;
import java.io.*;

public class SecureServlet extends HttpServlet
{
   public SecureServlet()
   {
      super();
   }

   public void doGet(HttpServletRequest req,
                     HttpServletResponse res)
                     throws IOException
   {
      PrintWriter pw = res.getWriter();

      pw.println("<html><head>");
      pw.println("<title>Declarative Security Example</title>");
      pw.println("</head>");
      pw.println("<body>");
      pw.println("Hello! HTTP GET request is open to all
                                                     users.");
```

```
        pw.println("</body></html>");

    }
    public void doPost(HttpServletRequest req,
                       HttpServletResponse res)
                       throws IOException
    {
        PrintWriter pw = res.getWriter();

        pw.println("<html><head>");
        pw.println("<title>Declarative Security Example</title>");
        pw.println("</head>");
        pw.println("<body>");
        String name = req.getParameter("username");
        pw.println("Welcome, "+name+"!");
        pw.println("<br>You are seeing this page because you are
                                              a supervisor.");
        pw.println("</body></html>");
    }
}
```

The servlet code in listing 9.2 is fairly simple and self-explanatory. We implemented the `doGet()` and `doPost()` methods for demonstration purposes only.

An important point to observe here is that the servlet does not have any security-related code. All of the security aspects are taken care of by the servlet container with the help of the deployment descriptor.

### *Running the example*

You can access the complete working code from the accompanying CD. Simply copy the `chapter09-declarative` directory to the `webapps` directory of your Tomcat installation and restart Tomcat.

- From your browser, go to `http://localhost:8080/chapter09-declarative/servlet/SecureServlet`. This sends a GET request to the servlet. Note that you are not asked for a username or password.
- To see the behavior of the POST method, go to `http://localhost:8080/chapter09-declarative/posttest.html`. This HTML file contains a FORM, which sends a POST request to the servlet. Observe that this time you get the login page (`formlogin.html`) because we have specified POST in `<http-method>` in the `<web-resource-collection>` section of the deployment descriptor (listing 9.1). The servlet's `doPost()` method is executed only if you enter `bob` and `bbb` as the user ID and password, since `bob` is the only user we have defined in the deployment descriptor with the role of `supervisor`. For other values, you will get the error page (`formerror.html`). The code for `posttest.html` is simple and contains the following six lines:

```
<html><body>
<form action="/servlet/SecureServlet" method="POST">
<input type="text" name="username">
<input type="submit">
</form>
</body></html>
```

Tomcat 4.0.1 does not handle the combination of FORM-based authentication and a constraint on the HTTP POST method for a resource correctly. It authenticates the user as expected but calls the `doGet()` method on the resource instead of `doPost()`. In the above example, if you use the FORM-based authentication and submit the FORM using `posttest.html`, Tomcat calls the `doGet()` method on `SecureServlet`. This combination works well in the Weblogic Application Server, though.

## 9.4 SECURING WEB APPLICATIONS PROGRAMMATICALLY

In some cases, declarative security is not sufficient or fine-grained enough for the application. For example, suppose we want a servlet to be accessed by all employees. However, we want the server to generate a certain output for managers and a different output for other employees.

For such cases, the Servlet specification allows the servlet to have security-related code. This is called *programmatic security*. In this approach, a servlet identifies the role that a user is playing and then generates the output according to the role. As shown in table 9.1, the `HttpServletRequest` interface provides three methods for identifying the user and the role.

**Table 9.1 HttpServletRequest methods for identifying a user**

| Method | Description |
|---|---|
| String getRemoteUser | This method returns the login name of the user, if the user has been authenticated, or null if the user has not been authenticated. |
| Principal getUserPrincipal() | This method returns a java.security.Principal object containing the name of the current authenticated user. It returns null if the user is not authenticated. |
| boolean isUserInRole(String rolename) | This method returns a Boolean indicating whether the authenticated user is included in the specified logical role. It returns false if the user is not authenticated. |

Let's modify the `SecureServlet` that we saw in section 9.3 to generate customized output. We will just change the `doPost()` method and leave the rest as is:

```
public void doPost(HttpServletRequest req,
                   HttpServletResponse res)
                   throws IOException
{
   PrintWriter pw = res.getWriter();
```

```
        pw.println("<html><head>");
        pw.println("<title>Programatic Security Example</title>");
        pw.println("</head>");
        pw.println("<body>");

        String username = req.getRemoteUser();   <-- Gets the username

        if(username != null)
                pw.println("<h4>Welcome, "+username+"!</h4>");

        if(req.isUserInRole("manager"))   <-- Determines if the user is a manager
        {
            pw.println("<b>Manager's Page!</b>");
        }
        else
        {
            pw.println("<b>Employee's Page!</b>");
        }
        pw.println("</body></html>");
    }
```

In this code, we retrieve the login name of the user using the `getRemoteUser()` method and determine whether or not the user is a manager.

Obviously, this requires hard-coding the role name `manager` in the servlet code. At the actual deployment location, however, users may be called supervisors instead of managers. To allow flexibility in defining the roles at deployment time, the servlet developer must convey the hard-coded values to the deployer. The deployer then maps these hard-coded values to the actual role values that are used in the deployment environment (as we'll see in the example that follows).

Now, let's modify the deployment descriptor of our previous example. Listing 9.3 contains the new deployment descriptor; the modified part appears in bold.

**Listing 9.3 web.xml for programmatic security configuration**

```
<?xml version="1.0" encoding="ISO-8859-1"?>

<!DOCTYPE web-app
  PUBLIC "-//Sun Microsystems, Inc.//DTD Web Application 2.3//EN"
    "http://java.sun.com/dtd/web-app_2_3.dtd">

<web-app>

 <servlet>
  <servlet-name>SecureServlet</servlet-name>
  <servlet-class>SecureServlet</servlet-class>

  <security-role-ref>
    <role-name>manager</role-name>          <-- Role name hard-coded in the servlet
    <role-link>supervisor</role-link>       <-- Role name defined in the servlet container
  </security-role-ref>

 </servlet>
```

```
  <security-constraint>
    <web-resource-collection>
      <web-resource-name>programmatic security test</web-resource-name>
      <url-pattern>/servlet/SecureServlet</url-pattern>
      <http-method>POST</http-method>
    </web-resource-collection>
    <auth-constraint>
      <role-name>employee</role-name>        <-- Gives access to all the employees
    </auth-constraint>
    <user-data-constraint>
      <transport-guarantee>NONE</transport-guarantee>
    </user-data-constraint>
  </security-constraint>

  <login-config>
    <auth-method>FORM</auth-method>
    <realm-name>sales</realm-name>
    <form-login-config>
      <form-login-page>/formlogin.html</form-login-page>
      <form-error-page>/formerror.html</form-error-page>
    </form-login-config>
  </login-config>

  <security-role>
    <role-name>supervisor</role-name>
  </security-role>
  <security-role>
    <role-name>employee</role-name>
  </security-role>

</web-app>
```

In the above code, the `<security-role-ref>` section is used to associate the hard-coded role name used by the servlet (`manager`) to the actual role name (`supervisor`). Since we now want the servlet to be accessed by all employees, we have also changed the `<security-constraint>` to let all staff access this servlet. That's all there is to the programmatic security model.

## 9.5 SUMMARY

As companies conduct more of their business over the Internet, security issues will continue to increase in importance. In this chapter, we learned how to make a web application secure. We first introduced some important security-related terms. *Authentication* is validating who a user is, *authorization* is verifying what the user can do, and *auditing* holds the user accountable for her actions. We also discussed *confidentiality* and *data integrity*, and how these terms apply to web applications. The Servlet specification defines four mechanisms to authenticate users: `BASIC`, `CLIENT`, `FORM`, and `DIGEST`. The authentication mechanism is defined in the deployment descriptor (`web.xml`) of the web application.

We also learned how to secure a web application declaratively by configuring its security aspects in the deployment descriptor, and we learned how to implement security-related code in a servlet in order to secure a web application programmatically. Finally, we presented a complete web application that uses all the security features provided by the Servlet specification.

You should now be able to answer questions that require an understanding of authorization, authentication, data integrity, auditing, malicious code, and web site attacks. You should know how to specify the security requirements of an application in the deployment descriptor and how to identify incorrectly written security constraints. In the next chapter, we will learn about multithreaded and single-threaded servlets. We'll also learn how to develop thread-safe servlets.

## 9.6 REVIEW QUESTIONS

1. Which of the following correctly defines data integrity? (Select one)

   **a** It guarantees that information is accessible only to certain users.
   **b** It guarantees that the information is kept in encrypted form on the server.
   **c** It guarantees that unintended parties cannot read the information during transmission between the client and the server.
   **d** It guarantees that the information is not altered during transmission between the client and the server.

2. What is the term for determining whether a user has access to a particular resource? (Select one)

   **a** Authorization
   **b** Authentication
   **c** Confidentiality
   **d** Secrecy

3. Which one of the following must be done before authorization takes place? (Select one)

   **a** Data validation
   **b** User authentication
   **c** Data encryption
   **d** Data compression

4. Which of the following actions would you take to prevent your web site from being attacked? (Select three)

   **a** Block network traffic at all the ports except the HTTP port.
   **b** Audit the usage pattern of your server.
   **c** Audit the Servlet/JSP code.
   **d** Use HTTPS instead of HTTP.

e Design and develop your web application using a software engineering methodology.

f Use design patterns.

5. Identify the authentication mechanisms that are built into the HTTP specification. (Select two)

   a Basic

   b Client-Cert

   c FORM

   d Digest

   e Client-Digest

   f HTTPS

6. Which of the following deployment descriptor elements is used for specifying the authentication mechanism for a web application? (Select one)

   a `security-constraint`

   b `auth-constraint`

   c `login-config`

   d `web-resource-collection`

7. Which of the following elements are used for defining a security constraint? Choose only those elements that come directly under the `security-constraint` element. (Select three)

   a `login-config`

   b `role-name`

   c `role`

   d `transport-guarantee`

   e `user-data-constraint`

   f `auth-constraint`

   g `authorization-constraint`

   h `web-resource-collection`

8. Which of the following *web.xml* snippets correctly identifies all HTML files under the `sales` directory? (Select two)

   a
```
<web-resource-collection>
    <web-resource-name>reports</web-resource-name>
    <url-pattern>/sales/*.html</url-pattern>
</web-resource-collection>
```

   b
```
<resource-collection>
    <web-resource-name>reports</web-resource-name>
    <url-pattern>/sales/*.html</url-pattern>
</resource-collection>
```

**c**
```
<resource-collection>
    <resource-name>reports</resource-name>
    <url-pattern>/sales/*.html</url-pattern>
</resource-collection>
```

**d**
```
<web-resource-collection>
    <web-resource-name>reports</web-resource-name>
    <url-pattern>/sales/*.html</url-pattern>
    <http-method>GET</http-method>
</web-resource-collection>
```

9. You want your `PerformanceReportServlet` to be accessible only to managers. This servlet generates a performance report based on a FORM submitted by a user. Which of the following correctly defines a security constraint for this purpose? (Select one)

**a**
```
<security-constraint>
 <web-resource-collection>
    <web-resource-name>performance report</web-resource-name>
    <url-pattern>/servlet/PerformanceReportServlet</url-pattern>
    <http-method>GET</http-method>
 </web-resource-collection>

 <auth-constraint>

    <role-name>manager</role-name>
 </auth-constraint>

 <user-data-constraint>
    <transport-guarantee>NONE</transport-guarantee>
 </user-data-constraint>

 </security-constraint>
```

**b**
```
<security-constraint>

 <web-resource-collection>
    <web-resource-name>performance report</web-resource-name>
    <url-pattern>/servlet/PerformanceReportServlet</url-pattern>

    <http-method>*</http-method>
 </web-resource-collection>

 <accessibility>
    <role-name>manager</role-name>
 </accessibility>

 <user-data-constraint>
    <transport-guarantee>CONFIDENTIAL</transport-guarantee>
 </user-data-constraint>

 </security-constraint>
```

**c**
```
<security-constraint>

  <web-resource-collection>
    <web-resource-name>performance report</web-resource-name>
    <url-pattern>/servlet/PerformanceReportServlet</url-pattern>
    <http-method>POST</http-method>
  </web-resource-collection>

  <accessibility>
    <role-name>manager</role-name>
  </accessibility>

  <user-data-constraint>
    <transport-guarantee>CONFIDENTIAL</transport-guarantee>
  </user-data-constraint>

  </security-constraint>
```

**d**
```
<security-constraint>

  <web-resource-collection>
    <web-resource-name>performance report</web-resource-name>
    <url-pattern>/servlet/PerformanceReportServlet</url-pattern>
    <http-method>POST</http-method>
  </web-resource-collection>

  <auth-constraint>
    <role-name>manager</role-name>
  </auth-constraint>

  </security-constraint>
```

10. Which of the following statements regarding authentication mechanisms are correct? (Select two)

   **a** The HTTP Basic mechanism transmits the username/password "in the open."
   
   **b** The HTTP Basic mechanism uses HTML FORMs to collect usernames/passwords.
   
   **c** The transmission method in the Basic and FORM mechanisms is the same.
   
   **d** The method of capturing the usernames/passwords in the Basic and FORM mechanisms is the same.

11. Which of the following statements are correct for an unauthenticated user? (Select two)

   **a** `HttpServletRequest.getUserPrincipal()` returns null.
   
   **b** `HttpServletRequest.getUserPrincipal()` throws `SecurityException`.
   
   **c** `HttpServletRequest.isUserInRole()` returns false.
   
   **d** `HttpServletRequest.getRemoteUser()` throws a `SecurityException`.

CHAPTER 10

# Developing thread-safe servlets



## EXAM OBJECTIVES

**7.1** Identify which attribute scopes are thread-safe:

- Local variables
- Instance variables
- Class variables
- Request attributes
- Session attributes
- Context attributes.

(Sections 10.3–10.4)

**7.2** Identify correct statements about differences between the multi-threaded and single-threaded servlet models. (Sections 10.1–10.2)

**7.3** Identify the interface used to declare that a servlet must use the single thread model. (Sections 10.2)

## INTRODUCTION

In a large production environment, a servlet container receives thousands of simultaneous requests from multiple clients. Servicing each request quickly is very important. In such situations, processing each request one by one is usually not an option; doing so would make the response time unacceptably high. The only solution is to service the requests concurrently using multiple threads.

In this chapter, we will learn how a servlet container handles simultaneous requests and what care should be taken in developing servlets that service requests in parallel. We will also look at cases in which a servlet cannot handle multiple requests simultaneously and the best way to implement servlets in these instances. To do well on the exam, it is important that you understand the behavior of the two threading models discussed in this chapter.

## 10.1 UNDERSTANDING THE MULTITHREADED SERVLET MODEL

In the multithreaded servlet model, the container maintains a thread pool to service requests. A thread pool is nothing but a set of threads waiting to execute any code. These threads are called *worker threads*. A servlet container also has a thread (the *dispatcher thread*) that manages the worker threads. When the container receives a request for a servlet, the dispatcher thread picks up a worker thread from the pool and dispatches the request to the worker thread. The worker thread then executes the `service()` method of the servlet (see figure 10.1).

If the container receives another request while this thread is still working, it picks up another thread from the pool and uses it to service the new request. Note that the servlet container does not care whether the second request is for the same servlet or another

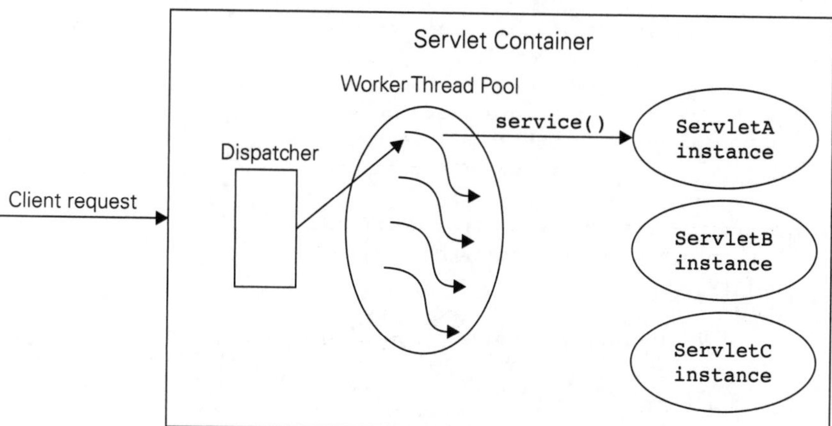


**Figure 10.1 The dispatcher assigns a request to a worker thread.**

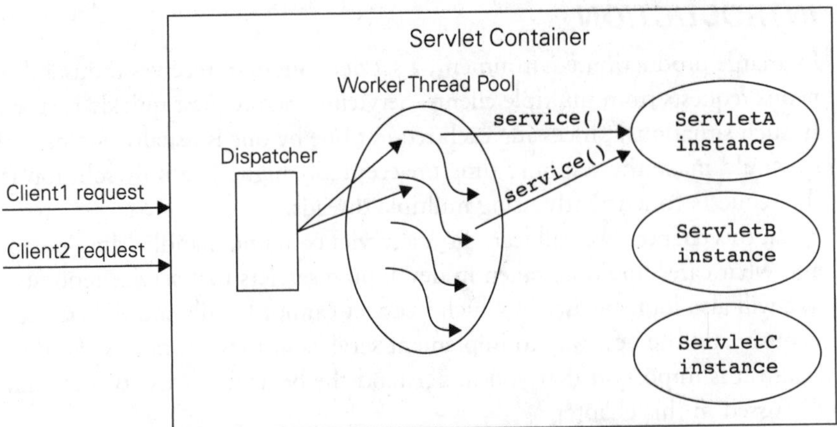


**Figure 10.2 Two threads may execute the service() method simultaneously.**

servlet. Therefore, if the container receives multiple requests for one servlet simultaneously, the `service()` method of that servlet will be executed concurrently in multiple threads. Figure 10.2 shows two worker threads both executing the `service()` method of a servlet. This is the default behavior of the servlet container, and it improves the response time considerably without any extra hardware cost.

To see the effect of multithreading, consider listing 10.1, which contains code for a servlet that takes a lot of time to generate a response.

**Listing 10.1 A multithreaded servlet**

```
import java.io.*;
import javax.servlet.http.*;

public class SlowServlet extends HttpServlet
{

   public void doGet(HttpServletRequest req,
                     HttpServletResponse res)
                     throws IOException
   {
      PrintWriter htmlout = res.getWriter();
      htmlout.println("<html><body>");
      try
      {
         //simulate excessive processing by sleeping for
                                                  10 seconds.

         Thread.sleep(10000);
      }
      catch(Exception e)
      {
      }
```

```
            htmlout.println("<h2>Hello World.</h2>");
            htmlout.println("</body></html>");
        }
    }
```

The doGet() method of this servlet is simple. We have inserted a call to Thread.sleep() to simulate a situation in which it takes 10 seconds to process a request. Now, assume that 10 clients simultaneously send requests to this servlet. Without multithreading, each request would be processed sequentially, and one of the clients would get a response after a staggering 100 seconds! However, since the servlet container processes the requests in multiple threads, each of the clients will receive a response in approximately 10 seconds (assuming that the container has at least 10 worker threads in the pool).

## 10.2 UNDERSTANDING THE SINGLE-THREADED MODEL

While multithreaded servlets greatly improve performance, some servlets perform tasks that cannot be done in parallel. For example, consider the servlet shown in listing 10.2, which retrieves information from a request and writes it to a file.

**Listing 10.2 The wrong way to write to a file**

```
import java.io.*;
import javax.servlet.http.*;

public class BadRequestInfoWriterServlet extends HttpServlet
{
   PrintWriter pw = null;
   pw = new PrintWriter(new FileOutputStream("testdata.txt"));

   public void doGet(HttpServletRequest req,
                     HttpServletResponse res)
                     throws IOException
   {
     String name = req.getParameter("name");
     String data = req.getParameter("data");

     pw.println("START REQUEST DATA");
     pw.println(name+"="+data);
     pw.println("END REQUEST DATA");

     PrintWriter htmlout = res.getWriter();
     htmlout.println("<html><body>");
     htmlout.println("<h2>Data is written to the file.</h2>");
     htmlout.println("</body></html>");
   }
}
```

Upon receiving multiple simultaneous requests for this servlet, the container will call the `doGet()` method in multiple threads. However, executing the `doGet()` method of this servlet concurrently would definitely corrupt the file because all the threads would be writing data to the file simultaneously. To avoid this, the servlet should only service requests sequentially. Clearly, the default behavior of the container is not suitable for this servlet.

The Servlet specification helps us in such situations by defining an interface called `SingleThreadModel` in the `javax.servlet` package. Let's see what this interface offers.

### 10.2.1 The javax.servlet.SingleThreadModel interface

The `javax.servlet.SingleThreadModel` interface does not declare any methods, and it signifies that a servlet implementing this interface cannot service requests concurrently. The specification guarantees that if a servlet implements this interface, the container will not execute the `service()` method (and hence the do*XXX*() methods of the servlet) in more than one thread simultaneously. However, as we saw in the previous section, servicing requests sequentially seriously hurts performance. To avoid the performance problem, a servlet container may create multiple instances of the servlet class. In short, multiple requests will still be processed simultaneously but by different servlet instances. Figure 10.3 shows two requests for a servlet named `STMServlet`, which implements the `SingleThreadModel` interface. In this case, the two requests are serviced by two different instances of the servlet.

In listing 10.3, we use this interface to improve our `RequestInfoWriterServlet`.

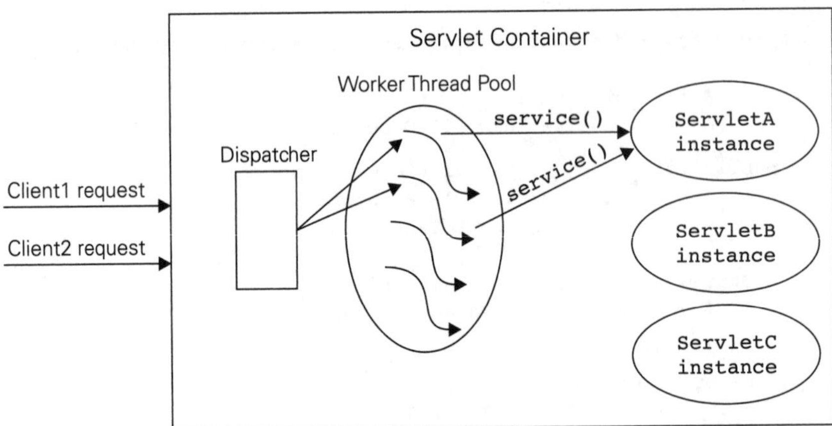


**Figure 10.3 A container may create multiple instances of a servlet if the servlet implements SingleThreadModel.**

**Listing 10.3 A better way to write to a file**

```
import java.io.*;
import javax.servlet.*;
import javax.servlet.http.*;
public class RequestInfoWriterServlet extends HttpServlet
            implements SingleThreadModel
{
   static int instanceNumber = 1;

   //instance block to increment instanceNumber.
   //A static block will not work here because a static block
   //will be executed only once when the class is loaded. So,
   //the instanceNumber variable will not be incremented if a
   //new instance of this class is created.
   {
      instanceNumber++;

   }

   String filename = "testdata"+instanceNumber+".txt";
   PrintWriter pw = new PrintWriter(
                  new FileOutputStream(filename)
                                 );

   public void doGet(HttpServletRequest req,
                  HttpServletResponse res)
                  throws IOException
   {
     String name = req.getParameter("name");
     String data = req.getParameter("data");

     pw.println("START REQUEST DATA");
     pw.println(name+"="+data);
     pw.println("END REQUEST DATA");

     PrintWriter htmlout = res.getWriter();
     htmlout.println("<html><body>");
     htmlout.println("<h2>Data is written to the file.</h2>");
     htmlout.println("</body></html>");
   }
}
```

To prevent running multiple threads in its `doGet()` method, the servlet in listing 10.3 implements the `SingleThreadModel` interface. Because the container may create multiple instances of this servlet, we use a static variable, which is incremented in an instance block for each new instance of the servlet, to create a different filename for each instance.

Although very convenient, this interface is not highly recommended for the following reasons:

- *Performance.* The creation of multiple instances consumes time as well as memory. Also, not all servlet containers will create multiple instances of a `SingleThreadModel` servlet. This leads to the sequential processing of the requests, which degrades the performance drastically.
- *A false sense of thread safety.* Many novice developers think that implementing the `SingleThreadModel` interface allows them to forget about thread safety altogether. However, implementing this interface does not alleviate the problems associated with sharing the data through common means such as `HttpSession` and `ServletContext` because the requests may still be processed simultaneously by multiple instances. We will learn about the multithreading issues associated with `HttpSession` and `ServletContext` in the next section.
- *Data sharing.* Instance variables cannot be used to share data among multiple requests, since different requests may be serviced by different instances.

### Synchronizing the service method

Synchronizing the `service()` (or do*XXX*) method of a servlet instead of implementing the `SingleThreadModel` interface seems to be a very good solution if your servlet is not thread safe. It prevents the container from calling the `service()` method of your servlet from multiple threads. It also prevents the container from creating multiple instances of your servlet (because the servlet does not implement `SingleThreadModel`), which eliminates the issues with sharing data using `HttpSession` and `ServletContext`. However, these benefits also degrade the performance drastically. Synchronizing the `service()` method ensures that multiple requests can never be processed simultaneously, not even by multiple instances. For this reason, this approach is almost never used.

## 10.3 VARIABLE SCOPES AND THREAD SAFETY

When developing servlets using either the multithreaded or the single-threaded model, we must take care to ensure that they are thread safe. For example, consider the servlet shown in listing 10.4, which sends a welcome message to a user upon request.

**Listing 10.4 A thread-unsafe servlet**

```
import java.servlet.*;
import java.io.*;
import javax.servlet.http.*;

public class BadWelcomeServlet extends HttpServlet
{
   String username = "";

   public void doGet(HttpServletRequest req,
                     HttpServletResponse res)
                     throws IOException
   {
```

```
1:     PrintWriter htmlout = res.getWriter();
2:     htmlout.println("<html><body>");
3:     username = req.getParameter("name");

4:     htmlout.println("<h2>Welcome, "+ username +"</h2><br>");

5:     htmlout.println("</body></html>");
    }
}
```

This seemingly innocent servlet may not work as expected. Let's see what might happen when two users, A and B, send a request to this servlet simultaneously:

1. The servlet container assigns a worker thread (for example, T1) to service A's request and another worker thread (T2) to service B's request.
2. The OS schedules T1 to run.
3. T1 extracts the `name` parameter from the request and saves it in the `username` variable (lines 1, 2, and 3). The value of `username` is now `A`.
4. Just before T1 attempts to execute the next statement, the OS preempts T1 and schedules T2 to run.
5. T2 extracts the `name` parameter from the request and saves it in the `username` variable (lines 1, 2, and 3). Therefore, the value of `username` is now `B`. Notice that the value saved by T1 is now lost.
6. T2 executes the last two lines (4 and 5) and a valid response—that is, `"Welcome, B"`—is sent to user B.
7. Now, the OS schedules T1 again, which starts from where it was preempted. It executes the remaining two lines (4 and 5). Since the value of the `username` variable is `B`, it sends `"Welcome, B"` to user A.

The problem in listing 10.4 is that `username` is an instance variable. Since this variable is shared among multiple threads running the `doGet()` method simultaneously, its value does not remain constant throughout the processing of a request.

This example shows that although a servlet may not involve any threading code, it is still very much a part of the multithreaded servlet framework. In the following sections, we will see which variable and attribute scopes are thread safe and why. We will also look at two solutions for fixing this servlet. On the exam, you may be shown an example of servlet code and be asked to determine whether or not it is thread safe. You may even be asked to identify the thread-safe variables used by a given servlet.

### 10.3.1 Local variables

Each thread gets its own copy of the local variables, and changes made to these variables do not affect the copies of the local variables of other threads. We can easily fix `BadWelcomeServlet` in listing 10.4 by using a local variable instead of an instance variable, as shown in listing 10.5.

**Listing 10.5 A thread-safe servlet using a local variable**

```
import java.io.*;
import javax.servlet.http.*;

public class GoodWelcomeServlet extends HttpServlet
{

   public void doGet(HttpServletRequest req,
                     HttpServletResponse res)
                     throws IOException
   {
      String username = "";

      PrintWriter htmlout = res.getWriter();
      htmlout.println("<html><body>");
      username = req.getParameter("name");

      htmlout.println("<h2>Welcome, "+name+"</h2><br>");

      htmlout.println("</body></html>");
   }
}
```

In this servlet, each thread gets its own copy of the `username` variable. Therefore, the value of `username` remains constant throughout the request processing. This makes the servlet thread safe, no matter how many threads run the `doGet()` method simultaneously.

In short, local variables are always thread safe. Being thread safe, local variables are used to control the flow of logic in the servlet methods. As in any Java class, we use them as loop variables, temporary data holders, and so forth. Obviously, these variables cannot be used to share data between the threads, since each thread gets a different copy of the local variables.

### 10.3.2 Instance variables

There is only one copy of the instance variables per instance of the servlet, and all of the threads share this copy. In the case of the multithreaded model, multiple threads may access an instance variable simultaneously, as seen in listing 10.4, which makes it unsafe. However, in the case of the single-threaded model, only one thread executes the methods of a servlet instance at a time. Therefore, an instance variable is thread safe for the single-threaded model. For example, we can make our `BadWelcomeServlet` thread safe by implementing the `SingleThreadModel` interface, as shown in listing 10.6.

**Listing 10.6 A thread-safe servlet using SingleThreadModel**

```
import java.servlet.*;
import java.io.*;
import javax.servlet.http.*;

public class GoodWelcomeServlet extends HttpServlet
                                   implements SingleThreadModel
```

```
{
    String username = "";

    public void doGet(HttpServletRequest req,
                      HttpServletResponse res)
                      throws IOException
    {
        PrintWriter htmlout = res.getWriter();
        htmlout.println("<html><body>");
        username = req.getParameter("name");

        htmlout.println("<h2>Welcome, "+name+"</h2><br>");

        htmlout.println("</body></html>");
    }
}
```

Instance variables are used to cache objects that can be initialized at the servlet startup. Such variables can be used throughout the life of the servlet. For example, the servlet shown in listing 10.7 uses an instance variable to cache the database connection object.

**Listing 10.7 Using an instance variable to keep the connection to the database open**

```
import java.sql.*;
import java.io.*;
import javax.servlet.http.*;

public class TestServlet extends HttpServlet
{
   private Connection conn;
   public void init()
   {
     //initialize connection
     Class.forName(getInitParameter("driverClass"));
     conn = DriverManager.getConnection("dbUrl");
   }

   public void doGet(HttpServletRequest req,
                     HttpServletResponse res)
                     throws IOException
   {
     //use the connection object to get data from the db
     Statement stmt = conn.createStatement("...");
     ...
   }
}
```

Since creating a connection to the database is time-consuming, this servlet creates a connection object in its `init()` method instead of creating a new connection object for each request in the `doGet()` method and then reuses it for processing requests.

### 10.3.3 Class (or static) variables

Only one copy of a class variable exists across all the instances of the object belonging to the class for which it is declared. Not surprisingly, just like instance variables, class variables are not thread safe. In fact, class variables are unsafe even for the single-threaded model, because multiple threads may access the same class variable from different servlet instances.

Class variables are used to store "read-only," or constant, data. Such data is usually hard-coded in the class. For example, the servlet in listing 10.8 uses class variables to define some constants.

**Listing 10.8 Using class variables to store hard-coded constants**

```
import java.io.*;
import javax.servlet.http.*;
public class TestServlet extends HttpServlet
{
   final static int STORE    = 101;
   final static int DISPLAY = 102;
   final static int MODIFY  = 103;
   public void doGet(HttpServletRequest req,
                     HttpServletResponse res)
                     throws IOException
   {
      int command=Integer.parseInt(req.getParameter("command"));
      if(command == STORE)
      {
         ...
      }
      else if(command == DISPLAY)
      {
         ...
      }
      else if(command == MODIFY)
      {
         ...
      }
   }
}
```

## 10.4 ATTRIBUTE SCOPES AND THREAD SAFETY

You'll recall from chapter 4, "The Servlet model," that servlets can share data (objects) using any of three scopes:

- `context` (implemented by `ServletContext`)
- `session` (implemented by `HttpSession`)
- `request` (implemented by `ServletRequest`)

All of these scopes allow us to set and get objects using the `setAttribute()` and `getAttribute()` methods, respectively. Whether or not a scope is thread safe depends on whether the scope gives exclusive access to its data to a single thread. In the following sections, we will see which of these scopes are thread safe and why.

### 10.4.1 Context scope

The servlet context is accessible to all the servlets of a web application. Multiple threads can set and get attributes simultaneously from the servlet context, which may make the data stored in it inconsistent. For example, let's consider two servlets, named `LoginServlet` and `ReporterServlet`. `LoginServlet` authenticates the user and adds the username to a list stored in `ServletContext`. If the user logs out, `LoginServlet` removes the username from the list. The `service()` method of this servlet looks like this:

```
public void service(HttpServletRequest req,
                    HttpServletResponse res)
{
   String username = //authenticate user
   if(authenticated)
   {
      List list = (List)
             getServletContext().getAttribute("listofusers");
      list.add(userName);
   }
   else if(logout)
   {
      //remove username from the "listofusers" list.
   }
   ...
}
```

`ReporterServlet`, upon request, simply iterates through the username list and displays the names in the output page. Its `service()` method looks like this:

```
public void service(HttpServletRequest req,
                    HttpServletResponse res)
{
   PrintWriter pw = res.getWriter();
   List list =
       (List) getServletContext().getAttribute("listofusers");
   int noOfUsers = list.size();
   pw.println("<html><body>");
   for(int i=0; i<noOfUsers; i++)
   {
     pw.println(list.get(i)+ "<br>");
   }
   pw.println("</body></html>");
}
```

The `listofusers` attribute is accessible to both servlets at any time. Therefore, it is entirely possible that while `ReporterServlet` is iterating through a list of users,

LoginServlet may remove certain elements from it. This will cause list.get(i) to throw an IndexOutofBoundsException! This example shows that the context scope does not give exclusive access to its data to ReporterServlet, which means it is not thread safe.

We can make the two servlets thread safe by either synchronizing the use of the listofusers attribute or by making a copy of the listofusers attribute in ReporterServlet. Synchronizing the use of listofusers will be a bottleneck because all but one of the threads will have to keep waiting for the object. Making a local copy of the list is a better approach, but if there are a large number of users, creating the copy will be very costly.

Usually, context scope is used to share data that is seldom modified. For example, the context is a perfect place to store the information needed to connect to a database, such as the database URL and the driver class name.

### 10.4.2 Session scope

Unlike ServletContext, which is accessible to all of the threads of a web application, HttpSession is accessible only to the threads that are servicing requests belonging to that session. We may think that there can be only one request from the user at a time and, therefore, the session scope would be thread safe; however, that's not the case. A user can open multiple browser windows and send requests through multiple windows. In such instances, all the requests belong to the same session and all the threads processing these requests will be able to access the session attributes simultaneously. For example, consider the code for the doGet() method of a sample ShoppingCartServlet (listing 10.9).

**Listing 10.9 HttpSession may be accessed by multiple threads simultaneously**

```
public void service(HttpServletRequest req,
                    HttpServletResponse res)
{
   ...
   HttpSession session = req.getSession();
   List listOfItems =
               (List) session.getAttribute("listofitems");
   if("addItem".equals(command))
   {
      //add appropriate element to listOfItems
   }
   else if("removeItem".equals(command))
   {
      //remove appropriate element from listOfItems
   }
   else if("viewItems".equals(command))
   {
      int noOfItems = listOfItems.size();
      for(i=0; i<noOfItems; i++)
      {
```

```
            pw.println(listOfItems.get(i)+ "<br>");
        }
    }
    ...
}
```

This code has the same issue that we saw in the previous example. If the user deletes an item from one browser window and tries to view the list of items in another window simultaneously, this code will throw an `IndexOutofBoundsException`. This means that the session scope is not thread safe.

A quick way to fix this servlet would be to synchronize the access to the `listofitems` attribute. This approach will work without causing any bottleneck because most times only one thread will be attempting to access this object.

Session scope, used to store the state of the user session, is implemented by an `HttpSession` object. Hence, access to the `HttpSession` object must be synchronized as shown in listing 10.10.

**Listing 10.10 A valid thread-safe use of HttpSession**

```
public void service(HttpServletRequest req,
                    HttpServletResponse res)
{
   ...
   HttpSession session = req.getSession();
   synchronized(session)
   {
      List listOfItems =
                (List) session.getAttribute("listofitems");
      if("addItem".equals(command))
      {
         //add appropriate element to listOfItems
      }
      else if("removeItem".equals(command))
      {
         //remove appropriate element from listOfItems
      }
      else if("viewItems".equals(command))
      {
         int noOfItems = listOfItems.size();
         for(i=0; i<noOfItems; i++)
         {
            pw.println(listOfItems.get(i)+ "<br>");
         }
      }
   }
   ...
}
```

### 10.4.3 Request scope

Unlike a ServletContext and an HttpSession, a ServletRequest object is accessed by only one thread because the servlet container creates a new ServletRequest object[1] for each request that it receives. Since only one thread services the request, the request scope object is thread safe, unless we create threads in the do*XXX*() methods and try to access the request object from such threads.

An important point to keep in mind is that the ServletRequest object is passed as a parameter to the service() method and is valid only for the scope of the service() method of the servlet. We should not try to hold a reference to this object beyond the scope of this method; otherwise, there is no guarantee as to how this object might behave. For example, we should not assign its reference to an instance variable and try to use the reference for another request.

The request scope is used when a request is to be forwarded to another resource (servlet/JSP page). One resource (usually a servlet) computes or retrieves data from the database, adds it to the request, and forwards it to another resource (usually a JSP page). The second resource uses these values to generate an HTML page. We will learn more about this approach in chapter 17, "Design patterns," when we discuss the MVC pattern.

## 10.5 SUMMARY

The Servlet specification defines the default behavior of servlets as multithreaded. In this chapter, we looked at the way a servlet container supports the multithreaded servlet model, allowing one servlet to process multiple requests concurrently in separate threads. At times, it is necessary for a servlet to implement the SingleThreadModel interface in order to ensure that only one request at a time is handled by one servlet instance. However, in this case as well, multiple requests can be serviced simultaneously using multiple servlet instances.

We also discussed the thread safety of local, instance, and static variables and context, session, and request scopes. Local variables are always thread safe, static variables never are, and the thread safety of instance variables depends on the threading model of the servlet. The context and session scopes are not thread safe, while the request scope is thread safe for all practical purposes because only one thread services one request.

At this point, you should be able to answer questions about multithreaded and single-threaded models. You should also be able to identify thread-safe usage of variable types and scopes.

In the next chapter, we will begin our investigation into another important technology used to build web applications: JavaServer Pages.

---

1 Actually, to increase performance, a servlet container may reuse a ServletRequest object, but for all practical purposes, it is as good as a newly created ServletRequest object.

## 10.6 REVIEW QUESTIONS

1. Consider the following servlet code:

```
public class TestServlet extends HttpServlet
{
   private static StringBuffer staticVar = new StringBuffer();
   private StringBuffer instanceVar = new StringBuffer();
   public void doGet(HttpServletRequest req, HttpServletResponse res)
   {
      private StringBuffer localVar = new StringBuffer();
   }
}
```

Which of the variables used in the above servlet reference objects is thread safe? (Select one)

**a** `staticVar`

**b** `instanceVar`

**c** `localVar`

**d** None

2. Consider the following servlet code:

```
public class TestServlet extends HttpServlet
{
   public void doGet(HttpServletRequest req, HttpServletResponse res)
   {
      private HttpSession session = req.getSession();
      private ServletContext ctx = getServletContext();

   }
}
```

Which of the variables used in the above servlet reference objects that are thread safe? (Select two)

**a** `req`

**b** `res`

**c** `session`

**d** `ctx`

3. Consider the following servlet code:

```
public class TestServlet extends HttpServlet
                         implements SingleThreadModel
{
   private static Hashtable staticHash = new StringBuffer();
   private Hashtable instanceHash = new StringBuffer();

   public void doGet(HttpServletRequest req, HttpServletResponse res)
   {
```

```
            StringBuffer sb = new StringBuffer()

            HttpSession session = request.getSession();
            servletContext ctx =getServletContext();

            // 1
        }
    }
```

Which of the following lines can be inserted at `//1` so that the `StringBuffer` object referred to by the variable `sb` can only be accessed from a single thread at a time? (Select two)

**a** `staticHash.put("sb", sb);`

**b** `instanceHash.put("sb", sb);`

**c** `session.setAttribute("sb", sb);`

**d** `ctx.setAttribute("sb", sb);`

**e** `req.setAttribute("sb", sb);`

4. Which of the following statements is correct? (Select one)

   **a** By default, the servlets are executed in the single-threaded model.

   **b** The threading model of a servlet can be set through the deployment descriptor.

   **c** The threading model of a servlet depends on the interfaces that it implements.

   **d** Servlets developed for the multithreaded model are not thread safe while servlets developed for the single-threaded model are.

   **e** A servlet can be made thread safe by running it in the single-threaded model.

5. Which of the following statements is correct for a servlet that implements `SingleThreadModel`? (Select one)

   **a** The servlet container cannot handle multiple requests simultaneously.

   **b** The servlet container cannot create multiple instances of the servlet class.

   **c** The servlet container will not run multiple threads on one instance simultaneously.

   **d** It is thread safe.

6. What is the requirement for a servlet that implements the `SingleThreadModel` interface? (Select one)

   **a** Its `service(HttpServletRequest, HttpServletResponse)` must be synchronized.

   **b** It must implement the `service(HttpServletRequest, HttpServletResponse)` method.

   **c** It must implement the `release()` method.

   **d** It must implement the `destroy()` method.

   **e** None of the above.

# PART 3

# *Java Server Pages*

In developing web components, we normally use JavaServer Pages for the presentation. In this part of the book, we focus on the exam objectives related to JSP pages.

CHAPTER 11

# The JSP technology model—the basics



## EXAM OBJECTIVES

**8.1** Write the opening and closing tags for the following JSP tag types:

- Directive
- Declaration
- Scriptlet
- Expression

(Section 11.1)

**8.2** Given a type of JSP tag, identify correct statements about its purpose or use. (Section 11.1)

**8.5** Identify and put in sequence the following elements of the JSP page lifecycle:

- Page translation
- JSP page compilation
- Load class
- Create instance

- Call jspInit
- Call _jspService
- Call jspDestroy

  (Section 11.2)

**8.4** Identify the page directive attribute, and its values, that:

- Import a Java class into the JSP page
- Declare that a JSP page exists within a session
- Declare that a JSP page uses an error page
- Declare that a JSP page is an error page

  (Section 11.3)

## INTRODUCTION

In the J2EE suite of specifications that includes Servlets, JavaServer Pages (JSP), the Java Naming and Directory Interface (JNDI), Enterprise JavaBeans (EJB), and so forth, the JSP is a web-tier specification that supplements the Servlet specification and is useful in the development of web interfaces for enterprise applications. JSP is a technology that combines the HTML/XML markup languages and elements of the Java programming language to return dynamic content to a web client. For this reason, it is commonly used to handle the presentation logic of a web application, although the JSP pages may also contain business logic.

In this chapter, we will discuss the basic syntax of the JSP scripting language and the JSP page life cycle. This chapter gives you the basics you need to understand the JSP technology model and will help you grasp the more complex topics covered in the next chapter.

## 11.1 JSP SYNTAX ELEMENTS

Just like any other language, the JSP scripting language has a well-defined grammar and includes syntax elements for performing various tasks, such as declaring variables and methods, writing expressions, and calling other JSP pages. At the top level, these syntax elements, also called JSP tags, are classified into six categories. Table 11.1 summarizes the element categories and their basic use.

**Table 11.1 JSP element types**

| JSP Tag Type | Brief Description | Tag Syntax |
|---|---|---|
| Directive | Specifies translation time instructions to the JSP engine. | <%@ Directives %> |
| Declaration | Declares and defines methods and variables. | <%! Java Declarations %> |

*continued on next page*

**Table 11.1 JSP element types *(continued)***

| JSP Tag Type | Brief Description | Tag Syntax |
|---|---|---|
| Scriptlet | Allows the developer to write free-form Java code in a JSP page. | <% Some Java code %> |
| Expression | Used as a shortcut to print values in the output HTML of a JSP page. | <%= An Expression %> |
| Action | Provides request-time instructions to the JSP engine. | <jsp:actionName /> |
| Comment | Used for documentation and for commenting out parts of JSP code. | <%-- Any Text --%> |

The exam objectives covered in this chapter require you to know the syntax and purpose of the first four element types: directives, declarations, scriptlets, and expressions. We will briefly introduce actions in section 11.1.5, and explain them in detail in chapters 13 through 14. Although you don't need to be familiar with comments to do well on the exam, they are very useful when writing JSP pages, and we will discuss them briefly in section 11.1.6.

Listing 11.1 is a simple JSP page that counts the number of times it is visited. It demonstrates the use of the different elements, which we will explain in the sections following the listing.

**Listing 11.1 counter.jsp**

```
<html><body>

<%@ page language="java" %>    <— Directive
<%! int count = 0;       %>    <— Declaration
<%  count++;             %>    <— Scriptlet

Welcome! You are visitor number
<%= count                %>    <— Expression

</body></html>
```

When this file is accessed for the first time via the URL `http://localhost:8080/chapter11/counter.jsp`, it displays the following line in the browser window:

```
Welcome! You are visitor number 1
```

On subsequent requests, the counter is incremented by 1 before the message is printed.

### 11.1.1 Directives

Directives provide general information about the JSP page to the JSP engine. There are three types of directives: `page`, `include`, and `taglib`.

A `page` directive informs the engine about the overall properties of a JSP page. For example, the following `page` directive informs the JSP engine that we will be using Java as the scripting language in our JSP page:

```
<%@ page language="java" %>
```

An `include` directive tells the JSP engine to include the contents of another file (HTML, JSP, etc.) in the current page. Here is an example of an `include` directive:

```
<%@ include file="copyright.html" %>
```

A `taglib` directive is used for associating a prefix with a tag library. The following is an example of a `taglib` directive:

```
<%@ taglib prefix="test" uri="taglib.tld" %>
```

See section 11.3 for details on the page directive. In chapter 13, "Reusable web components," we will take a close look at the `include` directive. Because the concept of a tag library is a vast topic in itself, the exam objectives devote two sections to it. We will learn about the `taglib` directive in detail in chapter 15, "Using custom tags," and chapter 16, "Developing custom tag libraries."

A directive always starts with `<%@` and ends with `%>`. The general syntax of the three directives is:

```
<%@ page    attribute-list %>
<%@ include attribute-list %>
<%@ taglib  attribute-list %>
```

In the sample tags above, `attribute-list` represents one or more attribute-value pairs that are specific to the directive. Here are some important points to remember about the syntax of the directives:

- The tag names, their attributes, and their values are all case sensitive.
- The value must be enclosed within a pair of single or double quotes.
- A pair of single quotes is equivalent to a pair of double quotes.
- There must be no space between the equals sign (=) and the value.

### 11.1.2 Declarations

Declarations declare and define variables and methods that can be used in the JSP page.[1] The following is an example of a JSP declaration:

```
<%! int count = 0; %>
```

This declares a variable named `count` and initializes it to 0. The variable is initialized only once when the page is first loaded by the JSP engine, and retains its value in subsequent client requests. That is why the `count` variable in listing 11.1 is not reset to 0 each time we access the page.

---

[1] Theoretically, a JSP declaration can contain any valid Java declaration including inner classes and static code blocks. However, such declarations are rarely used.

A declaration always starts with `<%!` and ends with `%>`. It can contain any number of valid Java declaration statements. For example, the following tag declares a variable and a method in a single tag:

```
<%!
    String color[] = {"red", "green", "blue"};

    String getColor(int i)
    {
       return color[i%3];
    }
%>
```

We can also write the above two Java declaration statements in two JSP declaration tags:

```
<%! String color[] = {"red", "green", "blue"}; %>

<%!
    String getColor(int i)
    {
       return color[i%3];
    }
%>
```

Note that since the declarations contain Java declaration statements, each variable's declaration statement must be terminated with a semicolon.

### 11.1.3 Scriptlets

*Scriptlets* are Java code fragments that are embedded in the JSP page. For example, this line from the `counter.jsp` example (listing 11.1) is a JSP scriptlet:

```
<% count++; %>
```

The scriptlet is executed each time the page is accessed, and the `count` variable is incremented with each request.

Since scriptlets can contain any Java code, they are typically used for embedding computing logic within a JSP page. However, we can use scriptlets for printing HTML statements, too. The following is equivalent to the code in listing 11.1:

```
<%@ page language="java" %>
<%! int count = 0;       %>

<%
   out.print("<html><body>");
   count++;
   out.print("Welcome! You are visitor number " + count);
   out.print("</body></html>");
%>
```

Instead of writing normal HTML code directly in the page, we are using a scriptlet to achieve the same effect. The variable `out` refers to an object of type `javax.servlet.jsp.JspWriter`. We will learn about `out` in chapter 12, "The JSP technology model—advanced topics."

A scriptlet always starts with <% and ends with %>. Note, however, that unlike the other elements, the opening tag of a scriptlet does not have any special character following <%. The code within the scriptlet must be valid in the Java programming language. For example, this is an error because it does not terminate the print statement with a semicolon:

```
<% out.print(count) %>
```

### 11.1.4 Expressions

Expressions act as placeholders for Java language expressions. This is an example of a JSP expression:

```
<%= count %>
```

The expression is evaluated each time the page is accessed, and its value is then embedded in the output HTML. For instance, in the previous `counter.jsp` example (listing 11.1), instead of incrementing the `count` variable in a scriptlet, we could have incremented it in the expression itself:

```
<html><body>
<%@ page language="java" %>
<%! int count = 0;        %>

Welcome! You are visitor number <%= ++count %>     <-- Evaluates the expression and prints it out

</body></html>
```

A JSP expression always starts with <%= and ends with %>. Unlike variable declarations, expressions must not be terminated with a semicolon. Thus, the following is not valid:

```
<%= count; %>
```

We can print the value of any object or any primitive data type (`int`, `boolean`, `char`, etc.) to the output stream using an expression. We can also print the value of any arithmetic or Boolean expression or a value returned by a method call. The exam may ask you to identify valid JSP expressions. Tables 11.2 and 11.3 contain some examples of valid and invalid JSP expressions based on the following declarations:

```
<%!
   int anInt = 3;
   boolean aBool = true;
   Integer anIntObj = new Integer(3);
   Float aFloatObj = new Float(12.6);

   String str = "some string";
   StringBuffer sBuff = new StringBuffer();

   char getChar(){ return 'A'; }
%>
```

**Table 11.2 Valid JSP expressions**

| Expression | Explanation |
|---|---|
| <%= 500 %> | An integral literal |
| <%= anInt*3.5/100-500 %> | An arithmetic expression |
| <%= aBool %> | A Boolean variable |
| <%= false %> | A Boolean literal |
| <%= !false %> | A Boolean expression |
| <%= getChar() %> | A method returning a char |
| <%= Math.random() %> | A method returning a double |
| <%= aVector %> | A variable referring to a Vector object |
| <%= aFloatObj %> | A Float object |
| <%= aFloatObj.floatValue() %> | A method returning a Float object |
| <%= aFloatObj.toString()%> | A method that returns a String object |

**Table 11.3 Invalid JSP expressions**

| Expression | Explanation |
|---|---|
| <%= aBool; %> | You cannot use a semicolon in an expression. |
| <%= int i = 20 %> | You cannot define anything inside an expression. |
| <%= sBuff.setLength(12); %> | The method does not return any value. The return type is void. |

### 11.1.5 Actions

Actions are commands given to the JSP engine. They direct the engine to perform certain tasks during the execution of a page. For example, the following line instructs the engine to include the output of another JSP page, `copyright.jsp`, in the output of the current JSP page:

```
<jsp:include page="copyright.jsp" />
```

There are six standard JSP actions:

- `jsp:include`
- `jsp:forward`
- `jsp:useBean`
- `jsp:setProperty`
- `jsp:getProperty`
- `jsp:plugin`

The first two, `jsp:include` and `jsp:forward`, enable a JSP page to reuse other web components. We will discuss these two actions in chapter 13, "Reusable web components."

The next three, `jsp:useBean`, `jsp:setProperty`, and `jsp:getProperty`, are related to the use of JavaBeans in JSP pages. We will discuss these three actions in chapter 14, "Using JavaBeans."

The last action, `jsp:plugin`, instructs the JSP engine to generate appropriate HTML code for embedding client-side components, such as applets. This action is not specified in the exam objectives, and its details are beyond the scope of this book.

In addition to the six standard actions, a JSP page can have user-defined actions. These are called custom tags. We will learn about custom tags in chapters 15 ("Using custom tags") and 16 ("Developing custom tag libraries").

The general syntax of a JSP action is:

```
<jsp:actionName attribute-list />
```

In the sample tag above, `actionName` is one of the six actions mentioned and `attribute-list` represents one or more attribute-value pairs that are specific to the action. As with directives, you should keep in mind these points:

- The action names, their attributes, and their values are case sensitive.
- The value must be enclosed within a pair of single or double quotes.
- A pair of single quotes is equivalent to a pair of double quotes.
- There must be no space between the equals sign (=) and the value.

### 11.1.6 Comments

Comments do not affect the output of a JSP page in any way but are useful for documentation purposes. The syntax of a JSP comment is:

```
<%-- Anything you want to be commented --%>
```

A JSP comment always starts with `<%--` and ends with `--%>`.

We can comment the Java code within scriptlets and declarations by using normal Java-style comments and the HTML portions of a page by using HTML-style comments, as shown here:

```
<html><body>
   Welcome!
   <%-- JSP comment      --%>
   <%   //Java comment    %>
   <!-- HTML comment      -->
</body></html>
```

As we mentioned earlier, the exam does not cover comments, but they can be quite useful when you're debugging JSP pages. The JSP engine drops everything between `<%--` and `--%>`, so it is easy to comment out large parts of a JSP page—including nested HTML and other JSP tags. However, remember that you cannot nest JSP comments within other JSP comments.

*Quizlet*

**Q:** Which of the following page directives are valid?

**a** `<%  page language="java"  %>`

**b** `<%! page language="java"  %>`

**c** `<%@ page language="java"  %>`

**A:** Only option c is correct. Directives use an @ in the opening tag.

**Q:** What is wrong with the following code?

```
<!% int i = 5;                    %>
<!% int getI() { return i; }     %>
```

**A:** The opening tag for a declaration is `<%!` and not `<!%`.

**Q:** Assuming that `myObj` refers to an object and `m1()` is a valid method on that object, tell why each of the following are valid or invalid JSP constructs.

**a** `<%  myObj.m1()  %>`

**b** `<%= myObj.m1()  %>`

**c** `<% =myObj.m1()  %>`

**d** `<% =myObj.m1(); %>`

**A:** The following table explains why an option is valid or invalid.

| Construct | Explanation |
|---|---|
| <% myObj.m1() %> | Invalid: It is not an expression because it does not have an = sign. It is an invalid scriptlet because a semicolon is missing at the end of the method call. |
| <%=myObj.m1() %> | Depends: The = sign makes it an expression. But if the return type of the method m1() is void, it is invalid. A method call inside an expression is valid if and only if the return type of the method is not void. |
| <% =myObj.m1() %> | Invalid: There is a space between <% and =. Hence, it is not an expression but a scriptlet. However, the scriptlet construct is not valid because =myObj.m1(), by itself, is not a valid Java statement. |
| <% =myObj.m1();%> | Invalid: Same as previous example except that it has a semicolon. |

The valid way to write this as a scriptlet is:

```
<% myObj.m1(); %>
```

However, this will just call the method; it will not generate any output. If the method `m1()` returns a value, then the correct way to write this as an expression is:

```
<%= myObj.m1() %>
```

This will print the return value of the method call to the output HTML.

## 11.2 THE JSP PAGE LIFE CYCLE

A JSP page goes through seven phases in its lifetime. These phases are called *life-cycle phases*. The exam requires you to know the sequence of the phases and the activity that takes place in each of the phases. But before we start discussing the life cycle of a JSP page, we need to understand the two important points regarding JSP pages that are explained in the following sections.

### 11.2.1 JSP pages are servlets

Although, structurally, a JSP page *looks* like an HTML page, it actually runs as a servlet. The JSP engine parses the JSP file and creates a corresponding Java file. This file declares a servlet class whose members map directly to the elements of the JSP file. The JSP engine then compiles the class, loads it into memory, and executes it as it would any other servlet. The output of this servlet is then sent to the client. Figure 11.1 illustrates this process.

### 11.2.2 Understanding translation units

Just as an HTML page can include the contents of other HTML pages (for example, when using frames), a JSP page can include the contents of other JSP pages and HTML pages. This is done with the help of the `include` directive (see chapter 13 for more information). But an important thing to remember here is that when the JSP engine generates the Java code for a JSP page, it also inserts the contents of the included pages into the servlet that it generates. The set of pages that is translated into a single servlet class is called a *translation unit*. Some of the JSP tags affect the whole translation unit and not just the page in which they are declared.

Keep in mind these other points regarding a translation unit:

- The page directives explained in section 11.3 affect the whole translation unit.
- A variable declaration cannot occur more than once in a single translation unit. For example, we cannot declare a variable in an included page using the `include` directive if it is already declared in the including page since the two pages constitute a single translation unit.
- The standard action `<jsp:useBean>` cannot declare the same bean twice in a single translation unit. We examine the `jsp:useBean` action further in chapter 14.

### 11.2.3 JSP life-cycle phases

You might have observed that when a JSP page is accessed for the first time, the server is slower in responding than it is in the second, third, and subsequent accesses. This is because, as we mentioned previously, every JSP page must be converted into an instance of a servlet class before it can be used to service client requests. For each request, the JSP engine checks the timestamps of the source JSP page and the corresponding servlet class file to determine if the JSP page is new or if it has already been converted into a

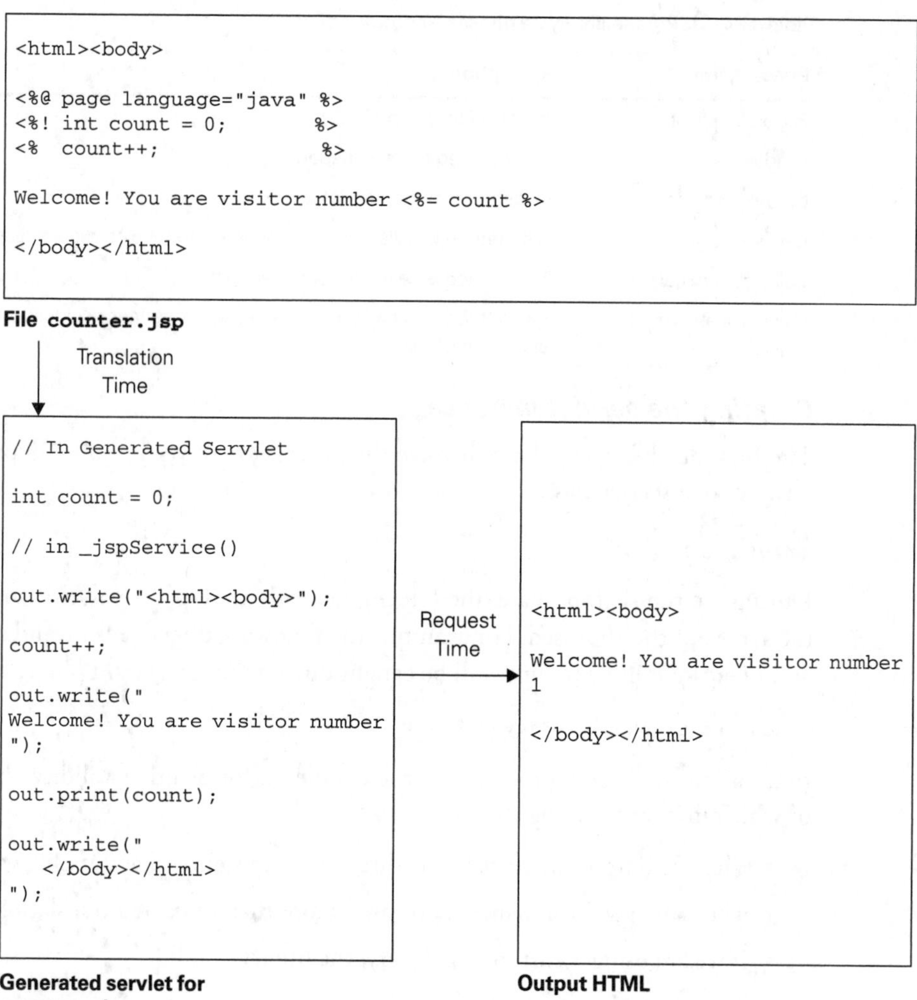

<html><body>
<%@ page language="java" %>
<%! int count = 0; %>
<% count++; %>
Welcome! You are visitor number <%= count %>
</body></html>
File counter.jsp
Translation Time
// In Generated Servlet
int count = 0;
// in _jspService()
out.write("<html><body>");
count++;
out.write(" Welcome! You are visitor number ");
out.print(count);
out.write(" </body></html> ");
Request Time
<html><body>
Welcome! You are visitor number 1
</body></html>
Generated servlet for counter.jsp
Output HTML


**Figure 11.1 A JSP page as a servlet.**

class file. Therefore, if we modify a JSP page, the whole process of converting the JSP page into a servlet is performed again. This process consists of seven phases, and you need to understand their order and significance for the exam. Table 11.4 lists the phases in the order in which they occur.

**Table 11.4 JSP page life-cycle phases**

| Phase Name | Description |
|---|---|
| Page translation | The page is parsed and a Java file containing the corresponding servlet is created. |

*continued on next page*

**Table 11.4 JSP page life-cycle phases *(continued)***

| Phase Name | Description |
|---|---|
| Page compilation | The Java file is compiled. |
| Load class | The compiled class is loaded. |
| Create instance | An instance of the servlet is created. |
| Call jspInit() | This method is called before any other method to allow initialization. |
| Call _jspService() | This method is called for each request. |
| Call jspDestroy() | This method is called when the servlet container decides to take the servlet out of service. |

### *Creating the servlet instance*

The first four life-cycle phases involve the process of converting the JSP page into an instance of a servlet class.

#### *Translation*

During the translation phase, the JSP engine reads a JSP page, parses it, and validates the syntax of the tags used. For example, the following directive is invalid since it uses an uppercase *P* in `Page` and will be caught during the translation phase:

```
<%@ Page language="java" %>
```

In addition to checking the syntax, the engine performs other validity checks, some of which involve verifying that:

- The attribute-value pairs in the directives and standard actions are valid.
- The same JavaBean name is not used more than once in a translation unit.
- If we are using a custom tag library, the library is valid.
- The usage of custom tags is valid.

Once the validations are completed, the engine creates a Java file containing a public servlet class.

#### *Compilation*

In the compilation phase, the Java file generated in the previous step is compiled using the normal Java compiler javac (or using a vendor-provided compiler or even a user-specified compiler[2]). All the Java code that we write in declarations, scriptlets, and expressions is validated during this phase. For example, the following declaration tag is a valid JSP tag and will pass the translation phase, but the declaration statement is

[2] This varies from container to container. Please consult the servlet container documentation for more information.

not a valid Java declaration statement because it does not end with a semicolon and will be caught during the compilation phase:

```
<%! int count = 0 %>
```

Scripting language errors (Java, in this case) are caught during the compilation phase. We can force a compilation of a JSP page without actually executing it by using the precompilation request parameter `jsp_precompile`. For example, if we want to compile the `counter.jsp` page without executing it, we must access the page as:

```
http://localhost:8080/chapter11/counter.jsp?jsp_precompile=true
```

The engine will translate the JSP page and compile the generated servlet class without actually executing the servlet. This can be quite useful during the development phase if we have complex JSP pages that create database connections or access other J2EE services. Also, it is always a good idea to precompile all the pages. In this way, we check for syntax errors and keep the pages ready to be served, thus reducing the response time for the first request to each page.

**NOTE** The parameter `jsp_precompile` takes a Boolean value, `true` or `false`. If the value is `false`, the precompilation will not occur. The parameter can also be specified without any value, in which case the default is `true`:

```
http://localhost:8080/chapter11/counter.jsp?jsp_precompile
```

In either case, `true` or `false`, the page will not be executed.

Also, this would be a good place to point out that all of the request parameter names that include the prefix `jsp` are reserved and must not be used for user-defined values. Thus, the following usage is not recommended and may result in unexpected behavior:

```
http://localhost:8080/chapter11/counter.jsp?jspTest=myTest
```

*Loading and instantiation*

After successful compilation, the container loads the servlet class into memory and instantiates it.

### Calling the JSP life-cycle methods

The generated servlet class for a JSP page implements the `HttpJspPage` interface of the `javax.servlet.jsp` package. The `HttpJspPage` interface extends the `JspPage` interface of the same package, which in turn extends the `Servlet` interface of the `javax.servlet` package. The generated servlet class thus implements all the methods of these three interfaces and is also known as the page's implementation class.

The `JspPage` interface declares only two methods—`jspInit()` and `jspDestroy()`—that must be implemented by all JSP pages regardless of the client-server protocol. However, the JSP specification has provided the `HttpJspPage` interface specifically for JSP pages serving HTTP requests. This interface declares one method: `_jspService()`. Here are the signatures of the three JSP methods:

```
public void jspInit();

public void _jspService(HttpServletRequest request,
                        HttpServletResponse response)
                  throws
                        javax.servlet.ServletException,
                        javax.IO.IOException;

public void jspDestroy();
```

These methods are called the life-cycle methods of the JSP pages. The `jspInit()`, `_jspService()`, and `jspDestroy()` methods of a JSP page are equivalent to the `init()`, `service()`, and `destroy()` methods of a servlet, respectively.

Every JSP engine vendor provides a vendor-specific class that is used as a base class for the page's implementation class. This base class provides the default implementations of all the methods of the `Servlet` interface and the default implementations of both methods of the `JspPage` interface: `jspInit()` and `jspDestroy()`. During the translation phase, the engine adds the `_jspService()` method to the JSP page's implementation class, thus making the class a concrete subclass of the three interfaces.

#### *jspInit()*

The container calls `jspInit()` to initialize the servlet instance. It is called before any other method, and is called only once for a servlet instance. We normally define this method to do initial or one-time setup, such as acquiring resources and initializing the instance variables that have been declared in the JSP page using `<%! ... %>` declarations.

#### *_jspService()*

The container calls the `_jspService()` for each request, passing it the request and the response objects. All of the HTML elements, the JSP scriptlets, and the JSP expressions become a part of this method during the translation phase. We discuss the details of this method in chapter 12.

#### *jspDestroy()*

When the container decides to take the instance out of service, it calls the `jspDestroy()` method. This is the last method that is called on the servlet instance, and it is used to clean up the resources acquired in the `jspInit()` method.

We are not required to implement the `jspInit()` and `jspDestroy()` methods, since they have already been implemented by the base class. If we need to override them, we can do so using the JSP declaration tag `<%! ... %>`. However, we cannot define our own `_jspService()` method because the engine generates it automatically.

### 11.2.4 JSP life-cycle example

Let's modify our counter example to add persistence capabilities to it so that the counter does not start from 1 each time the server is shut down and restarted. Listing 11.2 illustrates how we can:

- Use `jspInit()` to load the previous value of the counter from a file when the server starts.
- Use `jspDestroy()` to save the final value to the file when the server shuts down.

**Listing 11.2 persistent_counter.jsp**

```
<%@ page language="java" import="java.io.*" %>

<%!
   // A variable to maintain the number of visits.
   int count = 0;

   // Path to the file, counter.db, which stores the count
   // value in a serialized form. The file acts like a database.
   String dbPath;

   // This is the first method called by the container,
   // when the page is loaded.
   // We open the db file, read the integer value, and
   // initialize the count variable.
   public void jspInit()
   {
      try
      {
         dbPath = getServletContext().getRealPath("/WEB-INF/counter.db");
         FileInputStream fis = new FileInputStream(dbPath);
         DataInputStream dis = new DataInputStream(fis);
         count = dis.readInt();
         dis.close();
      }
      catch(Exception e)
      {
        getServletContext().log("Error loading persistent counter", e);
      }
   }
%>

<%--
  The main content that goes to the browser.
  This will become a part of the generated _jspService() method
--%>
<html><body>
<% count++; %>
Welcome! You are visitor number
<%= count   %>
</body></html>

<%!

   // This method is called by the container only once when the
   // page is about to be destroyed. We open the db file in this
   // method and save the value of the count variable as an integer.

   public void jspDestroy()
```

```
    {
        try
        {
            FileOutputStream fos = new FileOutputStream(dbPath);
            DataOutputStream dos = new DataOutputStream(fos);
            dos.writeInt(count);
            dos.close();
        }
        catch(Exception e)
        {
          getServletContext().log("Error storing persistent counter", e);
        }
    }
%>
```

This example illustrates three things: the use of the `jspInit()` method, the use of the `jspDestroy()` method, and the use of the `getServletContext()` method.

When the page is first loaded into the servlet container, the engine will call the `jspInit()` method. In this method, we initialize the `count` variable to the value read in from the resource database file `"/WEB-INF/counter.db"`. During its lifetime, the JSP page may be accessed zero or more times, and each time the `_jspService()` method will be executed. Since the scriptlet `<% count++; %>` becomes a part of the `_jspService()` method, the expression `count++` is evaluated each time, increasing the counter by 1. Finally, when the page is about to be destroyed, the container will call the `jspDestroy()` method. In this method, we open the resource database file again, and save the latest value of the variable `count` into it.

Because the JSP page is converted into a servlet, we can call all the methods in a JSP page that we can call on a servlet. Thus, in both methods, `jspInit()` and `jspDestroy()`, we get the `ServletContext` object by using the method `getServletContext()`, which is actually defined in the `javax.servlet.Servlet` interface. The returned `ServletContext` object can then be used in a JSP page exactly the way we use it in normal servlets. In our example, we are using the `ServletContext` object to convert the relative path of a resource into its real path and to log error information in case of exceptions. If the web application is installed in the directory `C:\jakarta-tomcat-4.0.1\webapps\chapter11`, then a call to `getServletContext().getRealPath("/WEB-INF/counter.db");` will return `C:\jakarta-tomcat-4.0.1\webapps\chapter11\WEB-INF\counter.db`.

When the server is started the very first time and the page is first accessed, the file `counter.db` does not exist and a `FileNotFoundException` is thrown. We catch this exception and log the error message by using the `ServletContext.log()` method.[3] When the server is shut down the first time, the `jspDestroy()` method

3 Tomcat uses <TOMCAT_HOME>\logs\ directory as the default directory to create log files.

creates a new file, and the current value of the variable is written into it. When the server is started the second time and the JSP page is loaded, the `jspInit()` method will find the file and initialize the `count` variable to its previously saved value.

The JSP technology thus combines the best of both worlds: the ease of use offered by the web scripting methodology and the object-oriented features of the servlet technology.

## 11.3 UNDERSTANDING JSP PAGE DIRECTIVE ATTRIBUTES

A `page` directive informs the JSP engine about the overall properties of a JSP page. This directive applies to the entire translation unit and not just to the page in which it is declared. Table 11.5 describes the 12 possible attributes for the `page` directive.

**Table 11.5 Attributes for the page directive**

| Attribute name | Description | Default Value/s |
|---|---|---|
| import | A comma-separated list of Java classes and packages that we want to use in the JSP page. | java.lang.*;<br>javax.servlet.*;<br>javax.servlet.jsp.*;<br>javax.servlet.http.*; |
| session | A Boolean literal specifying whether the JSP page takes part in an HTTP session. | true |
| errorPage | Specifies a relative URL to another JSP page that is capable of handling errors on behalf of the current page. | null |
| isErrorPage | A Boolean literal specifying whether the current JSP page is capable of handling errors. | false |
| language | Any scripting language supported by the JSP engine. As of JSP 1.2, *java* is the only one allowed. | java |
| extends | Any valid Java class that implements javax.servlet.jsp.JspPage. | Implementation dependent |
| buffer | Specifies the size of the output buffer. If a buffer size is specified, it must be in kilobytes (kb). If buffering is not required, specify the string *none*. | Implementation dependent |
| autoFlush | A Boolean literal indicating whether the buffer should be flushed when it is full. | true |
| isThreadSafe | A Boolean literal indicating whether the JSP page is thread safe. | true |
| info | Any informative text about the JSP page. | Implementation dependent |
| contentType | Specifies the MIME type and character encoding for the output. | text/html;charset=ISO-8859-1 |
| pageEncoding | Specifies the character encoding of the JSP page. | ISO-8859-1 |

While the exam requires that you know all of the valid page directive attributes and their values, it focuses more on the usage of the first four: import, session, errorPage, and isErrorPage.

### 11.3.1 The import attribute

The import attribute of a page directive is similar to the import statement in a Java class. For example, if we want to use the Date class of the package java.util, then we have to either use the fully qualified class name in the code or import it using the page directive. At the time of translation, the JSP engine inserts an import statement into the generated servlet for each of the packages declared using this attribute.

We can import multiple packages in a single tag by using a comma-separated list of package names, as shown here:

```
<%@ page import="java.util.*, java.io.*, java.text.*,
                 com.mycom.*, com.mycom.util.MyClass " %>
```

We can also use multiple tags for readability. For example, the above page directive can also be written as:

```
<%@ page import="java.util.* " %>
<%@ page import="java.io.* "   %>
<%@ page import="java.text.* " %>
<%@ page import="com.mycom.*, com.mycom.util.MyClass " %>
```

Since the order of import statements in a Java class does not matter, the order of import tags shown here does not matter, either. A JSP engine always imports the java.lang.*, javax.servlet.*, javax.servlet.jsp.*, and javax.servlet.http.* packages, so we do not have to import them explicitly.

**NOTE** import is the only attribute of the page directive that can occur multiple times in a translation unit. Duplicate values are ignored.

### 11.3.2 The session attribute

The session attribute indicates whether or not the JSP page takes part in an HTTP session. The default value is true, in which case the JSP engine declares the implicit variable session. (We will learn more about implicit variables in chapter 12.) If we do not want the page to participate in a session, then we have to explicitly add the following line:

```
<%@ page session="false" %>
```

### 11.3.3 The errorPage and isErrorPage attributes

During the execution of a page, it is possible that the embedded Java code will throw exceptions. Just as in normal Java programs, we can handle the exceptions in JSP pages using try-catch blocks. However, the JSP specification defines a better approach, which separates the error-handling code from the main page and thus promotes reusability of the exception-handling mechanism. In this approach, a JSP page uses the errorPage attribute to delegate the exception to another JSP page that has the error-handling code. In listing 11.3, errorHandler.jsp is specified as the error handler.

**Listing 11.3 hello.jsp: Using errorPage to delegate exceptions**

```
<%@ page errorPage="errorHandler.jsp" %>
<html>
<body>
   <%
      if (request.getParameter("name")==null)
      {
         throw new RuntimeException("Name not specified");
      }
   %>
   Hello, <%=request.getParameter("name")%>
</body>
</html>
```

The above JSP page throws an exception if the parameter name is not supplied in the request, but it does not catch the exception itself. Instead, with the help of the errorPage attribute, it instructs the JSP engine to delegate the error handling to errorHandler.jsp.

The isErrorPage attribute conveys whether or not the current page can act as an error handler for any other JSP page. The default value of the isErrorPage attribute is false. For example, the errorHandler.jsp that we used in the previous example must explicitly set this attribute to true, as shown in listing 11.4. In this case, the JSP engine declares the implicit variable exception in the page's servlet class.

**Listing 11.4 errorHandler.jsp: Handling exceptions**

```
<%@ page isErrorPage="true" %>
<html>
<body>
   Unable to process your request: <%=exception.getMessage()%><br>
   Please try again.
</body>
</html>
```

Notice that this page only extracts the information from the exception and generates an appropriate error message. Because it does not implement any business logic, it can be reused for different JSP pages.

In JSP 1.2, it is not necessary that the errorPage value be a JSP page. It can also be a static file, such as an HTML page:

```
<%@ page errorPage="errorHandler.html" %>
```

Obviously, we cannot write a scriptlet or an expression in the HTML file `errorHandler.html` to generate dynamic messages.

**NOTE** In general, it is always a good programming practice to specify an error page in all the JSP pages. This prevents unanticipated error messages from being displayed on the client's browser.

### 11.3.4 The language and extends attributes

The `language` attribute specifies the language used by a page in declarations, scriptlets, and expressions. The default value is `java`, which is also the only value allowed by the JSP Specification 1.2. Needless to say, adding the following line to a JSP page is redundant:

```
<%@ page language="java" %>
```

The `extends` attribute specifies that the supplied class be used as a base class of the generated servlet. This is useful only if we want to customize the behavior of the generated servlet class. The default base class is vendor specific and is designed to work efficiently with the rest of the framework. Consequently, this attribute is seldom used. The following line shows the syntax for this attribute:

```
<%@ page extends="mypackage.MySpecialBaseServlet" %>
```

### 11.3.5 The buffer and autoFlush attributes

The `buffer` attribute specifies the minimum size required by the output buffer that holds the generated content until it is sent to the client. The default size of the buffer is JSP engine implementation dependent, but the specification mandates it to be at least `8kb`. The following line sets the buffer size to `32kb`:

```
<%@ page buffer="32kb" %>
```

The value of the buffer is in kilobytes and the suffix `kb` is mandatory. To send the data directly to the client without any buffering, we can specify the value as `none`.

The `autoFlush` attribute specifies whether the data in the output buffer should be sent to the client automatically as soon as the buffer is full. The default value for `autoFlush` is `true`. If it is set to `false` and the buffer is full, an exception is raised when we attempt to add more data to the buffer. Here is the syntax for this attribute:

```
<%@ page autoFlush="false" %>
```

Obviously, the following combinations occurring in a JSP page are invalid and may either cause an error at translation time or have an unknown behavior at runtime:

```
<%@ page buffer="none" autoFlush="false" %>
<%@ page buffer="0kb" autoFlush="false" %>
```

### 11.3.6 The isThreadSafe attribute

The `isThreadSafe` attribute specifies whether a page can handle multiple requests concurrently. Although this attribute is not mentioned in the exam objectives, you should understand how it works. For instance, neither of our examples, counter.jsp (listing 11.1) or persistent_counter.jsp (listing 11.2), is thread safe. If multiple client requests arrive simultaneously, then it is possible that two or more clients will receive the same value for the visit count.

This is because, by default, the value of isThreadSafe attribute is true. This tells the container that it can dispatch multiple requests to the page's servlet concurrently in different threads. When this happens, each thread will attempt to increment the same instance of the variable count simultaneously that is declared using the declarations tags. Since the access to the variable is not synchronized, it is possible that two threads will access it at the same time, one incrementing the value and the other printing its value in the output. One way we can avoid this situation is by adding the following line in our counter.jsp and persistent_counter.jsp pages:

```
<%@ page isThreadSafe="false" %>
```

If isThreadSafe is set to false, the container dispatches the requests to the page one at a time in the order they are received. This is equivalent to implementing the SingleThreadModel interface for servlets, which we discussed in chapter 10, "Developing thread-safe servlets." In this case, only one thread will execute the servlet code at a time, incrementing the value of count and then printing it in the output HTML.

However, note that even this is not a totally foolproof method of synchronizing the counter. It will work when there is only one instance of the servlet serving the requests. But if the container decides to create a pool of instances of the thread-unsafe servlet, then each servlet instance will have its own copy of the count variable. A request to the same JSP page will then return the count depending on which servlet instance was used from the pool. In such cases, it is better to use a programmatic synchronization mechanism for incrementing the count and leave the page as thread safe:

```
<%@ page isThreadSafe="true" %>
<%
   synchronized(this)//this refers to the servlet instance
   {
      count++;
      out.print("Welcome! You are visitor number " + count);
   }
%>
```

In this code, the attribute-value pair isThreadSafe=true will ensure that the servlet does not implement SingleThreadModel; that way, only a single instance of the servlet is created. The this keyword refers to the servlet instance, and the synchronized block on the instance will make sure that the two operations—incrementing the count and printing its value—are executed by a single thread at a time, thus printing a unique value of the count in the output HTML for each request.

For those of you who want to experiment with the behavior of this attribute, listing 11.5 contains another example that you can use.

**Listing 11.5 threadSafety.jsp**

```
<html><body>

<%@ page isThreadSafe="true" %>

<%! int j=0; %>

<%
   for (int i=0; i<10; i++)
   {
      out.print("The value of j is " + j + "<br>");
      j++;
      Thread.currentThread().sleep(1000);
   }
%>

</body></html>
```

Open two browser windows and go to the URL `http://localhost:8080/chapter11/threadSafety.jsp` from each window. Analyze the code listing and guess what will happen before you try this. If you are not sure about the outcome, you should go over chapter 10. Then, set the value of `isThreadSafe` to `false` and repeat the above steps.

### 11.3.7 The info attribute

The `info` attribute allows to us to specify the value of the string returned by the `getServletInfo()` method of the generated servlet. The following line shows one possible use:

```
<%@ page info="This is a sample Page. " %>
```

The default value of this attribute is implementation dependent.

### 11.3.8 The contentType and pageEncoding attributes

The `contentType` attribute specifies the MIME type and character encoding of the output. The default value of the MIME type is `text/html`; the default value of the character encoding is `ISO-8859-1`. The MIME type and character encoding are separated by a semicolon, as shown here:

```
<%@ page contentType="text/html;charset=ISO-8859-1" %>
```

This is equivalent to writing the following line in a servlet:

```
response.setContentType("text/html;charset=ISO-8859-1");
```

The `pageEncoding` attribute specifies the character encoding of the JSP page. The default value is `ISO-8859-1`. The following line illustrates the syntax:

```
<%@ page pageEncoding="ISO-8859-1" %>
```

*Quizlet*

**Q:** Which of the following page directives are valid and which are invalid?

```
a <%@ page import="java.util.* java.text.* "     %>
b <%@ page import="java.util.*", "java.text.* " %>
c <%@ page buffer="8kb", session="false"        %>
d <%@ page import="com.manning.servlets.* "     %>
  <%@ page session="true"                       %>
  <%@ page import="java.text.*"                 %>
e <%@ page bgcolor="navy"                       %>
f <%@ page buffer="true"                        %>
g <%@ Page language='java'                      %>
```

**A:** The following table explains why an option is valid or invalid.

| Page Directive | Valid/ Invalid | Reasons |
|---|---|---|
| <%@ page import="java.util.* java.text.* " %> | Invalid: | A comma is required between the values. <%@ page import="java.util.*, java.text.* " %> |
| <%@ page import="java.util.*", "java.text.* " %> | Invalid: | Both packages must be specified in the same string. |
| <%@ page buffer="8kb", session="false" %> | Invalid: | A comma is not allowed between attributes. |
| <%@ page import="com.manning.scwcd.servlets.* " %><br><%@ page session="true" %><br><%@ page import="java.text.*" %> | Valid: | The order and placement of page directives do not matter.<br>The import attribute can occur multiple times. |
| <%@ page bgcolor="navy" %> | Invalid: | bgcolor is not a valid attribute. |
| <%@ page buffer="true" %> | Invalid: | true is not a valid value for the buffer attribute. The value must specify the size of the buffer in kb. |
| <%@ Page language='java' %> | Invalid | Directive names, attributes, and values, are case sensitive. We must use page and not Page. |

## 11.4 SUMMARY

In this chapter, we examined JavaServer Pages as a web scripting methodology. We learned the basic rules of the six JSP syntax elements—directives, declarations, scriptlets, expressions, actions, and comments—and we examined the first four in depth. We learned that JavaServer Pages are translated into servlet instances before serving the client's requests, and we reviewed the seven phases of the JSP page life cycle. We then looked at the three life-cycle methods—`jspInit()`, `_jspService()`, and `jspDestroy()`—and how they are used in the initialization, servicing, and destruction of a JSP page.

Through its 12 attributes, a page directive provides information about the overall properties of a JSP page to the JSP engine. We need to understand all of the attributes for writing real-life JSP pages, but in preparing for the exam, it is especially important to understand `import`, `session`, `errorPage`, and `isErrorPage`.

In the next chapter, we will continue our discussion of JavaServer Pages as we examine some of the more advanced features that form a logical extension of the servlet technology.

## 11.5 REVIEW QUESTIONS

1. Consider the following code and select the correct statement about it from the options below. (Select one)

```
<html><body>
   <%! int aNum=5 %>
   The value of aNum is <%= aNum %>
</body></html>
```

**a** It will print `"The value of aNum is 5"` to the output.

**b** It will flag a compile-time error because of an incorrect declaration.

**c** It will throw a runtime exception while executing the expression.

**d** It will not flag any compile time or runtime errors and will not print anything to the output.

2. Which of the following tags can you use to print the value of an expression to the output stream? (Select two)

**a** `<%@     %>`

**b** `<%!     %>`

**c** `<%      %>`

**d** `<%=     %>`

**e** `<%--  --%>`

3. Which of the following methods is defined by the JSP engine? (Select one)

**a** `jspInit()`

**b** `_jspService()`

**c** `_jspService(ServletRequest, ServletResponse)`

**d** `_jspService(HttpServletRequest, HttpServletResponse)`

**e** `jspDestroy()`

4. Which of the following exceptions may be thrown by the `_jspService()` method? (Select one)

**a** `javax.servlet.ServletException`

**b** `javax.servlet.jsp.JSPException`

**c** `javax.servlet.ServletException` and `javax.servlet.jsp.JSPException`

**d** `javax.servlet.ServletException` and `java.io.IOException`

**e** `javax.servlet.jsp.JSPException` and `java.io.IOException`

5. Write the name of the method that you can use to initialize variables declared in a JSP declaration in the space provided. (Write only the name of the method. Do not write the return type, parameters, or parentheses.)

   [_______________]

6. Which of the following correctly declares that the current page is an error page and also enables it to take part in a session? (Select one)

   **a** `<%@ page pageType="errorPage" session="required"  %>`

   **b** `<%@ page isErrorPage="true"   session="mandatory" %>`

   **c** `<%@ page errorPage="true"     session="true"      %>`

   **d** `<%@ page isErrorPage="true"   session="true"      %>`

   **e** None of the above.

CHAPTER 12

# The JSP technology model—advanced topics



## EXAM OBJECTIVES

**8.7** Distinguish correct and incorrect scriptlet code for:

- A conditional statement
- An iteration statement

(Section 12.1)

**8.6** Match correct descriptions about purpose, function, or use with any of the following implicit objects:

- request
- response
- out
- session
- config
- application

- page
- pageContext
- exception

  (Sections 12.2 and 12.3)

**8.3** Given a JSP tag type, identify the equivalent XML-based tags. (Section 12.4)

## INTRODUCTION

In chapter 11, "The JSP technology model—the basics," we reviewed the basic elements of JSP pages. In this chapter, we will continue our discussion of the JSP technology model by examining some of the more advanced features of the JSP framework.

## 12.1 UNDERSTANDING THE TRANSLATION PROCESS

As we discussed in chapter 11, the first phase of the life cycle of a JSP page is the translation phase, in which the JSP page is translated into a Java file containing the corresponding servlet. The JSP engine parses the JSP page and applies the following rules for translating the JSP elements to the servlet code:

- Some directives are used by the JSP engine during the translation phase to generate Java code. For example, the `import` attribute of the `page` directive aids in generating import statements, while the `info` attribute aids in implementing the `getServletInfo()` method of the generated servlet class. Some directives just inform the engine about the overall properties of the page; for instance, the `language` attribute informs the engine that we are using Java as the scripting language, and the `pageEncoding` attribute informs the engine of the character encoding of the page.
- All JSP declarations become a part of the generated servlet class. They are copied as is. Thus, variables declared in a JSP declaration become instance variables, and the methods declared in a JSP declaration become instance methods of the servlet.
- All JSP scriptlets become a part of the generated `_jspService()` method. They are copied as is. Thus, variables declared in a scriptlet become local variables of the `_jspService()` method. We cannot declare a method in a scriptlet since we cannot have methods declared inside other methods in Java.
- All JSP expressions become a part of the `_jspService()` method. They are wrapped inside `out.print()`.
- All JSP actions are replaced by calls to vendor-specific classes.
- All JSP comments are ignored.
- Any other text becomes part of the `_jspService()` method. It is wrapped inside `out.write()`. This text is also called *template text.*

In the following sections, we will look at some of the implications of these translation rules.

### 12.1.1 Using scripting elements

Since the declarations, scriptlets, and expressions allow us to write scripting language code in JSP pages, these elements are collectively referred to as the *scripting elements*. We use Java as the scripting language, and consequently, the rules of the Java programming language govern the compile-time and runtime behavior of the code in the scripting elements. Let's examine them one by one with examples.

#### *Order of declarations*

Because all the variables and methods defined in the declarations of a JSP page become members of the generated servlet class, their order of appearance in a page does not matter. The following example (listing 12.1) highlights this behavior.

**Listing 12.1 area.jsp**

```
<html>
<body>
   Using pi = <%=pi%>, the area of a circle<br>
   with a radius of 3 is <%=area(3)%>

<%!
   double area(double r)
   {
      return r*r*pi;
   }
%>

<%! final double pi=3.14159; %>
</body>
</html>
```

In this case, even though the constant `pi` and the method `area()` are used before they are defined, the page will translate, compile, and run just fine, printing the following output:

```
Using pi = 3.14159, the area of a circle
with a radius of 3 is 28.27431
```

#### *Order of scriptlets*

Since scriptlets become a part of the `_jspService()` method in the generated servlet, the variables declared in a scriptlet become local variables of the method; consequently, their order of appearance is important. The following code demonstrates this:

```
<html>
<body>
<%  String s  = s1+s2;     %>   <-- Error: undefined variable s2
<%! String s1 = "hello"; %>   <-- Member variable sl
<%  String s2 = "world"; %>   <-- Local variable s2
```

```
<%  out.print(s);          %>
</body>
</html>
```

In this example, s and s2 are declared in a scriptlet while s1 is declared in a declaration. Because s2 is used before it is declared, this code will not compile.

### *Initialization of the variables*

In Java, instance variables are automatically initialized to their default values, while local variables must be initialized explicitly before they are used. Hence, the variables declared in JSP declarations are initialized to their default values, while the variables declared in JSP scriptlets must be initialized explicitly before they are used. Consider the following example:

```
<html>
<body>
   <%! int i; %>
   <%  int j; %>
   The value of i is <%= i++ %> <br>     <-- OK: i is 0 by default
   The value of j is <%= j++ %> <br>     <-- Error: j not initialized
</body>
</html>
```

The variable i, declared using a declaration (<%!...%>), becomes an instance variable of the generated class and is initialized to 0. The variable j, declared using a scriptlet (<%...%>), becomes a local variable of the generated method _jspService() and remains uninitialized. Since Java requires local variables to be initialized explicitly before use, this code is invalid and will not compile.

Another important thing to remember is that the instance variables are created and initialized only once, when the JSP container instantiates the servlet. Thus, variables declared in JSP declarations retain their values across multiple requests. On the other hand, local variables are created and destroyed for every request. Thus, variables declared in a scriptlet do not retain their values across multiple requests and are re-initialized each time the JSP container calls _jspService().

To make the above code compile, we have to initialize j as:

```
<% int j=0; %>
```

Now, if we access the above page multiple times, the value of i will get incremented, printing a new value each time, while the value of j will always be printed as 0.

## 12.1.2 Using conditional and iterative statements

Scriptlets are used for embedding computational logic, and frequently this logic includes conditional and iterative statements. For example, the following scriptlet code uses a conditional statement to check a user's login status, and based on that status, it displays an appropriate message:

```
<%
   boolean isUserLoggedIn = ... //get login status
   if (isUserLoggedIn)
   {
      out.print("<h3>Welcome!</h3>");
   }
   else
   {
      out.println("Hi! Please log in to access the member's area.<br>");
      out.println("<A href='login.jsp'>Login</A>");
   }
%>
```

If we want to include a large amount of HTML within the body of a conditional statement, we can avoid writing multiple `out.println()` statements by spanning the conditional statement across multiple scriptlets in the JSP page, as shown in the following example:

```
<html><body>

<%
   boolean isUserLoggedIn = ... //get login status
   if (isUserLoggedIn)
   {
%>
   <h3>Welcome!</h3>
   A lot of HTML here...

<%
   }
   else
   {
%>
    Hi! Please log in to access the member's area.
    <A href="login.jsp">login</A>
    A lot of HTML here...

<%
   }
%>

</body></html>
```

In the above code snippet, the `if-else` statement is spread across three scriptlets. At runtime, the first scriptlet gets the login status of the user and assigns it to the `boolean` variable `isUserLoggedIn`. If the value of this variable is `true`, then the HTML code between the first scriptlet and the second scriptlet is included in the output stream. If the value is `false`, then the HTML code between the second scriptlet and the third scriptlet is included in the output stream.

Note the usage of the curly braces to mark the beginning and end of the Java programming language code blocks. Omitting the braces might cause an error at compile time or an undesired behavior at runtime. For example:

```
<% if  (isUserLoggedIn) %>
Welcome, <%= userName %>!
```

will be translated to:

```
if (isUserLoggedIn)
out.write("Welcome, ");
out.print(userName);
```

In this case, the statement `out.print(userName);` will be executed even if the value of `isUserLoggedIn` is `false`. The correct way to write this is:

```
<% if (isUserLoggedIn)
   {
%>
       Welcome, <%= userName %>!
<%
   }
%>
```

Like conditional statements, iterative statements can also span across multiple scriptlets, with regular HTML code in between the scriptlets. Such constructs are commonly used for displaying long lists of values in a tabular format. The following example illustrates this usage:

```
<html><body>
   List of logged in users:
<table>

<tr>
   <th> Name </th>
   <th> email </th>
</tr>

<%
   User[] users = //get an array of logged in users

   for(int i=0; i< users.length; i++)
   {

%>

  <tr>
     <td> <%= users[i].name %> </td>
     <td> <%= users[i].email %> </td>
  </tr>

<%
   } // For loop ends
%>

</table>
</body></html>
```

The above code uses two scriptlets to enclose HTML code within a `for` loop; the first scriptlet opens the loop block and the second scriptlet closes the loop block. Notice that the HTML code between the two scriptlets contains only one row and that it embeds JSP expressions that use the loop variable `i` declared by the previous scriptlet.

At request time, the loop may be executed zero or more times based on the length of the `users` array. For each execution, the HTML code will insert one row into the table. Thus, if the length of the `users` array is 9, it will create a table with nine rows in the output stream. Also, since the scriptlet will increment the value of the variable `i` each time after the loop is executed, the expressions within the HTML code will index into a different element in the `users` array with each iteration.

Thus, we can generate a variable-sized table containing dynamic rows and columns with the help of multiple scriptlets and expressions.

### 12.1.3 Using request-time attribute expressions

JSP expressions are not always written to the output stream of the JSP page; they can also be used to pass values to action attributes:

```
<% String pageURL = "copyright.html"; %>
<jsp:include page="<%=pageURL%>" />
```

In this case, the value of the JSP expression `<%=pageURL%>` does not go into the output stream. It is evaluated at request time, and its value is assigned to the page attribute of the `jsp:include` action. An expression used in this way to pass a value to an action attribute is called a *request-time attribute expression.*

An important point to remember here is that such a mechanism of providing request-time attribute values cannot be used in directives, because directives have translation time semantics; this means that the JSP engine uses the directives during the page translation time only. Thus, the two directives in the following example are not valid:

```
<%!
   String bSize = "32kb";
   String pageUrl = "copyright.html";
%>

<%@ page buffer="<%=bSize%>" %>
<%@ include file="<%=pageUrl%>" %>
```

### 12.1.4 Using escape sequences

Like any programming language, the JSP scripting language also has special characters that have a specific meaning from the JSP parser's point of view. These characters are the single quote, the double quote, the backslash, and the character sequences `<%@`, `<%!`, `<%=`, `<%`, %>, `<%--`, and `--%>`. To use them in a manner other than as special characters, we have to use a backslash and create an escape sequence in order to instruct the parser not to use them as special characters. Let's examine the different situations where we must use the escape sequences.

### In template text

All scripting elements—declarations (<%!), scriptlets (<%), and expressions (<%=)—start with the characters <%. Hence, while parsing the JSP page, the parser looks for the character sequence <% to find the start of a tag. If we want to use the string literal <% in a normal template text as is, we have to escape the character % with a backslash (\), as shown in the following example:

```
<html><body>
   The opening tag of a scriptlet is <\%
   The closing tag of a scriptlet is %>
</body></html>
```

Note in this example that we can use the sequence %> without using an escape character, because the parser is not looking for that sequence while parsing the text.

### In scripting elements

All scripting elements end with the tag %>. Therefore, after reading the opening tag, the parser looks for the character sequence %> to find the end of the tag. If we want to use the string literal %> within a scripting element as is, we have to escape the character > with a backslash, as shown in the following example:

```
<html><body>
   <%= "The opening tag of a scriptlet is <%"  %>
   <%= "The closing tag of a scriptlet is %\>" %>
</body></html>
```

Note that we can use the sequence <% without an escape character, because the parser is not looking for that sequence; it is already in the middle of parsing the scripting element, which is an expression.

### In attributes

For string literals used in attribute values, we have to escape the special characters with a backslash character. Consider the following snippet:

```
<%@ page info="A sample use of ', \", \\, <\%, and %\> characters. " %>
<html><body>
   <%= getServletInfo() %>
</body></html>
```

This code will generate the following into the output HTML:

```
A sample use of ', ", \, <%, and %> characters.
```

Note that we have used a backslash for the double quote but not for the single quote. This is because the value is enclosed in a pair of double quotes. If we use a pair of single quotes to enclose the entire value, then we have to escape the single quote appearing within the value as shown here:

```
<%@ page info='A sample use of \', ", \\, <\%, and %\> characters. ' %>
```

In case of request-time attribute expressions, we cannot use a pair of double quotes within a pair of double quotes or a pair of single quotes enclosed within a pair of single quotes. Thus, the following is invalid:

```
<jsp:include page="<%= "copyright.html" %>" />
```

It can be rectified either by using the escape sequence `\"` or by using a pair of single quotes for the entire value and a pair of double quotes for the string literal in the JSP expression:

```
<jsp:include page='<%= "copyright.html" %>' />

<jsp:include page="<%= \"copyright.html\" %>" />
```

### *Quizlet*

**Q:** Explain whether the following are valid or invalid JSP constructs.

**a** `<%=myObj.m1(); %>`

**b** `<% int x=4, y=5; %>`
`<%=x=y%>`

**c** `<% myObj.m1(); %>`

**A:** **a** Invalid: The = sign makes it a JSP expression. However, JSP expressions are not terminated with a semicolon. The generated servlet code will cause a syntax error:

```
out.print(myObj.m1(););
```

**b** Valid: `<%=x=y%>` will be translated to:

```
out.print(x=y);
```

The value of `y` is assigned to `x`, and the new value of `x` is then printed out. The output will be `5`.

**c** Valid: It is a valid scriptlet because a semicolon ends the method call statement. It would be valid even if the method returns a value, because the value would be ignored. Let's look at a similar example:

```
Welcome! You are visitor number <% ++count; %>
```

This is a very common mistake, and it is often difficult to debug. The above code will compile and run without any errors, but it will not print the desired output. This is how the JSP engine will translate the code:

```
out.write("Welcome! You are visitor number ");
++count;
```

It increments the count variable, but does not use `out.print()` to print its value. To print the value, we have to make it an expression by inserting an equals sign (=) after the opening tag (<%) and removing the semicolon (;) from the end, as shown here:

```
Welcome! You are visitor number <%= ++count %>
```

**Q:** What is wrong with the following code?

```
<%@ page language='java' %>
<%
   int x = 0;
   int incr() { return ++x; }
%>
The value of x is <%=incr()%>
```

**A:** We cannot define methods in a scriptlet. Upon translation of the above code into a servlet, the `_jspService()` method will look like this:

```
public void _jspService(...)
{
      ...other code

      int x = 0;
      int incr() { return ++x; }
      out.write("The value of x is ");
      out.print(incr());
 }
```

Since the `incr()` method is declared inside the `_jspService()` method, the code will not compile.

**Q:** Will the following code compile?

```
<%  int x = 3; %>
<%! int x = 5; %>
<%! int y = 6; %>
The sum of x and y is <%=x+y%>
```

**A:** Yes. It will compile and print:

```
The sum of x and y is 9
```

Upon translation of the above code into a servlet, the variable x will be declared twice: once global to the class because of the declaration `<%!int x = 5; %>` and once local to the `_jspService()` method because of the scriptlet `<% int x = 3; %>`:

```
public class xyz ...
{
   ...other code

   int x = 5;
   int y = 6;

   public void _jspService(...)
   {
      ...other code

      int x = 3;
      out.write("The sum of x and y is ");
      out.print(x+y);
   }
}
```

Since local variables have precedence over global variables, the expression x+y evaluates as 3+6.

**Q:** What is the output of the following code?

```
<% int i; %>
<%
   for(i=0; i<3; i++)
%>
The value of i is <%=i%>
```

**A:** This code will translate into:

```
int i = 0;
for (int i=0; i<3; i++)
out.write("The value of i is ");
out.print(i);
```

Since we have not enclosed the body of the loop in a block { ... }, it will print:

```
The value of i is The value of i is The value of i is 3
```

## 12.2 UNDERSTANDING JSP IMPLICIT VARIABLES AND JSP IMPLICIT OBJECTS

During the translation phase, the JSP engine declares and initializes nine commonly used variables in the _jspService() method. We have already seen the use of one of them, out, in some of our previous examples:

```
<html><body>
   <%
      out.print("Hello World! ");
   %>
</body></html>
```

Even though we have not defined the variable out in this example, the code will translate, compile, and execute without errors. This is because out is one of the nine variables that the JSP engine implicitly makes available to the JSP page. Table 12.1 describes these variables.

**Table 12.1 Implicit variables available to JSP pages**

| Identifier Name | Class or Interface | Description |
|---|---|---|
| application | interface javax.servlet.ServletContext | Refers to the web application's environment |
| session | interface javax.servlet.http.HttpSession | Refers to the user's session |
| request | interface javax.servlet.http.HttpServlet-Request | Refers to the current request to the page |

*continued on next page*

**Table 12.1 Implicit variables available to JSP pages *(continued)***

| Identifier Name | Class or Interface | Description |
|---|---|---|
| response | interface javax.servlet.http.HttpServlet-Response | Used for sending a response to the client |
| out | class javax.servlet.jsp.JspWriter | Refers to the output stream for the page |
| page | class java.lang.Object | Refers to the page's servlet instance |
| pageContext | class javax.servlet.jsp.PageContext | Refers to the page's environment |
| config | interface javax.servlet.ServletConfig | Refers to the servlet's configuration |
| exception | class java.lang.Throwable | Used for error handling |

Let's take a look at the way Tomcat 4.0.1 declares these variables in the generated servlet for a JSP file. Follow these steps:

1 Create a blank file in the `C:\jakarta-tomcat-4.0.1\webapps\chapter12` directory and name it `implicit.jsp`.
2 Start Tomcat.
3 From your browser, navigate to the URL `http://localhost:8080/chapter12/implicit.jsp`.

Although you will not see any content in the browser window, the JSP engine will create a Java file named `implicit$jsp.java` in the `C:\Jakarta-tomcat-4.0.1\work\localhost\chapter12` directory. This file contains the servlet that corresponds to the JSP file, `implicit.jsp`. The `_jspService()` method of the servlet is shown in Listing 12.2.

**Listing 12.2 implicit$jsp.java**

```
public void _jspService(
                    HttpServletRequest request,
                    HttpServletResponse response)
                       throws java.io.IOException,
                              ServletException
{
   ...other code

   PageContext pageContext = null;
   HttpSession session = null;
   ServletContext application = null;
   ServletConfig config = null;
   JspWriter out = null;
   Object page = this;

   ...other code

   pageContext = ...//get it from somewhere
   session     = pageContext.getSession();
```

```
    application = pageContext.getServletContext();
    config      = pageContext.getServletConfig();
    out         = pageContext.getOut();

    ...other code
}
```

As you can see, eight variables are already declared and available within the `_jspService()` method. To declare the ninth one, open the `implicit.jsp` file and add the following line:

```
<%@ page isErrorPage="true" %>
```

Save the file and go to the same URL again. Now you should see the following line added to the generated `implicit$jsp.java` file:

```
Throwable exception =
     (Throwable) request.getAttribute("javax.servlet.jsp.jspException");
```

Because the page author does not (and cannot) declare these variables explicitly, they are called *implicit variables*. The objects that these variables refer to are created by the servlet container and are called *implicit objects*. The exam may ask you to state their types, scopes, and uses. We will discuss the use of these nine implicit variables first, and then talk about their scopes in section 12.3.

### 12.2.1 application

The `application` variable is of type `javax.servlet.ServletContext`, and it refers to the environment of the web application to which the JSP page belongs. (We discussed the `ServletContext` class at length in chapter 6, "The servlet container model.") Thus, the following two scriptlets are equivalent:

```
<%
  String path = application.getRealPath("/WEB-INF/counter.db");
  application.log("Using: "+path);
%>

<%
  String path = getServletContext().getRealPath("/WEB-INF/counter.db");
  getServletContext().log("Using: "+path);
%>
```

### 12.2.2 session

Before we discuss the `session` implicit variable, let's clarify that the word *session* refers to four different but related things in JSP:

- Session, as in an HTTP session, is a concept that logically groups multiple requests from the same client as part of one conversation. We discussed HTTP sessions in chapter 8, "Session management."
- `session`, as used in a `page` directive, refers to the attribute named *session*.

  ```
  <@ page session="true" >
  ```

Its value, which is `true` or `false`, determines whether or not the JSP page participates in an HTTP session.

- `session`, as an implicit object (which we will talk about in this section), refers to the variable session of type `javax.servlet.http.HttpSession`.
- Session, as a scope of an object, refers to the lifetime and availability of the object. A session-scoped object persists throughout the life of an HTTP session. We will discuss scope in the next section.

The implicit variable `session` is declared if the value of the `session` attribute of the `page` directive is `true`. Since by default, the value of the `session` attribute is `true`, this variable is declared and is made available to the page even if we do not specify the `page` directive. However, if we explicitly set the `session` attribute to `false`, the JSP engine does not declare this variable, and any use of the variable results in an error. The following example demonstrates this:

```
<html>
<body>
   <%@ page session="false" %>    <-- session is not used

   Session ID = <%=session.getId()%>   <-- Error: undefined
</body>                                    symbol session
</html>
```

In the above example, the `page` directive sets the `session` attribute to `false` in order to indicate that the current page will not participate in an HTTP session. This makes the implicit variable `session` unavailable in the page. So the line `session.getId()` will generate a compile-time error.

### 12.2.3 request and response

The request and response implicit variables are of type `javax.servlet.http.HttpServletRequest` and `javax.servlet.http.HttpServletResponse`, respectively. They are passed in as parameters to the `_jspService()` method when the page's servlet is executed upon a client request. We use them in JSP pages in exactly the same way we use them in servlets—that is, to analyze the request and send a response:

```
<html><body>
<%
   String remoteAddr = request.getRemoteAddr();
   response.setContentType("text/html;charset=ISO-8859-1");
%>

Hi! Your IP address is <%=remoteAddr%>

</body></html>
```

### 12.2.4 page

The implicit variable page is of class java.lang.Object, and it refers to the instance of the generated servlet. It is declared as:

```
Object page = this;    //this refers to the instance of this servlet.
```

This variable is rarely used. In fact, since it is a variable of type Object, it cannot be used to directly call the servlet methods:

```
<%= page.getServletInfo()              %>    <-- Error
<%= ((Servlet)page).getServletInfo() %>    <-- OK: typecast
<%= this.getServletInfo()              %>    <-- OK
```

The first expression will generate a compile-time error indicating that getServletInfo() is not a method of java.lang.Object.

In the second expression, we have typecast the page reference to Servlet. Since page refers to the generated class and the class implements the Servlet interface, it is a valid cast. Also, because getServletInfo() is a method of the Servlet interface, the expression will compile and execute without errors. Note that, in this case, the page variable could also be cast to JspPage or HttpJspPage since these two interfaces are derived from the Servlet interface and are implemented by the generated servlet class.

In the third expression, we are using the Java keyword this to refer to the generated servlet. Therefore, it will also compile and execute without errors.

### 12.2.5 pageContext

The pageContext variable is of type javax.servlet.jsp.PageContext. The PageContext class is an abstract class, and the JSP engine vendor provides its concrete subclass. It does three things:

- Stores references to the implicit objects. If you look at the generated servlet code for the implicit.jsp file (listing 12.2), you will see that the session, application, config, and out implicit variables are initialized using the objects retrieved from pageContext. The pageContext object acts as a one-stop place for managing all the other objects, both user-defined and implicit, used by the JSP page, and it provides the getter methods to retrieve them.
- Provides convenience methods to get and set attributes in different scopes. These are explained in section 12.3.4.
- Provides convenience methods, described in table 12.2, for transferring requests to other resources in the web application.

**Table 12.2 Convenience methods of javax.servlet.jsp.PageContext for transferring requests to other resources**

| Method | Description |
|---|---|
| void include(String relativeURL) | Includes the output of another resource in the output of the current page. Same as ServletRequest.getRequestDispatcher().include(); |
| void forward(String relativeURL) | Forwards the request to another resource. Same as ServletRequest.getRequestDispatcher().forward(); |

For example, to forward a request to another resource from a servlet, we have to write the following two lines:

```
RequestDispatcher rd = request.getRequestDispatcher("other.jsp");
rd.forward(request, response);
```

In a JSP page, we can do that in just one line by using the `pageContext` variable:

```
pageContext.forward("other.jsp");
```

For a complete list of all the methods of the `PageContext` class, please refer to the JSP API.

### 12.2.6 out

The implicit variable `out` is of type `javax.servlet.jsp.JspWriter`. This variable is the workhorse of JSP pages. We use it directly in scriptlets and indirectly in expressions to generate HTML code:

```
<%  out.print("Hello 1"); %>
<%= "Hello 2"            %>
```

For both of the above lines, the generated servlet code will use the `out` variable to print the values:

```
public void _jspService(...)
{
   //other code
   out.print("Hello 1");
   out.print("Hello 2");
}
```

The `JspWriter` class extends `java.io.Writer` and inherits all the overloaded `write()` methods. On top of these methods, `JspWriter` adds its own set of overloaded `print()` and `println()` methods for printing out all the primitive data types, `Strings`, and the user-defined objects in the output stream. The following example prints out different data types using the `out` variable:

```
<%
   int anInt = 3;
   Float aFloatObj = new Float(12.6);

   out.print(anInt);                    //int
```

```
        out.print(anInt > 0);                //boolean
        out.print(anInt*3.5/100-500);        //float expression
        out.print(aFloatObj);                //object
        out.print(aFloatObj.floatValue()); //float method
        out.print(aFloatObj.toString());     //String method
    %>
```

### 12.2.7 config

The implicit variable `config` is of type `javax.servlet.ServletConfig`. As we saw in chapter 5 ("Structure and deployment"), each servlet can be passed a separate set of configuration parameters in the deployment descriptor, and the servlet can then retrieve this information using its own copy of the `ServletConfig` object.

Similarly, we can also pass configuration parameters that are specific to a JSP page, which the page can retrieve using the implicit variable `config`. To achieve this, we have to first declare a servlet with a `<servlet-name>` in the deployment descriptor `web.xml`. Then, instead of providing a `<servlet-class>`, we associate the named servlet with the JSP file, using the element `<jsp-file>`. All of the initialization parameters for this named servlet will then be available to the JSP page via the page's `ServletConfig` implicit object. The `web.xml` file shown in listing 12.3 illustrates this.

**Listing 12.3 Configuring InitTestServlet and mapping it to a JSP page in web.xml**

```
<?xml version="1.0" encoding="ISO-8859-1"?>

<!DOCTYPE web-app
   PUBLIC "-//Sun Microsystems, Inc.//DTD Web Application 2.3//EN"
   "http://java.sun.com/dtd/web-app_2_3.dtd">

<web-app>

   <servlet>
      <servlet-name>InitTestServlet</servlet-name>
      <jsp-file>/initTest.jsp</jsp-file>

      <init-param>
         <param-name>region</param-name>
         <param-value>North America</param-value>
      </init-param>
   </servlet>

</web-app>
```

The above deployment descriptor declares a servlet named `InitTestServlet` and maps it to the JSP file `<document root>/initTest.jsp`. Then it specifies an initialization parameter named `region` with the value of `North America` for the servlet. This information can be retrieved by `initTest.jsp` using the implicit variable `config`, as shown in listing 12.4.

**Listing 12.4 initTest.jsp**

```
<html><body>
   Servlet Name = <%=config.getServletName()%><br>
   Parameter region = <%=config.getInitParameter("region")%>
</body></html>
```

When the JSP page `initTest.jsp` is accessed as a servlet, using the URL `http://localhost:8080/chapter12/servlet/InitTestServlet` it will print the following output:

```
Servlet Name = InitTestServlet
Parameter region = North America
```

However, if this page is accessed directly using the `initTest.jsp` page's actual URL, `http://localhost:8080/chapter12/initTest.jsp`, then the above configuration for `InitTestServlet` is not used. This is because the JSP engine creates two different instances of the generated servlet class—one for accessing it as a named servlet and one for accessing it as a JSP page—and will pass each servlet instance a different `ServletConfig` object. In order to be able to use the same servlet instance—and hence the same configuration—when using either of the URLs mentioned above, we have to explicitly map the JSP page's URL in the deployment descriptor file using the `<servlet-mapping>` element:

```
<servlet-mapping>
   <servlet-name>InitTestServlet</servlet-name>
   <url-pattern>/initTest.jsp</url-pattern>
</servlet-mapping>
```

When mapped this way, the container will create only one instance of the generated servlet class and requests for both the URLs will be served by the same instance, thus guaranteeing the same configuration.

The rules for the `<servlet-mapping>` for JSP pages are the same as in the case of normal servlets. We can provide just about any URL pattern, and each time the pattern matches the client's request URL, the container will execute the specified JSP page (actually, the generated servlet for the JSP page).

### 12.2.8 exception

This implicit variable is of type `java.lang.Throwable`. The `exception` variable is available to the pages that act as error handlers for other pages. Recall from chapter 11 that error-handler pages have the page directive attribute `isErrorPage` set to `true`. Consider the following two JSP code examples:

*Example 1*

```
<html><body>
   <%@ page isErrorPage='true' %>
   Msg: <%=exception.toString()%>      <-- OK: exception defined implicitly
</body></html>
```

*Example 2*

```
<html><body>
   Msg: <%=exception.toString()%>
</body></html>
```

**Error: exception not defined**

In example 1, the engine defines the `exception` variable implicitly because the attribute `isErrorPage` is set to `true`. The `exception` variable refers to the uncaught `java.lang.Throwable` object thrown by a page that uses this page as its error handler.

In example 2, the engine does not define the variable `exception` implicitly because the attribute `isErrorPage` has a default value of `false`.

*Quizlet*

**Q:** What is wrong with the following code?

```
<%!
    jspInit(){
       application.getInitParameter("Region");
    }
%>
```

**A:** Recall that all the implicit variables are automatically declared by the JSP engine in the generated `_jspService()` method, which means they are available only in scriptlets and expressions. In a declaration, we have to explicitly declare the variables:

```
<%!
    jspInit(){
       ServletContext application = this.getServletContext();
       application.getInitParameter("Region");
    }
%>
```

## 12.3 UNDERSTANDING JSP PAGE SCOPES

In chapter 4, "The Servlet model," we introduced the concept of *scope*, which is the way that data is shared between servlets using the three container objects, `ServletContext`, `HttpSession`, and `ServletRequest`. The scopes associated with these three container objects are, respectively, the application scope, the session scope, and the request scope. The JSP technology, since it is based on servlet technology, also uses the three scopes, which are referred to in JSP pages as *application*, *session*, and *request* scopes. In addition, JSP pages have a fourth scope, the *page* scope, which is maintained by the container object `PageContext`.

All of the implicit objects as well as the user-defined objects in a JSP page exist in one of these four scopes, described in table 12.3. These scopes define the existence and accessibility of objects from within the JSP pages and servlets.

**Table 12.3 Scopes of objects in JSP pages**

| Scope Name | Existence and Accessibility |
|---|---|
| Application | Limited to a single web application |
| Session | Limited to a single user session |
| Request | Limited to a single request. |
| Page | Limited to a single page (translation unit) and a single request. |

As shown in table 12.3, objects in the *application* scope are the most accessible and objects in the *page* scope are the least accessible. Let's take a closer look at these scopes.

### 12.3.1 Application scope

Application-scoped objects are shared across all the components of the web application and are accessible for the life of the application. These objects are maintained as attribute-value pairs by an instance of the `ServletContext` class. In a JSP page, this instance is available in the form of the implicit object `application`. Thus, to share objects at the application level, we use the `setAttribute()` and `getAttribute()` methods of the `ServletContext` interface.

### 12.3.2 Session scope

Objects in the session scope are shared across all the requests that belong to a single-user session and are accessible only while the client is active. These objects are maintained as attribute-value pairs by an instance of the `HttpSession` class. In a JSP page, this instance is available in the form of the implicit object `session`. Thus, to share objects at the session level, we can use the `session.setAttribute()` and `session.getAttribute()` methods.

In the following example, the `login.jsp` page adds the user ID to the session scope so that the `userProfile.jsp` page can retrieve it:

```
<%--
   Add the userId to the session
--%>
<%
   String userId = // getUserLoggedIn
   session.setAttribute("userId", userId);
%>
```

In the file `userProfile.jsp`:

```
<%--
   Retrieve the userId from the session
--%>
<%
   String userId = (String) session.getAttribute("userId")

   //use the userId to retrieve user details.
   String name = getUserNameById(userId);
%>
User Name is: <%=name%>
```

Here, the session scope is used to make the username and ID available to all the requests in the session.

### 12.3.3 Request scope

Objects in the request scope are shared across all the components that process the same request and are accessible only while that request is being serviced. These objects are maintained as attribute-value pairs by an implementation instance of the interface `HttpServletRequest`. In a JSP page, this instance is available in the form of the implicit object `request`. Thus, we can add attributes to the request in one page and forward the request to another page. The second page can then retrieve these attributes to generate a response.

In this example, the file `login.jsp` creates a user object and adds it to the request, and then forwards the request to `authenticate.jsp`:

```
<%
   //Get login and password information from the request object
   //and file it in a User Object.

   User user = new User();
   user.setLogin(request.getParameter("login"));
   user.setPassword(request.getParameter("password"));

  //Set the user object in the request scope for now
  request.setAttribute("user", user);

  //Forward the request to authenticate.jsp
   pageContext.forward("authenticate.jsp");
   return;
%>
```

In the file `authenticate.jsp`:

```
<%
     //Get user from the forwarding page
     User user = (User) request.getAttribute("user");

     //Check against the database.
     if (isValid(user))
     {
        //remove the user object from request scope
        //and maintain it in the session scope
        request.removeAttribute("user");
        session.setAttribute("user",user);

        pageContext.forward("account.jsp");
     }
     else
     {
        pageContext.forward("loginError.jsp");
     }
     return;
%>
```

Here, the page (`login.jsp`) adds a `User` object to the request scope and forwards the request to `authenticate.jsp`. At that point, `authenticate.jsp` validates the user information against the database and, depending on the outcome of the authentication process, either transfers the object into the session scope and forwards the request to `account.jsp`, or forwards the request to `loginError.jsp`, which generates an appropriate response by using the `User` object. We call `return;` after forwarding the request to prevent writing anything to the output stream after the request is forwarded because doing so would throw an `IllegalStateException`.

### 12.3.4 Page scope

Objects in the page scope are accessible only in the translation unit in which they are defined. They do not exist outside the processing of a single request within a single translation unit. These objects are maintained as attribute-value pairs by an instance of a concrete subclass of the abstract class `PageContext`. In a JSP page, this instance is available in the form of the implicit object `pageContext`.

The use of the page scope and the `pageContext` container object may not be obvious right now, but it will become clearer when we will learn about the use of JavaBeans in chapter 14, "Using JavaBeans," and custom tags in chapter 16, "Developing custom tag libraries." The only way for actions (standard JSP actions and user-defined custom tags) to share data and JavaBean objects with other actions or custom tags appearing in the same JSP page (translation unit) and in the same request thread is to use the `pageContext` implicit object and the page scope.

To share objects in the page scope, we can use the two methods defined by `PageContext`, shown in table 12.4.

**Table 12.4 Convenience methods of javax.servlet.jsp.PageContext**

| Method | Description |
|---|---|
| void setAttribute(String name, Object attribute) | Adds an attribute to the page scope |
| java.lang.Object getAttribute(String name) | Returns the object associated with the name in the page scope or null if not found |

The `PageContext` object also provides a common and convenient way to handle all of the objects in all of the scopes. Table 12.5 describes the defined constants and methods used for this purpose.

**Table 12.5 Convenience scope-handling constants and methods of javax.servlet.jsp.PageContext**

| Member | Description |
|---|---|
| **Integer constants that work with scopes** | |
| static final int APPLICATION_SCOPE | Indicates application scope |
| static final int SESSION_SCOPE | Indicates session scope |

*continued on next page*

**Table 12.5 Convenience scope-handling constants and methods of javax.servlet.jsp.PageContext *(continued)***

| Member | Description |
|---|---|
| static final int REQUEST_SCOPE | Indicates request scope |
| static final int PAGE_SCOPE | Indicates page scope |
| **Methods that accept scope constants** | |
| void setAttribute(String name, Object object, int scope); | Sets the attribute in the specified scope |
| java.lang.Object getAttribute(String name, int scope); | Returns the object associated with the name in the specified scope or null if not found |
| void removeAttribute(String name, int scope) | Removes the object associated with the specified name from the given scope |
| java.util.Enumeration getAttributeNamesInScope(int scope) | Enumerates all the attributes in a given scope |
| **Convenience scope search methods** | |
| Object findAttribute(java.lang.String name) | Searches for the named attribute in page, request, session (if valid), and application scope(s) in this order and returns the associated value |
| int getAttributesScope(String name) | Gets the scope in which a given attribute is defined |

The six implicit objects—`response`, `out`, `page`, `pageContext`, `config`, and `exception`—are also considered to have page scope by the JSP specification. They are all maintained by the `pageContext` container object and can be obtained using their respective getter methods.

However, their existence and accessibility is somewhat different from the user-defined objects. Although the JSP specification defines these implicit objects as being in the page scope, they are not logically restricted to that scope. For example, the `page` implicit object refers to the generated servlet instance. For the same servlet instance, if there are multiple threads that are serving multiple requests, possibly even in multiple sessions, then the same implicit object `page` is shared by all those threads and is thus accessible by all the requests and in all the sessions. Similarly, the `ServletConfig` object, referred to as the implicit variable `config`, is also shared by multiple threads that are serving multiple requests, possibly in multiple sessions.

### *Quizlet*

**Q:** Objects in which scope are accessible to all of the web applications of a servlet container?

**A:** There is no scope defined in Servlets and JSP specification that can share objects across multiple web applications. To do that, we have to either use `ServletContext.getContext()` as explained in chapter 4 or use other mechanisms, such as an external database.

## 12.4 JSP PAGES AS XML DOCUMENTS

The JSP specification defines two sets of syntax for authoring JSP pages: standard JSP syntax format and XML syntax format. JSP files that use the standard syntax are called JSP pages, while the JSP files that use the XML syntax are called JSP documents.

We have already seen the standard syntax of the elements of a JSP page in the previous chapter. In this section, we will learn about the XML-style tags that make up a JSP document. The exam does not require you to know all the details of the XML format, but you are expected to know the XML-based tags for writing the directives and the scripting elements.

The best way to learn and remember the XML-style tags is to compare them with their JSP-style counterparts. So let's first look at the code for the JSP document `counter_xml.jsp` (listing 12.5), which is an XML equivalent of the code for the JSP page `counter.jsp` that we saw in chapter 11 (listing 11.1).

**Listing 12.5 counter_xml.jsp**

```
<jsp:root
        xmlns:jsp="http://java.sun.com/JSP/Page"
        version="1.2">

   <html><body>


   <jsp:directive.page language="java" />


   <jsp:declaration>
         int count = 0;
   </jsp:declaration>


   <jsp:scriptlet>
         count++;
   </jsp:scriptlet>


   <jsp:text>
         Welcome! You are visitor number
   </jsp:text>


   <jsp:expression>
         count
   </jsp:expression>


   </body></html>
</jsp:root>
```

The above JSP document counts the number of times it is visited during a server session. We will discuss its XML elements and tags in the following sections.

You should remember two important points about using the XML and JSP syntax together:

- The standard JSP tags and XML-based tags cannot be mixed within a single JSP page.
- A page written in one syntax format can, however, include or forward to a page in the other syntax format by using either directives or actions.

Like directives and actions in the JSP syntax format, the following rules apply to all of the elements in XML syntax format:

- The tag names, attribute names, and attribute values are all case sensitive.
- The value must be surrounded by a pair of single or double quotes.
- A pair of single quotes is equivalent to a pair of double quotes.
- There must be no space between the equals sign (=) and the value.

### 12.4.1 The root element

As seen in listing 12.5, the XML syntax requires that the entire JSP page be enclosed in a single root element:

```
<jsp:root
        xmlns:jsp="http://java.sun.com/JSP/Page"
        version="1.2" >

   Rest of the page

</jsp:root>
```

The attribute-value pair `xmlns:jsp="http://java.sun.com/JSP/Page"` tells the JSP engine that the prefix `jsp` is used to identify the tags in the library specified by the URI `http://java.sun.com/JSP/Page`. This library contains the standard elements defined by the JSP specification. Thus, all the JSP tags in listing 12.5 are of the form `<jsp:...>`. The attribute `version` informs the engine about the version of the JSP specification used in the page. Both of the attributes are mandatory.

`xmlns` stands for *XML Name Space*. Functionally, it is the same as the `prefix` attribute of a `taglib` directive in the JSP syntax. Hence, it is also used to specify the use of the custom tag libraries in the page:

```
<jsp:root
        xmlns:jsp="http://java.sun.com/JSP/Page"
        xmlns:myLib="www.someserver.com/someLib"
        version="1.2" >

   Rest of the page

</jsp:root>
```

The attribute-value pair `xmlns:myLib="www.someserver.com/someLib"` tells the JSP engine that the page uses custom tags of the form `<myLib:...>` and that the details of these custom tags are located in the library indicated by the URI `www.someserver.com/someLib`.

Tag libraries will be discussed in chapter 15, "Using custom tags," and chapter 16, "Developing custom tag libraries."

**NOTE** There is no equivalent to `<jsp:root>` in the JSP syntax.

### 12.4.2 Directives and scripting elements

There are only two directives in the XML format: `page` and `include`:

```
<jsp:directive.page ...attributeList... />
<jsp:directive.include ...attributeList... />
```

There is no `taglib` directive in the XML format since the tag library information is specified in the root element. The attributes and use of the `page` and `include` directives are the same in both XML syntax and JSP syntax.

The three scripting elements—declarations, scriptlets, and expressions—use the following syntax, respectively:

```
<jsp:declaration>
   Any valid Java declaration statements
</jsp:declaration>

<jsp:scriptlet>
   Any valid Java code
</jsp:scriptlet >

<jsp:expression>
   Any valid Java expression
</jsp:expression >
```

This syntax for `expression` is used when we want to write the expression values to the output HTML. For a request-time attribute expression, we have to use `%= ...%`, as in the following example:

```
<jsp:scriptlet>
   String pageURL = "copyright.html";
</jsp:scriptlet>

<jsp:include page="%=pageURL%" />
```

In this case, the value of the `pageURL` variable is sent as a parameter to the `include` action.

Compare this with the JSP style, where the same syntax, `<%= ... %>`, is used for both purposes.

### 12.4.3 Text, comments, and actions

A major difference between the JSP and XML syntax is the placement of normal text. The JSP syntax allows us to incorporate text into the page without using any special tags. However, the XML syntax requires us to embed the text between `<jsp:text>` and `</jsp:text>`, as shown here:

```
<html><body>
   <jsp:text>Have a nice day!</jsp:text>
</body></html>
```

The JSP specification does not stipulate any special tag for writing comments in XML format. However, since XML-based JSP pages are treated as XML documents, we should use the standard XML-style comments:

```
<!-- comment here -->
```

The standard JSP actions use the same tags in both the JSP syntax and XML syntax. This is an example of an `include` action in either syntax:

```
<jsp:include page="someOtherPage.jsp" />
```

### *Quizlet*

**Q:** What is wrong with the following code?

```
<jsp:root
            "xmlns:jsp=http://java.sun.com/JSP/Page"
            version="1.2" >

      2 + 3 = <jsp:expression>=2+3</jsp:expression>

</jsp:root>
```

**A:** Unlike JSP syntax elements, XML syntax elements do not use any extra characters in their tags.

```
<%=2+3%>     <— Valid JSP expression
<jsp:expression>=2+3</jsp:expression>    <— Error: = not required
<jsp:expression>2+3</jsp:expression>     <— Valid XML expression
```

Also, the text must be enclosed in `<jsp:text>`:

```
<jsp:text>2 + 3 = </jsp:text><jsp:expression>2+3</jsp:expression>
```

**Q:** What is wrong with the following code?

```
<jsp:root
        xmlns:jsp="http://java.sun.com/JSP/Page"
        version="1.2" >

    <jsp:Text>2 + 3 = </jsp:Text>
    <jsp:Expression>2+3</jsp:Expression>

</jsp:root>
```

**A:** All the tags are case sensitive. We must use `jsp:text` and `jsp:expression` instead of `jsp:Text` and `jsp:Expression`, respectively.

## 12.5 SUMMARY

In this chapter, we continued our discussion on the JSP technology by looking more closely at the translation phase rules that a JSP engine applies during the page's conversion into a servlet. We started by discussing the various traps and pitfalls involved in using the scripting elements (declarations, scriptlets, and expressions) to declare and initialize variables and to write conditional and iterative statements. A good grasp of these issues is essential when combining the Java programming language with HTML to develop error-free and effective JSP pages.

The JSP engine declares and initializes nine commonly used variables and makes them available to the JSP page's generated servlet code. These are called implicit variables, and they refer to the implicit objects that are created by the servlet container. We discussed the use of these nine implicit variables with examples, and we also saw how they relate to the four scopes: page, request, session, and application.

The JSP specification also supports the use of XML syntax to create JSP pages. Although much of the exam focuses on standard JSP syntax, some knowledge of the XML syntax is expected. We reviewed the XML tags for writing JSP documents, including directives and scripting elements, and compared them with their JSP counterparts.

With the end of this chapter, you should be ready to answer questions about the structure of a JSP page in both the standard and the XML format, the mapping of its elements into a servlet, and the implicitly provided objects with their scopes.

In the next chapter, we will learn different mechanisms provided by the JSP specification for reusing the JSP pages.

## 12.6 REVIEW QUESTIONS

1. What will be the output of the following code? (Select one)

```
<html><body>
   <%  x=3;      %>
   <%  int x=5; %>
   <%! int x=7; %>
   x = <%=x%>, <%=this.x%>
</body></html>
```

**a** `x = 3, 5`

**b** `x = 3, 7`

**c** `x = 5, 3`

**d** `x = 5, 7`

**e** Compilation error

2. What will be the output of the following code? (Select one)

```
<html><body>
   The value is <%=""%>
</body></html>
```

**a** Compilation error

**b** Runtime error

**c** `The value is`

**d** `The value is null`

3. Which of the following implicit objects is not available to a JSP page by default? (Select one)

   **a** `application`

   **b** `session`

   **c** `exception`

   **d** `config`

4. Which of the following implicit objects can you use to store attributes that need to be accessed from all the sessions of a web application? (Select two)

   **a** `application`

   **b** `session`

   **c** `request`

   **d** `page`

   **e** `pageContext`

5. The implicit variable `config` in a JSP page refers to an object of type: (Select one)

   **a** `javax.servlet.PageConfig`

   **b** `javax.servlet.jsp.PageConfig`

   **c** `javax.servlet.ServletConfig`

   **d** `javax.servlet.ServletContext`

6. A JSP page can receive context initialization parameters through the deployment descriptor of the web application.

   **a** True

   **b** False

7. Which of the following will evaluate to `true`? (Select two)

   **a** `page == this`

   **b** `pageContext == this`

   **c** `out instanceof ServletOutputStream`

   **d** `application instanceof ServletContext`

8. Select the correct statement about the following code. (Select one)

```
<%@ page language="java" %>
<html><body>
   out.print("Hello ");
   out.print("World ");
</body></html>
```

**a** It will print `Hello World` in the output.

**b** It will generate compile-time errors.

**c** It will throw runtime exceptions.

**d** It will only print `Hello`.

**e** None of above.

9. Select the correct statement about the following code. (Select one)

```
<%@ page language="java" %>
<html><body>
<%
   response.getOutputStream().print("Hello ");
   out.print("World");
%>
</body></html>
```

**a** It will print `Hello World` in the output.

**b** It will generate compile-time errors.

**c** It will throw runtime exceptions.

**d** It will only print `Hello`.

**e** None of above.

10. Which of the following implicit objects does not represent a scope container? (Select one)

**a** `application`

**b** `session`

**c** `request`

**d** `page`

**e** `pageContext`

11. What is the output of the following code? (Select one)

```
<html><body>
   <% int i = 10 ;%>
   <%  while(--i>=0) { %>
      out.print(i);
   <% } %>
</body></html>
```

**a** `9876543210`

**b** `9`

**c** `0`

**d** None of above

12. Which of the following is not a valid XML-based JSP tag? (Select one)

```
a <jsp:directive.page    />
b <jsp:directive.include />
c <jsp:directive.taglib  />
d <jsp:declaration></jsp:declaration>
e <jsp:scriptlet></jsp:scriptlet>
f <jsp:expression></jsp:expression>
```

13. Which of the following XML syntax format tags do not have an equivalent in JSP syntax format? (Select two)

```
a <jsp:directive.page/>
b <jsp:directive.include/>
c <jsp:text></jsp:text>
d <jsp:root></jsp:root>
e </jsp:param>
```

14. Which of the following is a valid construct to declare that the implicit variable session should be made available to the JSP page? (Select one)

```
a <jsp:session>true</jsp:session>
b <jsp:session required="true" />
c <jsp:directive.page>
      <jsp:attribute name="session" value="true" />
  </jsp:directive.page>
d <jsp:directive.page session="true" />
e <jsp:directive.page attribute="session" value="true" />
```

CHAPTER 13

# Reusable web components



## EXAM OBJECTIVES

**9.1** Given a description of required functionality, identify the JSP page directive or standard tag in the correct format with the correct attributes required to specify the inclusion of a Web component into the JSP page. (Sections 13.1–13.2)

## INTRODUCTION

Instead of building a case for reusing software components, in this chapter we will reiterate the well-acknowledged fact that reusable components enhance the productivity and maintainability of applications. In this respect, the JSP specification defines mechanisms that allow us to reuse web components.

Our aim in this chapter is to understand how web components can be reused. Although the exam objective corresponding to this topic looks narrow, it requires that you know a lot more than just syntax in order to answer the questions in the exam.

In the JSP world, reusing web components essentially means including the content or the output of another web component in a JSP page. This can be done in one of two ways: statically or dynamically. Static inclusion involves including the contents of the web component in a JSP file at the time the JSP file is translated, while in dynamic inclusion, the output of another component is included within the output of the JSP page when the JSP page is requested.

# 13.1 STATIC INCLUSION

In static inclusion, the contents of another file are included with the current JSP file at translation time to produce a single servlet. We use the JSP `include` directive to accomplish this. We have already seen the JSP syntax of the `include` directive in chapter 11, "The JSP technology model—the basics," and the XML syntax in chapter 12, "The JSP technology model—advanced topics." Here is a review of that syntax:

```
<%@ include file="relativeURL" %>

<jsp:directive.include file="relativeURL" />
```

The `file` attribute is the only attribute of the `include` directive, and it is mandatory. It refers to the file that contains the static text or code that will be inserted into the including JSP page. It can refer to any text-based file—HTML, JSP, XML, or even a simple .txt file—using a relative URL. A relative URL means that it cannot have a protocol, a hostname, or a port number. It can either be a path relative to the current JSP file—that is, it does not start with a /—or it can be a path relative to the document root of the web application—that is, it starts with a /. Figure 13.1 illustrates the way the `include` directive works.

Figure 13.1 shows two JSP files: `a.jsp` and `b.jsp`. The `a.jsp` file contains an `include` directive that refers to the `b.jsp` file.

While generating the servlet code for `a.jsp`, the JSP engine includes all the elements of `b.jsp`. The resulting code, which is a combination of the including page and the included page, is then compiled as a single translation unit.

When a request is made for `a.jsp`, it will be processed by the servlet generated for `a.jsp`. However, because this servlet also contains the code from `b.jsp`, the resulting HTML page will contain the generated output from `a.jsp` as well as `b.jsp`.

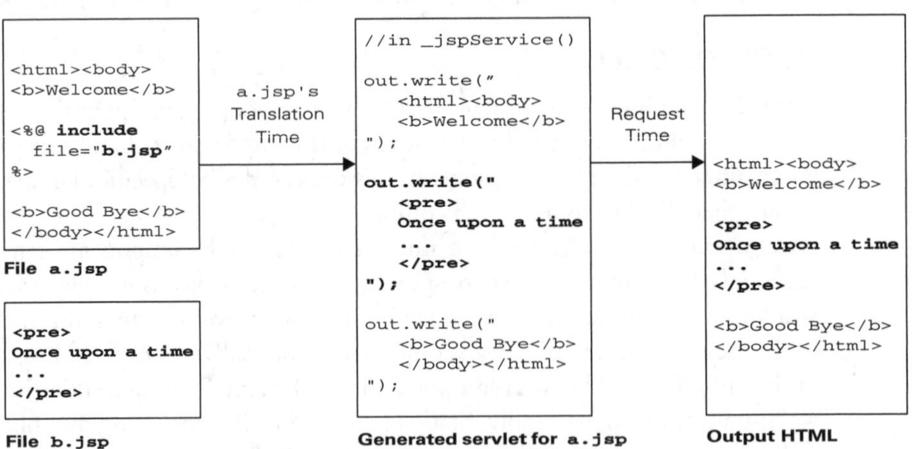


**Figure 13.1 Static inclusion using the include directive.**

### 13.1.1 Accessing variables from the included page

Since the code of the included JSP page becomes a part of the including JSP page, each page can access the variables and methods defined in the other page. They also share all of the implicit objects, as shown in listing 13.1.

**Listing 13.1 productsSearch.jsp**

```
<html><body>

   <%

      //Get the search criteria from the request.
      String criteria = request.getParameter("criteria");

      //Search the product database and get the product IDs.
      String productId[] = getMatchingProducts(criteria);
   %>

   The following products were found that match your criteria:<br>

   <!--
      Let productDescription.jsp generate the description
      for each of the products
   -->

   <%@ include file="productDescription.jsp" %>


   New Search:
   <!--
      FORM for another search
   -->
   <form>...</form>

</body></html>
```

In listing 13.1, the `productsSearch.jsp` file processes the search criteria entered by the user and retrieves the matching products from the database. It then includes the `productDescription.jsp` file to generate the product description.

The code for `productDescription.jsp` is shown in listing 13.2.

**Listing 13.2 productDescription.jsp**

```
<%
   // The implicit variable request used here is
   // actually that of the including page.
   String sortBy = request.getParameter("sortBy");

   // Use the productId array defined by productsSearch.jsp
   // to sort and generate the description of the products
   productId = sort(productId, sortBy);

   for(int i=0; i<productId.length; i++)
```

```
    {
        // Generate a tabular description
        // for the products.
    }
%>
```

The productDescription.jsp file uses the implicit request object and the productId array defined in productsSearch.jsp to generate a tabular display of the products.

### 13.1.2 Implications of static inclusion

When an include directive includes a file, the following rules apply:

- No processing can be done at translation time, which means the file attribute value cannot be an expression. Therefore, the following use of the include directive is invalid:

  ```
  <% String myURL ="copyright.html"; %>
  <%@ include file="<%=myURL%>" %>
  ```

- Because request parameters are a property of the requests and do not make any sense at translation time, the file attribute value cannot pass any parameters to the included page. Thus, the value of the file attribute in the following example is invalid:

  ```
  <%@ include file="other.jsp?abc=pqr" %>
  ```

- The included page may or may not be able to compile independently. If you look at listing 13.2, the productDescription.jsp file cannot be compiled, since it does not define the variable productId. In general, it is better to avoid such dependencies and use the implicit variable pageContext to share objects across statically included pages by using the pageContext.setAttribute() and pageContext.getAttribute() methods.

## 13.2 DYNAMIC INCLUSION

In dynamic inclusion, when the JSP page is requested, it sends a request to another object, and the output from that object is included in the requested JSP page. We use the standard JSP actions <jsp:include> and <jsp:forward> to implement dynamic inclusion. Their syntax is as follows:

```
<jsp:include page="relativeURL" flush="true" />

<jsp:forward page="relativeURL" />
```

The page attribute is mandatory. It must be a relative URL, and it can refer to any static or dynamic web component, including a servlet. It can also be a request-time expression, such as:

```
<% String pageURL = "other.jsp" %>
<jsp:include page="<%=pageURL%>" />
```

The `flush` attribute is only valid for `<jsp:include>` and not for `<jsp:forward>`. It is optional and specifies that if the output of the current JSP page is buffered, then the buffer should be flushed before passing the output stream to the included component. The default value for the flush attribute is `false`.

Functionally, the `<jsp:include>` and `<jsp:forward>` actions are equivalent to the `RequestDispatcher.include()` and `RequestDispatcher.forward()` methods that are used in servlets to include and forward the requests to other components.

### 13.2.1 Using jsp:include

The `<jsp:include>` action delegates the control of the request processing to the included component temporarily. Once the included component finishes its processing, the control is transferred back to the including page. Figure 13.2 illustrates this process.

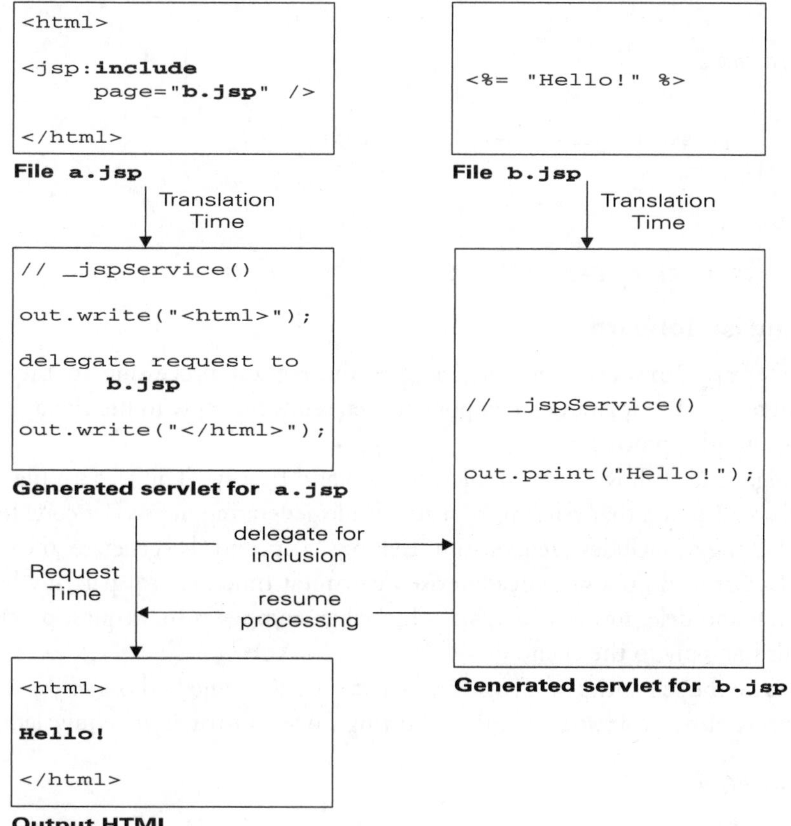


**Figure 13.2 Dynamic inclusion using the include action.**

Figure 13.2 shows two JSP files, `a.jsp` and `b.jsp`. The `a.jsp` file contains an `include` action that refers to `b.jsp` file. While generating the servlet code for `a.jsp`, the JSP engine includes a request-time call to `b.jsp`, and also generates the servlet code for `b.jsp` if it does not already exist. When a request is made for `a.jsp`, it will be received and processed by the servlet generated for `a.jsp`. However, since this servlet contains a call to the `b.jsp` file, the resulting HTML page will contain the output from the servlet generated for `b.jsp` as well as the servlet generated for `a.jsp`.

Because the semantics of `<jsp:include>` are the same as those of `RequestDispatcher.include()`, the following three constructs are equivalent:

*Construct 1*

```
<%
   RequestDispatcher rd =
      request.getRequestDispatcher("other.jsp");
   rd.include(request, response);
%>
```

*Construct 2*

```
<%
   pageContext.include("other.jsp");
%>
```

*Construct 3*

```
<jsp:include page="other.jsp" flush="true"/>
```

### 13.2.2 Using jsp:forward

The `<jsp:forward>` action delegates the request processing to the forwarded component. The forwarded component then sends the reply to the client. Figure 13.3 illustrates this process.

Figure 13.3 shows two JSP files, `a.jsp` and `b.jsp`. The `a.jsp` file contains a `forward` action that refers to `b.jsp`. While generating the servlet code for `a.jsp`, the JSP engine includes a request-time call to `b.jsp`, and also generates the servlet code for `b.jsp` if it does not already exist. At request time, `a.jsp` partially handles the request and delegates it to `b.jsp`, which then completes the request processing and sends the reply to the client.

Since the semantics of `<jsp:forward>` are the same as those of the `RequestDispatcher.forward()`, the following three constructs are equivalent:

*Construct 1*

```
<%
   RequestDispatcher rd =
      request.getRequestDispatcher("other.jsp");
   rd.forward(request, response);
%>
```

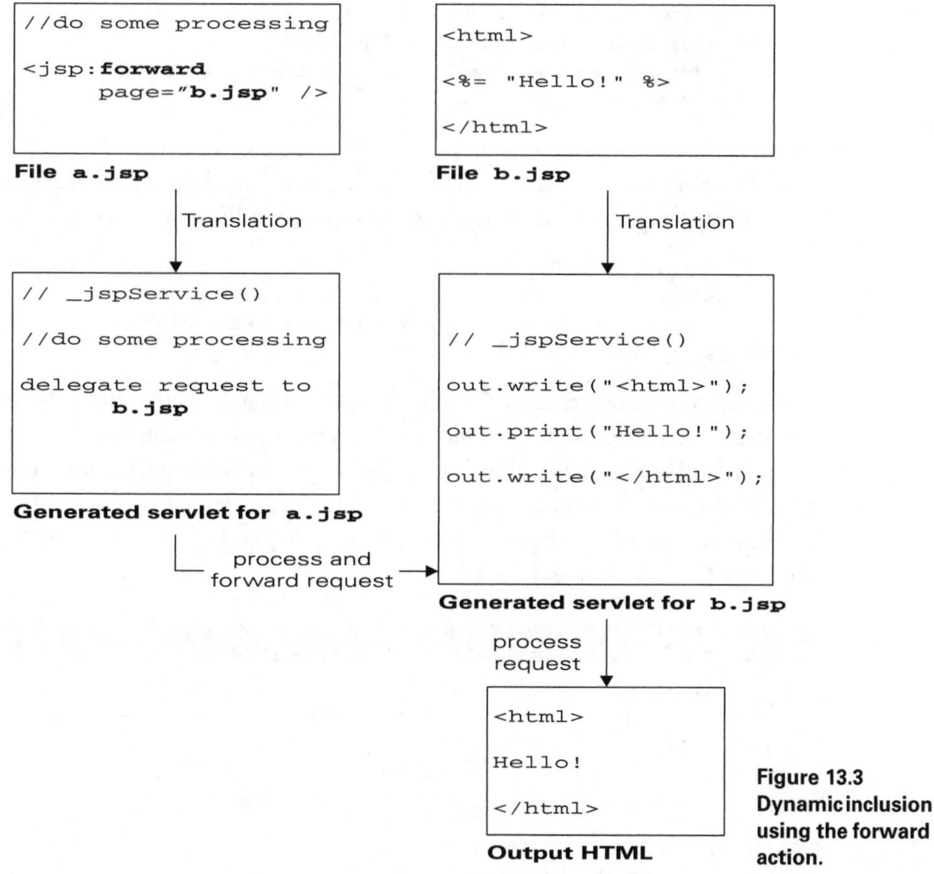


**Figure 13.3 Dynamic inclusion using the forward action.**

*Construct 2*

```
<%
   pageContext.forward("other.jsp");
%>
```

*Construct 3*

```
<jsp:forward page="other.jsp" />
```

In all three cases, if the output is buffered, it is first cleared, and then the request is forwarded to the other resource. However, if the output is not buffered and/or if the response is already committed by the forwarding resource, then a `java.lang.IllegalStateException` is raised when we attempt to forward the request.

### 13.2.3 Passing parameters to dynamically included components

We can pass parameters to the dynamically included components by using the `<jsp:param />` tags. The following examples illustrate the use of the `<jsp:param>` tag to pass two parameters to the included page:

```
<jsp:include page="somePage.jsp">
   <jsp:param name="name1" value="value1" />
   <jsp:param name="name2" value="value2" />
</jsp:include>
```

There can be any number of `<jsp:param>` elements nested within the `<jsp:include>` or `<jsp:forward>` element. The value of the `value` attribute can also be specified using a request-time attribute expression in the following way:

```
<jsp:include page="somePage.jsp">
   <jsp:param name="name1" value="<%=someExpr1%>" />
   <jsp:param name="name2" value="<%=someExpr2%>" />
</jsp:include>
```

In addition to parameters that are explicitly passed using the above methods, the included components have access to parameters that were originally present in the request to the including component. However, if the original parameter names are repeated in the explicitly passed parameters, the new values take precedence over the old values. For example, consider the two files `paramTest1.jsp` and `paramTest2.jsp` (shown in listings 13.3 and 13.4).

**Listing 13.3 The file paramTest1.jsp**

```
<html><body><pre>

In paramTest1:
First name is <%=request.getParameter("firstname")%>
Last  name is <%=request.getParameter("lastname")%>

<jsp:include page="paramTest2.jsp" >
  <jsp:param name="firstname" value="mary" />
</jsp:include>

</pre></body></html>
```

**Listing 13.4 The file paramTest2.jsp**

```
In paramTest2:
First name is <%=request.getParameter("firstname")%>
Last  name is <%=request.getParameter("lastname")%>

Looping through all the first names
<%
   String first[] = request.getParameterValues("firstname");
   for (int i=0; i<first.length; i++)
   {
      out.println(first[i]);
   }
%>
```

If you access the paramTest1.jsp file with the URL

```
http://localhost:8080/chapter13/paramTest1.jsp?firstname=john&lastname=smith
```

the output to the browser will be:

```
In paramTest1:
First name is john
Last name is smith

In paramTest2:
First name is mary
Last name is smith

Looping through all the first names
mary
john
```

This is because when we call paramTest1.jsp (listing 13.3) using the URL given above, it receives the request parameters as firstname=john&lastname=smith. It prints out these values and then passes a new name-value pair, firstname=mary, to the included page paramTest2.jsp (listing 13.4) using the <jsp:param> element.

In the included page, the new value of the firstname parameter takes precedence over the original value and therefore receives the parameters as firstname=mary&firstname=john&lastname=smith. Thus, a call to request.getParameter("firstname") will return "mary", while a call to request.getParameterValues("firstname") will return an array of Strings containing the values "mary" and "john". Since no new value for lastname was supplied, paramTest2.jsp uses the original value, "smith".

The name-value pairs passed in via the <jsp:param> tag exist within the request object and are available only for the included component. After the included component has finished processing, the engine removes these values from the request object. Thus, if the file paramTest1.jsp calls request.getParameterValues("first") after paramTest2.jsp returns, the call will return an array of Strings containing only one value: "john".

All of the above examples used <jsp:include>, but this discussion is equally applicable to <jsp:forward>.

### 13.2.4 Sharing objects with dynamically included components

The dynamically included pages execute separately, so they do not share the variables and methods defined by the including page. However, they process the same request and thus share all the objects present in the request scope, as shown in listing 13.5.

**Listing 13.5 productsSearch.jsp**

```
<html><body>

   <%
      //Get the search criteria from the request.
```

```
      String criteria = request.getParameter("criteria");

      //Search the product database and get the product IDs.
      String productId[] = getMatchingProducts(criteria);

      request.setAttribute("productIds", productId);
   %>


   The following products were found that match your criteria:<br>

   <!--
      Let productDescription.jsp generate the description
      for each of the products
   -->

   <jsp:include page="productDescription.jsp" />


   New Search:
   <!--
      FORM for another search
   -->
   <form>...</form>

</body></html>
```

Listing 13.5 produces the same results as listing 13.1, but it uses dynamic inclusion instead of static inclusion. The including file, `productSearch.jsp`, adds the `productId` object into the `request` scope by calling the `request.setAttribute()` method. The included file, `productDescription.jsp` (listing 13.6), then retrieves this object by calling the `request.getAttribute()` method.

**Listing 13.6 productDescription.jsp**

```
<%
   //The implicit variable request used here is
   //not the same as that of the including page.
   //But the objects in the request scope are shared.

   String sortBy = request.getParameter("sortBy");

   String[] productIds = (String[])
               request.getAttribute("productIds");

   //Use the productId array here
   for(int i=0; i<productIds.length; i++)
   {
      // Generate a tabular description
      // for the products.
   }
%>
```

Here, the implicit variable `request` in `productsDescription.jsp` is accessing the same `request` scope objects as the implicit variable `request` in the `productSearch.jsp` file. The same mechanism can also be used with the `<jsp:forward>` action.

Note that in addition to `request`, we could use the implicit variables `session` and `application` to share objects with included and forwarded pages, but they are not meant for sharing request-dependent values. For example, if we use `application` instead of `request` in listings 13.5 and 13.6, then the product IDs generated for a search request from one client could affect the result of a search for another client because they share the value of the attribute `productIds` in the application scope.

### *Quizlet*

**Q:** Explain whether each of the following are valid or invalid.

```
a <jsp:include url="catalog.jsp" />
b <jsp:include page="http://myserver/catalog.jsp" />
c <jsp:include flush="true" />
d <jsp:forward flush="false" page="catalog.jsp" />
e <jsp:include page="/servlets/catalogServlet" />
f <%@ include page="catalog.jsp" %>
g <%@ include file="/servlets/catalogServlet" %>
h <%@ include file="catalog.jsp?category=gifts" %>
i <% String fileURL = "catalog.jsp"; %>
  <%@ include file="<%=fileURL%>" %>
```

**A:** The following table explains why an option is valid or invalid.

| Example | Construct | Valid/ Invalid | Explanation |
|---|---|---|---|
| a | `<jsp:include url="catalog.jsp" />` | Invalid | There is no attribute named *url* in jsp:include or jsp:forward. Use *page*. |
| b | `<jsp:include page="http://myserver/catalog.jsp" />` | Invalid | The value of *page* has to be a relative URL. We cannot specify a protocol, hostname, or port number. |
| c | `<jsp:include flush="true" />` | Invalid | The mandatory attribute *page* is missing. |
| d | `<jsp:forward flush="false" page="catalog.jsp" />` | Invalid | The attribute *flush* is only for jsp:include, not for jsp:forward. |
| e | `<jsp:include page="/servlets/catalogServlet" />` | Valid | The attribute *page* can point to a servlet. |
| f | `<%@ include page="catalog.jsp" %>` | Invalid | The include directive uses *file*, not *page*. |

*continued on next page*

| Example | Construct | Valid/ Invalid | Explanation |
|---|---|---|---|
| g | <%@ include file="/servlets/catalogServlet" %> | Invalid | When using the include directive, you can include XML, text, HTML, or even JSP files, but not a servlet. |
| h | <%@ include file="catalog.jsp?category=gifts" %> | Invalid | Query strings cannot be used with the include directive. |
| i | <% String fileURL = "catalog.jsp"; %><br><%@ include file="<%=fileURL%>" %> | Invalid | The include directive cannot use a request-time attribute expression. |

**Q:** What is the difference between the following constructs?

```
<% pageContext.include("other.jsp"); %>

<jsp:include page="other.jsp" />
```

**A:** They are functionally similar but with a minor difference. The `pageContext.include()` method always flushes the output of the current page before including the other components, while `<jsp:include>` flushes the output of the current page only if the value of `flush` is explicitly set to `true`, as in this example:

```
<jsp:include page="other.jsp" flush="true" />
```

**Q:** What is wrong with the following JSP document?

```
<jsp:root
        xmlns:jsp=http://java.sun.com/JSP/Page
        version="1.2">

   <jsp:scriptlet>
      String pageURL = "other.jsp";
   </jsp:scriptlet>

   <jsp:include page="<%=pageURL%>" />

</jsp:root>
```

**A:** The expression `<%=pageURL%>` is in the JSP syntax format. Recall from the previous chapter that the correct syntax for a request-time expression in XML syntax format is `%= expr %`. Thus, the `<jsp:include>` action in the above code must be written as:

```
<jsp:include page="%=pageURL%" />
```

**Q:** The following code does not work. Identify the problem and rectify it. In the `main.jsp` file:

```
<html><body>

   <%
      Integer oneHundred = new Integer(100);
      Integer twoHundred = new Integer(200);
   %>
```

```
    <jsp:include page="display.jsp" >
       <jsp:param name="one" value="<%= oneHundred %>" />
       <jsp:param name="two" value="<%= twoHundred %>" />
    </jsp:include>

 </body></html>
```

In the display.jsp file:

```
 <%@ page import="java.lang.* " %>

 <%
    Integer oneHundred = (Integer) request.getParameter("one");
    Integer twoHundred = (Integer) request.getParameter("two");
 %>
```

**A:** We can use only String to pass and retrieve parameters using the <jsp:param> and request.getParameter() mechanisms. To pass any other type of object, we have to use request.setAttribute() in the including component and request.getAttribute() in the included component.

## 13.3 SUMMARY

JSP technology reuses web components by including the content or output of the components in a JSP page. There are two ways to do this: static inclusion and dynamic inclusion.

Static inclusion happens during the translation process, and it uses the include directive: <%@ include %>. The included file gets translated together with the including JSP file into a single servlet class. In this way, the pages are able to share all variables and methods.

Dynamic inclusion occurs at the time the including JSP page is requested, and it is accomplished by the standard actions, <jsp:include> and <jsp:forward>. In this chapter, we reviewed the techniques for passing parameters to the included components. Even though a dynamically included component does not share variables and methods with the including JSP page, they both process the same request and therefore share all the objects present in the request scope.

At this point, you should be able to answer questions based on the concepts of static and dynamic inclusion of web components in JSP pages.

In the next chapter, we will examine the way JSP pages use JavaBeans.

## 13.4 REVIEW QUESTIONS

1. Which of the following JSP tags can be used to include the output of another JSP page into the output of the current page at request time? (Select one)

   **a** `<jsp:insert>`

   **b** `<jsp:include>`

   **c** `<jsp:directive.include>`

   **d** `<jsp:directive:include>`

   **e** `<%@ include %>`

2. Consider the contents of the following two JSP files:

   File 1: `test1.jsp`

```
<html><body>
      <% String message = "Hello"; %>

      //1 Insert LOC here.

      The message is <%= message %>
</body></html>
```

   File 2: `test2.jsp`

```
<% message = message + " world!"; %>
```

   Which of the following lines can be inserted at `//1` in `test1.jsp` so that it prints `"The message is Hello world!"` when requested? (Select one)

   **a** `<%@ include  page="test2.jsp" %>`

   **b** `<%@ include  file="test2.jsp" />`

   **c** `<jsp:include page="test2.jsp" />`

   **d** `<jsp:include file="test2.jsp" />`

3. Which of the following is a correct way to pass a parameter equivalent to the query string `user=mary` at request time to an included component? (Select one)

   **a**
```
<jsp:include page="other.jsp" >
    <jsp:param paramName="user" paramValue="mary" />
</jsp:include>
```

   **b**
```
<jsp:include page="other.jsp" >
    <jsp:param name="mary" value="user" />
</jsp:include>
```

   **c**
```
<jsp:include page="other.jsp" >
    <jsp:param value="mary" name="user" />
</jsp:include>
```

   **d**
```
<jsp:include page="other.jsp" >
    <jsp:param param="user" value="mary"/>
</jsp:include>
```

**e** 
```
<jsp:include page="other.jsp" >
    <jsp:param user="mary" />
</jsp:include>
```

4. Identify the JSP equivalent of the following code written in a servlet. (Select one)

```
RequestDispatcher rd = request.getRequestDispatcher("world.jsp");
rd.forward(request, response);
```

**a** `<jsp:forward page="world.jsp"/>`

**b** `<jsp:action.forward page="world.jsp"/>`

**c** `<jsp:directive.forward page="world.jsp"/>`

**d** `<%@ forward file="world.jsp"%>`

**e** `<%@ forward page="world.jsp"%>`

5. Consider the contents of two JSP files:

File 1: `test1.jsp`

```
<html><body>
   <% pageContext.setAttribute("ninetyNine", new Integer(99));  %>

   //1

</body></html>
```

File 2: `test2.jsp`

```
The number is <%= pageContext.getAttribute("ninetyNine") %>
```

Which of the following, when placed at line `//1` in the `test1.jsp` file, will allow the `test2.jsp` file to print the value of the attribute when `test1.jsp` is requested? (Select one)

**a** `<jsp:include page="test2.jsp" />`

**b** `<jsp:forward page="test2.jsp" />`

**c** `<%@ include file="test2.jsp" %>`

**d** None of the above because objects placed in `pageContext` have the `page` scope and cannot be shared with other components.

6. Consider the contents of two JSP files:

File 1: `this.jsp`

```
<html><body><pre>
   <jsp:include page="that.jsp" >
      <jsp:param name="color" value="red" />
      <jsp:param name="color" value="green" />
   </jsp:include>
</pre></body></html>
```

File 2: `that.jsp`

```
<%
   String colors[] = request.getParameterValues("color");
   for (int i=0; i<colors.length; i++)
   {
      out.print(colors[i] + " ");
   }
%>
```

What will be the output of accessing the `this.jsp` file via the following URL? (Select one)

```
http://localhost:8080/chapter13/this.jsp?color=blue
```

**a** `blue`

**b** `red green`

**c** `red green blue`

**d** `blue red green`

**e** `blue green red`

7. Consider the contents of two JSP files:

File 1: `this.jsp`

```
<html><body>

   <%= request.getParameter("color")  %>

   <jsp:include page="that.jsp" >
      <jsp:param name="color" value="red" />
   </jsp:include>

   <%= request.getParameter("color")  %>

</body></html>
```

File 2: `that.jsp`

```
<%= request.getParameter("color")  %>
```

What will be the output of accessing the `this.jsp` file via the following URL? (Select one)

```
http://localhost:8080/chapter13/this.jsp?color=blue
```

**a** `blue red blue`

**b** `blue red red`

**c** `blue blue red`

**d** `blue red null`

8. Consider the contents of three JSP files:

File 1: `one.jsp`

```
<html><body><pre>

   <jsp:include page="two.jsp" >
      <jsp:param name="color" value="red" />
   </jsp:include>

</pre></body></html>
```

File 2: `two.jsp`

```
<jsp:include page="three.jsp" >
   <jsp:param name="color" value="green" />
</jsp:include>
```

File 3: `three.jsp`

```
<%= request.getParameter("color")  %>
```

What will be the output of accessing the `one.jsp` file via the following URL? (Select one)

`http://localhost:8080/chapter13/one.jsp?color=blue`

**a** `red`

**b** `green`

**c** `blue`

**d** The answer cannot be determined.

CHAPTER 14

# Using JavaBeans



## EXAM OBJECTIVES

**10.1** For any of the following tag functions, match the correctly constructed tag, with attributes and values as appropriate, with the corresponding description of the tag's functionality:

- Declare the use of a JavaBean component within the page.
- Specify, for jsp:useBean or jsp:getProperty tags, the name of an attribute.
- Specify, for a jsp:useBean tag, the class of the attribute.
- Specify, for a jsp:useBean tag, the scope of the attribute.
- Access or mutate a property from a declared JavaBean.
- Specify, for a jsp:getProperty tag, the property of the attribute.
- Specify, for a jsp:setProperty tag, the property of the attribute to mutate, and the new value.

(Section 14.2)

**10.2** Given JSP page attribute scopes: request, session, application, identify the equivalent servlet code. (Section 14.3)

**10.3** Identify techniques that access a declared JavaBean component. (Section 14.4)

## *INTRODUCTION*

JavaBeans are independent software components that we can use to assemble other components and applications. JSP technology uses standard tags to access JavaBeans components, which allow us to encapsulate code, perform complex operations, and leverage existing components to save time. In this chapter, we will give you a brief overview of JavaBeans from the JSP perspective, and show you how they are used in JSP pages.

## 14.1 *JAVABEANS: A BRIEF OVERVIEW*

The JavaBeans component model architecture is both a specification and a framework of APIs that supports a set of features that includes component introspection, properties, events, persistence, and so forth. Since it is platform independent, it enables us to write portable and reusable components.

Components developed according to this specification are called *beans*. From a developer's perspective, a bean is a Java class object that encapsulates data in the form of instance variables. These variables are referred to as *properties* of the bean. The class then provides a set of methods for accessing and mutating its properties. The actual strength of a bean as a reusable component lies in its ability to allow programmatic introspection of its properties. This ability facilitates automated support for bean customization using software programs called *bean containers*.

### 14.1.1 JavaBeans from the JSP perspective

In the JSP technology, the JSP engine acts as a bean container. Any class that follows these two conventions can be used as a JavaBean in JSP pages:

- The class must have a public constructor with no arguments. This allows the class to be instantiated as needed by the JSP engine.
- For every property, the class must have two publicly accessible methods, referred to as the *getter* and the *setter*, that allow the JSP engine to access or mutate the bean's properties.

The name of the method that accesses the property should be get*XXX*() and the name of the method that mutates the property should be set*XXX*(), where *XXX* is the name of the property with the first character capitalized. Here are the signatures of the methods:

```
public property-type getXXX();
public void setXXX(property-type);
```

In the following getter and setter methods, the name of the property is `color` and its data type is `String`:

```
public String getColor();
public void setColor(String);
```

Let's look at a simple example of a Java class that can be used as a JavaBean in a JSP page. In listing 14.1, the class `AddressBean` encapsulates the address information in four private attributes and provides access to them via the corresponding setter and getter methods.

**Listing 14.1 A simple JavaBean class named AddressBean**

```
public class AddressBean
{
   //properties
   private String street;
   private String city;
   private String state;
   private String zip;

   //setters
   public void setStreet(String street){ this.street = street; }
   public void setCity(String city)     { this.city   = city;   }
   public void setState(String state)   { this.state  = state;  }
   public void setZip(String zip)       { this.zip    = zip;    }

   //getters
   public String getStreet(){ return this.street; }
   public String getCity()  { return this.city;   }
   public String getState() { return this.state;  }
   public String getZip()   { return this.zip;    }

}
```

Note that the name of our class `AddressBean` ends with the word *Bean.* Although this is not a requirement, many developers like to follow this convention (`UserBean`, `AccountBean`, etc.) to differentiate between JavaBean classes and ordinary classes, thus making their intent clear to co-developers.

The rules for placing the bean classes are the same as for any other class, such as servlets, utility classes, or third-party tools. They must be present in the classpath of the web application—which means we can keep them directly in the `/WEB-INF/classes` directory, or in a JAR file under the `/WEB-INF/lib` directory. Then, to use these classes within the JSP pages, we have to import them via the `import` attribute of the `page` directive.

### 14.1.2 The JavaBean advantage

Let's look at an example of using the `AddressBean` class in a JSP page. In this example, we want to capture the address information of visitors to our web site and maintain it during the lifetime of a session. Listing 14.2 shows an HTML page code with an input form that will collect this information.

**Listing 14.2 addressForm.html**

```
<html>
<body>
Please give your address:<br>
   <form action="address.jsp">
      Street: <input type="text" name="street"><br>
```

```
        City:    <input type="text" name="city"><br>
        State:   <input type="text" name="state"><br>
        Zip:     <input type="text" name="zip"><br>

                  <input type="submit"><br>
    </form>
</body>
</html>
```

When the user fills out the form and submits the page, we need to perform the following tasks on the server:

1. Check if an AddressBean object already exists in the session.
2. If not, create a new AddressBean object and add it to the session.
3. Call request.getParameter() for all the HTML FORM fields.
4. Set the respective values into the AddressBean object.

If there were no support from the JSP engine, we would have to code the above steps in a scriptlet, as shown here:

```
<%@ page import="AddressBean" %>
<%
   AddressBean address = null;

   synchronized(session)
   {
      //Get an existing instance
      address = (AddressBean) session.getAttribute("address");

      //Create a new instance if required
      if (address==null)
      {
         address = new AddressBean();
         session.setAttribute("address", address);
      }

      //Get the parameters and fill up the address object
      address.setStreet(request.getParameter("street"));
      address.setCity(request.getParameter("city"));
      address.setState(request.getParameter("state"));
      address.setZip(request.getParameter("zip"));
   }
%>
```

However, the JSP specification defines standard actions that provide a convenient means of handling HTML FORM input and sharing information across the JSP pages using JavaBeans. The scriptlet code shown above can be replaced with the following lines using the JavaBean and the standard JSP actions:

```
<%@ page import="AddressBean" %>
<jsp:useBean id="address" class="AddressBean" scope="session" />
<jsp:setProperty name="address" property="*" />
```

Shorter code is not the only incentive to use JavaBeans in JSP pages; JavaBeans also help to increase code reusability. Suppose that after setting all the fields of the `AddressBean` to the values retrieved from the request parameters we want to persist this information into a database. We could write a scriptlet and include the logic of opening the database connection and saving the bean's properties in that scriptlet. But what if this functionality is required by more than one JSP page? We have to repeat the same scriptlet code in all the JSP pages. And then, what if the logic to access the database changes? We have to modify all the affected pages to adapt to the new database logic. However, if we build that logic into a method in the `AddressBean` class itself, then all the pages can use that method. Furthermore, if the database access logic changes, only the `AddressBean` class and its method change; the JSP pages remain unaffected.

Another advantage of using beans is that they are Java programming language objects, which means we can fully utilize the object-oriented features provided by the language. Let's suppose the application needs to maintain two different types of addresses: one for businesses and one for residences. We can have two separate beans, `BusinessAddressBean` and `ResidentialAddressBean`, both derived from a common base class, `AddressBean`. The base class can implement all the logic common to both beans, while the derived classes can handle the logic that is specific to each bean independently.

### 14.1.3 Serialized JavaBeans

Usually, in an enterprise application we use some form of a database to store and retrieve persistent data. For example, we can have a relational database with a table for storing address information captured in our `AddressBean` when a visitor first goes to the site. The same address information can be retrieved from the database when we want to display the address at a later date. Storing JavaBean properties in a database is one way of persisting JavaBeans. The JavaBeans specification also allows us to persist JavaBeans in the file system as serialized objects.

A *serialized bean* is a bean instance that is converted into a data stream and stored in a file so that its attributes and values are saved permanently and can be retrieved later as required. The process of serialization is achieved using the standard *Object Serialization* mechanism of Java. First, we make our bean class capable of being serialized by implementing the `java.io.Serializable` interface.[1] Then we can serialize the individual bean instances by using the `java.io.ObjectOutputStream` class.

---

[1] It can also done by implementing the java.io.Externalizable interface. Please see the JDK API for more details.

Serialized beans are considered to be resources and have the following requirements:

- The file that stores a serialized bean must have the extension `.ser`. For example, we can serialize instances of the `AddressBean` class in files and name the files after the person to which the address belongs, such as `John.ser` or `Mary.ser`.
- The file that stores the bean must be present in the classpath of the web application. Since the `/WEB-INF/classes` directory is always present in the classpath of a web application, we can create and save all the beans in either the `/WEB-INF/classes` directory or a subdirectory of the `/WEB-INF/classes` directory. For example:

  ```
  /WEB-INF/classes/John.ser
  /WEB-INF/classes/businessData/visitorAddresses/Mary.ser
  ```

- The combination of the path and the filename that stores the bean is treated as the *name* of the bean, similar to the way classes and packages are treated.

Thus, in the examples shown above, the names of the two serialized beans are `John` and `businessData.visitorAddresses.Mary`. This is because `/WEB-INF/classes/` is in the classpath of the web application. If we also add the `businessData` directory to the classpath so that any file under `<WEB-INF>/classes/businessData` is available as a resource, we can refer to Mary's bean as `visitorAddresses.Mary`.

Once saved as serialized beans, these objects can be loaded in any Java program using the `java.beans.Beans.instantiate()`[2] method.

In the following example, we will assume that we have a directory structure called `/WEB-INF/classes/businessData/visitorAddresses/`, and we will create the serialized beans in that directory.

First, let's make our `AddressBean` class serializable as follows:

```
public class AddressBean implements java.io.Serializable
{
   ...
}
```

Listing 14.3, `beanSaver.jsp`, accepts the user's name and address information in the request parameter, creates an instance of `AddressBean`, and serializes it to a file that is given the name of the user.

---

2 See the JDK documentation of the package java.beans for more details

**Listing 14.3 beanSaver.jsp**

```
<%@ page import="AddressBean, java.io.* " %>

<%
   String message="";

   try
   {
      //Create an instance. Set the properties
      AddressBean address = new AddressBean();
      address.setCity(request.getParameter("city"));
      address.setState(request.getParameter("state"));

      //Get the user's name to build the file path
      String name = request.getParameter("name");

      String appRelativePath =
            "/WEB-INF/classes/businessData/visitorAddresses/"
            + name
            + ".ser";

      String realPath = application.getRealPath(appRelativePath);

      //Serialize the object into the file
      FileOutputStream fos = new FileOutputStream(realPath);
      ObjectOutputStream oos = new ObjectOutputStream(fos);
      oos.writeObject(address);
      oos.close();

      message = "Successfully saved the bean as " + realPath;
   }
   catch(Exception e){
      message = "Error: Could not save the bean";
   }
%>
<html><body>
  <h3><%= message %></h3>
</body></html>
```

In this example, we first import the `AddressBean` class and the `java.io` package via the `import` attribute of the `page` directive. Then, we create an instance of the `AddressBean` class and set its `city` and `state` properties as specified in the `request` parameter. Next, using the value of the `request` parameter `name`, we build the path to a filename. Finally, using the `FileOutputStream` and `ObjectOutputStream` classes of the `java.io` package, we serialize the bean into the file.

We can access the above page via the following URL:

```
http://localhost:8080/chapter14/
   beanSaver.jsp?name=John&city=Topeka&state=Kansas
```

If all goes well, it will create a file named `John.ser` under the directory `/WEB-INF/classes/businessData/visitorAddresses` and will print the message with the filename on the browser window.

Thus, we can create as many serialized beans as we want with different sets of property values as long as the names of the bean files are different. We can then use these serialized beans in other components of the application.

In the following sections, we will explain the standard JSP actions that help us use JavaBeans in JSP pages effectively.

## 14.2 USING JAVABEANS WITH JSP ACTIONS

Table 14.1 summarizes the three standard actions for using JavaBeans in a JSP page.

**Table 14.1 Standard JSP actions for using JavaBeans**

| Action | Description |
|---|---|
| <jsp:useBean> | Declares the use of a JavaBean instance in a JSP page |
| <jsp:setProperty> | Sets new values to the bean's properties |
| <jsp:getProperty> | Gets the current value of the bean's properties |

In the sections that follow, we will describe each of these actions in details.

### 14.2.1 Declaring JavaBeans using <jsp:useBean>

The `jsp:useBean` action declares a variable in the JSP page and associates an instance of a JavaBean with it. The association is a two-step process. First, the action tries to find an existing instance of the bean. If an instance is not found, a new instance is created and associated with the declared variable. We can customize the behavior of this action using the five attributes shown in table 14.2.

**Table 14.2 <jsp:useBean> attributes**

| Attribute Name | Description | Examples |
|---|---|---|
| id | The name by which the bean is identified in the JSP page. | id="address" |
| scope | The scope of the bean's instance—*page*, *request*, *session*, or *application*. The default value is *page*. | scope="session" |
| class | The Java class of the bean. | class="BusinessAddressBean" |
| type | Specifies the type of the variable to be used to refer to the bean. | type="AddressBean" |
| beanName | The name of a serialized bean if we are loading from a file or the name of a class if we are creating a new instance. | beanName="business-Data.John" beanName="AddressBean" |

Of the five attributes in table 14.2:

- The `id` attribute is mandatory.
- The `scope` attribute is optional.
- The three attributes `class`, `type`, and `beanName` can only be used in one of the following four combinations, and at least one of these attributes or combinations of attributes must be present in a `useBean` action:
  - `class`
  - `type`
  - `class` and `type`
  - `beanName` and `type`

To make it easier to understand and remember the usage of these attributes, let's first examine their meaning in the following sections. Then, we will look at some examples that will demonstrate how we can use the different combinations.

### The id attribute

The `id` attribute uniquely identifies a particular instance of a bean. It is mandatory because its value is required by the other JSP actions, `<jsp:setProperty>` and `<jsp:getProperty>`, to identify the particular instance of the bean. In the generated Java servlet, the value of `id` is treated as a Java language variable; therefore, we can use this variable name in expressions and scriptlets in the JSP page. Note that since the value of the `id` attribute uniquely identifies a particular instance of a bean, we cannot use the same value for the `id` attribute in more than one `<jsp:useBean>` action within a single translation unit.

### The scope attribute

The `scope` attribute specifies the scope in which the bean instance resides. Like implicit objects, the existence and accessibility of JavaBeans from JSP pages are determined by the four JSP scopes: *page*, *request*, *session*, and *application*. This attribute is optional, and if not specified, the page scope is used by default.

We cannot use the session scope for a bean in a JSP page if we set the value of the `page` directive attribute `session` to `false`.

### The class attribute

The `class` attribute specifies the Java class of the bean instance. If the `<jsp:useBean>` action cannot find an existing bean in the specified scope, it creates a new instance of the bean's class as specified by the value of the `class` attribute using the class's publicly defined no-argument constructor. Therefore, the class specified by the `class` attribute must be a `public` non-abstract class and must have a `public` no-argument constructor. If the class is part of a package, then the fully qualified class name must be specified as `mypackage.MyClass`.

### The type attribute

The `type` attribute specifies the type of the variable declared by the `id` attribute. Since the declared variable refers to the actual bean instance at request time, its type must be the same as the bean's class, or a superclass of the bean's class, or an interface implemented by the bean's class. Again, if the class or the interface is part of a package, then the fully qualified name must be specified as `mypackage.MyClass`.

### The beanName attribute

The `beanName` attribute specifies the name of a bean as expected by the `instantiate()` method of the `java.beans.Beans` class. For this reason, `beanName` can refer either to a serialized bean or to the name of a class whose instance is to be created.

If the `beanName` attribute refers to a serialized bean, then the bean is loaded from the file that holds the bean. For example, if the attribute is specified as `beanName="businessData.visitorAddresses.John"`, the bean is loaded from the file `businessData/visitorAddresses/John.ser`. Note that we do not use the extension `.ser` in the value for the `beanName` attribute.

If the `beanName` attribute refers to a class, the class is loaded into the memory, an instance of the class is created, and the instance is used as a bean. For example, if the attribute is specified as `beanName="myBeans.AddressBean"`, then the class is loaded from the file `myBeans/AddressBean.class`. Note that we do not use the extension `.class` in the value for the `beanName` attribute.

Both `class` and `beanName` can be used to create new instances from the specified class. However, the advantage of using `beanName` over `class` is that the value of the `beanName` attribute can also be specified as a request-time attribute expression, so it can be decided at request time and need not be specified at translation time.

### Using the combinations of attributes

Now that we have introduced the five attributes of the `<jsp:useBean>` action, let's take a look at the way they are used in JSP pages.

#### *A simple useBean declaration*

This action uses three attributes—`id`, `class`, and `scope`—to declare the use of a JavaBean:

```
<jsp:useBean id="address" class="AddressBean" scope="session" />
```

This informs the JSP engine that the variable that refers to the bean should be named `address` and that the bean should be an instance of the `AddressBean` class. The `scope` attribute specifies the bean's scope as `session`.

At request time, if an object named `address` is already present in the session scope, it is assigned to the variable `address`. Otherwise, a new object of the class `Address` is created, which is then assigned to the variable and added to the session. It is equivalent to the following code:

```
AddressBean address = (AddressBean) session.getAttribute("address");
if (address == null)
{
   address = new AddressBean();
   session.setAttribute("address", address);
}
```

*The default scope*

The following declaration uses only two attributes—id and class:

```
<jsp:useBean id="address" class="AddressBean" />
```

This is similar to the previous example, except that we have not specified the scope attribute. In this case, the page scope is used by default. Thus, this bean is available only in the JSP page in which it is defined and only for the request for which it is created. It is equivalent to the following code:

```
AddressBean address = (AddressBean)
                      pageContext.getAttribute("address");

if (address == null)
{
   address = new AddressBean();
   pageContext.setAttribute("address", address);
}
```

*The typecast problem*

Suppose we have two classes, BusinessAddressBean and ResidentialAddressBean, both derived from a common base class, AddressBean. We have two JSP pages, both declaring a bean with the same id value, but each with a different class value, as shown below:

In residential.jsp:

```
<jsp:useBean id="address"
             scope="session"
             class="ResidentialAddressBean" />
```

In business.jsp:

```
<jsp:useBean id="address"
             scope="session"
             class="BusinessAddressBean" />
```

If the page residential.jsp is accessed first, its <jsp:useBean> action will add an object of the ResidentialAddressBean class into the session scope with the name address. Now, if the business.jsp page is accessed within the same session, the <jsp:useBean> action of business.jsp will locate the address object in the session scope and will try to cast it to the BusinessAddressBean class. Since the two classes do not have a class-subclass relationship, it will raise a java.lang.ClassCastException. Similarly, if the business.jsp page is accessed first, then the <jsp:useBean> action in the residential.jsp page will raise a java.lang.ClassCastException.

### *Using the class and type attributes*

The following declaration uses the `class` attribute as well as the `type` attribute:

```
<jsp:useBean id="address"
             type="AddressBean"
             class="BusinessAddressBean"
             scope="session"   />
```

In this action, the variable named `address` that refers to the bean is declared of type `AddressBean`. As we mentioned earlier, before creating an instance using the `class` attribute, the engine looks for an existing bean by the name `address` in the session scope. If an existing bean is found, then it is assigned to the `address` variable. Note that, in this case, since the `address` variable is declared of type `AddressBean`, the actual class of the existing instance may be `AddressBean` or any subclass of `AddressBean`. Therefore, the actual class of the existing instance need not be of type `BusinessAddressBean`.

However, if an existing instance is not found and a new instance has to be created, then the value of the `class` attribute specifies that the actual instance of the bean that is created must be of the `BusinessAddressBean` class. This `useBean` declaration is equivalent to the following code:

```
AddressBean address = (AddressBean)
                      session.getAttribute("address");

if (address == null)
{
   address = new BusinessAddressBean();
   session.setAttribute("address", address);
}
```

If we do not explicitly specify the `type` attribute, it is considered to be the same as `class`. The following two tags are equivalent:

```
<jsp:useBean id="address"
             class="BusinessAddressBean"
             scope="session"  />

<jsp:useBean id="address"
             type="BusinessAddressBean"
             class="BusinessAddressBean"
             scope="session" />
```

### *Using serialized beans*

In the following `useBean` declaration, the `beanName` attribute specifies the use of a serialized bean, `businessData.Address.John`:

```
<jsp:useBean id="address"
             type="AddressBean"
             beanName="businessData.Address.John"
             scope="session" />
```

In this case, the action first tries to locate an existing instance of the bean in the session scope. If the bean is not found, then the action creates an instance and initializes it with the serialized data present in the businessData/visitorAddresses/John.ser file. This method of locating and creating a bean is equivalent to the following code:

```
AddressBean address = (AddressBean)
            session.getAttribute("address");

if (address == null)
{
   ClassLoader classLoader = this.getClass().getClassLoader();

   address = (AddressBean)
             java.beans.Beans.instantiate(
                      classLoader,
                      "businessData.visitorAddresses.John");

   session.setAttribute("address", address);
}
```

In the following useBean declaration, the beanName attribute specifies the name of a class instead of a serialized bean:

```
<jsp:useBean id="address"
             type="AddressBean"
             beanName="AddressBean"
             scope="session" />
```

Here, the action first tries to locate an existing instance of the bean in the specified scope. If the bean is not found, the action creates an instance of the class specified by the beanName attribute. This action is equivalent to the following:

```
java.beans.Beans.instantiate(classLoader, "AddressBean");
```

Note that we do not specify the class attribute with the beanName attribute, because the class of the bean is determined either by the bean's serialized data itself or by the value of the beanName attribute. But the type attribute is required in order to determine the type of the declared variable. Thus, the value of the type attribute must be same as the class of the bean, a superclass of the bean, or an interface implemented by the bean.

### *Using a request-time attribute expression with the beanName attribute*

Since the value of the beanName attribute can also be specified as a request-time attribute expression, it can be useful in deciding the resource to be used as a bean at request time. Consider the following example:

```
<%@ page import="AddressBean, java.io.*" %>
<%
   String theBeanName = null;

   String name = request.getParameter("name");
```

```
    if (name!=null && !name.equals(""))
    {
       theBeanName = "businessData.visitorAddresses. " + name;
    }
    else
    {
        //Name not specified.

       if ("Business".equals(request.getParameter("newType")))
       {
          theBeanName = "BusinessAddressBean";
       }
       else
       {
          theBeanName = "ResidentialAddressBean";
       }
    }
%>

<jsp:useBean id="address"
             type="AddressBean"
             beanName="<%=theBeanName%>" />
```

If the value of the request parameter name is John (or Mary), then the action will try to locate a serialized file named businessData/visitorAddresses/John.ser (or businessData/visitorAddresses/Mary.ser) in the classpath.

If the name request parameter is not specified, the useBean action will try to create an instance of the BusinessAddressBean or ResidentialAddressBean class, depending on the newType request parameter.

Notice that the type attribute in the action specifies the type as AddressBean. This ensures that the code will work regardless of the actual type of the instance at runtime. For example, the serialized bean of John may be of the type BusinessAddressBean, while that of Mary may be of the type ResidentialAddressBean. This is true even for the new instances created based on the newType parameter. Also, the import directive imports only one class, AddressBean. Since the two derived classes are used only within String literals, we do not have to import them explicitly.

In either of the two cases, if the specified resource, serialized bean, or class is not found, then a java.lang.InstantiationException is thrown.

*Using the type attribute*

The following action uses the type attribute without the class or beanName attribute. This is useful if we want to locate an existing bean object but do not want to create a new instance even if an existing instance is not available:

```
<jsp:useBean id="address" type="AddressBean" scope="session" />
```

If the located object is not of type AddressBean, and if it is not a subtype of AddressBean, a ClassCastException is thrown. On the other hand, if the object could not be located in the specified scope at all, no new object is created and a java.lang.InstantiationException is thrown.

### Initializing bean properties

A limitation of using JavaBeans is that they are instantiated by the JSP engine using a no-argument constructor. Because of this limitation, we cannot initialize the beans by passing parameters to constructors. To overcome this, the JSP specification allows us to provide a body for the <jsp:useBean> tag, as shown by this example:

```
<jsp:useBean id="address" scope="session" class="AddressBean" >
   <%
      address.setStreet("123 Main St. ");
   %>
</jsp:useBean>
```

The above code conveys two things to the JSP engine:

1 If the bean named address is already present in the session scope, then the JSP engine should skip the body of the <jsp:useBean> tag and use the bean object as it is. In this case, the nested scriptlet code is not executed.

2 If the bean named address is not already present in the session scope, then the JSP engine should create a new instance of the bean class AddressBean, add the instance to the session scope with the name address, and execute the body of the <jsp:useBean> tag before continuing. In this case, the nested scriptlet code is executed, allowing us to set the street property to an initial value of "123 Main St." each time the bean is instantiated.

It is the second point that gives us the ability to initialize newly created beans. In this example, we have used a scriptlet to set the street property of the bean. However, a cleaner way to initialize the properties is to use the <jsp:setProperty> action. We will discuss this action in section 14.2.2.

In practice, in addition to initializing the bean, the body of the <jsp:useBean> tag can be used to write any valid JSP code (HTML, scriptlets, expressions, and so forth). Just remember that it is executed only when the <jsp:useBean> tag requires that a bean be created.

### Scope of the declared variable

When a <jsp:useBean> declaration is enclosed inside a Java programming language block using scriptlets and a pair of curly braces, the scope of the variable declared by the action also gets restricted to the enclosing block. Consider the following code, which will not execute correctly:

```
<%@ page language="java" import="AddressBean" %>
<html><body>

   <%
      if (true)
      {
   %>
         <jsp:useBean id="address" class="AddressBean" />
   <%
       }
   %>

<B>Some HTML here</B>

   <%
      if (true)
      {
         out.print("Zip: "+ address.getZip(); //error here
      }
%>

</body></html>
```

In this example, the <jsp:useBean> declaration is enclosed inside a block using a pair of curly braces. This marks the scope of the address variable declared by the action. When this variable is used within the out.print() method, which is in a different block, the compiler flags an error indicating that the address variable is not defined.

However, even though the address variable is out of scope because of the pair of curly braces, the address bean is still reachable in the page scope. We can access it by using the implicit variable pageContext:

```
<%
      if (true)
      {
         AddressBean address = (AddressBean)
                  pageContext.getAttribute("address");

         out.print("Zip: "+ address.getZip(); //ok
      }
%>
```

If the <jsp:useBean> action specifies a different scope, such as the request, session, or application scope, then we can use the corresponding implicit variable and the getAttribute() method to access the declared bean in that scope.

### 14.2.2 Mutating properties using <jsp:setProperty>

The <jsp:setProperty> action assigns new values to the bean's properties. It has four attributes, as described in table 14.3.

**Table 14.3 The <jsp:setProperty> attributes**

| Attribute Name | Description |
|---|---|
| name | The name by which the bean is identified in the JSP page |
| property | The name of the property of the bean, which is to be given a new value |
| value | The new value to be assigned to the property |
| param | The name of the parameter available in the HttpServletRequest, which is to be assigned as a new value to the property of the bean |

### *The name attribute*

The `name` attribute identifies a particular instance of an existing bean. Therefore, the `name` attribute is mandatory. The bean must have already been declared by a previous `<jsp:useBean>` action, and the value of the `name` attribute must be the same as the value of the `id` attribute specified by the `<jsp:useBean>` action.

### *The property attribute*

The `property` attribute specifies the property of the bean to be set. The JSP engine calls the set*XXX*() method on the bean based on the specified property. Thus, this attribute is also mandatory.

### *The value attribute*

The `value` attribute specifies the new value to be set for the bean's property. This attribute can also accept a request-time attribute expression.

### *The param attribute*

The `param` attribute specifies the name of the request parameter. If the request contains the specified parameter, then the value of that parameter is used to set the bean's property.

The `value` and `param` attributes are never used together and are both optional. If neither of the two is specified, it is equivalent to having the same value for both `param` and `property`, and the JSP engine searches for a request parameter with the name that is same as the `property` attribute.

Let's look at the following examples to understand how these attributes are used. For each of the examples, assume that we have already declared the use of the bean as follows:

```
<%@ page import="AddressBean" %>
<jsp:useBean id="address" class="AddressBean" />
```

Note that in all the examples below, we have shown the equivalent scriptlet code that we can write instead of the standard actions, `getProperty` and `setProperty`. The JSP engine, however, does not always translate these actions into such code. It uses reflection to check if the bean has the specified properties and then calls the appropriate methods.

*Using the value attribute*

These two actions instruct the JSP engine to use the bean named `address` and set its `city` and `state` properties to the values `"Albany"` and `"NY"`, respectively.

```
<jsp:setProperty name="address" property="city" value="Albany" />
<jsp:setProperty name="address" property="state" value="NY" />
```

They are equivalent to the scriptlet code:

```
<%
   address.setCity("Albany");
   address.setState("NY");
%>
```

The following example uses a request-time expression for the `value` attribute:

```
<% String theCity = getCityFromSomewhere();  %>

<jsp:setProperty name="address"
                 property="city"
                 value="<%=theCity%>" />
```

*Using the param attribute*

In this case, instead of specifying the values using the `value` attributes, we have specified the request parameter names using the `param` attributes:

```
<jsp:setProperty name="address" property="city"  param="myCity" />
<jsp:setProperty name="address" property="state" param="myState"/>
```

This instructs the engine to get the values of the `myCity` and `myState` request parameters and set them to the `"city"` and `"state"` properties, respectively. Thus, the above tags are equivalent to the following scriptlet code:

```
<%
   address.setCity(request.getParameter("myCity"));
   address.setState(request.getParameter("myState"));
%>
```

*Using the default param mechanism*

The technique of setting the properties shown in the previous example is used when the names of the request parameters do not match the names of the bean properties. If the names of the request parameters match the names of the bean properties, we do not need to specify either the `param` or the `value` attribute, as shown here:

```
<jsp:setProperty name="address" property="city"  />
<jsp:setProperty name="address" property="state" />
```

In this case, the bean properties are set using the corresponding values from the request parameters. The above tags are equivalent to:

```
<jsp:setProperty name="address" property="city"  param="city"  />
<jsp:setProperty name="address" property="state" param="state" />
```

These in turn are equivalent to the following scriptlet code:

```
<%
   address.setCity(request.getParameter("city"));
   address.setState(request.getParameter("state"));
%>
```

You might ask, “What if there is no such parameter in the request?” If the parameter is not present in the request, or if it has a value of "" (empty string), the `<jsp:setProperty>` action has no effect and the property retains its original value.

*Setting all the properties in one action*

The following is a shortcut to set all the properties of a bean in a single action:

```
<jsp:setProperty name="address" property="*"  />
```

Instead of setting each property of the address bean one by one, we can set all the properties to the respective values present in the request parameters using a value of "*" for the property attribute. The above tag is equivalent to the following scriptlet code:

```
<%
   address.setStreet(request.getParameter("street"));
   address.setCity(request.getParameter("city"));
   address.setState(request.getParameter("state"));
   address.setZip(request.getParameter("zip"));
%>
```

Obviously, the names of the request parameters must match the names of the properties. As we mentioned earlier, if there is no matching parameter in the request for a particular property, the value of that property remains unchanged. Also, in all the above cases where we use the param attribute, if the request parameter has multiple values, then only the first value is used.

### 14.2.3 Accessing properties using <jsp:getProperty>

The `<jsp:getProperty>` action is used to retrieve and print the values of the bean properties to the output stream. The syntax of this action is quite simple:

```
<jsp:getProperty name="beanInstanceName"
                 property="propertyName" />
```

It has only two attributes, name and property, which are both mandatory. As in the `<setProperty>` action, the name attribute specifies the name of the bean instance as declared by a previous `<jsp:useBean>` action and the property attribute specifies the property whose value is to be printed.

The following actions instruct the JSP engine to print out the values of the state and the zip properties of the address bean:

```
<jsp:getProperty name="address" property="state" />
<jsp:getProperty name="address" property="zip" />
```

They are equivalent to the scriptlet code:

```
<%
   out.print(address.getState());
   out.print(address.getZip());
%>
```

The code in listing 14.4 locates an instance of AddressBean in the session scope and prints out its properties in a tabular format.

**Listing 14.4 addressDisplay.jsp**

```
<%@ page import="AddressBean" %>
<jsp:useBean id="address" class="AddressBean" scope="session"/>
<html><body>
<table>
   <tr>
      <td>Street</td>
      <td><jsp:getProperty name="address" property="street"/></td>
   </tr>
   <tr>
      <td>City</td>
      <td><jsp:getProperty name="address" property="city"/></td>
   </tr>
   <tr>
      <td>State</td>
      <td><jsp:getProperty name="address" property="state"/></td>
   </tr>
   <tr>
      <td>Zip</td>
      <td><jsp:getProperty name="address" property="zip"/></td>
   </tr>
</table>
</body></html>
```

### *Quizlet*

**Q:** Consider the following code from a file named addressInput.jsp:

```
<%@ page import="AddressBean" %>
<jsp:useBean id="address" class="AddressBean" scope="request" />
<jsp:setProperty name="address" property="*"  />
<jsp:forward page="addressDisplay.jsp"   />
```

Can the addressDisplay.jsp file access the address bean declared in the addressInput.jsp file and print its values using <jsp:getProperty>?

**A:** Yes, the page `addressDisplay.jsp` file can print the values of the bean properties using `<jsp:getProperty>` provided it also contains a `<jsp:useBean>` declaration that is identical to the one shown in `addressInput.jsp` and that the declaration appears before the `<jsp:getProperty>` declaration.

## 14.3 JAVABEANS IN SERVLETS

We know that JSP pages are converted into servlets at translation time, which means that the beans that we use in our JSP pages are actually used from a servlet. This implies that we can use JavaBeans from servlets, too. This section discusses the ways in which we can share beans between JSP pages and servlets. The exam requires you to know the servlet code that is equivalent to using beans in the different scopes: request, session, and application.

Suppose a JSP page uses three beans, each with a different scope, request, session, and application, declared as:

```
<jsp:useBean id="address1" class="AddressBean" scope="request" />
<jsp:useBean id="address2" class="AddressBean" scope="session" />
<jsp:useBean id="address3" class="AddressBean" scope="application" />
```

Listing 14.5 shows how to achieve the same functionality in the servlet code.

**Listing 14.5 Using JavaBeans in servlets**

```
import javax.servlet.*;
import javax.servlet.http.*;
import AddressBean;

public class BeanTestServlet extends HttpServlet
{

   public void service(HttpServletRequest request,
                       HttpServletResponse response)
                         throws java.io.IOException,
                                ServletException
   {

      AddressBean address1 = null;
      AddressBean address2 = null;
      AddressBean address3 = null;

      //Get address1 using the parameter request
      synchronized(request)
      {
         address1 = (AddressBean)
                     request.getAttribute("address1");

         if (address1==null)
         {
            address1 = new AddressBean();
            request.setAttribute("address1", address1);
```

```
            }
        }

        //Get address2 using HttpSession
        HttpSession session = request.getSession();

        synchronized(session)
        {
            address2 = (AddressBean)
                        session.getAttribute("address2");

            if (address2==null)
            {
                address2 = new AddressBean();
                session.setAttribute("address2", address2);
            }
        }

        // Get address3 using ServletContext
        ServletContext servletContext = this.getServletContext();

        synchronized(servletContext)
        {
            address3 = (AddressBean)
                        servletContext.getAttribute("address3");

            if (address3==null)
            {
                address3 = new AddressBean();
                servletContext.setAttribute("address3", address3);
            }
        }
    }//service
}//class
```

This simple example demonstrated the use of the three container objects— `HttpServletRequest`, `HttpSession`, and `ServletContext`—that allow us to share JavaBeans between servlets and JSP pages in the three scopes—`request`, `session`, and `application`. An important point to remember here is that we have to synchronize access to the three container objects because other servlets and JSP pages may be accessing the same objects simultaneously in more than one thread. If we want to use serialized beans from a servlet, we can use the following method:

```
java.beans.Beans.instantiate(
            this.getClass().getClassLoader(),
            "businessData.John");
```

We will not discuss this method because you are not required to know its details for the exam. Please refer to the API documentation for more information.

*Quizlet*

**Q:** Consider the following servlet code. How will you achieve the same effect in a JSP page?

```
AddressBean address;
ServletContext servletContext =
                                    this.getServletContext ();

synchronized(servletContext)
{
    address = (AddressBean)
                servletContext.getAttribute("address");

    if (address==null)
    {
        address = new BusinessAddressBean();
        address.setCity("Greenwich");
        address.setState("Connecticut");
        servletContext.setAttribute("address", address);
    }
}
```

**A:** You should notice four points about this code. First, the code uses `ServletContext` to get and set the named object `address`. This means that it uses the `application` scope. Second, if the object is not found, the code creates a new instance of the class with the `new` keyword and does not use the `java.beans.Beans` mechanism. This means we should use the `class` attribute instead of the `beanName` attribute. Third, the declared variable `address` is of type `AddressBean`, while the new instance created is of type `BusinessAddressBean`. This means we must use the `type` attribute with `AddressBean` as its value but the `class` attribute must have `BusinessAddressBean` as its value. Fourth, it sets two properties, `city` and `state`, whenever the object address is not found in the application scope and a new instance is created. This means we must initialize the bean using `<jsp:setProperty>` tags within the opening and closing `<jsp:useBean>` tags. Thus, it is equivalent to the following JSP code:

```
<jsp:useBean id="address"
             type="AddressBean"
             class="BusinessAddressBean"
             scope="application" >
    <jsp:setProperty name="address" property="city"
                                    value="Greenwich" />
    <jsp:setProperty name="address" property="state"
                                    value="Connecticut" />
</jsp:useBean>
```

## 14.4 ACCESSING JAVABEANS FROM SCRIPTING ELEMENTS

As we have seen, one of the main advantages of using JavaBeans in JSP pages is that they help to keep the code clean when they are used with the standard actions. However, JavaBeans can also be used in scripting elements. Say, for instance, that a bean has some processing capabilities in addition to its normal function of holding a set of properties. The bean may retrieve values from the database as it is initialized; in such cases, it may have methods that are not, or cannot be, implemented as setters and getters. For example, suppose we have a `UserBean` that stores user profiles, and we need to set the login and password properties submitted by the user and then load the user information from the database. The following code snippet shows how to do this:

```
<%@ page import="UserBean" %>

<jsp:useBean id="user" class="UserBean" scope="session">

   <jsp:setProperty name="user" property="login"     />
   <jsp:setProperty name="user" property="password" />

   <%
      //The bean is used in a scriptlet here.
      //Load the user information from the database.
      user.initialize();
   %>

</jsp:useBean>
```

Here, we first create an instance of the `UserBean` using the `<jsp:useBean>` action. Then we set its login and password properties using the `<jsp:setProperty>` action. But after that we want to initialize it using its `initialize()` method. Since there is no standard JSP action that can be used to achieve this, we have to use a scriptlet[3] as shown above. Within the scriptlet, we can use the `user` variable to refer to the bean instance since the `<jsp:useBean>` action declares it automatically.

Another reason for using beans in scriptlets and expressions is that the standard action `<jsp:getProperty>` writes out the property value directly into the output stream. It cannot be used for writing conditional logic or for passing it as a value to an attribute. For example, suppose `UserBean` has a property, named `loginStatus`, which is set to `true` or `false` depending on whether the login attempt was successful. We cannot use the `<jsp:getProperty>` action in an `if` condition to test it. The following is not valid:

---

3 We can also define and use custom tags to work with beans instead of scriptlets. Custom tags are explained in chapters 15 and 16.

```
<%
   if (<jsp:getProperty                              //error here
                  name="user"
                  property="loginStatus" />)
   {
   }
%>
```

Similarly, if UserBean has a property named preferredHomePage that stores a URL to the user's preferred home page, then <jsp:getProperty> cannot be used to pass request-time values to the <jsp:forward> action. The following is not valid:

```
<jsp:forward  page="<jsp:getProperty                   //error here
                       name="user"
                       property="preferredHomePage" />"
/>
```

In such cases, we have to use the bean in a scriptlet and an expression in this way:

```
<% if (user.getLoginStatus()) { %>
   <jsp:forward page="<%=user.getPreferredHomePage()%>" />
   } else {
   <jsp:forward page="loginError.jsp" >
<% } %>
```

### *Quizlet*

**Q:** What is wrong with the following code?

```
<jsp:useBean id="address"
             class="AddressBean"
             beanName="businessData.visitorAddresses.John" />
```

**A:** We cannot use the attributes beanName and class in the same <jsp:useBean> declaration.

**Q:** What is wrong with the following code?

```
<jsp:setProperty name="address"
                 param="state"
                 value="FL" />
```

**A:** We have to use the mandatory attribute property to specify the property of the bean. param specifies the request parameter whose value is to be used. We cannot use the param and value attributes in the same <jsp:setProperty> action.

**Q:** How can we get all of the properties of a bean in a single JSP action?

**A:** We can set all of the properties of a bean in a single action:

```
<jsp:setProperty name="beanName" property="*" />
```

But there is no way to get all of the properties of a bean in a single action.

## 14.5 MORE ABOUT PROPERTIES IN JAVABEANS

In the AddressBean example we have used throughout this chapter, all of the properties have been of type java.lang.String. However, a bean can have any type of property, such as:

- Primitive data types (int, char, boolean, etc.)
- Wrapper object types (java.lang.Integer, java.lang.Character, java.lang.Boolean, etc.)
- Other object types
- Array types (int [], Integer [], etc.)

In this section, we will take a closer look at the way JSP pages manage these non-string data types in JavaBeans. To illustrate this in the short examples that follow, we will be using a UserBean class that stores three different types of data:

```
public class UserBean{

   private int visits;            //An example of primitive type
   private Boolean valid;         //An example of wrapper type
   private char[] permissions;    //An example of index type
   //appropriate setters and getters go here
}
```

The visits variable counts the number of visits by this user. The valid property indicates whether this bean instance has been initialized and is valid or not. Notice that the permissions property is an array of char. Such properties are called *indexed properties*. We will learn more about them in section 14.5.2.

### 14.5.1 Using non-string data type properties

Request parameters are always of the type String. Hence, if we are expecting a value that is of a type other than String, then we have to do the necessary conversions in scriptlets before using the value. For example, the following scriptlet converts an incoming request parameter from a String to an int and to an Integer:

```
<%
   String  numAsString  = null;
   int     numAsInt     = 0;
   Integer numAsInteger = null;
   try{
      numAsString  = request.getParameter("num");
      numAsInt     = Integer.parseInt(numAsString);
      numAsInteger = Integer.valueOf(numAsString);
   }
   catch(NumberFormatException nfe){
   }
%>
```

However, if a JavaBean has non-string properties, then the standard JSP actions `<jsp:setProperty>` and `<jsp:getProperty>` perform the necessary conversions automatically, as explained below.

### *Automatic type conversion in <jsp:setProperty>*

When we use literal values to set non-string properties in a bean using the `<jsp:getProperty>` action, the container performs the appropriate conversion from `String` to the property type. For example, in the following actions, the engine converts the literals `30` and `true` to `int` and `Boolean`, respectively:

```
<jsp:setProperty name="user" property="visits" value="30" />
<jsp:setProperty name="user" property="valid" value="true" />
```

These actions are equivalent to the following scriptlet:

```
<%
   user.setVisits(Integer.valueOf("30").intValue());
   user.setValid(Boolean.valueOf("true"));
%>
```

The type conversion occurs automatically even in the case of request parameters. For example, if we do not specify any value in the `<setProperty>` action as shown below but pass the values using a query string in the URL, the JSP engine automatically performs the conversions:

```
<jsp:setProperty name="user" property="visits" />
<jsp:setProperty name="user" property="valid" />
```

This will work without errors when we call the JSP page using the following URL:

```
http://localhost:8080/chapter14/test.jsp?visits=30&valid=true
```

However, if we use request-time attribute expressions in the `<jsp:setProperty>` action, then no such automatic conversion happens. Consider the following:

```
<%
   String anIntAsString = "30";
   String aBoolAsString = "true";
%>

<jsp:setProperty name="user"
                 property="visits"
                 value="<%=anIntAsString%>" />


<jsp:setProperty name="user"
                 property="valid"
                 value="<%=aBoolAsString%>" />
```

This example will not compile because we have passed a request-time attribute expression value that evaluates to a `String` in both actions instead of an `int` and a `Boolean`, respectively. To make it work, we have to explicitly convert the values from a

String to int for the visits property and from a String to a Boolean for the valid property, as follows:

```
<jsp:setProperty
   name="user"
   property="visits"
   value="<%=Integer.valueOf(anIntAsString).intValue()%>" />


<jsp:setProperty
   name="user"
   property="valid"
   value="<%=Boolean.valueOf(aBoolAsString) %>" />
```

#### *Automatic type conversion in <jsp:getProperty>*

When we use non-string data type properties of a bean in the <jsp:getProperty> action, the action takes care of the conversion from the given type to String. For example, the following actions use an int and a Boolean to print the values:

```
<jsp:getProperty name="user" property="visits" />
<jsp:getProperty name="user" property="valid" />
```

They are equivalent to the following scriptlet:

```
<%
   out.print(user.getVisits()); //getVisits() returns int
   out.print(user.getValid());  //getValid() returns Boolean
%>
```

### 14.5.2 Using indexed properties

Indexed properties can be used to associate multiple values to a single property. We can set an indexed property in one of two ways:

- We can set it automatically from the request parameter.
- We can set it using a request-time expression and explicitly pass an array of the desired type.

#### *Setting an indexed property from request parameters*

The following action sets the indexed property permissions to the values received in the request parameter:

```
<jsp:setProperty name="user" property="permissions" />
```

Suppose we access the JSP page with this URL:

```
http://localhost:8080/chapter14/test.jsp?
   permissions=XYZ&permissions=PQR&permissions=L
```

The engine will create an array of chars with the length of the array equal to the number of request parameter values for the parameter named permissions. Since the URL specifies three values for permissions as permissions=XYZ&permissions=PQR&permissions=L, it will create an array of three chars. Then, for each individual element of the char array, it will convert the parameter value from String to char using String.charAt(0). Thus, the <jsp:setProperty> action will use the values X, P, and L. It is equivalent to:

```
char charArr[] = new char[3];

charArr[0] = (request.getParameterValues("permissions"))[0].charAt(0);
// "XYZ".charAt(0)

charArr[1] = (request.getParameterValues("permissions"))[1].charAt(0);
// "PQR".charAt(0)

charArr[2] = (request.getParameterValues("permissions"))[2].charAt(0);
// "L".charAt(0)
```

### *Setting an indexed property using request-time attribute expressions*

The following action sets the indexed property permissions using a request-time attribute expression:

```
<%!
   char myPermissions[] = {'A', 'B', 'C' };
%>

<jsp:setProperty
             name="user"
             property="permissions"
             value="<%=myPermissions%>" />
```

This action is simple and will use the values A, B, and C.

The approaches we have discussed for setting indexed properties apply to all of the data types. Whether they are String, primitive data types, wrapper objects, or other objects, the parameter values are converted to their respective types for each individual element of the array.

### *Getting indexed properties*

When we get indexed properties from a bean using the <jsp:getProperty> action, it is equivalent to calling out.print(property-type []), where property-type is the data type of the indexed property. Consider the following example:

```
<jsp:getProperty name="user" property="permissions" />
```

This is equivalent to the following scriptlet:

```
<%
   out.print(user.getPermissions()); // getPermissions returns char[]
%>
```

However, since an array in Java is considered to be an Object, the `<jsp:getProperty>` action is not very useful for indexed properties; it simply prints the internal reference of the Object in memory. The output of the action might look something like this:

```
char[]@0xcafebabe
```

Thus, to print a particular property, or all the properties, we have to use scripting elements:

```
<%
   char[] permissions = user.getPermissions();
   if (permissions != null)
   {
      for (int p = 0; p<permissions.length; p++ )
      {
%>
   Permission is <%= permissions[p] %>  <br>
<%
      }
   }
%>
```

Here we are using scriptlets to get the permissions, and we are using an expression to print them.

## 14.6 SUMMARY

JSP technology is designed to take advantage of the power of JavaBeans components. In this chapter, we discussed JavaBeans from the JSP developer's point of view. We noted the value they provide by reducing the code in JSP pages, thereby increasing the readability of the pages. In JSP pages, any class can be used as a JavaBean as long as it has a public constructor with no arguments and private properties that are accessed by public getter and setter methods. The JSP specification provides the following standard actions to use JavaBeans in JSP pages: `<jsp:useBean>`, `<jsp:setProperty>`, and `<jsp:getProperty>`.

Servlets can also access JavaBeans objects. We reviewed the servlet code to access JavaBeans in the different scopes, and we compared it with the equivalent JSP code. At times, we need to access a JavaBean from scripting elements, so we discussed using beans with scriptlets and expressions and under what circumstances we would do that.

Not all properties of JavaBean are of the type `java.lang.String`. We reviewed the way that the `<jsp:setProperty>` and `<jsp:getProperty>` standard actions handle using non-string data types, and then we looked at indexed properties and how they are managed in JSP pages.

With the end of this chapter, you should be ready to answer exam questions about the way JavaBeans can be declared, initialized, and used in JSP pages as well as in servlets and how the standard actions—`<jsp:useBean>`, `<jsp:setProperty>`, and `<jsp:getProperty>`—help us to reduce the use of scriptlets and write cleaner JSP pages.

Now that we have a good understanding of the standard tags, in the next chapter we will explore the use of custom tags in JSP pages.

## 14.7 REVIEW QUESTIONS

1. Which of the following is a valid use of the `<jsp:useBean>` action? (Select one)

   a `<jsp:useBean id="address" class="AddressBean" />`

   b `<jsp:useBean name="address" class="AddressBean"/>`

   c `<jsp:useBean bean="address" class="AddressBean" />`

   d `<jsp:useBean beanName="address" class="AddressBean" />`

2. Which of the following is a valid way of getting a bean's property? (Select one)

   a `<jsp:useBean action="get" id="address" property="city" />`

   b `<jsp:getProperty id="address" property="city" />`

   c `<jsp:getProperty name="address" property="city" />`

   d `<jsp:getProperty bean="address" property="*" />`

3. Which of the following are valid uses of the `<jsp:useBean>` action? (Select two)

   a
   ```
   <jsp:useBean id="address" class="AddressBean" name="address"          />
   ```
   b
   ```
   <jsp:useBean id="address" class="AddressBean"
                             type="AddressBean"          />
   ```
   c
   ```
   <jsp:useBean id="address" beanName="AddressBean"
                             class="AddressBean"     />
   ```
   d
   ```
   <jsp:useBean id="address" beanName="AddressBean"
                             type="AddressBean"      />
   ```

4. Which of the following gets or sets the bean in the `ServletContext` container object? (Select one)

   a `<jsp:useBean id="address" class="AddressBean" />`

   b `<jsp:useBean id="address" class="AddressBean" scope="application" />`

   c `<jsp:useBean id="address" class="AddressBean" scope="servlet" />`

   d `<jsp:useBean id="address" class="AddressBean" scope="session" />`

   e None of the above

5. Consider the following code:

   ```
   <html><body>
   <jsp:useBean id="address" class="AddressBean" scope="session" />
   state = <jsp:getProperty name="address" property="state" />
   </body></html>
   ```

   Which of the following are equivalent to the third line above? (Select three)

   a `<% state = address.getState();                                  %>`

   b `<% out.write("state = "); out.print(address.getState()); %>`

   c `<% out.write("state = "); out.print(address.getstate()); %>`

   d `<% out.print("state = " + address.getState());             %>`

   e `state = <%= address.getState()                                  %>`

   f `state = <%! address.getState();                                 %>`

6. Which of the options locate the bean equivalent to the following action? (Select three)

```
<jsp:useBean id="address" class="AddressBean" scope="request" />
```

**a** `request.getAttribute("address");`

**b** `request.getParameter("address");`

**c** `getServletContext().getRequestAttribute("address");`

**d** `pageContext.getAttribute("address",PageContext.REQUEST_SCOPE);`

**e** `pageContext.getRequest().getAttribute("address");`

**f** `pageContext.getRequestAttribute("address");`

**g** `pageContext.getRequestParameter("address");`

7. Consider the following code for `address.jsp`:

```
<html><body>
<jsp:useBean id="address" class="AddressBean" />
<jsp:setProperty name="address" property="city" value="LosAngeles" />
<jsp:setProperty name="address" property="city" />
<jsp:getProperty name="address" property="city" />
</body></html>
```

What is the output if the above page is accessed via the URL

```
http://localhost:8080/chap14/address.jsp?city=Chicago&city=Miami
```

Assume that the `city` property is not an indexed property. (Select one)

**a** `LosAngeles`

**b** `Chicago`

**c** `Miami`

**d** `ChicagoMiami`

**e** `LosAngelesChicagoMaimi`

**f** It will not print anything because the value will be `null` or `""`.

8. Consider the following code:

```
<html><body>
<%{%>
<jsp:useBean id="address" class="AddressBean" scope="session" />
<%}%>
//1
</body></html>
```

Which of the following can be placed at line `//1` above to print the value of the `street` property? (Select one)

**a** `<jsp:getProperty name="address" property="street" />`

**b** `<% out.print(address.getStreet()); %>`

**c** `<%= address.getStreet() %>`

**d** `<%= ((AddressBean)session.getAttribute("address")).getStreet() %>`

**e** None of the above; the bean is nonexistent at this point.

9. Consider the following code:

```
<html><body>

<%{%>
<jsp:useBean id="address" class="AddressBean" scope="session" />
<%}%>

<jsp:useBean id="address" class="AddressBean" scope="session" />
<jsp:getProperty name="address" property="street" />

</body></html>
```

Which of the following is true about the above code? (Select one)

**a** It will give translation-time errors.
**b** It will give compile-time errors.
**c** It may throw runtime exceptions.
**d** It will print the value of the `street` property.

10. Consider the following servlet code:

```
//...

public void service (HttpServletRequest request,
                     HttpServletResponse response)
        throws IOException, ServletException
    {
    //1
    }
```

Which of the following can be used at `//1` to retrieve a JavaBean named `address` present in the application scope? (Select one)

**a** `getServletContext().getAttribute("address");`
**b** `application.getAttribute("address");`
**c** `request.getAttribute("address",APPLICATION_SCOPE);`
**d** `pageContext.getAttribute("address",APPLICATION_SCOPE);`

11. Consider the following code, contained in a file called `this.jsp`:

```
<html><body>
<jsp:useBean id="address" class="AddressBean" />
<jsp:setProperty name="address" property="*"  />
<jsp:include page="that.jsp"   />
</body></html>
```

Which of the following is true about the `AddressBean` instance declared in this code? (Select one)

**a** The bean instance will not be available in `that.jsp`.
**b** The bean instance may or may not be available in `that.jsp`, depending on the threading model implemented by `that.jsp`.

**c** The bean instance will be available in `that.jsp`, and the `that.jsp` page can print the values of the beans properties using `<jsp:getProperty />`.

**d** The bean instance will be available in `that.jsp` and the `that.jsp` page can print the values of the bean's properties using `<jsp:getProperty />` only if `that.jsp` also contains a `<jsp:useBean/>` declaration identical to the one in `this.jsp` and before using `<jsp:getProperty/>`.

12. Consider the following code contained in a file named `this.jsp` (the same as above, except the fourth line):

```
<html><body>
<jsp:useBean id="address" class="AddressBean" />
<jsp:setProperty name="address" property="*"  />
<%@ include file="that.jsp"   %>
</body></html>
```

Which of the following is true about the `AddressBean` instance declared in the above code? (Select one)

**a** The bean instance will not be available in `that.jsp`.

**b** The bean instance may or may not be available in `that.jsp`, depending on the threading model implemented by `that.jsp`.

**c** The bean instance will be available in `that.jsp`, and the `that.jsp` page can print the values of the bean's properties using `<jsp:getProperty />`.

**d** The bean instance will be available in `that.jsp`, and the `that.jsp` page can print the values of the bean's properties using `<jsp:getProperty />` only if `that.jsp` also contains a `<jsp:useBean/>` declaration identical to the one in `this.jsp` and before using `<jsp:getProperty/>`.

C H A P T E R 1 5

# Using custom tags



## EXAM OBJECTIVES

**11.1** Identify properly formatted tag library declarations in the Web application deployment descriptor. (Section 15.2)

**11.2** Identify properly formatted taglib directives in a JSP page. (Section 15.2)

**11.3** Given a custom tag library, identify properly formatted custom tag usage in a JSP page. Uses include:

- An empty custom tag
- A custom tag with attributes
- A custom tag that surrounds other JSP code
- Nested custom tags

(Section 15.3)

## *INTRODUCTION*

As we saw in chapter 13, "Reusable web components" and chapter 14, "Using JavaBeans," the JSP specification provides standard XML type tags, called JSP actions, that instruct the JSP engine to take some action in a predefined manner.

Although very useful, the standard tags provide just a basic set of features. As your web application grows, you will find that these standard JSP tags are somewhat restrictive and don't provide support for the presentation logic that is required for formatting dynamic data. For instance, you may be forced to write too much of your presentation code in JSP scriptlets. Moreover, you may have to copy and paste those presentation scriptlets onto multiple pages of the application. At this point, you need a way to put that presentation logic in one place and reuse it wherever it is required. The JSP technology provides a feature that allows you to do just that. You can create new tags and define their behavior according to your needs. These user-defined tags are called *custom tags*.

# 15.1 GETTING STARTED

Custom tags do not introduce any new syntax. They are similar to the standard JSP actions and follow the same XML syntax format. In that sense, it may be more accurate to refer to them as custom *actions* rather than *tags*. Custom tags allow us to move the presentation logic outside the JSP pages into independent Java classes, thereby centralizing the implementation of the presentation logic and increasing maintainability. By using custom tags in JSP pages instead of scriptlets, we avoid duplicating the presentation logic; removing the scriptlets also makes the pages less cluttered and easier to read.

## 15.1.1 New terms

New concepts bring new terms. So let's begin our foray into the world of custom tags by becoming familiar with the terminology.

### *Tag handler*

The JSP specification defines a *tag handler* as a runtime, container-managed object that evaluates custom actions during the execution of a JSP page.

In practical terms, a tag handler is a Java class that implements one of the tag interfaces—`Tag`, `IterationTag`, or `BodyTag`—of the package `javax.servlet.jsp.tagext`. We will learn about these interfaces in chapter 16, "Developing custom tag libraries." For now, just remember that while executing a JSP file, if the JSP engine encounters a custom tag, it calls the methods on the tag's handler class to do the actual work.

### *Tag library*

The JSP specification defines a *tag library* as a collection of actions that encapsulate some functionality to be used from within a JSP page.

Typically, we would not create just one tag to fulfill a particular requirement. Rather, we would design and develop a set of custom tags that work together and help solve a recurring requirement. Such a set of custom tags is called a tag library.

#### *Tag library descriptor*

When we use custom tags in a JSP page, the JSP engine needs to know the tag handler classes for these tags, in which tag library they are located, and how are they used. This meta-information is stored in a file called the *tag library descriptor* (TLD).

#### *Types of URIs*

In a JSP page, we reference the tag libraries through URIs. Table 15.1 describes the three types of URIs that are used in a JSP page.

**Table 15.1 Types of URIs for referring to a tag library**

| Type | Description | Examples |
|---|---|---|
| Absolute URI | A URI that has a protocol, a hostname, and optionally a port number. | http://localhost:8080/taglibs<br>http://www.manning.com/taglibs |
| Root Relative URI | A URI that starts with a / and that does not have a protocol, a hostname, or a port number. It is interpreted as relative to the document root of the web application. | /helloLib<br>/taglib1/helloLib |
| Non-root Relative URI | A URI that does not start with a / and that does not have a protocol, a hostname, or a port number. It is interpreted as relative to either the current JSP page or the WEB-INF, depending on where it is used. | HelloLib<br>taglib2/helloLib |

### 15.1.2 Understanding tag libraries

You do not need to create your own tag libraries to handle many common functions. A variety of custom tag libraries are available on the Internet that you can use in our JSP pages. For example, the libraries provided by the Jakarta Apache Project at `http://jakarta.apache.org/taglibs` contain several frequently used features, such as text manipulation or date manipulation. Sun Microsystems is also developing a group of standard tag libraries for Java (JSTL); for more information, visit the Sun site at `http://java.sun.com/products/jsp/taglibraries.html`.

To use an existing tag library, you need to know two things:

- How to inform the JSP engine of the location of the TLD file of a tag library
- How to use the custom tags provided by the tag library in JSP pages

The exam objectives covered in this chapter focus on these two points.

However, if none of the existing libraries suits your needs and if you plan to implement a custom tag library on your own, you need to know two more things:

- How to implement the tag handlers for your tag library
- How to describe your tag library in a TLD file

We will discuss these two topics in the next chapter, where we will develop a simple tag library.

## 15.2 INFORMING THE JSP ENGINE ABOUT A CUSTOM TAG LIBRARY

In the JSP syntax, we can import a new tag library into a JSP page using a `taglib` directive:

```
<%@ taglib prefix="test" uri="sampleLib.tld" %>
```

If we are using the XML syntax, the library information in the JSP document is included in the `<jsp:root>` element:

```
<jsp:root
   xmlns:jsp="http://java.sun.com/JSP/Page"
   xmlns:test="sampleLib.tld"
   version="1.2" >

   ...JSP PAGE...

</jsp:root>
```

The above declarations inform the engine that the page uses custom tags with the prefix `test` and that these tags are described in the file `sampleLib.tld`. In this example, the value of the URI attribute provides a non-root, or page-relative path, to the TLD file. The JSP engine searches for the file in the same directory as the JSP page.

Though keeping all the JSP pages and the TLD files in the same directory is the simplest way to use a `taglib` directive, it has two major drawbacks: security and flexibility.

Let's look at security first. Suppose the URL of the JSP page is `http://www.someserver.com/sample.jsp`. A visitor can view the contents of your library without much effort by typing the URL `http://www.someserver.com/sampleLib.tld`.

Of course, we can configure the web server to restrict access to all the TLD files, or better yet, we can put the TLD files under the `/WEB-INF` directory and use the path `/WEB-INF/sampleLib.tld` to access them. However, we would still have the problem of flexibility. If we wanted to switch to a newer version of the library, say `sampleLib_2.tld`, then we would have to manually modify all the JSP pages that are affected by this change. Further, third-party custom tag libraries are packaged and shipped as JAR files. How would we indicate the location of a TLD file in such cases?

To avoid such problems, JSP provides a cleaner solution for indicating the use of tag libraries. The JSP container maintains a map between the URIs that we use in taglib directives and the actual physical location of the TLD files in the file system. With this approach, instead of using a page-relative path, we use an absolute URI path:

```
<%@ taglib prefix="test"
           uri="http://www.someserver.com/sampleLib" %>
```

When the JSP engine reads the above URI, it refers to its internal map to find the corresponding TLD file location.

Thus, by creating a level of indirection, this approach solves both the security and the flexibility problems. The actual TLD file can reside in the WEB-INF directory or even in a JAR file, hidden away from the visitors. If a newer version is released, all we have to do is update the mapping between the URI and the actual path.

**NOTE** The use of an absolute URL does not mean that the JSP engine will actually download the TLD file or the tag library classes from the specified URL. Thus, in the above example, the JSP engine will not try to locate the library at http://www.someserver.com/sampleLib. Consider the URI as just a name that is mapped to the actual location of the TLD file somewhere on the local machine.

In the following sections, we will discuss the possible locations for TLD files, how the mappings between the URIs and TLD locations are created, and how the JSP engine interprets the different values of URIs specified in the taglib directives.

### 15.2.1 Location of a TLD file

A TLD file can reside in one of two types of places. First, it can be placed in any directory of a web application; for example:

```
<docroot>/sampleLib.tld
<docroot>/myLibs/sampleLib.tld
<docroot>/WEB-INF/sampleLib.tld
<docroot>/WEB-INF/myLibs/sampleLib.tld
```

We usually keep the TLD file in a directory, instead of a JAR file, during the development of a tag library. This speeds up the development and testing cycles, during which we design new tags, add new handler classes, and modify the TLD file frequently. However, once development is finished, we package the handler classes and the TLD file of the library as a JAR file. This file is then deployed under the <doc-root>/web-inf/lib directory along with other jarred classes, such as servlets and third-party tools.

The JSP specification mandates that, when deployed in a JAR file, a TLD file be placed either directly under or inside a subdirectory of the META-INF directory. In addition, the name of the TLD file must be taglib.tld. Thus, a JAR file containing a packaged tag library is typically structured like this:

```
myPackage/myTagHandler1.class
myPackage/myTagHandler2.class
myPackage/myTagHandler3.class
META-INF/taglib.tld
```

The JSP container will recognize either of these two locations, a directory or a JAR, as a path to a TLD file. This path is called the *TLD resource path*.

Let's return for a moment to our discussion on the mapping between a URI and the location of a TLD file. We can now see that this mapping is actually between a URI and a TLD resource path, where the TLD resource path is either the path to the TLD file or to the JAR file containing the TLD file. This mapping is referred to as the *taglib map*.

### 15.2.2 Associating URIs with TLD file locations

The JSP container populates the taglib map in three ways:

- First, the container reads the user-defined mapping entries present in the deployment descriptor. This is called *explicit mapping*. We will learn how to add new entries to the deployment descriptor in the next section.
- Then, the container reads all the `taglib.tld` files present in the packaged JARs. For each jarred TLD file that contains information about its own URI, the JSP container automatically creates a mapping between the specified URI and the current location of the JAR file. This is called *implicit mapping*. We will learn how to add the URI information to a TLD file in the next chapter, where we will create a custom tag library.
- Finally, the JSP container adds entries for the URIs that are known to the container by default. These URIs are called *well-known URIs*. The `<jsp:root>` element of a JSP document contains an example of a well-known URI:

```
http://java.sun.com/JSP/Page
```

The container itself provides the implementation for all the tags in this library. This is actually another form of implicit mapping.

### 15.2.3 Understanding explicit mapping

We use the `<taglib>` element of the deployment descriptor file, `web.xml`, to associate user-defined URIs with TLD resource paths. This is the syntax:

```
<!ELEMENT taglib (taglib-uri, taglib-location)>
```

Each `<taglib>` element associates one URI with one location. It contains two subelements:

- `<taglib-uri>`. This is the user-defined URI. Its value can be an absolute URI, a root-relative URI, or a non-root relative URI.
- `<taglib-location>`. This is the TLD resource path. Its value can be either a root-relative URI or a non-root relative URI, and it must point to a valid TLD resource path.

Listing 15.1 illustrates the use of the `<taglib>` element in the deployment descriptor.

**Listing 15.1 web.xml**

```
<?xml version="1.0" encoding="ISO-8859-1"?>

<!DOCTYPE web-app
  PUBLIC "-//Sun Microsystems, Inc.//DTD Web Application 2.3//EN"
  "http://java.sun.com/dtd/web-app_2_3.dtd">

<web-app>

  <!-- other elements ... -->

  <!-- Taglib 1 -->

  <taglib>
    <taglib-uri>
      http://www.manning.com/studyKit
    </taglib-uri>
    <taglib-location>
      /myLibs/studyKit.tld
    </taglib-location>
  </taglib>


  <!-- Taglib 2 -->

  <taglib>
    <taglib-uri>
      http://www.manning.com/sampleLib
    </taglib-uri>
    <taglib-location>
      yourLibs/sample.jar
    </taglib-location>
  </taglib>

</web-app>
```

In the above code, there are two `<taglib>` elements. The first `<taglib>` element associates the URI `http://www.manning.com/studyKit` with the TLD resource path `/myLibs/studyKit.tld`, while the second `<taglib>` element associates the URI `http://www.manning.com/sampleLib` with the TLD resource path `yourLibs/sample.jar`.

### 15.2.4 Resolving URIs to TLD file locations

Once the taglib mapping between the URIs and the TLD resource paths has been created, the JSP pages can refer to these URIs using the `taglib` directives:

```
<%@ taglib prefix="study" uri="http://www.manning.com/studyKit" %>
<%@ taglib prefix="sample" uri="http://www.manning.com/sampleLib" %>
```

When the JSP engine parses a JSP file and encounters a `taglib` directive, it checks its taglib map to see if a mapping exists for the `uri` attribute of the `taglib` directive:

- If the value of the `uri` attribute matches any of the `<taglib-uri>` entries, the engine uses the value of the corresponding `<taglib-location>` to locate the actual TLD file.
  - If the `<taglib-location>` value is a root-relative URI (that is, it starts with a /), the JSP engine assumes the location to be relative to the web application's document root directory. Thus, the location for the URI `http://www.manning.com/studyKit` in listing 15.1 will resolve to the TLD file `<doc-root>/myLibs/studyKit.tld`.
  - If the `<taglib-location>` value is a non-root relative URI (that is, it starts without a /), the JSP engine prepends `/WEB-INF/` to the URI and assumes the location to be relative to the web application's document root directory. Thus, the location for the URI `http://www.manning.com/sample.jar` in listing 15.1 will resolve to the TLD file `<doc-root>/WEB-INF/yourLibs/studyKit.tld`.
- If the value of the `uri` attribute of the `taglib` directive does not match any of the `<taglib-uri>` entries, then the following three possibilities arise:
  - If the specified `uri` attribute is an absolute URI, then it is an error and is reported at translation time.
  - If the specified `uri` attribute is a root-relative URI, it is assumed to be relative to the web application's document root directory.
  - If the specified `uri` attribute is a non-root-relative URI, it is assumed to be relative to the current JSP page. Thus, if the JSP file `<doc-root>/jsp/test.jsp` contains the directive `<%@ taglib prefix="test" uri="sample.tld" %>`, the engine will expect to find the `sample.tld` file at `<doc-root>/jsp/sample.tld`.

### *Quizlet*

**Q:** Consider the following `taglib` directive appearing in a JSP file. What will happen if the URI used in this directive is not mapped to a TLD file in the deployment descriptor?

```
<%@ taglib uri="www.manning.com/hello.tld" prefix="a" %>
```

**A:** The URI `www.manning.com/hello.tld` does not contain a protocol; therefore, it is not an absolute URI. It does not start with a /, so it is not a root-relative URI either. It is a page-relative URI. After failing to find an entry in the map, the engine will search for the file `hello.tld` at the location relative to the current page. Suppose the JSP page is at location

```
C:\tomcat\webapps\chapter15\test.jsp
```

The engine will look for the file at

```
C:\tomcat\webapps\chapter15\www.manning.com\hello.tld
```

If it is unable to find `hello.tld` at this location either, it will flag an error.

**Q:** What is wrong with the following `taglib` declaration?

```
<taglib>
   <taglib-uri>http://myLibs.com</taglib-uri>
   <taglib-location>http://yourLibs.com</taglib-location>
</taglib>
```

**A:** The value of `<taglib-location>` cannot be an absolute URI.

### 15.2.5 Understanding the prefix

As we discussed in chapter 11, "The JSP technology model—the basics," each standard JSP action tag has a tag name that is made up of two parts, a prefix and an action, separated by a colon. For example, in `<jsp:include>` and `<jsp:forward>`, the prefix is `jsp`, while the actions are `include` and `forward`, respectively. Custom tags use the same syntax:

```
<myPrefix:myCustomAction>
```

Since we can use multiple libraries in one JSP page, the prefix differentiates between tags that belong to different libraries. For example:

```
<%@ taglib prefix="compA" uri="mathLibFromCompanyA" %>
<%@ taglib prefix="compB" uri="mathLibFromCompanyB" %>

<!-- Uses a tag from Company A -->
<compA:random/>

<!-- Uses a tag from Company B-->
<compB:random/>
```

In the above code snippet, the prefixes `compA` and `compB` enable the JSP engine to identify the libraries to which the tags belong.

In order to avoid conflicts between the user-defined tags and the standard tags provided by the JSP implementations, there are certain restrictions on the value of the `prefix` attribute. For example, we cannot use `jsp` as a prefix for custom tag libraries because it is already used as a prefix for standard actions, such as `<jsp:include>`, `<jsp:forward>`, and `<jsp:useBean>`.

In addition to `jsp`, the specification has reserved the following prefix values, which means we cannot use them in a `taglib` directive: `jspx`, `java`, `javax`, `servlet`, `sun`, and `sunw`. Thus, the following directive is invalid:

```
<%@ taglib prefix="sun" uri="myLib" %>
```

## 15.3 USING CUSTOM TAGS IN JSP PAGES

In section 15.2, we learned how to import custom tags using a `taglib` directive. Now, we will see how to use different types of custom tags in a JSP page. These types include:

- Empty tags
- Tags with attributes

- Tags with JSP code
- Tags with nested tags

To illustrate the usage of these tag types, we have used the tags of a simple tag library in the following sections. We will learn how to build these tags in the next chapter.

### 15.3.1 Empty tags

Empty tags do not have any body content. They are written in two ways. They can consist of a pair of opening and closing tags without anything in between:

```
<prefix:tagName></prefix:tagName>
```

They can also be formatted as a single self-tag:

```
<prefix:tagName />
```

The self-tag has a forward slash / at the end of the tag.

In listing 15.2, we have an empty tag named `required` that embeds the character `*` in the output HTML. This tag is useful while accepting `<FORM>` input from users.

**Listing 15.2 Usage of an empty tag**

```
<%@ taglib uri="sampleLib.tld" prefix="test" %>

<html>
Please enter your address and click submit.<br>
The fields marked with a <test:required /> are mandatory.

<form action="validateAddress.jsp">
<table>

<tr>
      <td><test:required /> Street 1</td>
      <td><input TYPE='text' NAME='street1'></td>
</tr>

<tr>
      <td>           Street 2</td>
      <td><input TYPE='text' NAME='street2'></td>
</tr>

<tr>
      <td>           Street 3</td>
      <td><input TYPE='text' NAME='street3'></td>
</tr>

<tr>
      <td><test:required/> City    </td>
      <td><input TYPE='text' NAME='city'></td>
</tr>

<tr>
      <td><test:required/> State   </td>
      <td><input TYPE='text' NAME='state'></td>
```

```
    </tr>

    <tr>
          <td><test:required /> Zip      </td>
          <td><input TYPE='text' NAME='zip'></td>
    </tr>

    </table>

    <input TYPE='submit' >

    </form>
    </html>
```

Figure 15.1 shows the output of listing 15.2 in a browser.

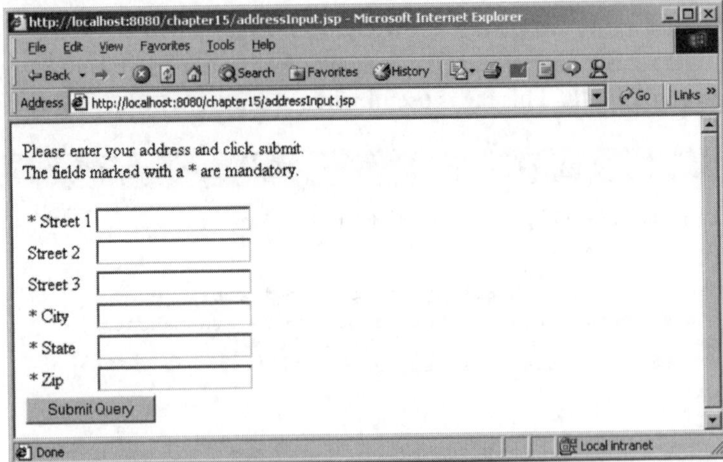


**Figure 15.1 A JSP page using the *required* tag.**

Although simple, this tag is quite useful. The page author does not have to scatter `<font color='#FF0000'>*</font>` everywhere in the JSP page. In addition, if you decide later on that you want to use a different color for the `*` or you want to use an image instead of `*`, you can just modify the tag handler class and the change will be reflected application-wide without modifying any JSP page.

### 15.3.2 Tags with attributes

Just like standard tags, custom tags can have attributes. In our sample library, we have a tag named `greet` that prints the greeting `Hello` in the output. It accepts an attribute named `user` to print the user's name:

```
<html><body>

   <%@ taglib prefix="test" uri="sampleLib.tld" %>

   <h3><test:greet user="john" /></h3>

</body></html>
```

When used this way, it will print the user's name in the greeting as `Hello john!` in the browser.

In the same way that standard tags may have attributes that are mandatory, attributes for custom tags also may be defined as mandatory. If we do not specify the mandatory attributes, the JSP engine flags an error at translation time. On the other hand, if we do not specify the non-mandatory attributes, the tag handler uses the default values. The default values depend on the implementation of the tag handler. The attribute values can be either constants or JSP expressions:

```
<prefix:tagName attrib1="fixedValue"
                attrib2="<%=someJSPExpresson%>"
                attrib3= ...
/>
```

The expressions are evaluated at request time and passed to the corresponding tag handler. Instead of passing a string literal `john`, we can use a JSP expression to make it more flexible:

```
<html><body>
   <%@ taglib prefix="test" uri="sampleLib.tld" %>

   <h3>
   <test:greet
      name='<%=request.getParameter("username")%>'
   />
   </h3>
</body></html>
```

Thus, attributes to a tag are like parameters to a method call. The tag designer can customize the behavior of a tag by specifying attributes and values. However, we cannot pass in any arbitrary attribute-value pairs. As we will see in the next chapter, the tag library designer defines the following in a TLD file:

- A set of valid attributes names
- Whether or not an attribute is mandatory
- The data type of the values
- Whether the value of an attribute has to be specified at translation time using a string literal or if it can be specified as a request-time expression

### 15.3.3 Tags with JSP code

A tag may contain JSP code enclosed within the opening and closing tags. This code is called the *body content* of the tag. It can be any valid JSP code, which means it can be text, HTML, a scriptlet, an expression, and so forth. Our sample library has a tag named `if` that accepts a Boolean attribute. It either includes the body in the output or skips the body altogether based on the value of the attribute passed:

```
<html><body>
   <%@ taglib uri="sampletaglib.tld" prefix="test" %>

   <test:if condition="true">
     Anything that is to be printed when the condition is true goes here.
      Name is: <%=request.getParameter("name")%>
   </test:if>

</body></html>
```

In the above code, the `<test:if>` tag is passed a value of `true` for the attribute `condition`. It executes the body of the tag, and the contents are included in the output. If we set the value of the `condition` attribute to `false`, it will skip the body and the contents will not be included in the output.

### 15.3.4 Tags with nested custom tags

Non-empty tags can also include other custom tags in their body. These types of tags are called *nested tags*. In our sample library, we have three tags—`<switch>`, `<case>`, and `<default>`—that help us write `switch-case` statements in JSP pages:

```
<html><body>
   <%@ taglib uri="sampleLib.tld" prefix="test" %>

   <test:switch conditionValue='<%=request.getParameter("action")%>' >

      <test:case caseValue="sayHello">
         Hello!
      </test:case>

      <test:case caseValue="sayGoodBye" >
         Good Bye!!
      </test:case>

      <test:default>
         I am Dumb!!!
      </test:default>

   </test:switch>

</body></html>
```

In the above code, the `<case>` and `<default>` tags are nested inside the `<switch>` tag. Depending on the value of the `conditionValue` attribute, the body of an appropriate case tag executes.

Note that the opening and closing tags of a nested tag and its enclosing tag cannot overlap. The following is syntactically incorrect:

```
<test:tag1>
   <test:tag2>
</test:tag1>
   </test:tag2>
```

## 15.4 SUMMARY

Custom tags are action elements on JSP pages that are mapped to tag handler classes in a tag library. Tag libraries allow us to use independent Java classes to manage the presentation logic of the JSP pages, thereby reducing the use of scriptlets and leveraging existing code to accelerate development time. In this chapter, we learned the basic terms and usage of tag libraries, including how to explicitly associate a URI with a TLD file using the `<taglib>` element in the deployment descriptor.

We discussed the use of the `taglib` directive to import custom tags into a JSP page. Then we examined several different types of custom tags that we use in JSP pages: empty tags, tags with attributes, tags with a body, and tags that contain nested tags.

You should now be able to answer exam questions about the declaration of a tag library in the deployment descriptor, the various ways of importing a custom tag library for use in JSP pages, and the use of different types of custom tags in JSP pages.

In the next chapter, we will learn more about the TLD file and how to implement our own custom tags.

## 15.5 REVIEW QUESTIONS

1. Which of the following elements are required for a valid `<taglib>` element in `web.xml`? (Select two)

   **a** `uri`

   **b** `taglib-uri`

   **c** `tagliburi`

   **d** `tag-uri`

   **e** `location`

   **f** `taglib-location`

   **g** `tag-location`

   **h** `tagliblocation`

2. Which of the following `web.xml` snippets correctly defines the use of a tag library? (Select one)

   **a**
   ```
   <taglib>
       <uri>http://www.abc.com/sample.tld</uri>
       <location>/WEB-INF/sample.tld</location>
   </taglib>
   ```

   **b**
   ```
   <tag-lib>
       <taglib-uri>http://www.abc.com/sample.tld</taglib-uri>
       <taglib-location>/WEB-INF/sample.tld</taglib-location>
   </tag-lib>
   ```

   **c**
   ```
   <taglib>
       <taglib-uri>http://www.abc.com/sample.tld</taglib-uri>
       <taglib-location>/WEB-INF/sample.tld</taglib-location>
   </taglib>
   ```

**d**
```
<tag-lib>
    <taglib>http://www.abc.com/sample.tld</taglib-uri>
    <taglib>/WEB-INF/sample.tld</taglib-location>
</tag-lib>
```

3. Which of the following is a valid `taglib` directive? (Select one)

**a** `<% taglib uri="/stats" prefix="stats" %>`

**b** `<%@ taglib uri="/stats" prefix="stats" %>`

**c** `<%! taglib uri="/stats" prefix="stats" %>`

**d** `<%@ taglib name="/stats" prefix="stats" %>`

**e** `<%@ taglib name="/stats" value="stats" %>`

4. Which of the following is a valid `taglib` directive? (Select one)

**a** `<%@ taglib prefix="java" uri="sunlib"%>`

**b** `<%@ taglib prefix="jspx" uri="sunlib"%>`

**c** `<%@ taglib prefix="jsp" uri="sunlib"%>`

**d** `<%@ taglib prefix="servlet" uri="sunlib"%>`

**e** `<%@ taglib prefix="sunw" uri="sunlib"%>`

**f** `<%@ taglib prefix="suned" uri="sunlib"%>`

5. Consider the following `<taglib>` element, which appears in a deployment descriptor of a web application:

```
<taglib>
   <taglib-uri>/accounting</taglib-uri>
   <taglib-location>/WEB-INF/tlds/SmartAccount.tld</taglib-location>
</taglib>
```

Which of the following correctly specifies the use of the above tag library in a JSP page? (Select one)

**a** `<%@ taglib uri="/accounting" prefix="acc"%>`

**b** `<%@ taglib uri="/acc" prefix="/accounting"%>`

**c** `<%@ taglib name="/accounting" prefix="acc"%>`

**d** `<%@ taglib library="/accounting" prefix="acc"%>`

**e** `<%@ taglib name="/acc" prefix="/accounting"%>`

6. You are given a tag library that has a tag named `printReport`. This tag may accept an attribute, `department`, which cannot take a dynamic value. Which of the following are correct uses of this tag? (Select two)

**a** `<mylib:printReport/>`

**b** `<mylib:printReport department="finance"/>`

**c** `<mylib:printReport attribute="department" value="finance"/>`

**d**
```
<mylib:printReport attribute="department"
                   attribute-value="finance"/>
```

**e**
```
<mylib:printReport>
    <jsp:attribute name="department" value="finance" />
</mylib:printReport>
```

7. You are given a tag library that has a tag named `getMenu`, which requires an attribute, `subject`. This attribute can take a dynamic value. Which of the following are correct uses of this tag? (Select two)

**a**
```
<mylib:getMenu />
```
**b**
```
<mylib:getMenu subject="finance"/>
```
**c**
```
<% String subject="HR";%>
<mylib:getMenu subject="<%=subject%>"/>
```
**d**
```
<mylib:getMenu> <jsp:param subject="finance"/> </mylib:getMenu>
```
**e**
```
<mylib:getMenu>
    <jsp:param name="subject" value="finance"/>
</mylib:getMenu>
```

8. Which of the following is a correct way to nest one custom tag inside another? (Select one)

**a**
```
<greet:hello>
    <greet:world>
    </greet:hello>
</greet:world>
```
**b**
```
<greet:hello>
    <greet:world>
    </greet:world>
</greet:hello>
```
**c**
```
<greet:hello
    <greet:world/>
/>
```
**d**
```
<greet:hello>
    </greet:hello>
    <greet:world>
</greet:world>
```

9. Which of the following elements can you use to import a tag library in a JSP document? (Select one)

**a** `<jsp:root>`

**b** `<jsp:taglib>`

**c** `<jsp:directive.taglib>`

**d** `<jsp:taglib.directive>`

**e** We cannot use custom tag libraries in XML format.

CHAPTER 16

# Developing custom tag libraries



## EXAM OBJECTIVES

**12.1** Identify the tag library descriptor element names that declare the following:

- The name of the tag
- The class of the tag handler
- The type of content that the tag accepts
- Any attributes of the tag

(Section 16.1.3)

**12.2** Identify the tag library descriptor element names that declare the following:

- The name of a tag attribute
- Whether a tag attribute is required

- Whether or not the attribute's value can be dynamically specified
  (Section 16.1.4)

**12.3** Given a custom tag, identify the necessary value for the <body-content> TLD element for any of the following tag types:
- Empty-tag
- Custom tag that surrounds other JSP code
- Custom tag that surrounds content that is used only by the tag handler.
  (Section 16.1.5)

**12.4** Given a tag event method (doStartTag, doAfterBody, and doEndTag), identify the correct description of the method's trigger. (Sections 16.3, 16.4)

**12.5** Identify valid return values for the following methods:
- doStartTag
- doAfterBody
- doEndTag
- PageContext.getOut.
  (Sections 16.3, 16.4)

**12.6** Given a "BODY" or "PAGE" constant, identify a correct description of the constant's use in the following methods:
- doStartTag
- doAfterBody
- doEndTag.
  (Sections 16.3, 16.4, 16.5)

**12.7** Identify the method in the custom tag handler that accesses:
- A given JSP page's implicit variable
- The JSP page's attributes
  (Section 16.6)

**12.8** Identify methods that return an outer tag handler from within an inner tag handler. (Sections 16.3.1, 16.6.1)

## *INTRODUCTION*

In chapter 15, "Using custom tags," we introduced JSP custom tags and tag libraries. We discussed the way that we use custom tags in JSP pages and the process of importing an existing tag library into a JSP page using the `taglib` directive. In this chapter, we will continue our discussion about implementing the different types of tags as we learn how to develop our own custom tag libraries.

## 16.1 UNDERSTANDING THE TAG LIBRARY DESCRIPTOR

The tag library descriptor (TLD) file contains the information that the JSP engine needs to know about the tag library in order to interpret the custom tags on a JSP page. Let's take a close look at the elements of the TLD and how they are used to describe a tag library.

A *tag library descriptor* is an XML document that follows the DTD designated by the JSP specification so that it can be created, read, and understood by all kinds of users, including human users and the JSP engine, as well as other development tools. In essence, it informs the user of a tag library about the usage and behavior of the tags that the library provides.

On the exam, you may be asked to identify the correct format and usage of the different elements in a TLD file. In addition, given a properly formatted TLD file, you may be asked to identify the correct usage of the corresponding tags and their attributes in JSP pages.

Listing 16.1 is an example of a TLD. We have bolded four elements—`<taglib>`, `<tag>`, `<body-content>`, and `<attribute>`—which you need to be familiar with to do well on the exam. We will discuss all of these elements in the following sections.

**Listing 16.1 sampleLib.tld: A sample tag library descriptor**

```
<?xml version="1.0" encoding="ISO-8859-1">

<!DOCTYPE taglib PUBLIC
   "-//Sun Microsystems, Inc.//DTD JSP Tag Library 1.2//EN"
   "http://java.sun.com/dtd/web-jsptaglibrary_1_2.dtd" >

<taglib>

   <tlib-version>1.0</tlib-version>
   <jsp-version>1.2</jsp-version>
   <short-name>test</short-name>
   <uri>http://www.manning.com/sampleLib</uri>

   <tag>
         <name>greet</name>
         <tag-class>sampleLib.GreetTag</tag-class>
         <body-content>empty</body-content>
         <description>Prints Hello and the user name</description>

         <attribute>
            <name>user</name>
            <required>false</required>
            <rtexprvalue>true</rtexprvalue>
         </attribute>
   </tag>

</taglib>
```

This code demonstrates three important things:

- First, a tag library descriptor file, like all XML files, starts with the line `<?xml version="1.0" encoding="ISO-8859-1">`, which specifies the version of XML and the character set that the file is using.
- Second, it has a `DOCTYPE` declaration that identifies the DTD for this document. In the case of a tag library descriptor that conforms to the JSP 1.2 specification, the `DOCTYPE` declaration must be:

```
<!DOCTYPE taglib PUBLIC
"-//Sun Microsystems, Inc.//DTD JSP Tag Library 1.2//EN"
"http://java.sun.com/dtd/web-jsptaglibrary_1_2.dtd" >
```

- Finally, it shows that all the contents of the TLD come under the `<taglib>` element. In other words, the `<taglib>` element is the root element of a TLD.

**NOTE** Unlike the deployment descriptor (`web.xml`), the extension of a TLD file is typically `.tld` and not `.xml`.

For all of the examples in this chapter, assume that the name of the TLD file is `sampleLib.tld`, that it resides in the `WEB-INF` directory of the web application named `chapter16`, and that the JSP code snippets that use the custom tags follow the `taglib` directive declared as:

```
<%@ taglib prefix="test" uri="/WEB-INF/sampleLib.tld" %>
```

Therefore, all of the tags in these examples will be qualified with the prefix `test`.

### 16.1.1 The <taglib> element

The `<taglib>` element is the top-level, or root, element of the tag library descriptor. It contains other second-level elements that provide information about the library as a whole, such as the version of the library and the version of the JSP specification the library conforms to. The following is the DTD for the `<taglib>` element:

```
<!ELEMENT taglib (tlib-version, jsp-version, short-name,
                  uri?, display-name?, small-icon?, large-icon?,
                  description?, validator?, listener*, tag+) >
```

As we can see from this DTD, the three subelements—`<tlib-version>`, `<jsp-version>`, and `<short-name>`—are mandatory and appear exactly once. There must be at least one `<tag>` subelement and zero or more `<listener>` elements. All other subelements are optional and can occur no more than once. Table 16.1 briefly describes their use.

Table 16.1 **The subelements of <taglib>**

| Element | Description | Occurrence |
|---|---|---|
| tlib-version | Specifies the version of the tag library. | Exactly once |
| jsp-version | Specifies the version of JSP (1.1 or 1.2 ) that this tag library depends on. For example, a value of 1.2 informs the JSP container that the implementation classes are using features of the JSP Specification 1.2 and that the container must be 1.2 compatible to be able to use this library. | Exactly once |
| short-name | Specifies a preferred prefix value for the tags in the library. Usually used by page authoring tools. | Exactly once |
| uri | A URI for identifying this tag library. This is the implicit way of adding <taglib-uri> and <taglib-location> pair entries into the taglib map. The value of this element is used as the URI for this library and the actual physical location of this TLD file is used as the location of the library. | At most once |
| display-name | A short name that can be displayed by page authoring tools. | At most once |
| small-icon | A small icon that can be used by tools. | At most once |
| large-icon | A large icon that can be used by tools. | At most once |
| description | Any text describing the use of this taglib. | At most once |
| validator | Information about this library's TagLibraryValidator. | At most once |
| listener | Specifies event listener classes. We saw in the Servlet Sections that we can specify listeners such as HttpSessionListener or ServletContextListener in the web.xml file. Similarly, if a tag library needs such listeners, we can specify the listener classes using this element. The container obtains these listener classes in exactly the way it obtains them from web.xml. | Any number of times |
| tag | Consists of subelements providing descriptions of a single tag. For multiple tags, we use multiple <tag> elements. | At least once |

Notice that the file `sampleLib.tld` shown in listing 16.1 contains a `<uri>` element:

```
<uri>http://www.manning.com/sampleLib</uri>
```

This is the implicit way of adding a `<taglib-uri>` and `<taglib-location>` pair entry into the taglib map. If you recall the discussion of the taglib map in chapter 15, the JSP engine reads all of the `taglib.tld` files present in the packaged JAR files. For each jarred TLD file that contains information about its own URI, the JSP container automatically creates a mapping between the specified URI and the current location of the JAR file. In this case, if the `sampleLib.tld` file is renamed as `taglib.tld` and kept in the `META-INF` directory inside a JAR file, the above `<uri>` element will cause the JSP container to create an implicit mapping of the URI `http://www.manning.com/sampleLib` with the actual location of the JAR file. We can then import the library into JSP pages using the `taglib` directive, as shown here:

```
<%@ taglib prefix="test" uri=" http://www.manning.com/sampleLib" %>
```

However, if the deployment descriptor file contains an explicit mapping for the same URI, then the explicit mapping takes precedence over such implicit mappings.

### 16.1.2 The <tag> element

The `<taglib>` element may contain one or more `<tag>` elements. Each `<tag>` element provides information about a single tag, such as the tag's name, that will be used in the JSP pages, the tag's handler class, the tag's attributes, and so forth. The `<tag>` element is defined as follows:

```
<!ELEMENT tag (name, tag-class, tei-class?, body-content?,
               display-name?, small-icon?, large-icon?,
               description?, variable*, attribute*, example?) >
```

As we can see from this definition, the two subelements, `<name>` and `<tag-class>`, are mandatory and appear exactly once. There can be zero or more `<variable>` and `<attribute>` elements. All other subelements are optional and can occur at most once. Table 16.2 gives a brief description of each of the subelements.

**Table 16.2 The subelements of <tag>**

| Element | Description | Occurrence |
|---|---|---|
| name | The unique tag name | Exactly once |
| tag-class | The tag handler class that implements javax.servlet.jsp.tagext.Tag. | Exactly once |
| tei-class | An optional subclass of javax.servlet.jsp.tagext.TagExtraInfo. | At most once |
| body-content | The content type for the body of the tag. Can be *empty, JSP,* or *tagdependent*. The default is *JSP.* | At most once |
| display-name | A short name that is intended to be displayed by development tools. | At most once |
| small-icon | A small icon that can be used by development tools. | At most once |
| large-icon | A large icon that can be used by development tools. | At most once |
| description | Specifies any tag-specific information. | At most once |
| variable | Specifies the scripting variable information. | Any number of times |
| attribute | Describes an attribute that this tag can accept. | Any number of times |
| example | Optional informal description of an example of using this tag. | At most once |

The `<name>` element specifies the name of the tag that is to be used in the JSP pages, and the `<tag-class>` element specifies the fully qualified class name that implements the functionality of this tag. The class that we specify here must implement the `javax.servlet.jsp.tagext.Tag` interface.

We can define multiple tags that have different names and the same tag class. For example:

```
<tag>
  <name>greet</name>
  <tag-class>sampleLib.GreetTag</tag-class >
</tag>

<tag>
  <name>welcome</name>
  <tag-class>sampleLib.GreetTag</tag-class>
</tag>
```

In a JSP page, both of the tags, `<test:greet>` and `<test:welcome>`, will invoke the same handler class, `sampleLib.GreetTag` (assuming that the JSP page uses `test` as the prefix for this tag library).

However, we cannot define more than one tag with the same name, because the engine would not be able to resolve the tag handler class while de-referencing the tag name. Thus, the following is illegal:

```
<tag>
  <name>greet</name>
  <tag-class>sampleLib.GreetTag</tag-class >
</tag>

<tag>
  <name>greet</name>
  <tag-class>sampleLib.WelcomeTag</tag-class>
</tag>
```

### 16.1.3 The <attribute> element

The `<attribute>` element is a third-level element in a TLD and is a child of the `<tag>` element. If a custom tag accepts attributes, then the information about each attribute is specified using an `<attribute>` element. Each `<attribute>` element can have five subelements that provide the following information about the attribute:

- The attribute's name that will be used in the JSP pages
- The attribute's data type (`int`, `Boolean`, etc.)
- Whether or not the attribute is mandatory
- Whether or not the attribute can accept values at request time
- A brief description of the attribute

Here is the definition for the `<attribute>` element:

```
<!ELEMENT attribute (name, required? , rtexprvalue?,
                     type?, description?) >
```

As we can see from the definition, only the `<name>` subelement is mandatory and must appear exactly once. All other subelements are optional and can occur no more than once. Table 16.3 describes each of the subelements.

**Table 16.3 The subelements of <attribute>**

| Element | Description |
|---|---|
| name | The name of the attribute. |
| required | A value that specifies whether the attribute is required or optional. The default is false, which means optional. If this is set to true, then the JSP page must pass a value for this attribute. Possible values are true, false, yes, and no. |
| rtexprvalue | A value that specifies whether or not the attribute can accept request-time expression values. The default is false, which means it cannot accept request-time expression values. Possible values are true, false, yes, and no. |
| type | The data type of the attribute. This may be used only when <rtexprvalue> is set to true. It specifies the return type of the expression, using a request-time attribute expression: <%= %>. The default value is java.lang.String. |
| description | Some text describing the attribute for documentation purposes. |

Consider a tag element that is defined as follows:

```
<tag>
   <name>greet</name>
   <tag-class>sampleLib.Greet</tag-class>
   <attribute>
      <name>user</name>
      <required>false</required>
      <rtexprvalue>true</rtexprvalue>
   </attribute>
</tag>
```

The above tag indicates that it accepts an attribute named `user`. Since the value of the `<required>` tag is `false`, a JSP page author may choose not to use the attribute-value pair. Further, since `<rtexprvalue>` is `true`, a JSP page author may use a request-time expression value. Therefore, the following lines from a JSP page are valid usages of this tag:

```
<test:greet />                                          <-- Does not use user attribute

<test:greet user='<%=request.getParameter("user")%>' />  <-- Uses request-time expression
```

In the previous tag definition, if we were to use a value of `true` for the `<required>` element, then we would have to specify the attribute-value pair for the given attribute in the JSP page. Thus, the first tag, `<test:greet />`, would generate a translation-time error because it does not specify a value for the `user` attribute. Moreover, if we were to use a value of `false` for the `<rtexprevalue>` element, then we must provide a value for the attribute in the JSP page that is not a request-time expression. Therefore, `<test:greet user="john"/>` is fine, but the second line in the code, `<test:greet user="<%=...%>"/>`, which uses a request-time attribute value, will generate a translation-time error.

### 16.1.4 The <body-content> element

The `<body-content>` element is a third-level element in a TLD and is a direct child of the `<tag>` element. This element does not have any subelements and can have one of three values:

- `empty`. Specifies that the body of the tag must be empty
- `JSP`. Specifies that the body of the tag can accept any normal JSP code
- `tagdependent`. Specifies that the content is not to be interpreted by the JSP engine and is tag dependent

Let's look at the details for each of these.

#### *empty*

Some tags require a body, while others do not. In chapter 15 (section 15.3), we discussed the tags `<test:required>`, `<test:greet>`, and `<test:if>`. The `<test:required>` and `<test:greet>` tags did not have any body content. By their mere presence, they generated some output in the final HTML. On the other hand, the purpose of the `<test:if>` tag was to contain a set of statements that could either be skipped or executed as required.

A value of `empty` for the `<body-content>` element indicates that the tag does not support any body content. If the page author provides any content, the JSP engine flags an error at translation time. The following example declares the `<greet>` tag and specifies that its body content should be empty.

```
<tag>
   <name>greet</name>
   <tag-class>sampleLib.GreetTag</tag-class>
   <body-content>empty</body-content>

   <attribute>
      <name>user</name>
      <required>false</required>
      <rtexprvalue>true</rtexprvalue>
   </attribute>

</tag>
```

Therefore, the following are valid usages of the `<test:greet>` tag shown above:

```
<test:greet />

<test:greet user="john" />

<test:greet></test:greet>

<test:greet user="john"></test:greet>
```

The following usages of the tag are invalid since they contain some body content between the start and end tags:

```
<test:greet>john</test:greet>

<test:greet><%="john"%></test:greet>

<test:greet> </test:greet>    <— Space is not the same as empty

<test:greet>                  New Line is not
</test:greet>          <—     the same as empty
```

### JSP

A value of JSP for the <body-content> element indicates that the tag can have any valid JSP code in its body. This means that it can take plain text, HTML, scripting elements, standard actions, or even other custom tags nested inside this tag. The body could even be empty. The following example declares the <if> tag and specifies that its body can contain any kind of JSP content:

```
<tag>
   <name>if</name>
   <tag-class>sampleLib.IfTag</tag-class>
   <body-content>JSP</body-content>

   <attribute>
      <name>condition</name>
      <required>true</required>
      <rtexprvalue>true</rtexprvalue>
   </attribute>

</tag>
```

At request time, the nested scriptlets and expressions are executed and the actions and the custom tags are invoked as usual. Thus, the following are valid usages for the <if> tag declared above:

```
<test:if condition="true" />

<test:if condition="true"> </test:if>

<test:if condition="true">  </test:if>

<test:if condition="true">

   <test:greet user="john" />

   <% int x = 2+3; %>
   2+3 = <%= x %>

</test:if>
```

### tagdependent

A value of tagdependent for the <body-content> element indicates that the tag is expecting the body to contain text that may not be valid JSP code. The JSP engine does not attempt to execute the body and passes it as is to the tag handler at request time. It is up to the tag handler class to process the body content as needed.

This value for the body content element is required if we want to introduce code snippets from other languages. For example, we can develop a tag that executes SQL statements and inserts the result set into the output:

```
<test:dbQuery>
   SELECT count(*) FROM USERS
</test:dbQuery>
```

The tag handler class of the dbQuery tag would handle everything regarding the database, such as opening a connection, firing an SQL query, and so forth. It will only need the actual SQL query string that is specified as the body of the above tag. For such a tag, the <body-content> element must be specified as tagdependent.

**NOTE** Since a TLD is an XML document, the following rules apply:

- The order of the different elements and subelements is important. For example, the <body-content> element must appear before the <attribute> element under the <tag> element.
- The tag names are case sensitive. Thus, <Attribute> is not a valid element; we must use <attribute>.
- The character - appearing in many of the elements is important. Thus, <bodycontent> and <tagclass> are both valid in JSP 1.1 but invalid in JSP 1.2. Questions on version-specific issues may not appear on the exam, but it is good to know these points because while practicing the examples with a JSP 1.2–compliant container, you will have to use <body-content> and <tag-class> if you use the following DOCTYPE:

```
<!DOCTYPE taglib PUBLIC
    "-//Sun Microsystems, Inc.//DTD JSP Tag Library 1.2//EN"
    "http://java.sun.com/dtd/web-jsptaglibrary_1_2.dtd" >
```

## 16.2 THE TAG EXTENSION API

The Tag Extension API is a set of interfaces and classes that forms a contract between the JSP container and the tag handler classes. Just as we need to know the Servlet API to write servlets, we need to know the Tag Extension API to write custom tags. This API consists of just one package: javax.servlet.jsp.tagext. It has four interfaces and 13 classes. Of these, the most important ones are shown in table 16.4.

**Table 16.4 Important classes and interfaces of the javax.servlet.jsp.tagext package**

| Interface Name | Description |
|---|---|
| Tag | The Tag interface is the base interface for all tag handlers and is used for writing simple tags. It declares six tag life-cycle methods, including the two most important ones: doStartTag() and doEndTag(). We implement this interface if we want to write a simple tag that does not require iterations or processing of its body content. |

*continued on next page*

**Table 16.4 Important classes and interfaces of the javax.servlet.jsp.tagext package *(continued)***

| Interface Name | Description |
|---|---|
| IterationTag | IterationTag extends the Tag interface and adds one more method for supporting iterations: doAfterBody(). |
| BodyTag | BodyTag extends IterationTag and adds two methods for supporting the buffering of body contents: doInitBody() and setBodyContent(). |

| Class Name | Description |
|---|---|
| TagSupport | TagSupport implements the IterationTag interface and provides a default implementation for all its methods, acting as an IterationTag adapter class. We can use it as a base class for implementing simple and iterative custom tags. |
| BodyTagSupport | BodyTagSupport implements the BodyTag interface and provides a default implementation for all its methods, acting as a BodyTag adapter class. We can use it as a base class for implementing custom tags that process the contents of the body. |
| BodyContent | BodyContent extends the JspWriter class and acts as a buffer for the temporary storage of the evaluated body of a tag. This object is used only with the BodyTag interface or the BodyTagSupport class. |

All custom tag handlers must implement one of these three interfaces either directly or indirectly (by extending from the adapter classes).

In addition to the interfaces and classes in table 16.4, the `Tag` handler classes use the exception classes shown in table 16.5, which are defined in the `javax.servlet.jsp` package.

**Table 16.5 Exception classes of javax.servlet.jsp**

| Class Name | Description |
|---|---|
| JspException | JspException is derived from java.lang.Exception. It is a generic exception that is known to the JSP engine. All uncaught JspExceptions result in an invocation of the error-page machinery. The important methods—doStartTag(), doInitBody(), doAfterBody(), and doEndTag()—all throw JspException. |
| JspTagException | JspTagException extends JspException. Tag handler classes can use this exception to indicate unrecoverable errors. |

Observe that the `JspTagException` class belongs to the `javax.servlet.jsp` package and not to the `javax.servlet.jsp.tagext` package, as you might expect.

In the next few sections, we are going to examine the interfaces and classes that are listed in table 16.4, using examples from the `sampleLib` package that is included in the CD that accompanies this book. Figure 16.1 shows the inheritance relationship between the interfaces and classes of the API and our sample classes. The oval-shaped objects represent the interfaces, the square objects represent the classes, and the arrows represent generalization. The names of the standard classes and interfaces present in the `javax.servlet.jsp.tagext` package are in bold. The other nine classes are the examples that we are going to look at in the following sections.

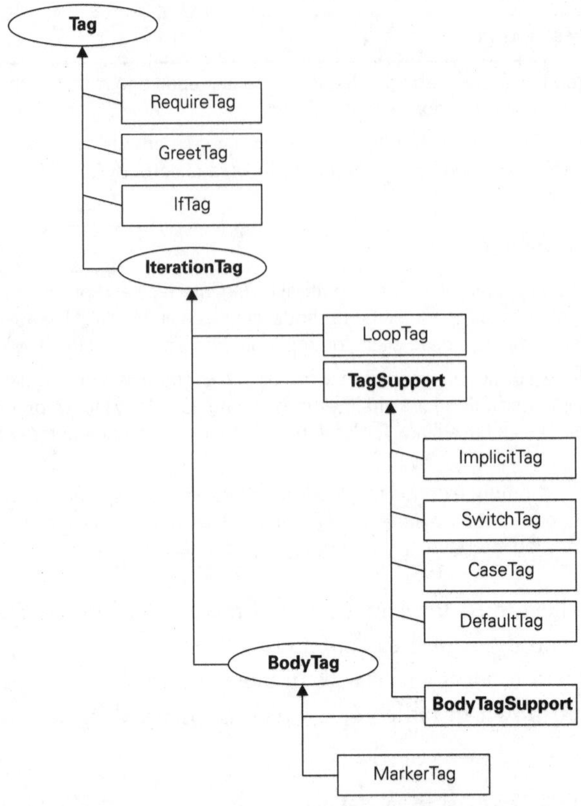


**Figure 16.1**
**A diagram of the Tag Extension API and the examples in this chapter.**

## 16.3 IMPLEMENTING THE TAG INTERFACE

The `Tag` interface is the base interface for all custom tag handlers. It provides the basic life-cycle methods that the JSP engine calls on the tags. Table 16.6 gives a brief description of the methods and constants defined by the `Tag` interface.

**Table 16.6 Methods and constants of the javax.servlet.jsp.tagext.Tag interface**

| Method Name | Description |
|---|---|
| int doStartTag() | Called when the opening tag is encountered. |
| int doEndTag() | Called when the closing tag is encountered. |
| Tag getParent() | Returns the handler class object of the closest enclosing tag of this tag. |
| void release() | Called on a tag handler to release resources. |
| void setPageContext(PageContext) | Sets the current page context. |
| void setParent(Tag) | Sets the parent (closest enclosing tag handler) of this tag handler. |

*continued on next page*

**Table 16.6 Methods and constants of the javax.servlet.jsp.tagext.Tag interface *(continued)***

| Constant | Description |
|---|---|
| EVAL_BODY_INCLUDE | Return value for doStartTag()<br>Instructs the JSP engine to evaluate the tag body and include it in the output. |
| SKIP_BODY | Return value for doStartTag()<br>Instructs the JSP engine not to evaluate the tag body and not to include it in the output. |
| EVAL_PAGE | Return value for doEndTag()<br>Instructs the JSP engine to evaluate the rest of the page and include it in the output. |
| SKIP_PAGE | Return value for doEndTag()<br>Instructs the JSP engine not to evaluate the rest of the page and not to include it in the output. |

## 16.3.1 Understanding the methods of the Tag interface

Let's take a closer look at the methods in the life cycle of a custom tag. They are presented here in the sequence in which they are normally called.

### *The setPageContext() method*

The `setPageContext()` method is the first method that is called in the life cycle of a custom tag. The signature of `setPageContext()` is:

```
public void setPageContext(PageContext);
```

The JSP container calls this method to pass the `pageContext` implicit object of the JSP page in which the tag appears. A typical implementation of this method is to save the `pageContext` reference in a private member for future use.

### *The setParent() and getParent() methods*

These methods are used when custom tags are nested one inside the other. In such cases, the outer tag is called the *parent* tag, while the inner tag is called the *child* tag. The signatures of these methods are:

```
public void setParent(Tag);
public Tag getParent();
```

The JSP container calls the `setParent()` method on the child tag and passes it a reference to the parent tag. The `getParent()` method is usually called by one of the child tags and not directly by the JSP container. A typical implementation of these methods is to save the reference to the parent tag in a private member and return it when required. For example, if a JSP page has multiple tags at more than two levels of nesting, then the JSP engine passes each child tag a reference to its immediate parent. This allows the innermost tag to get a reference to the outermost tag by calling `getParent()` on its immediate parent and then again calling `getParent()` on the returned reference, working its way up the nested hierarchy.

### The setter methods

Attributes in custom tags are handled in exactly the same way properties are handled in JavaBeans. If a custom tag has any attributes, then for each attribute, the JSP engine calls the appropriate setter method to set its value at request time. Since the method signatures depend on the attribute names and types, these methods are not defined in the `Tag` interface but are invoked using the standard introspection mechanism that is used in JavaBeans. The setter methods are called after the calls to the `setPageContext()` and `setParent()` methods but before the call to `doStartTag()`.

### The doStartTag() method

After setting up the tag with appropriate references by calling the `setPageContext()`, `setParent()`, and setter methods, the container calls the `doStartTag()` method on the tag. The signature of `doStartTag()` is:

```
public int doStartTag() throws JspException;
```

This method marks the beginning of the tag's actual processing, giving the tag handler a chance to do initial computations and to verify whether or not the attribute values passed in the setter methods are valid. If the initialization fails, the method may throw a `JspException` or a subclass of `JspException`, such as `JspTagException`, to indicate the problem, depending on application requirement.

After initialization, the `doStartTag()` method decides whether or not to continue evaluating its body content. As a result, it returns one of the two integer constants defined in the `Tag` interface: `EVAL_BODY_INCLUDE` or `SKIP_BODY`. A return value of `Tag.EVAL_BODY_INCLUDE` indicates that the body must be executed and that its output must be included in the response, while a return value of `Tag.SKIP_BODY` indicates that the body must be skipped and that it is not to be evaluated at all. This method cannot return any other value.

### The doEndTag() method

After the body of the tag is evaluated or skipped (depending on the return value of `doStartTag()`), the container calls the `doEndTag()` method. The signature of `doEndTag()` is:

```
public int doEndTag() throws JspException;
```

This marks the end of the processing of the tag and gives the tag handler a chance to do the final cleanup for the tag. If anything fails during the cleanup process, the method may throw a `JspException` or a subclass of `JspException`, such as `JspTagException`, to indicate the problem.

Finally, the `doEndTag()` method decides whether or not to continue evaluating the rest of the JSP page. As a result, it returns one of the two integer constants defined in the `Tag` interface: `EVAL_PAGE` or `SKIP_PAGE`. A return value of `Tag.EVAL_PAGE` indicates that the rest of the JSP page must be evaluated and its output be included in the response, while a return value of `Tag.SKIP_PAGE` indicates that the rest of the JSP page must not be evaluated at all and that the JSP engine should return immediately from the current `_jspService()` method. If this page was forwarded or included from another JSP page or a servlet, only the current page evaluation is terminated, and if the page was included, the processing resumes from the calling component. The tag cannot return any other value from this method.

### *The release() method*

Finally, the container calls the `release()` method on the handler class when the tag handler object is no longer required. The signature of `release()` is:

```
public void release();
```

A custom tag may occur multiple times on a JSP page. A single instance of the tag handler may be used to handle all of these occurrences. The JSP container calls the `release()` method on the handler class when the handler object is no longer required. It is important to note that this method is not called after every call to `doEndTag()`. It is called only once, when the container decides to put this instance out of service. For example, if the container implementation maintains a pool of tag handler instances, the container may reuse an instance of a tag by calling the sequence `setPageContext()`, `doStartTag()`, `doEndTag()` multiple times. The container calls the `release()` method only when the tag is to be removed permanently from the pool. This method can be used to release all resources acquired by the tag handler during its lifetime.

The flowchart in figure 16.2 shows the order of processing in a tag handler class that implements the `Tag` interface.

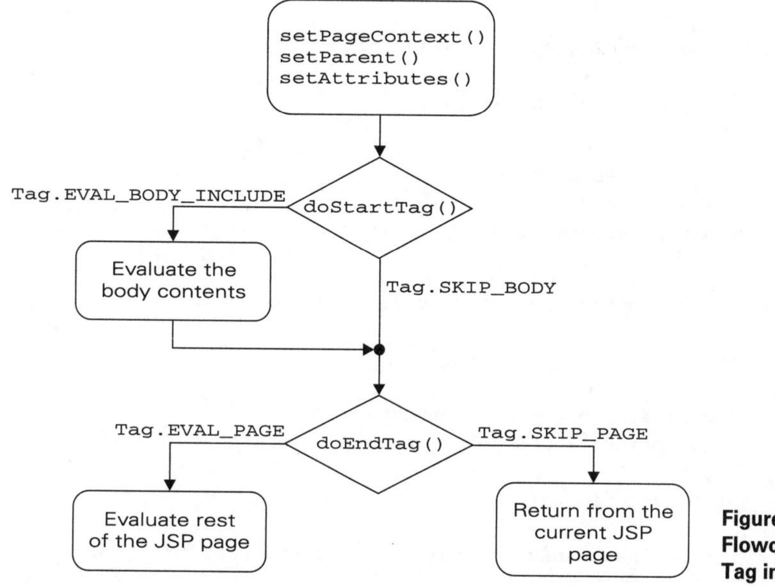


**Figure 16.2 Flowchart for the Tag interface.**

Let's now look at some examples of using the `Tag` interface. We will write tag handlers for the following cases:

- An empty tag that just prints HTML text
- An empty tag that accepts an attribute
- A non-empty tag (a tag with a body) that skips or includes its body content

### 16.3.2 An empty tag that prints HTML text

In chapter 15 (section 15.3), we used a tag named `required` on a JSP page to demonstrate the use of an empty tag. It prints the `*` character wherever it is placed on the page:

```
<test:required />
```

Listing 16.2 shows the implementation of the tag handler for this tag.

**Listing 16.2 RequiredTag.java**

```
package sampleLib;

import javax.servlet.jsp.*;
import javax.servlet.jsp.tagext.*;

public class RequiredTag implements Tag
{
   private PageContext pageContext;
   private Tag parentTag;

   public void setPageContext(PageContext pageContext)
   {
      this.pageContext = pageContext;
   }

   public void setParent(Tag parentTag)
   {
      this.parentTag = parentTag;
   }

   public Tag getParent()
   {
      return this.parentTag;
   }

   public int doStartTag() throws JspException
   {
      try
      {
         JspWriter out = pageContext.getOut();
         out.print("<font color='#ff0000'>*</font>");
      }
      catch(Exception e)
      {
         throw new JspException("Error in RequiredTag.doStartTag()");
      }
```

```
        return SKIP_BODY;
    }

    public int doEndTag() throws JspException
    {
        return EVAL_PAGE;
    }

    //clean up the resources (if any)
    public void release()
    {
    }
}
```

This code shows a simple tag handler class, `RequiredTag`, that implements the `Tag` interface and defines all six methods. First, we save the references to `pageContext` and the parent tag in the `setPageContext()` and `setParent()` methods. Note that in this tag, we do not have any attributes, and so we have not defined any setter methods. Then, in the `doStartTag()` method, we use the saved `pageContext` reference to get the output writer of JSP page and print the HTML code:

```
JspWriter out = pageContext.getOut();
out.print("<font color='#ff0000'>*</font>");
```

We return `SKIP_BODY` in `doStartTag()` because we expect the page author to use this as an empty tag. Finally, we return `EVAL_PAGE` in `doEndTag()`, since we want the rest of the page to be executed normally. The following `<tag>` element describes this tag in a TLD file:

```
<tag>
    <name>required</name>
    <tag-class>sampleLib.RequiredTag</tag-class>
    <body-content>empty</body-content>
    <description>Prints * wherever it occurs</description>
</tag>
```

Notice that we have specified `<body-content>` as empty because we do not want to have any body content for this tag.

**NOTE** We could have gotten the output writer and written out the HTML code in `doEndTag()` instead of `doStartTag()`. In tags that are empty, or in tags where `doStartTag()` returns `SKIP_BODY`, such as the above one, it does not matter in which method you choose to print out the HTML code. However, if the tag has a body and if the `doStartTag()` method returns `EVAL_BODY_INCLUDE`, then anything that is printed in `doStartTag()` appears before the body content and anything that is printed in `doEndTag()` appears after the body content in the final output.

### 16.3.3 An empty tag that accepts an attribute

When a tag accepts attributes, there are three important things that we must do for each attribute:

- We must declare an instance variable in the tag class to hold the value of the attribute.
- If we do not want to make the attribute mandatory, we must either provide a default value or take care of the corresponding null instance variable in the code.
- We must implement the appropriate setter methods for each of the attributes.

Let's look at an implementation of the `<greet>` tag that accepts one attribute, `user`, and prints the word `Hello` followed by the user value, in the output HTML:

```
<test:greet />
<test:greet user='john' />
```

The tag prints only the word `Hello` if the `user` attribute is not specified. The following is a code snippet from the file `GreetTag.java`, which is on the accompanying CD. We have omitted the parts of the code that are common to all the examples, such as package declarations, import statements, and `setPageContext()`:

```
public class GreetTag implements Tag
{
   //other methods as before

   //A String that holds the user attribute
   private String user;

   //The setter method that is called by the container
   public void setUser(String user) { this.user = user;  }

   public int doStartTag() throws JspException
   {
      JspWriter out = pageContext.getOut();

      try
      {
         if (user==null)
            out.print("Hello!");
         else
            out.print("Hello "+user+"!");
      }
      catch(Exception e)
      {
         throw new JspException("Error in Greet.doStartTag()");
      }

      return SKIP_BODY;
   }
}
```

This code is similar to the code for RequiredTag except that it has two extra members: a variable and a setter method for the user attribute. If and when the JSP engine encounters the user attribute in the tag, it calls the setUser() method, passing it the attribute's value. The setUser() method stores this value in the private instance variable, which is then used by the doStartTag() method. In this example, if the page author does not specify the user attribute in the <test:greet> tag, the user variable remains null and we print the word Hello in the output without a username.

The following <tag> element describes this tag in a TLD file:

```
<tag>
   <name>greet</name>
   <tag-class>sampleLib.GreetTag</tag-class>
   <body-content>empty</body-content>
   <attribute>
      <name>user</name>
      <required>false</required>
      <rtexprvalue>true</rtexprvalue>
   </attribute>
   <description>Prints Hello user! wherever it occurs</description>
</tag>
```

You may have been surprised at the use of the user variable as an instance variable. Using instance variables to keep request-specific information is very dangerous in servlets since they are not thread safe. However, in the case of custom tags, the onus of thread safety is on the container. It ensures that either a new tag handler instance is created for each occurrence of the tag in a JSP page, or if the container maintains a pool of instances, then an appropriate instance is reused from a pool and the attributes are reset. Thus, in the following example, the second occurrence of the greet tag will not use the value of the user attribute passed into the first occurrence:

```
<html><body>
   <test:greet user="john" />
   <test:greet />
</body></html>
```

### 16.3.4 A non-empty tag that includes its body content

The doStartTag() method can return either EVAL_BODY_INCLUDE or SKIP_BODY to include or skip the body content. Let's look at a tag that uses this feature to provide functionality similar to that of an if statement in a programming language. The following is a code snippet from the IfTag.java file you can find on the accompanying CD:

```
public class IfTag implements Tag
{
   //other methods as before

   private boolean condition = false;

   public void setCondition(boolean condition)
```

```
    {
        this.condition = condition;
    }

    public int doStartTag() throws JspException
    {
        if (condition)
            return EVAL_BODY_INCLUDE;
        else
            return SKIP_BODY;
    }

}
```

In this example, we use a `boolean` attribute, `condition`, to determine whether the body needs to be included or skipped. In the `doStartTag()` method, depending on the condition value, we return either `Tag.EVAL_BODY_INCLUDE` or `Tag.SKIP_BODY`.

The following `<tag>` element describes the `<if>` tag in a TLD file:

```
<tag>
    <name>if</name>
    <tag-class>sampleLib.IfTag</tag-class>
    <body-content>JSP</body-content>

    <attribute>
        <name>condition</name>
        <required>true</required>
        <rtexprvalue>true</rtexprvalue>
    </attribute>
</tag>
```

Observe that we have specified the `<body-content>` as `JSP`. This allows us to write any valid JSP code in the body of the tag. If the `doStartTag()` method of the tag handler returns `EVAL_BODY_INCLUDE`, the body will be executed like normal JSP code; otherwise, it will be skipped altogether. We have specified the value of the `<required>` element as `true`, since we need it to decide whether or not to include the body content. The following code shows the usage of the `<if>` tag in the JSP page:

```
<%@ taglib prefix="test" uri="/WEB-INF/sampleLib.tld" %>
<% boolean debug =  "true".equals(request.getParameter("debug")); %>

<html><body>
Hello<br>

    <test:if condition="<%=debug%>" >
        DEBUG INFO:...
    </test:if>

</body></html>
```

When we access the above JSP page as

```
http://localhost:8080/chapter16/ifTest.jsp?debug=true
```

the output will be:

```
Hello
DEBUG INFO:...
```

If we pass `debug=false` in the query string of the URL, the output will not contain the second line.

## 16.4 IMPLEMENTING THE ITERATIONTAG INTERFACE

In the previous examples, we used the `Tag` interface to either include or skip the body content of the tag. However, if the body content was included, it was included only once. The `IterationTag` interface extends the `Tag` interface and allows us to include the body content multiple times, in a way that is similar to the loop functionality of a programming language. The `IterationTag` interface declares one method and one constant, as shown in table 16.7.

**Table 16.7 Methods of the javax.servlet.jsp.tagext.IterationTag interface**

| Method Name | Description |
|---|---|
| int doAfterBody() | This method is called after each evaluation of the tag body. It can return either of two values: IterationTag.EVAL_BODY_AGAIN or Tag.SKIP_BODY. The return value determines whether or not the body needs to be reevaluated. |
| **Constant** | **Description** |
| EVAL_BODY_AGAIN | Return value for doAfterBody().<br>This constant instructs the JSP engine to evaluate the tag body and include it in the output. |

### 16.4.1 Understanding the IterationTag methods

Since `IterationTag` extends `Tag`, it inherits all the functionality of the `Tag` interface. The container sets up the iterative tag with appropriate references by calling the `setPageContext()` and `setParent()` methods, passes the attribute values using the setter methods, and calls `doStartTag()`. Depending on the return value of `doStartTag()`, the container either includes or skips the body content.

If `doStartTag()` returns `SKIP_BODY`, then the body is skipped and the container calls `doEndTag()`. In this case, the `doAfterBody()` method is never called on the iterative tag. However, if `doStartTag()` returns `EVAL_BODY_INCLUDE`, the body of the tag is evaluated, the result is included in the output, and the container calls `doAfterBody()` for the very first time.

#### *The doAfterBody() method*

The `doAfterBody()` is the only method defined by the `IterationTag` interface. It gives the tag handler a chance to reevaluate its body. The signature of `doAfterBody()` is:

```
public int doAfterBody() throws JspException;
```

If an error occurs during the invocation of the doAfterBody() method, it may throw a JspException or a subclass of it, such as JspTagException, to indicate the problem. If everything goes fine, it decides whether or not to reevaluate its body. To evaluate the body again, it will return the integer constant EVAL_BODY_AGAIN, which is defined in the IterationTag interface. This will cause an evaluation of the tag's body the second time, and after the evaluation, the JSP container will call doAfterBody() for the second time. This process continues until doAfterBody() returns SKIP_BODY, which is defined in the Tag interface. We cannot return any other value from this method.

Finally, the doEndTag() method is called, either because doStartTag() returns SKIP_BODY, or because doAfterBody() returns SKIP_BODY. The purpose and functionality of the doEndTag() method in the IterationTag interface are the same as in the Tag interface.

The flowchart in figure 16.3 shows the order of processing in a tag handler class that implements the IterationTag interface.

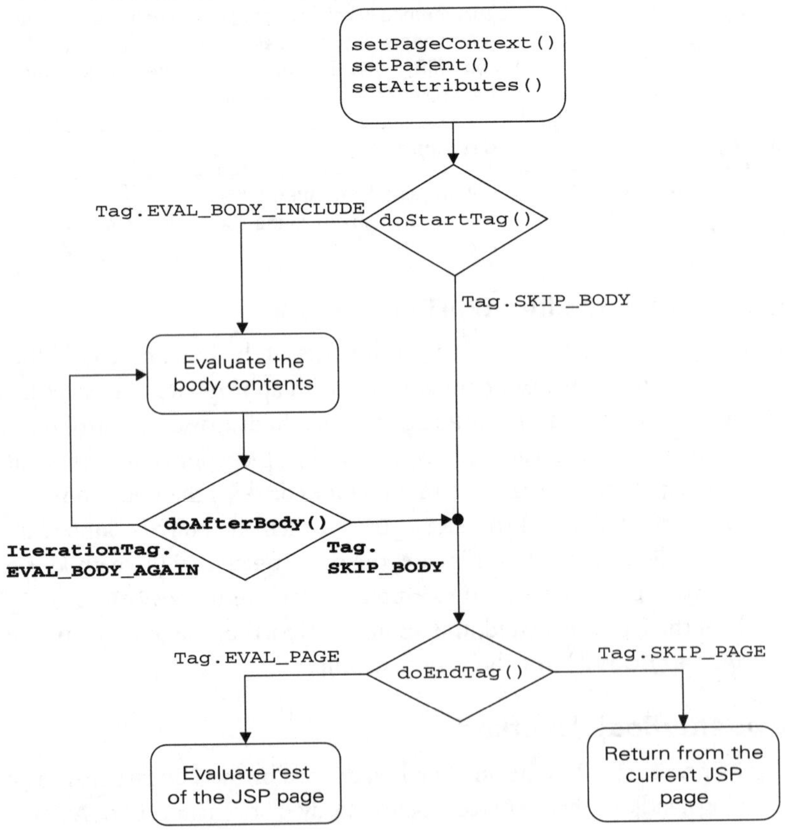


**Figure 16.3 Flowchart for the IterationTag interface.**

### 16.4.2 A simple iterative tag

Let's now look at a tag that provides the functionality similar to that of a looping construct in a programming language. The following code snippet from a JSP page demonstrates the use of the loop tag:

```
<%@ taglib prefix="test" uri="/WEB-INF/sampleLib.tld" %>
<html><body>
  <test:loop count="5" >
     Hello World!<br>
  </test:loop>
</body></html>
```

The above tag has an attribute named `count` that accepts integral values to specify the number of times the body of the tag should be executed. The above code prints `Hello World!` five times in the output.

Listing 16.3 shows the code for `LoopTag.java`. This tag handler class implements the `IterationTag` interface and thus provides implementation for the extra method `doAfterBody()` as well as the six methods of the `Tag` interface.

**Listing 16.3 LoopTag.java**

```
package sampleLib;

import javax.servlet.jsp.*;
import javax.servlet.jsp.tagext.*;

public class LoopTag implements IterationTag
{
   private PageContext pageContext;
   private Tag parentTag;

   public void setPageContext(PageContext pageContext)
   {
      this.pageContext = pageContext;
   }

   public void setParent(Tag parentTag)
   {
      this.parentTag = parentTag;
   }

   public Tag getParent()
   {
      return this.parentTag;
   }

   //Attribute to maintain looping count
   private int count = 0;

   public void setCount(int count)
   {
      this.count = count;
   }
```

```
    public int doStartTag() throws JspException
    {
       if (count>0)
          return EVAL_BODY_INCLUDE;
       else
          return SKIP_BODY;
    }

    public int doAfterBody() throws JspException
    {

       if (--count > 0)
          return EVAL_BODY_AGAIN;
       else
          return SKIP_BODY;
    }

    public int doEndTag() throws JspException
    {
       return EVAL_PAGE;
    }

    public void release()
    {
    }
}
```

In the above code, we have used the `count` variable to keep track of the number of iterations. For each invocation of the `doAfterBody()` method, we decrement the count by 1 and return `EVAL_BODY_AGAIN` until the count reaches 0. If the count reaches 0, we return `SKIP_BODY` to terminate the looping effect, which tells the container to skip further iterations and call `doEndTag()`.

The following `<tag>` element describes the loop tag in a TLD file:

```
<tag>
   <name>loop</name>
   <tag-class>sampleLib.LoopTag</tag-class>
   <body-content>JSP</body-content>
   <attribute>
      <name>count</name>
      <required>true</required>
      <rtexprvalue>true</rtexprvalue>
   </attribute>
</tag>
```

As you can see, describing an `IterationTag` is no different than defining a normal tag in a TLD. We have not informed the container explicitly whether or not this tag is iterative. The container introspects the interface implemented by the tag's class and calls `doAfterBody()` only if it finds that the class is an instance of `IterationTag`.

## 16.5 IMPLEMENTING THE BODYTAG INTERFACE

The BodyTag interface extends IterationTag and adds a new functionality that lets the tag handler evaluate its body content in a temporary buffer. This feature allows the tag to process the generated contents at will. For example, after evaluation, the tag handler can view the body content, discard it completely, modify it, or add more data to it before sending it to the output stream. Since it is derived from IterationTag, BodyTag can also handle the evaluation and processing of the content as many times as required.

The BodyTag interface declares two methods and a constant, as shown in table 16.8.

**Table 16.8 Methods of the javax.servlet.jsp.tagext.IterationTag Interface**

| Method Name | Description |
|---|---|
| void setBodyContent(BodyContent) | Called by the JSP container to pass a reference to a BodyContent object. |
| void doInitBody() | Called by the JSP container after calling setBodyContent(), to allow the tag handler class to perform initialization steps on BodyContent. |
| **Constant** | **Description** |
| EVAL_BODY_BUFFERED | A constant defined as a return value for doStartTag() and doAfterBody() for tags that want to buffer the evaluation of their content. |

**NOTE** In JSP 1.1, there was another return value for BodyTag.doAfterBody(): EVAL_BODY_TAG. This value is now deprecated. If the exam asks about it, you should treat it the same as IterationTag.EVAL_BODY_AGAIN or BodyTag.EVAL_BODY_BUFFERED, as the case may be.

### 16.5.1 Understanding the methods of BodyTag

The BodyTag interface adds two new methods to handle the processing of the tag's body: setBodyContent() and doInitBody().

#### *The setBodyContent() method*

The JSP container calls the setBodyContent() method to pass an instance of BodyContent to the tag. The signature of setBodyContent() is:

```
public void setBodyContent(BodyContent);
```

A typical implementation of this method is to save the BodyContent reference in a private member for future use.

#### *The doInitBody() method*

The JSP container calls the doInitBody() method after calling setBodyContent(). The signature of doInitBody() is:

```
public void doInitBody(BodyContent) throws JspException;
```

This method allows the tag handler class to initialize the `BodyContent` object, if required, before the actual evaluation process starts. Thus, if the initialization of `BodyContent` fails, the `doInitBody()` method may throw a `JspException` or a subclass of `JspException`, such as `JspTagException`, to indicate the problem.

Since `BodyTag` extends `IterationTag`, which in turn extends the `Tag` interface, `BodyTag` inherits all the functionality of `IterationTag` as well as `Tag`. The container sets up the implementation handler class with appropriate references by calling the `setPageContext()` and `setParent()` methods, passes the attribute values using the setter methods, and calls `doStartTag()`.

The `doStartTag()` method of a class that implements the `BodyTag` interface returns any one of three values: `EVAL_BODY_INCLUDE` or `SKIP_BODY` inherited from the `Tag` interface, or `EVAL_BODY_BUFFERED`, which is defined in the `BodyTag` interface. The actions taken by the JSP container for the return values `EVAL_BODY_INCLUDE` and `SKIP_BODY` are the same as for the `IterationTag` interface.

However, if `doStartTag()` returns `EVAL_BODY_BUFFERED`, the JSP container takes a different course of action. It first creates an instance of the `BodyContent` class. The `BodyContent` class is a subclass of `JspWriter` and overrides all the print and write methods of `JspWriter` to buffer any data written into it rather than sending it to the output stream of the response. The JSP container passes the newly created `BodyContent` instance to the tag handler using its `setBodyContent()` method, calls `doInitBody()` on the tag, and finally evaluates the body of the tag, filling the `BodyContent` buffer with the result of the body tag evaluation.

The container calls `doAfterBody()` after evaluating the body, writing the data directly into the output or buffering it, as the case may be. If the output was buffered, we can add, modify, or delete the contents of this buffer. Finally, this method returns `EVAL_BODY_AGAIN` or `EVAL_BODY_BUFFERED` to continue evaluating the body in a loop, or returns `SKIP_BODY` to terminate the loop.

Finally, the container calls `doEndTag()`, and, as with the other interfaces, the tag handler class that is implementing the `BodyTag` interface can return either `SKIP_PAGE` or `EVAL_PAGE`.

The flowchart in figure 16.4 shows the order of processing in a tag handler class that implements the `BodyTag` interface.

### 16.5.2 A tag that processes its body

Let's now look at a tag named `mark` that displays certain characters in its tag body in boldface when they are specified in the `search` attribute of the tag. For example:

```
<test:mark search="s">
   she sells sea shells on the sea shore!
</test:mark>
```

will print

```
she sells sea shells on the sea shore!
```

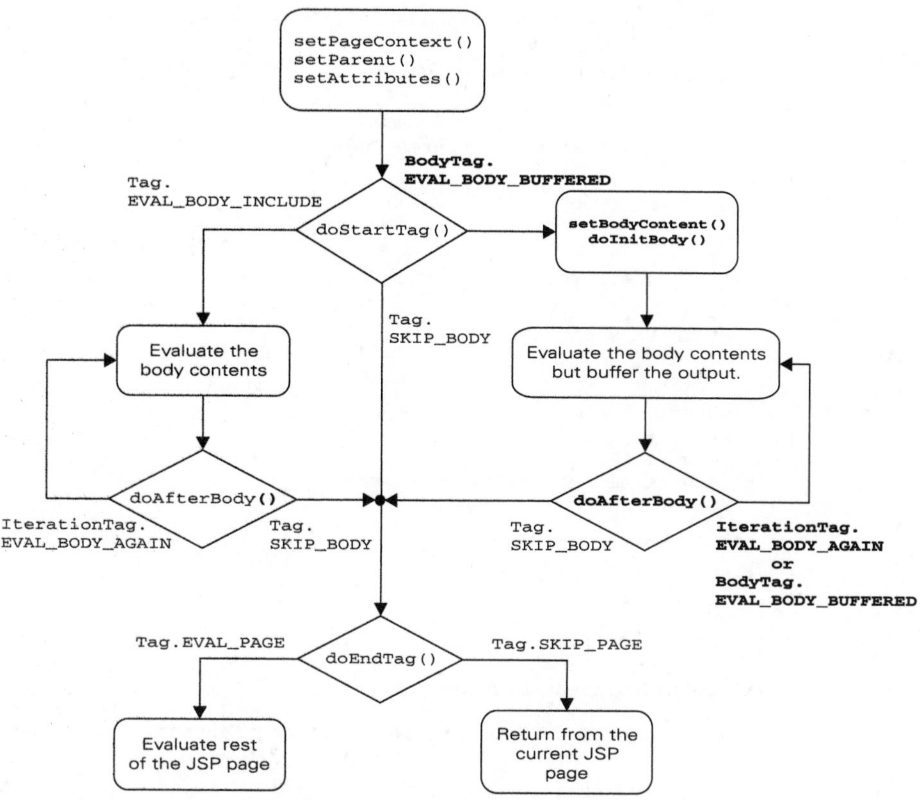


**Figure 16.4 A flowchart for the BodyTag interface.**

whereas if we pass sh to the search attribute, it will print

```
she sells sea shells on the sea shore!
```

This kind of feature is useful if your site maintains many informative documents and allows a search on them using a keyword. The output of the search engine can be nested inside the mark tag with the search string shown in bold.

Listing 16.4 contains the code for the tag handler class of this tag.

**Listing 16.4 MarkerTag.java**

```
package sampleLib;

import javax.servlet.jsp.*;
import javax.servlet.jsp.tagext.*;

public class MarkerTag implements BodyTag {

//INITIALIZATION
   private PageContext pageContext;
   private Tag parentTag;
```

```
    public void setPageContext(PageContext pageContext)
    {
        this.pageContext = pageContext;
    }

    public void setParent(Tag parentTag)
    {
        this.parentTag = parentTag;
    }

    public Tag getParent()
    {
        return this.parentTag;
    }

//attributes
    private String search = null;

    public void setSearch(String search)
    {
        this.search = search;
    }


//BODY CONTENT RELATED MEMBERS

    private BodyContent bodyContent;

    public void setBodyContent(BodyContent bodyContent)
    {
        this.bodyContent = bodyContent;

    public void doInitBody() throws JspException
    {
    }


//START, ITERATE, AND END METHODS

    public int doStartTag() throws JspException
    {
       return EVAL_BODY_BUFFERED;
    }

    public int doAfterBody() throws JspException
    {
        try{
            JspWriter out = bodyContent.getEnclosingWriter();

            String text = bodyContent.getString();

            int len = search.length();

            int oldIndex=0, newIndex=0;

            while((newIndex = text.indexOf(search,oldIndex))>=0){

                if (newIndex<=oldIndex)
```

```
            {
               break;
            }
            out.print(text.substring(oldIndex,newIndex));
            out.print("<b>"+search+"</b>");
            oldIndex = newIndex + len;
         }

         out.print(text.substring(oldIndex));
      }
      catch(Exception e){
         e.printStackTrace();
      }

      return SKIP_BODY;

   }

   public int doEndTag() throws JspException {
      return EVAL_PAGE;
   }

   public void release()
   {
   }
}
```

In the above example, we have used an object of type `BodyContent`.

Note that we have used `EVAL_BODY_BUFFERED` in the return value of `doStartTag()`. If we had returned `EVAL_BODY_INCLUDE` instead, it would have thrown a `NullPointerException` upon using the `bodyContent` object in the `doAfterBody()`:

```
JspWriter out = bodyContent.getEnclosingWriter();
```

This is because `setBodyContent()` is not called and the `bodyContent` object is not set if `doStartTag()` returns `EVAL_BODY_INCLUDE`.

## 16.6 EXTENDING TAGSUPPORT AND BODYTAGSUPPORT

Until now, we have been writing tag classes that directly implement the `Tag`, `IterationTag`, and `BodyTag` interfaces. We chose to do this in order to learn about the flow of events that occur during the execution of a tag in a JSP page. In practice, however, we do not need to write all of the methods ourselves. The API provides two adapter classes, `TagSupport` and `BodyTagSupport`, that implement the `IterationTag` interface and the `BodyTag` interface, respectively, and provide a default implementation of all the methods. Thus, we only need to override those methods that have to be customized.

### 16.6.1 The TagSupport class

The `TagSupport` class implements the `IterationTag` interface, and provides default implementations for each of the methods of the `Tag` and `IterationTag` interfaces. It adds some new convenience methods that allow us to maintain a list of named objects in a hashtable and a method to find an outer tag of a given class from an inner tag. Table 16.9 lists some of the important methods of the `TagSupport` class and a protected attribute.

**Table 16.9 Methods of the TagSupport class**

| Method | Description |
|---|---|
| **Important Overridden Methods and Their Default Return Values** | |
| void doStartTag() | Inherited from Tag. The default return value is SKIP_BODY. |
| void doAfterBody() | Inherited from IterationTag. The default return value is SKIP_BODY. |
| void doEndTag(); | Inherited from Tag. The default return value is EVAL_PAGE. |
| **Methods Useful for Convenient Handling of Nested Tags** | |
| void setParent(Tag); | Accepts and maintains a reference to the parent tag. |
| Tag getParent(); | Returns the reference to the parent tag. |
| Tag findAncestorWithClass(Tag, Class); | This is a static method. Given a reference to a tag and the desired class, it will find the closest ancestor of the given tag of the given class. Internally, it calls getParent() on each of the references returned. |
| **Convenience Methods Useful for Maintaining a Map of Name-Value Pairs, Especially for Accepting Tag Attributes** | |
| void setValue(String, Object) | Accepts a name-value pair. The name is a String and the value can be any Object. |
| Object getValue(String); | Returns the object for the supplied String name. |
| Enumeration getValues(); | Returns an Enumeration of all the values. |
| void removeValue(String); | Removes the name-value pair from the list for the given name. |
| **Protected Member That Can Be Used by Derived Classes** | |
| PageContext pageContext | A reference to the saved PageContext object. |

### 16.6.2 The BodyTagSupport class

The `BodyTagSupport` class extends the `TagSupport` class, inheriting all the functionality shown in table 16.9. In addition, it implements the `BodyTag` interface and provides default implementations of the `setBodyContent()` and `doInitBody()`

methods. It also provides two convenience methods for handling buffered output: `getBodyContent()` and `getPreviousOut()`. Table 16.10 lists some of the important methods of the `BodyTagSupport` class.

**Table 16.10 Methods of the BodyTagSupport class**

| Method | Description |
|---|---|
| **Important Overridden Methods and Their Default Return Values** | |
| void doStartTag() | Inherited from Tag. The default return value is EVAL_BODY_BUFFERED. |
| void doAfterBody() | Inherited from IterationTag. The default return value is SKIP_BODY. |
| void doEndTag(); | Inherited from Tag. The default return value is EVAL_PAGE. |
| **Methods Useful for Convenient Handling of the Buffered Output** | |
| void setBodyContent(BodyContent); | Accepts and maintains a reference to the BodyContent object. The BodyContent object is a wrapper around the actual JspWriter object. It acts as the current output stream, but does not write the output directly to the client. Instead, it buffers it for further processing. |
| BodyContent getBodyContent(); | Returns the reference to the BodyContent object. |
| JspWriter getPreviousOut(); | Returns the output writer object, which is wrapped inside the BodyContent object. |

### 16.6.3 Accessing implicit objects

One of the greatest features of custom tags is their ability to access all the objects that are accessible to the JSP page in which they appear from within the tag handler classes. This is done with the help of the `PageContext` object, which is set by the container using the `setPageContext()` method before calling the `doStartTag()` method. Using the `pageContext` object, we can access any other object available to the page. For example, we have used it to get the `JspWriter` object to write out HTML in some of the previous examples:

```
JspWriter out = pageContext.getOut();
```

Table 16.11 lists the methods to access the four implicit objects that act as scope containers for other objects.

**Table 16.11 The four implicit objects that act as scope containers**

| Scope | Implicit variable | Implicit Object Class | Getting the Object from within the Tag Class | |
|---|---|---|---|---|
| | | | Using Direct Getters | As Named Objects |
| Application | application | ServletContext | pageContext.getServletContext() | pageContext.getAttribute(PageContext.APPLICATION); |
| Session | session | HttpSession | pageContext.getSession() | pageContext.getAttribute(PageContext.SESSION); |
| Request | request | ServletRequest | pageContext.getRequest() | pageContext.getAttribute(PageContext.REQUEST); |
| Page | pageContext | PageContext | - | pageContext.getAttribute(PageContext.PAGECONTEXT); |

Let's now look at a tag named `<implicit>` that accepts two attributes: `attributeName` and `scopeName`. It searches for an object with the given name in the given scope and will print it out in the output stream. The following JSP page code shows the intended usage of this tag:

```
<%@ taglib prefix="test" uri="/WEB-INF/sampleLib.tld" %>
<html><body>
   <%
      application.setAttribute("attribute1", "somestring");
      session.setAttribute("attribute2", new Boolean(true));
      request.setAttribute("attribute3", new Integer(5));
   %>

<test:implicit attributeName="attribute1" scopeName="application"/>
<test:implicit attributeName="attribute2" scopeName="session"/>
<test:implicit attributeName="attribute3" scopeName="request"/>
</body></html>
```

In the above tag usage, we set `attribute1`, `attribute2`, and `attribute3` in the application, session, and request scopes, respectively. Our intention is now to print the values of these attributes in the output HTML through our `<implicit>` tag. To do this, we pass the `attributeName` and `scopeName` to the three `<test:implicit>` tags one by one. The tags use these values to generate the following output:

```
<html><body>
someString
true
5
</body></html>
```

Listing 16.5 contains the code for ImplicitTag.java, which implements the <implicit> tag by extending the TagSupport class.

**Listing 16.5 ImplicitTag.java**

```
package sampleLib;

import javax.servlet.*;
import javax.servlet.jsp.*;
import javax.servlet.jsp.tagext.*;

public class ImplicitTag extends TagSupport {

   public void setAttributeName(String name)
   {
      //Stores the passed object in the hashtable maintained by
      //TagSupport with the name "attributeName".
      setValue("attributeName",name);
   }

   public void setScopeName(String scope)
   {
      //Stores the passed object in the hashtable with
      //the name "scopeName".
      setValue("scopeName",scope);
   }

   //Our utility method to convert the scopeName String
   //to the integer constant defined in PageContext for each scope.
   //We need this method because we have to use
   //PageContext.getAttribute(String name, int scope) later.

   private int getScopeAsInt()
   {
      //Retrieve the scopeName value from the hashtable
      String scope = (String) getValue("scopeName");

      if ("request".equals(scope))
         return PageContext.REQUEST_SCOPE;

      if ("session".equals(scope))
         return PageContext.SESSION_SCOPE;

      if ("application".equals(scope))
         return PageContext.APPLICATION_SCOPE;

      //Default is page scope
      return PageContext.PAGE_SCOPE;
   }

   public int doStartTag() throws JspException
   {
      try
      {
         JspWriter out = pageContext.getOut();

         String attributeName = (String) getValue("attributeName");
```

```
            int scopeConstant = getScopeAsInt();

            out.print(pageContext.getAttribute(attributeName, scopeConstant));

            return SKIP_BODY;
        }
        catch(Exception e)
        {
            throw new JspException("Error in Implicit.doAfterBody()");
        }
    }
}
```

There are three points worth noting in the above code:

- We have implemented a setter method for each attribute. However, instead of defining a private instance variable for storing each attribute, we have used the hashtable maintained by the `TagSupport` class to store the attributes as name-value pairs.
- `getScopeAsInt()` is our utility method that returns the integer constant representing the scope name that is stored as a string in the hashtable. These constants are already defined by `PageContext` and are used by the `PageContext.getAttribute(String name, int scope)` method.
- Finally, in the `doStartTag()` method, we use the `PageContext.getAttribute(String name, int scope)` method to retrieve the value of the given attribute name from the given scope name. After printing the value of the attribute, we return `SKIP_BODY`, since we do not want to accept any body content for the `<implicit>` tag.

This tag can be easily described in a TLD as follows:

```
<tag>
    <name>implicit</name>
    <tag-class>sampleLib.ImplicitTag</tag-class>
    <body-content>empty</body-content>
    <attribute>
        <name>attributeName</name>
        <required>true</required>
    </attribute>
    <attribute>
        <name>scopeName</name>
        <required>true</required>
    </attribute>

</tag>
```

### 16.6.4 Writing cooperative tags

Since tags are usually designed and developed with a common pattern of problems in mind, we often build a group of tags that work together. Such tags are called *cooperative tags*. One of the simplest examples to demonstrate the usage of cooperative tags is to implement the switch-case functionality similar to the one provided by the Java programming language. Let us look at three tags—<switch>, <case>, and <default>—that can be used in a JSP page, as shown in listing 16.6.

**Listing 16.6 switchTest.jsp**

```
<html><body>

   <%@ taglib prefix="test" uri="/WEB-INF/sampleLib.tld" %>

   <% String action = request.getParameter("action"); %>

   <test:switch conditionValue="<%=action%>" >

      <test:case caseValue="sayHello">
         Hello!
      </test:case>

      <test:case caseValue="sayGoodBye" >
         Good Bye!!
      </test:case>

      <test:default>
         I am Dumb!!!
      </test:default>

   </test:switch>

</body></html>
```

The conditionValue attribute of the switch tag acts like the switch condition of the Java switch statement, while the caseValue attribute of the case tag acts like the case value of the Java switch statement. Only those case tags whose caseValue attribute value matches the value of the conditionValue attribute of the switch tag should print their body contents. Thus, the above page should print Hello! in the browser when accessed through the URL

```
http://localhost:8080/chapter16/switchTest.jsp?action=sayHello
```

Let's now look at SwitchTag.java, CaseTag.java, and DefaultTag.java, which implement these tags.

**Listing 16.7 SwitchTag.java**

```
package sampleLib;

import javax.servlet.jsp.*;
import javax.servlet.jsp.tagext.*;

public class SwitchTag extends TagSupport
{

   public void setPageContext(PageContext pageContext)
   {
      super.setPageContext(pageContext);
```

```
        //Sets the internal flag that tells whether or not a matching
        //case tag has been found to be false.
        setValue("caseFound", Boolean.FALSE);
    }

    //stores the value of the match attribute
    public void setConditionValue(String value)
    {
        setValue("conditionValue", value);
    }

    public int doStartTag() throws JspException
    {
        return EVAL_BODY_INCLUDE;
    }
}
```

The code for the `SwitchTag` class is quite simple and has just three methods: `setPageContext()`, a setter for the `conditionValue` attribute, and `doStartTag()`. The `caseFound` flag indicates whether or not a matching `case` tag has been found. The `pageContext()` method initializes it to `false`. We will show the use of this flag in the `case` and `default` tags shortly. The setter method stores the value of the `conditionValue` attribute using the `setValue()` method, as explained in the previous example. We don't want to do anything in the `doStartTag()` method, but we do want the body of the `switch` tag to be evaluated. However, the default implementation of `doStartTag()` provided by `TagSupport` returns `SKIP_BODY`, so we need to override it and return `EVAL_BODY_INCLUDE` instead.

Listing 16.8 is the code for the `case` tag handler.

**Listing 16.8 Case.java**

```
package sampleLib;

import javax.servlet.jsp.*;
import javax.servlet.jsp.tagext.*;

public class CaseTag extends TagSupport
{
    public void setCaseValue(String caseValue)
    {
        setValue("caseValue",caseValue);
    }
    public int doStartTag() throws JspException
    {
        //gets the reference of the enclosing switch tag handler.
        SwitchTag parent =
            (SwitchTag) findAncestorWithClass(this, SwitchTag.class);

        Object caseValue = this.getValue("caseValue");
        Object conditionValue = this.getValue("conditionValue");
```

```
        //If the value of the caseValue attribute of this case tag
        //matches with the value of the conditionValue attribute of
        //the parent switch tag, it sets the caseFound flag to true and
        //includes the body; otherwise, it skips the body.

        if (conditionValue.equals(caseValue))
        {
            //Sets the caseFound flag to true
            parent.setValue("caseFound",Boolean.TRUE);

            //Includes the body contents in the output HTML
            return EVAL_BODY_INCLUDE;
        }
        else
        {

            return SKIP_BODY;
        }
    }
}
```

There are two points worth noting in the above code:

- The `setCaseValue()` method stores the value attribute using the `setValue()` method of `TagSupport`.
- In `doStartTag()`, we first get a reference of the parent `switch` tag using the `findAncestorWithClass()` method of `TagSupport`. Next, we retrieve the value of the `conditionValue` attribute from the parent tag handler reference and the value of the `caseValue` attribute from the current tag. If the two values match, we set the `caseFound` flag to `true` and return `EVAL_BODY_INCLUDE` so that the body of this `case` tag is included in the output. Otherwise, if the values don't match, we return `SKIP_BODY`.

Now, let's look at the code for the `default` tag handler in listing 16.9.

**Listing 16.9 DefaultTag.java**

```
package sampleLib;

import javax.servlet.jsp.*;
import javax.servlet.jsp.tagext.*;


public class DefaultTag extends TagSupport
{

    public int doStartTag() throws JspException
    {

        SwitchTag parent = (SwitchTag)
                           findAncestorWithClass(this, SwitchTag.class);

        Boolean caseFound = parent.getValue("caseFound");
```

```
        //If the conditionValue attribute value of the switch tag
        //did not match with any of the caseValue attribute values,
        //then it includes the body of this tag; otherwise; it skips the body.

        if (caseFound.equals(Boolean.FALSE))
        {
           return EVAL_BODY_INCLUDE;
        }
        else
        {
           return SKIP_BODY;
        }
    }
}
```

The implentation of the default tag handler checks whether the `caseFound` attribute of the enclosing `SwitchTag` instance is set to `true`. If it is set to `false`, it means that none of the `caseValues` matched with the `conditionValue`, in which case the `DefaultTag` will include its own body. Otherwise, it will skip the body.

The following elements describe these tags in the TLD:

```
<tag>
   <name>switch</name>
   <tag-class>sampleLib.SwitchTag</tag-class>
   <body-content>JSP</body-content>
   <attribute>
      <name>conditionValue</name>
      <required>true</required>
      <rtexprvalue>true</rtexprvalue>
   </attribute>
</tag>

<tag>
   <name>case</name>
   <tag-class>sampleLib.CaseTag</tag-class>
   <body-content>JSP</body-content>
   <attribute>
      <name>caseValue</name>
      <required>true</required>
   </attribute>
</tag>

<tag>
   <name>default</name>
   <tag-class>sampleLib.DefaultTag</tag-class>
   <body-content>JSP</body-content>
</tag>
```

## 16.7 WHAT'S MORE?

We have discussed the various types of tags, interfaces, and classes provided by the Tag Extension API, which is information that you need to know in order to do well on the exam. However, the story of custom tags does not end here. To get maximum benefit from the use of custom tags, you should learn how to use other classes and the interfaces of the Tag Extension API as well. For example, you can learn how to use the `TagLibraryValidator` and the `PageData` classes to validate the semantics of the tags used in a JSP page at translation time, or how to make scripting variables in a JSP page available—in a manner similar to `<jsp:useBean>`—via the `TagExtraInfo` and `TagVariableInfo` classes. You can also learn how to handle resources more efficiently by implementing the `TryCatchFinally` interface, and many other techniques for working with custom tags.

### *The difference between custom tags and JavaBeans*

Many times developers ask when they should use custom tags and when they should use JavaBeans. They both are reusable components and help us to reduce the length of our scriptlets and make our JSP pages cleaner and more manageable. Then, how do we know when to use which type of component? For example, should the functionality of database access go into JavaBeans, or in custom tags?

After reading chapters 14, 15, and 16, you should know that the two types of components serve two different purposes. Here are some differences between the two that might help you determine which one to use:

- JavaBeans are the data handlers of JSP pages and aid in encapsulating data-management logic. They are used for storage. Tags, on the other hand, aid computational logic related to a particular request.
- Tags are thread safe; beans are not. Beans, like other separate utility classes, have to be made thread safe by the developers.
- Tags are aware of the environment (the page context) in which they execute. Beans are not.
- Tags remain in the translation unit. We can think of tags as events occurring in the execution of a JSP page. Beans are object stores that reside outside the translation unit.
- Tags can access implicit objects. Beans cannot.
- Tags only have page scope. They are created and destroyed within a single request and in a single page. They can access other objects in all the scopes, though. Beans, on the other hand, are themselves objects that reside in different scopes. Therefore, tags can access and manipulate beans, while beans do not access and manipulate tags.

- The Tag Extension API is designed closely with the concept of a JSP page in mind. They may not be used in other applications. Beans, on the other hand, are supposed to be reusable components and can be used by other containers.
- Tags are not persistent objects. Beans have properties, and properties have values. A set of values is called the *state* of the bean. This state can be persisted via serialization and reused later.

So to answer the question about whether to use beans or tags for database access, let's clarify that we can use beans to access a database, to encapsulate data, and to implement business logic rules to manipulate data in the beans. The code for managing the beans across scopes should be handled by custom tags. The code that uses the bean's properties and includes presentation logic should be placed in custom tags. Thus, tags are a preferred way of writing JSP pages that use JavaBeans.

## 16.8 SUMMARY

In this chapter, we learned how to create our own custom tab libraries. The tag library descriptor (TLD) file contains the information that the JSP engine needs to know about the tag library in order to successfully interpret the custom tags on JSP pages. We discussed the TLD file and its three important elements: `<tag>`, `<attribute>`, and `<body-content>`.

The Tag Extension API consists of one package: `javax.servlet.jsp.tagext`, with 4 interfaces and 13 classes. We examined in detail the methods and constants of the three interfaces: `Tag`, `IterativeTag`, and `BodyTag`. We then saw how we can implement those interfaces in classes. In addition, the JSP API provides two adapter classes, `TagSupport` and `BodyTagSupport`, that implement the `IterationTag` interface and `BodyTag` interface, respectively, and that provide default implementation of all the methods.

At this point, you should be able to answer exam questions about the structure and format of the TLD file elements as well as questions based on the Tag Extension API and implementation of custom tag libraries.

With the end of this chapter, we finish the second part of this book, in which we have discussed various aspects of the JSP technology. In the next part, we will learn about the design patterns that are widely used for developing web applications. We will also learn about the Filter API, which is a new concept that has been added recently to the Servlet specification.

## 16.9 REVIEW QUESTIONS

1. Which of the following is not a valid subelement of the <attribute> element in a TLD? (Select one)

   **a** <name>

   **b** <class>

   **c** <required>

   **d** <type>

2. What is the name of the tag library descriptor element that declares that an attribute can have a request-time expression as its value?

   [____________]

3. Consider the following code in a JSP page.

```
<% String message = "Hello "; %>

<test:world>
   How are you?
   <% message = message + "World! " %>
</test:world>

<%= message %>
```

   If doStartTag() returns EVAL_BODY_BUFFERED and doAfterBody() clears the buffer by calling bodyContent.clearBody(), what will be the output of the above code? (Select one)

   **a** Hello

   **b** Hello How are you?

   **c** Hello How are you? World!

   **d** Hello World!

   **e** How are you World!

4. Which of the following interfaces are required at a minimum to create a simple custom tag with a body? (Select one)

   **a** Tag

   **b** Tag and IterationTag

   **c** Tag, IterationTag, and BodyTag

   **d** TagSupport

   **e** BodyTagSupport

5. At a minimum, which of the following interfaces are required to create an iterative custom tag? (Select one)

   **a** Tag

   **b** Tag and IterationTag

c Tag, IterationTag, and BodyTag

d TagSupport

e BodyTagSupport

6. Which of the following methods is never called for handler classes that implement only the Tag interface? (Select one)

a setParent()

b doStartTag()

c doAfterbody()

d doEndTag()

7. Which of the following is a valid return value for doAfterBody()? (Select one)

a EVAL_BODY_INCLUDE

b SKIP_BODY

c EVAL_PAGE

d SKIP_PAGE

8. Which element would you use in a TLD to indicate the type of body a custom tag expects?

[________________]

9. If the doStartTag() method returns EVAL_BODY_INCLUDE one time and the doAfterBody() method returns EVAL_BODY_AGAIN five times, how many times will the setBodyContent() method be called? (Select one)

a Zero

b One

c Two

d Five

e Six

10. If the doStartTag() method returns EVAL_BODY_BUFFERED one time and the doAfterBody() method returns EVAL_BODY_BUFFERED five times, how many times will the setBodyContent() method be called? Assume that the body of the tag is not empty. (Select one)

a Zero

b One

c Two

d Five

e Six

11. How is the `SKIP_PAGE` constant used? (Select one)

   **a** `doStartTag()` can return it to skip the evaluation until the end of the current page.
   **b** `doAfterBody()` can return it to skip the evaluation until the end of the current page.
   **c** `doEndTag()` can return it to skip the evaluation until the end of the current page.
   **d** It is passed as a parameter to `doEndTag()` as an indication to skip the evaluation until the end of the current page.

12. Which of the following can you use to achieve the same functionality as provided by `findAncestorWithClass()`? (Select one)

   **a** `getParent()`
   **b** `getParentWithClass()`
   **c** `getAncestor()`
   **d** `getAncestorWithClass()`
   **e** `findAncestor()`

13. Consider the following code in a tag handler class that extends `TagSupport`:

```
public int doStartTag()
{
    //1
}
```

   Which of the following can you use at `//1` to get an attribute from the application scope? (Select one)

   **a** `getServletContext().getAttribute("name");`
   **b** `getApplication().getAttribute("name");`
   **c** `pageContext.getAttribute("name",PageContext.APPLICATION_SCOPE);`
   **d** `bodyContent.getApplicationAttribute("name");`

14. Which types of objects can be returned by `PageContext.getOut()`? (Select two)

   **a** An object of type `ServletOutputStream`
   **b** An object of type `HttpServletOutputStream`
   **c** An object of type `JspWriter`
   **d** An object of type `HttpJspWriter`
   **e** An object of type `BodyContent`

15. We can use the directive `<%@ page buffer="8kb" %>` to specify the size of the buffer when returning `EVAL_BODY_BUFFERED` from `doStartTag()`.

   **a** True
   **b** False

# PART 4

# *Patterns and filters*

This part contains two chapters. In the first chapter, we introduce design patterns and examine several patterns you need to know to do well on the exam. In the second chapter, we discuss filters, a topic that the exam does not cover (yet!). As you'll learn, filters are useful in developing real-life web applications.

CHAPTER 17

# Design patterns



## EXAM OBJECTIVES

**13.1** Given a scenario description with a list of issues, select the design pattern (Value Objects, MVC, Data Access Object, or Business Delegate) that would best solve those issues. (Sections 17.2.2–17.2.7)

**13.2** Match design patterns with statements describing potential benefits that accrue from the use of the pattern, for any of the following patterns:

- Value Objects
- MVC
- Data Access Object
- Business Delegate

(Sections 17.2.2–17.2.7)

## INTRODUCTION

In our daily lives as designers and programmers, we are continuously developing our problem-solving skills. With each problem we encounter, we immediately start considering the different ways it can be solved, including successful solutions that we have used in the past for similar problems. Out of many possible solutions, we pick the one that best fits our application. By documenting this solution, we can reuse and share the information that we have learned about the best way to solve the specific problem.

*Design patterns* address the recurring design problems that arise in particular design situations and propose solutions to them. Design patterns are thus successful solutions to known problems. There are various ways to implement design patterns. These implementation details are called *strategies.*

In this chapter, we will introduce the following J2EE design patterns that are named in the exam objectives: Value Object, Model-View-Controller, Data Access Object, and Business Delegate. We will also look at the Front Controller design pattern, since it is often mentioned on the exam.

## 17.1 DESIGN PATTERNS: A BRIEF HISTORY

A design pattern is an abstraction of a solution at a very high level. Many designers and architects have defined the term *design pattern* in various ways that suit the domain to which they apply the patterns. Further, they have divided the patterns into different categories according to their usage. Let's look at some of them before we go into the details of the J2EE patterns in the next section.

### 17.1.1 The civil engineering patterns

In the 1960s and 1970s, Christopher Alexander, professor of architecture and director of the Center for Environmental Structure, along with his colleagues, wrote a number of books describing and documenting the principles of civil engineering from a layperson's point of view. Of them, one of the most widely known books is *A Pattern Language: Towns, Buildings, Constructions.* It provides practical guidance on how to build houses, construct buildings and parking lots, design a good neighborhood, and so forth. The book examines how these simple designs integrate with each other to create well-planned towns and cities.

As its title suggests, the book describes 253 patterns that are split into three broad categories: towns, buildings, and construction.

### 17.1.2 The Gang of Four patterns

Software designers extended the idea of design patterns to software development. Since features provided by the object-oriented languages, such as inheritance, abstraction, and encapsulation, allowed them to easily relate programming language entities to real-world entities, designers started applying those features to create common and reusable solutions to recurring problems that exhibited similar patterns.

Around 1994, the now famous Gang of Four (GoF)—Erich Gamma, Richard Helm, Ralph Johnson, and John Vlissides—documented 23 such software design patterns in the book *Elements of Reusable Object-Oriented Software.* They classified the patterns at the very top level into three types of categories based on their purpose: creational, structural, and behavioral, as shown in table 17.1.

**Table 17.1 The GoF categories of design patterns**

| Type of GoF pattern | Description |
|---|---|
| Creational | Creational patterns deal with the ways to create instances of objects. The objective of these patterns is to abstract the instantiation process and hide the details of how objects are created or initialized. |
| Structural | Structural patterns describe how classes and objects can be combined to form larger structures and provide new functionality. These aggregated objects can be either simple objects or composite objects themselves. |
| Behavioral | Behavioral patterns help us define the communication and interaction between the objects of a system. The purpose of these patterns is to reduce coupling between objects. |

At the second level, they classified the patterns as falling into one of the two scopes: class or object. Thus, we have six types of patterns, as described in table 17.2.

**Table 17.2 The GoF categories and scopes of design patterns**

| GoF Pattern Category | Brief Description | Examples |
|---|---|---|
| **Creational** | | |
| Creational class | Creational class patterns use inheritance as a mechanism to achieve varying class instantiation. | Factory Method |
| Creational object | Creational object patterns are more scalable and dynamic compared to the class creational patterns. | Abstract Factory<br>Singleton |
| **Structural** | | |
| Structural class | Structural class patterns use inheritance to provide more useful program interfaces by combining the functionality of multiple classes. | Adapter (class) |
| Structural object | Structural object patterns create composite objects by aggregating individual objects to build larger structures. The composition of the structural object pattern can be changed at runtime, which gives us added flexibility over structural class patterns. | Adapter (object)<br>Facade<br>Bridge<br>Composite |

*continued on next page*

Table 17.2 The GoF categories and scopes of design patterns *(continued)*

| GoF Pattern Category | Brief Description | Examples |
|---|---|---|
| **Behavioral** | | |
| Behavioral class | Behavioral class patterns use inheritance to distribute behavior between classes. | Interpreter |
| Behavioral object | Behavioral object patterns allow us to analyze the patterns of communication between interconnected objects, such as the included objects of a composite object. | Iterator<br>Observer<br>Visitor |

### 17.1.3 The distributed design patterns

Though the GoF patterns served well in designing and developing object-oriented systems in both distributed and non-distributed environments, they were not created with the distributed nature of large-scale enterprise systems in mind. As the demands for more distributed enterprise applications grew, the architects felt the need to document the solutions to recurring problems as they experienced the same problem occurring over and over again. They started extending and refining the patterns over a larger scale and with a broader scope. One book that documents some 30 patterns at the architectural level is *CORBA Design Patterns*, by Thomas J. Mowbray and Raphael C. Malveau. Though the book focuses mainly on the Common Object Request Broker Architecture (CORBA), the patterns described are applicable to a wide range of distributed applications, including those that do not use CORBA.

The authors have categorized the design patterns at seven architectural levels:

- Global
- Enterprise
- System
- Application
- Macrocomponent
- Microcomponent
- Object

The authors have two basic arguments. The first is that software design involves making choices, such as which details of an object should be abstracted and what should be exposed, or which aspects of the objects are to be generalized and which one should be specialized. These decisions are based on the facts surrounding the problem at hand. The book terms such facts as *primal forces*, because they influence our choice of a particular pattern. The discussion on forces focuses on issues such as whether a pattern increases performance, whether it aids in enhanced functionality, or whether it helps to reduce complexity within modules.

The authors' second argument is that not all design patterns scale well at all seven architectural levels. Each pattern has a set of applicable levels, which is an important feature that must be considered when using the pattern.

### 17.1.4 The J2EE patterns

With the advent of the J2EE, a whole new catalog of design patterns cropped up. Since J2EE is an architecture in itself that comprises other architectures, including Servlets, JavaServer Pages, Enterprise JavaBeans, and so forth, it deserves its own set of patterns specifically tailored to the various types of enterprise applications that the architecture addresses.

The book *core J2EE PATTERNS Best Practices and Design Strategies*, by Deepak Alur, John Crupi, and Dan Malks, describes the five tiers of the J2EE architecture:

- Client
- Presentation
- Business
- Integration
- Resource

The book then explains 15 J2EE patterns that are divided among three of the tiers: presentation, business, and integration.

#### *The five tiers in J2EE*

A *tier* is a logical partition of the components involved in the system. Each tier is loosely coupled with the adjacent tier. It is easier to understand the role of design patterns once we fully grasp the different tiers involved in a J2EE application. The J2EE architecture identifies the five tiers described in table 17.3.

**Table 17.3 Tiers in the J2EE architecture**

| Tier Name | Description |
|---|---|
| Client | This tier comprises all the types of components that are clients of the enterprise application. Examples of client components are a web browser, a handheld device, or another application that accesses the services of the enterprise application remotely. |
| Presentation | This tier interfaces with the client tier and encapsulates the presentation logic. It accepts the requests, handles authentication and authorization, manages client sessions, delegates the business processing to the business tier, and presents the clients with the desired response. The components that make up this tier are filters, servlets, JavaBeans, JSP pages, and other utility classes. |
| Business | This tier is the heart of the enterprise application and implements the core business services. It is normally composed of the Enterprise JavaBeans components that handle all the business processing rules. |

*continued on next page*

**Table 17.3 Tiers in the J2EE architecture *(continued)***

| Tier Name | Description |
|---|---|
| Integration | The job of this tier is to seamlessly integrate different types of external resources in the resource tier with the components of the business tier. The components that make up the integration tier use various mechanisms like JDBC, J2EE connector technology, or proprietary middleware to access the resource tier. |
| Resource | This tier comprises the external resources that provide the actual data to the application. The resources can either be data stores such as relational databases and file-based databases, or systems such as applications running on mainframes, other legacy systems, modern business-to-business (B2B) systems, and third-party services like credit card authorization services. |

## *The J2EE pattern catalog*

Table 17.4 lists the 15 patterns of J2EE, with a brief description of each.

**Table 17.4 J2EE design patterns**

| Name (s) | Description |
|---|---|
| **Presentation Tier** | |
| Decorating Filter/ Intercepting Filter | An object that sits between the client and the web components. It pre-processes a request and post-processes the response. |
| Front Controller/ Front Component | An object that accepts all the requests from the client and dispatches or routes them to appropriate handlers. The Front Controller pattern may divide the above functionality into two different objects: the Front Controller and the Dispatcher. In that case, the Front Controller accepts all the requests from the client and does the authentication, and the Dispatcher dispatches or routes them to the appropriate handlers. |
| View Helper | A helper object that encapsulates data access logic on behalf of the presentation components. For example, JavaBeans can be used as View Helper patterns for JSP pages. |
| Composite View | A view object that is made up of an aggregate of other view objects. For example, a JSP page that includes other JSP and HTML pages using the include directive or the include action is a Composite View pattern. |
| Service To Worker | A kind of Model-View-Controller with the Controller acting as a Front Controller but with one important point: here the Dispatcher (which is a part of the Front Controller) uses View Helpers to a large extent and aids in view management. |
| Dispatcher View | A kind of Model-View-Controller with the controller acting as a Front Controller but with one important point: here the Dispatcher (which is a part of the Front Controller) does not use View Helpers and does very little work in view management. The view management is handled by the View components themselves. |

*continued on next page*

**Table 17.4 J2EE design patterns *(continued)***

| Name (s) | Description |
|---|---|
| **Business Tier** | |
| Business Delegate | An object that resides on the presentation tier and on behalf of other presentation-tier components calls remote methods on the objects in the business tier. |
| Value Object/ Data Transfer Object/ Replicate Object | A serializable object for transferring data over the network. |
| Session Façade/ Session Entity Façade/ Distributed Façade | An object that resides in the business tier, acts as an entry point into the business tier, and manages the workflow of business service objects, such as session beans, entity beans, and Data Access Objects. The Session Facade itself is usually implemented as a session bean. |
| Aggregate Entity | An object (entity bean) that is made up of or is an aggregate of other entity beans. |
| Value Object Assembler | An object that resides in the business tier and creates Value Objects on the fly as and when required. |
| Value List Handler/ Page-by-Page Iterator/ Paged List | An object that manages execution of queries, caching, and processing of results. Usually implemented as a Session Bean, serving a subset of the fetched result set to the client as and when needed. |
| Service Locator | An object that performs the task of locating business services on behalf of other components in the tier. Usually present in the presentation tier, it is used by Business Delegates to look up business service objects. |
| **Integration Tier** | |
| Data Access Object | An object that talks to the actual underlying database and provides other application components. It serves as a clean, simple, and common interface for accessing the data, and for reducing the dependency of other components on the details of using the database. |
| Service Activator | An object that helps in processing of business methods asynchronously. |

Of all the design patterns listed above, only three—Value Object, Data Access Object, and Business Delegate—are mentioned in the exam objectives. The exam objectives also cover the Model-View-Controller pattern, which is considered more of an architecture than a design pattern in J2EE. In the rest of this chapter, we will examine these four design patterns along with a fifth pattern that is often encountered in the exam, the Front Controller. Discussing the other 11 patterns is beyond the scope of this book. However, they are frequently used as possible options in the single-choice questions of the exam. It will be helpful if you study table 17.4 so that during the exam you can eliminate the incorrect choices, thereby making it easier for you to select the right answer.

## 17.2 PATTERNS FOR THE SCWCD EXAM

Table 17.5 lists the most important J2EE design patterns that you need to know for the exam.

**Table 17.5 Patterns required for the SCWCD exam**

| Name | Other Name(s) | Tier |
|---|---|---|
| Value Object | Data Transfer Object, Replicate Object | Presentation |
| Model-View-Controller | | Presentation |
| Data Access Object | Data Access Component | Integration |
| Business Delegate | | Business |
| Front Controller | Front Component | Presentation |

Even though Front Controller is not mentioned in the objectives, the exam frequently asks questions about it, which is why we have decided to include it in this section.

### 17.2.1 The pattern template

During the process of analyzing a problem, designing a solution, creating an action plan, and implementing the ideas that are born out of the process, one of the most important tasks is to document each and every aspect of the process. This facilitates preserving the ideas in a systematic manner so that they can be read, understood, and reused by others.

Design patterns are documented using a pattern template. The template is made up of headings; each heading explains a different aspect of the pattern, such as the cause of the problem, the situation in which the problem can occur, and the possible facts to look for. Different organizations and pattern catalog writers use different sets of headers and, therefore, their templates vary. However, their goal is the same: systematic documentation of the causes of the problems, the solutions provided by the patterns, their consequences and implications, examples, related patterns, and so forth.

So before we start explaining the design patterns required for the exams, let's first look at the template that we have used to explain the design patterns in the following sections. We have kept the template large enough to cover different aspects under different headings, while at the same time keeping it small enough to maintain simplicity. Also, wherever possible, we have avoided long paragraphs of text and used a bulleted-points approach while presenting the facts to make it easier to remember and reference. The following subsections describe the template headers.

#### *Context*

This section describes the context or the situation in which the problems can occur and the given pattern that we can apply.

Patterns, if not used wisely or if applied in the wrong context, can turn out to be anti-patterns. Various facts have to be sorted out, and the pros and cons of the pattern have to be evaluated against these facts before applying the pattern. Therefore, it is important to understand the situation in which the pattern may be applicable.

### *Problem*

This section provides a common, day-to-day problem that we face in the given context. Because so many developers and programmers have experienced this problem, designers have developed standard solutions for it.

In many books or tutorials, you may find a separate heading called *Intent* to describe the intent of the pattern. The *Intent* heading is suitable where the primary aim of the pattern is to enhance the design of the overall system rather than attacking a particular problem. In the patterns described below, we have provided a *Problem* heading instead, and the intent of the pattern is to solve the given problem.

### *Example*

This section provides a simple example of the specified problem type.

### *Facts or forces to consider*

Other than the given situation and the given type of problem, there may be various facts that need to be considered before using design patterns. These facts, usually business logic dependent, vary largely from system to system, depending on the requirements. They are also referred to as *forces* in the design pattern jargon, because they influence whether or not a design pattern is applicable in the given scenario. In some cases where more than one pattern can solve the problem, these forces can be helpful in determining the choice of using one pattern over the other. You can think of facts and forces as observations or requirements of the problem that you will take into consideration when you are evaluating the candidate design patterns for this particular situation.

### *Solution*

This section describes a typical solution that is tried, tested, and proven by experienced developers to solve the problem, taking into account the given facts or forces. The problem-solution pair forms a design pattern. However, the solution is really a high-level design guideline that we can follow. The actual implementation of the solution may vary from context to context, and each implementation of the solution is referred to as a *strategy* of the solution in the J2EE jargon. Thus, each design pattern can be implemented by applying different strategies depending on the context of the problem and the facts or forces surrounding the problem.

We have not provided a separate section of strategies, and we have discussed only the most common of the strategies for the patterns, since describing all the strategies is outside the scope of this book.

### Consequences/implications

This section describes the advantages, aftereffects, and hidden problems associated with the patterns. Every pattern has side effects inherent in the solution. Thus, a pattern may solve one problem but generate another. So we have to weigh the pros and cons of the pattern and find a balance between the two.

### Category

This section indicates which of the three categories the pattern falls into: creational, structural, or behavioral, with a brief description.

### Points to remember

These are the points we must take into account when considering a particular pattern as a solution. In the following discussions of the J2EE design patterns, we have provided a list of words, phrases, and terms that are related to the pattern, and which may help you to prepare for the exam. When you read a problem statement, see if you can identify any of the terms or phrases listed in this section in the statement. Another tactic is to restate the problem (without changing the meaning) and find any of these terms that match. This will aid you in selecting or eliminating the options in exam questions.

## 17.2.2 Value Object

### Context

In distributed applications, the following situation typically arises:

- The client-side and the server-side components reside at remote locations and communicate over the network.
- The server handles the database.
- The server provides getter methods to the clients so that the clients can call those getter methods one by one to retrieve database values.
- The server provides setter methods to the clients so that the clients can call those setter methods one by one to update database values.

### Problem

Every call between the client and the server is a remote method call with substantial network overhead. If the client application calls the individual getter and setter methods that retrieve or update single attribute values, it will require as many remote calls as there are attributes. These individual calls generate a lot of network traffic and degrade the system performance.

### Example

In the J2EE architecture, the business tier accesses the database directly or via the resource tier, and wraps the data access mechanism inside a set of entity beans and session beans. These entity and session beans expose the data via remote interfaces. The servlets and JSP pages in the presentation tier that need to access business data can do so by calling methods on the remote interfaces implemented by the beans.

As a specific example, suppose we maintain the address information in the database of the registered users of our enterprise application. In this case, the address information, which is a summation of four other pieces of data—street, city, state, and, zip—is a business entity. The access to this information is encapsulated by the application's business tier with the help of a session bean called `AddressSessionBean`. `AddressSessionBean` exposes methods for the remote clients, such as `getState()`, `setState()`, `getCity()`, and `setCity()`. The servlets and the JSP pages then have to call each of the methods one by one on the remote server, as shown in figure 17.1.

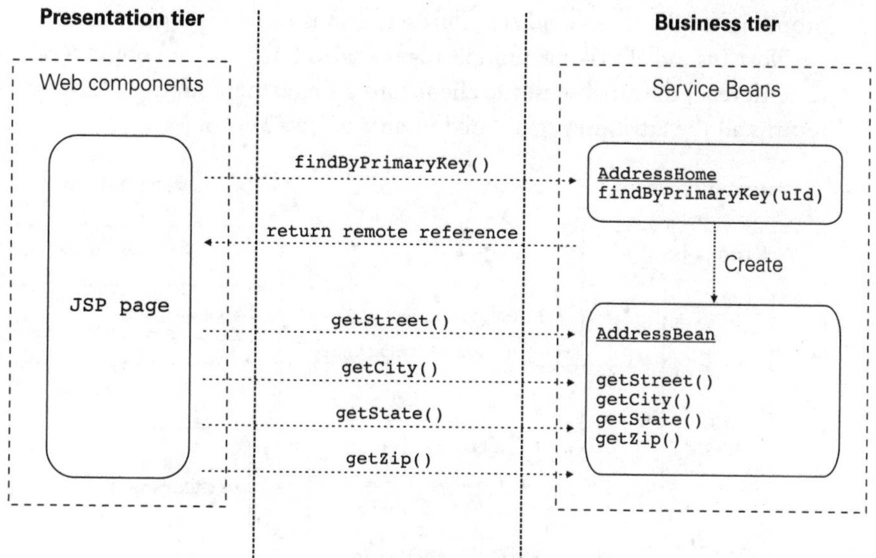


**Figure 17.1 Accessing attributes remotely.**

### Facts or forces to consider

In the context and the problem presented above, we observe the following facts:

- A single business object has many attributes.
- Most of the time, the client requires values for more than one attribute simultaneously rather than just an individual attribute.
- The rate of retrieving the data (calling the getter methods) is higher than the rate of updating the data (calling the setter methods).

For example, the address consists of the street, state, city, and zip. Each time the user buys a product online, we want to show the full address information for billing purposes. On the other hand, it is unlikely that the user's address changes very often.

### *Solution*

Create an object to encapsulate all of the attribute values that are required by the client application. This object is called the Value Object. When the client requests the data from the server, the server-side component gathers the data values and constructs the Value Object by setting the data values of the Value Object. This Value Object is then sent to the client by value (not by reference), which means that the whole object is serialized and each of its bits is transferred over the network.

The client on the other side reconstructs this object locally with all the values intact. It can then query this local instance for all the attribute values. Because the Value Object is local on the client, all of the calls to this object are local and do not incur any network overhead. The Value Object on the client serves as a proxy for the properties of the remote object. This scenario is shown in figure 17.2.

Now, instead of making multiple remote calls on the business object, `AddressBean`, to retrieve all the attributes, the client calls a single method, `getAddress()`, which returns all the attributes structured in an `AddressVO` object.

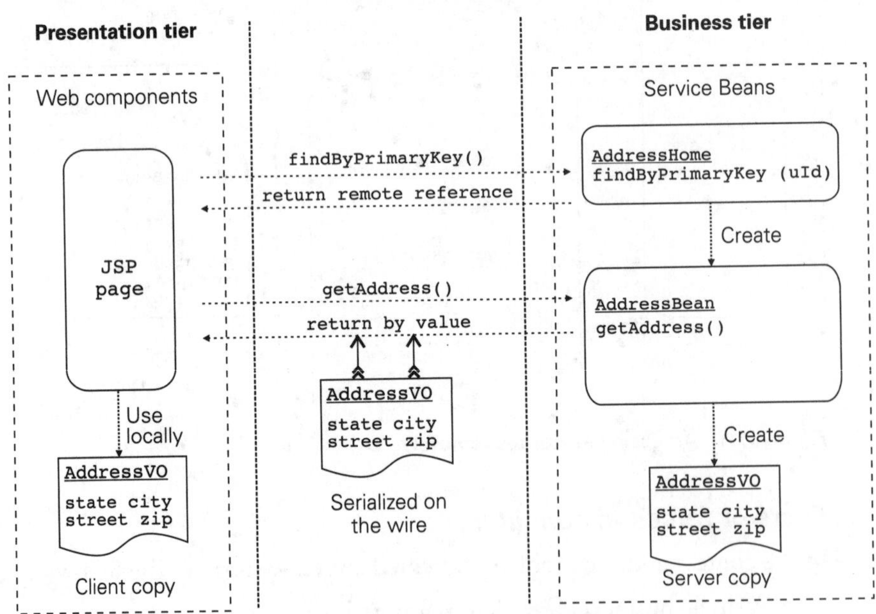


**Figure 17.2 Accessing attributes using the Value Object design pattern.**

Here are the responsibilities of the three components participating in this pattern:

- *Client.* The client can be a JSP page, a servlet, or a Java applet that makes remote calls to the business object on the business tier server.
- *Business object.* The business object is the server-side component that creates the Value Object. The client makes calls to the business object.
- *Value Object.* The Value Object is an object that has all the business values required by the client. The design of the Value Object depends on the application requirements. It can be mutable or immutable (no setter methods), depending on whether the application wants to allow updates to the Value Object.

### Consequences/implications

- The remote interfaces are simpler because the multiple methods returning single values are collapsed into one single method returning a group of multiple values.
- Because of the reduced number of calls across the network, the user response time improves.
- If the client wants to update the attribute values, it first updates the values in the local Value Object and then sends the updated Value Object to the server to persist the new values. This also happens using the pass-by-value mechanism.
- The Value Object can become stale—that is, if the client has acquired a Value Object for a long time, there is a possibility that the information may have been updated by another client.
- In the case of a mutable Value Object, requests for update from two or more clients can result in data conflict.

### Category

Since the Value Object pattern is concerned with communication between two other components, it falls in the category of a behavioral pattern.

In the J2EE pattern catalog, the Value Object is kept under the business tier because it represents the business object on the client side. However, note that even though the object that implements the Value Object pattern is created in the business tier, it is transferred to the presentation tier and is actually used in the presentation tier.

### Points to remember

A Value Object is a small-sized serializable Java *object* that is used for carrying grouped data (*values*) over the network from one component residing in one tier to another component residing in another tier of a multitier distributed application. Its purpose is to reduce communication overhead by reducing the number of remote calls between the distributed components.

Pay special attention to the following words, phrases, or terms appearing in the problem statement:

- Small object
- Grouped information
- Read-only data
- Reduce network traffic
- Increase response time
- Transfer data across networked tiers

### 17.2.3 Model-View-Controller (MVC)

#### *Context*

In systems involving user interfaces, the following situation typically arises:

- The system has to accept data from the user, update the database, and return the data to the user at a later point in time.
- There are several ways in which the data can be accepted from and presented to the system users.
- Data fed to the system in one form should be retrievable in another form.

#### *Problem*

If the system deploys a single component that interacts with the user as well as maintains the database, then a requirement to support a new type of display or view will necessitate the redesign of the component.

#### *Example*

Suppose a bank provides online stock trading facilities. When logged into the site, the web application allows the user to view the rates of the stocks over a period of time in various ways, such as a bar graph, a line graph, or a plain table. Here, the same data that represents the rates of the stocks is viewed in multiple ways, but is controlled by a single entity, the web application.

#### *Facts or forces to consider*

In the context and the problem presented above, we observe the following facts:

- There are three tasks to be done:
  1. Manage the user's interaction with the system.
  2. Manage the actual data.
  3. Format the data in multiple ways and present it to the user.
- Thus, a single component that does all the tasks can be split into three independent components.
- All three tasks can then be handled by different components.

### *Solution*

The solution is to separate the data presentation from the data maintenance and have a third component that coordinates the first two. These three components are called the Model, the View, and the Controller, and they form the basis of the MVC pattern. Figure 17.3 shows the relationship between the components of the MVC pattern.

Here are the responsibilities of the three MVC components:

- *Model.* The Model is responsible for keeping the data or the state of the application. It also manages the storage and retrieval of the data from the data source. It notifies all the Views that are viewing its data when the data changes.
- *View.* The View contains the presentation logic. It displays the data contained in the Model to the users. It also allows the user to interact with the system and notifies the Controller of the users' actions.
- *Controller.* The Controller manages the whole show. It instantiates the Model and the View and associates the View with the Model. Depending on the application requirements, it may instantiate multiple Views and may associate them with the same Model. It listens for the users' actions and manipulates the Model as dictated by the business rules.

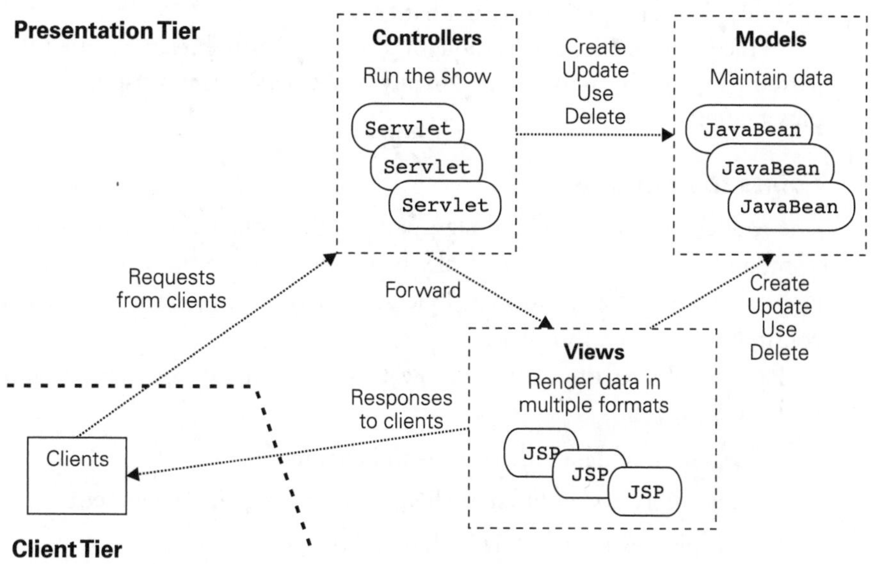


**Figure 17.3 The Model-View-Controller pattern.**

### *Consequences/implications*

- Separating the data representation (Model) from the data presentation (View) allows multiple Views for the same data. Changes can occur in both the Model and View components independently of each other as long as their interfaces remain the same. This increases maintainability and extensibility of the system.
- Separating the application behavior (Controller) from the data presentation (View) allows the controller to create an appropriate View at runtime based upon the Model.
- Separating the application behavior (Controller) from the data representation (Model) allows the users' requests to be mapped from the Controller to specific application-level functions in the Model.

### *Category*

Although MVC involves communication between the Model, View, and Controller components, it is not a behavioral pattern because it does not specify how the three components should communicate. The MVC pattern only specifies that the structure of a system of components be such that each individual component take up one of the three roles—Model, View, or Controller—and provide functionality only for its own role. As such, it is a structural pattern.

In the J2EE world, MVC is thought of more as an architecture rather than a design pattern. Though it can be applied in any of the tiers, it is most suitably applied in the presentation tier.

### *Points to remember*

The Model-View-Controller design pattern, consisting of three subobjects—Model, View, and Controller—is applicable in situations where the same data (Model) is to be presented in different formats (Views), but is to be managed centrally by a single controlling entity (Controller).

Pay special attention to the following words, phrases, or terms appearing in the problem statement:

- Separation of data presentation and data representation
- Provide services to different clients: web client, WAP client, etc.
- Multiple views, such as HTML or WML
- Single controller

## 17.2.4 Data Access Object (DAO)

### *Context*

In applications that access data from more than one data source, the following situations typically arise:

- The applications involve updating and retrieving data from different types of data sources—relational databases, object databases, legacy systems, and so forth.
- The applications involve updating and retrieving data from the same type of data source—for instance, relational databases—but the databases are from different vendors and therefore the access mechanism for each database implementation is different. For example, the database drivers are different, or the SQL data types of the database are different.
- Some of the databases allow data manipulation via stored procedures. The process of calling these procedures is dependent on the individual implementations of the database systems.

### Problem

It is difficult for the data consumers of the business tier to access the data in multiple data sources since each data source has a unique data access mechanism. Figure 17.4 shows a typical example. Even if the business tier needs to access only one data source,

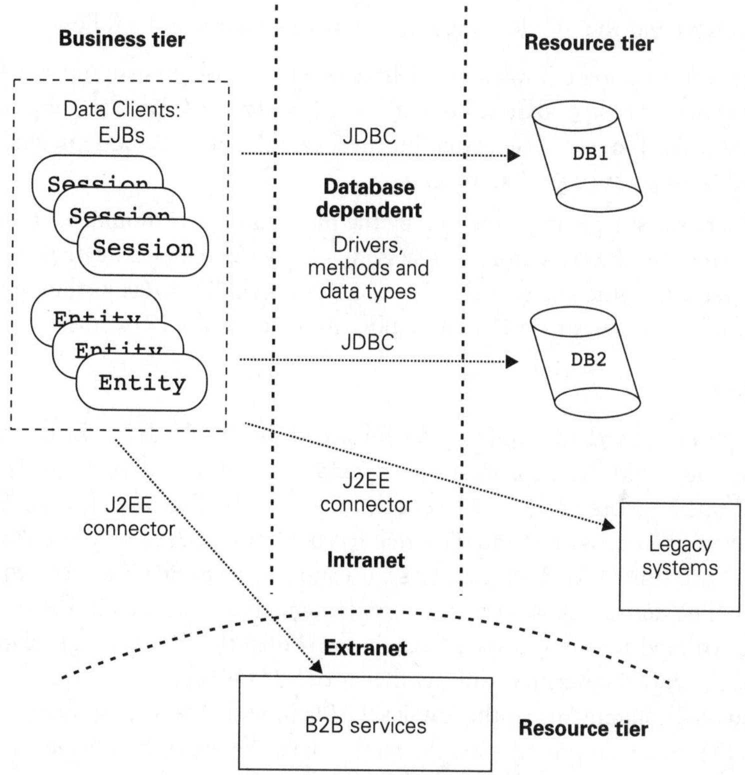


**Figure 17.4 Accessing data stores from the business tier.**

all the components of the business tier that access the data source directly need to be changed if the data source changes. The problem occurs when the type of the data source is not guaranteed or is expected to change with time.

This creates a need for a flexible and maintainable interface that encapsulates the data access mechanism and shields the data consumers from changes to the data source.

### Example

Until now, a company has been using an older type of database that uses Indexed Sequential Access Method (ISAM) techniques in a proprietary fashion. Now the business is growing, new services are to be added, and many services are to be made available on the Internet. The management feels a need to use a more scalable database system with a wide range of data-manipulation capabilities, and they decide to purchase a relational database. They will use the new database system for the new services that are added to their business, but at the same time, they must still have access to the large amount of data stored in the old database.

### Facts or forces to consider

In the context and the problem presented above, we observe the following facts:

- The business logic implemented by the business objects should not be dependent on the type of data store that is used—relational database, object database, ISAM, flat file, etc. The actual business calculations can be separated from the code that accesses the database.
- The business logic implemented by the business objects should not be dependent on the way the data store is accessed. The actual business calculations should remain the same whether the data is accessed via JDBC (as in the case of a relational database), or via JNI and a plug-in to access the ISAM files.

### Solution

Create special objects that only deal with accessing the database. In the case of the example, we could create a class called `AddressDAO`, and two subclasses called `RelationalAddressDAO` and `ISAMAddressDAO`. The base class `AddressDAO` can be an abstract class or an interface that has methods, such as `selectAddress()`, `updateAddress()`, `deleteAddress()`, and `insertAddress()`, used to retrieve the data. The derived classes can then implement these methods in the specific ways that are required by the individual databases. Thus, the DAOs encapsulate the data access logic, and the business objects that use the DAO classes do not need to know about any SQL statements or the low-level APIs provided by the database.

The DAO pattern provides an abstraction layer between the business tier and the data source. Business tier objects (the data consumers) access the data source via a Data Access Object. The Data Access Object encapsulates the details of the persistent storage and provides a standard set of interfaces to access the data. This object performs all

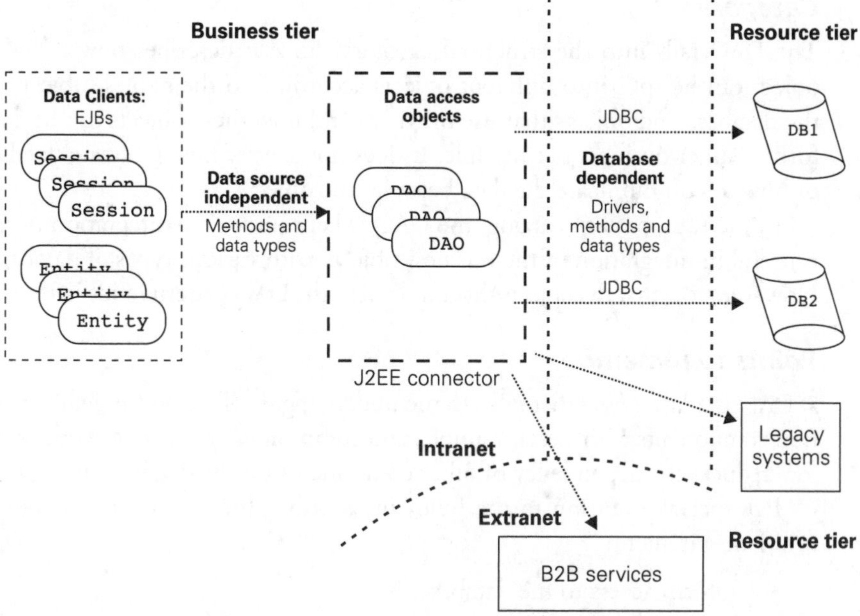


**Figure 17.5 Accessing data stores using the Data Access Objects.**

the data source–related operations, such as connection management and SQL queries. This limits the impact of a change on the data source to only the Data Access Object, and improves the readability and maintainability of the business objects. Figure 17.5 illustrates this approach.

The responsibilities of the components participating in this pattern are as follows:

- *Business object.* The business object uses the DAO to fetch the data.
- *Data Access Object (DAO).* The DAO is the main object of this pattern. It abstracts and encapsulates the features of the data source that the business tier needs to access. It maps the standardized data access call from the business tier to the actual data source specific call—for example, a SQL query.
- *Data source.* A data source can be any kind of database or Enterprise Integration System.

### *Consequences/implications*

- An application can dynamically select the data source by plugging in an appropriate DAO.
- The business tier is shielded from a change in the data source, since the DAO provides a standard interface to access the data.
- The DAO centralizes the data access logic in one place.

### *Category*

The DAO falls into the structural category, since it describes how a single business object can be split into different objects according to their roles (objects that access the database and objects that use the data) and how these objects can be combined to form a larger business tier module. It does not specify how to create database objects or how to communicate the data between the objects.

In the J2EE pattern catalog, the DAO is kept under the integration tier, because it is useful in integration of the business objects with various types of databases sources. However, note that the objects that implement the DAO pattern reside in the business tier.

### *Points to remember*

A DAO is a Java *object* that talks to the underlying database and provides other application components with a clean, simple, and common interface to *access* the *data*. It therefore reduces the dependency of other components on the details of using the database.

Pay special attention to the following words, phrases, or terms appearing in the problem statement:

- Uniform access to the database
- Transparent access to the database
- Centralized access to the database
- Reduce dependency on the type of database
- Reduce dependency on the database access mechanism
- Reduce coupling between the enterprise beans and the database
- Reduce coupling between the business objects and the database
- Shield business objects in case of migration of data from one database to another
- Multiple data sources, such as database systems on the intranet, database systems on the extranet with business partners who are B2B service providers, and so forth

## 17.2.5 Business Delegate

### *Context*

In an enterprise-scaled distributed application, typically the following situation arises:

- There are separate components to interact with the end users and to handle business logic.
- These separate components reside in different subsystems, separated by a network.
- The components that handle the business logic act as server components because they provide business services to the clients by exposing the business service API to the clients.
- The client components that use this API often reside in a remote system separated by a network.

- There is more than one client using the API.
- There is more than one server component providing similar services, but with minor differences in the API.

### Problem

Business services implemented by the business-tier components are accessed directly by the presentation-tier components through the exposed API of the services. However, the interfaces of such services keep changing as the requirements evolve. This affects all the components on the presentation tier. Furthermore, all the client-side components have to be aware of the location details of the business services—that is, each component has to use the JNDI lookup service to locate the required remote interfaces.

### Example

In the case of the J2EE architecture, the server components that expose the business service API are the session beans, the API is the remote interface implemented by the session beans, and the client components that use these services are servlets and the JavaBeans used in JSP pages. Figure 17.6 shows this relationship.

Let's look at a real-world example. A company is building a web-based application with JSP pages and servlets that need to access a set of business services. The management has decided not to develop the business services in-house, since they are readily available as off-the-shelf software from various vendors. In addition, the budget for the project is currently tight, so management has decided that they will purchase one of the more economical off-the-shelf solutions initially, and then when the money becomes available in a year, they will replace it with a more elaborate and expensive software solution.

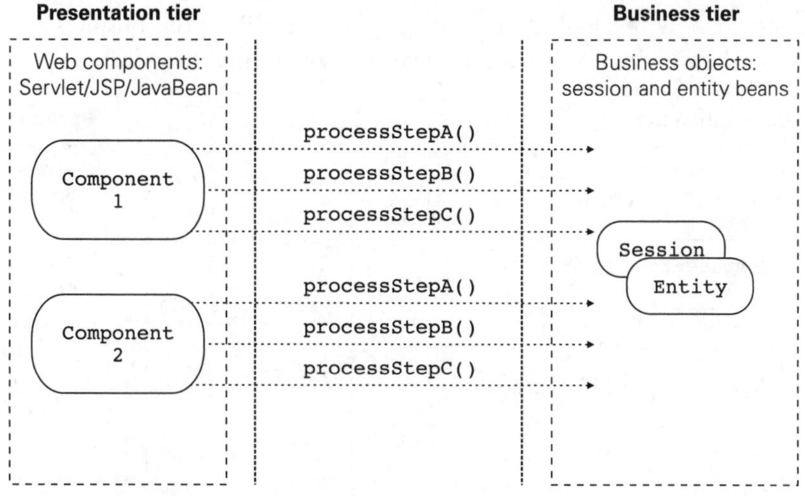


**Figure 17.6 Relationship of J2EE components in multiple tiers.**

### *Fact or forces to consider*

- The presentation-tier components, which in this case are the web components—servlets, JSP pages, and JavaBeans—perform two main tasks:
  - Handling the end user, which involves managing the web application logic, presenting the data, and so forth
  - Accessing the business services
- The code that handles the end user should not be dependent on the code that accesses the business services.
- Multiple presentation-tier components can call the same set of remote methods in the same sequence.
- It is expected that the business service APIs will change as business requirements evolve.

### *Solution*

Create a Business Delegate to handle all of the code that accesses the business services in the selected vendor software. When the vendor changes, the only changes that need to be made to the company's application software are changes to the Business Delegate, to access the business services in the new vendor software. The JSP pages and servlets will not have to be modified.

As shown in figure 17.7, we need to separate the code that accesses the remote service from the code that handles the presentation. We can put this service access code in a separate object. This separate object is called a *Business Delegate* object.

The Business Delegate object abstracts the business services API and provides a standard interface to all the client components. It hides the underlying implementation details, such as the lookup mechanism and the API of the business services. This reduces the coupling between the clients and the business services.

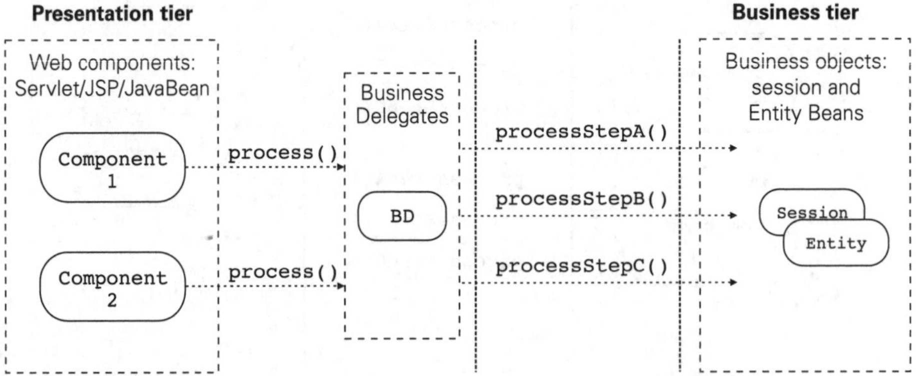


**Figure 17.7 The Business Delegate pattern.**

The responsibilities of the components participating in this pattern are:

- *Client components.* The client components, which are JSP pages and servlets in the presentation tier, delegate the work of locating the business service providers and the work of invoking the business service API methods to the Business Delegate objects.
- *Business Delegate.* The Business Delegate acts as a representative of the client components. It knows how to look up and access the business services. It invokes the appropriate business services methods in the required order. If the API of the business service component changes, only the Business Delegate needs to be modified, without affecting the client components.
- *Business service.* A business service component implements the actual business logic. Some examples of business service components are a stateless session EJB, an entity EJB, a CORBA object, or an RPC server.

### Consequences/implications

- Repetition of code is avoided. Each component does not have to include the code that will perform the lookup operation on the remote interfaces and invoke the methods.
- The server business logic API is hidden from the client components. Thus, it reduces the number of changes required in the client components when there is a change in the API of the server components.
- The Business Delegate can do all the business service–specific tasks, such as catching exceptions raised by the business services. For instance, it can catch remote exceptions and wrap them into application exceptions that are more user friendly.
- The results of remote invocations may be cached. This significantly improves performance, because it eliminates repetitive and potentially costly remote calls. The cached results may be used by multiple client components, again reducing code repetition and increasing performance.

It is worth mentioning here that the Business Delegate can either locate the business services itself or use another pattern, called the Service Locator pattern, to help locate the business service. In the instances when it uses the Service Locator pattern, the Business Delegate will deal only with the business service API invocation regardless of where the services are located, while the Service Locator does the job of locating the required named services. It is important to know that multiple Business Delegate objects can share a common Service Locator.

### Category

Since the Business Delegate pattern is concerned with the communication between two components—the presentation-tier and business-tier components—it falls into the category of a behavioral pattern. It describes how we can reduce the coupling between the two communicating parties by introducing the delegation layer in between, and how we can increase the flexibility of the design.

In the J2EE pattern catalog, the Business Delegate pattern is kept under the business tier category since it is more closely related to the business-tier components. However, note that the objects that implement the Business Delegate pattern reside in the presentation tier.

### *Points to remember*

A Business Delegate is an object that resides on the client side and communicates with the business service components residing on the server side. The client-side components can *delegate* the work of accessing the *business* services exposed by the business service components to the Business Delegate.

Pay special attention to the following words, phrases, or terms appearing in the problem statement:

- Reduce coupling between presentation and business tiers
- Proxy for the client
- Client-side facade
- Cache business service references for presentation-tier components
- Cache business service results for presentation-tier components
- Encapsulate business service lookup
- Encapsulate business service access
- Decouple clients from business service API

## 17.2.6 Front Controller

### *Context*

In component-based client-server applications, typically the following situation arises:

- A complete dialogue between the client and the server is a multistep request-response process.
- The steps have to be performed in well-defined sets of sequences.
- The next step in the sequence is decided dynamically based on the outcome of the previous step.
- Each step is performed by a different component.

### *Problem*

The client sends requests to each component as required. Before responding to a request, each component must authenticate the source of the request. Each component has to maintain the state of the current session and know which component to forward the request to. A change in the logic of the sequence may require a change in the actions of the components involved.

### *Example*

In a web application that accepts credit card information, several steps must be completed:

- Browse the catalog.
- Add items to the shopping cart.
- Confirm the checkout.
- Get the name and shipping address of the receiver.
- Get the name and billing address and the credit card information of the payer.

Each JSP page needs to know where to forward the request under normal circumstances and when to forward it to a different resource in the event of errors or in response to the user's actions. Each JSP page that needs to be a part of an HTTP session has to authenticate the request and ensure that the user is authorized to perform the requested task.

### *Facts or forces to consider*

In the context and the problem presented above, we observe the following facts:

- The Servlet API provides a mechanism that allows one component to partially process a request and forward the same request to other components for further processing.
- The authentication and authorization steps can be kept in separate specialized components and do not have to be mixed with other components.
- Components can be uncoupled from other components and focus only on a particular step in the overall process. For example, a JSP page that displays the shopping cart contents does not have to worry about the previous or next component in the user's navigational sequence.
- The same component may be used in different situations, and the component itself does not need to know the situation in which it is used. For example, a JSP page that captures and displays address information can be used to capture the shipping address in one of the steps, and the same JSP page can be used to capture the billing address in another step during the checkout process. The code that captures the address information itself does not need to know whether it is being used for capturing the shipping address or for capturing the billing address.

### *Solution*

We must create a web component object that is aware of all the steps of the shopping application, including the current state of the client, where the client is in the process, how the request will be authenticated, and the component to which the next step will be delegated. This object acts as a front door to the client and is called a Front Controller or a Front Component. Among the various strategies suggested by J2EE, the two simplest ones are using a servlet or a JSP page as front objects. All requests will be sent to the Front Controller and each request will have an action as a parameter.

### *Consequences/implications*

- The control of use cases is centralized. A change in the sequence of steps affects only the Front Controller component.
- Many web applications save the state of the client-server interaction if the user logs out in the middle of a process. When the user logs in at some other time, the previously saved state is reloaded and the process resumes from the point where it was left. In such cases, it is easier to maintain the state information using the Front Controller component because only one component handles the state management.
- Multiple Front Controller objects can be developed; each controller can concentrate on a different business use case.
- The reusability of worker components increases. Since the code that manages navigation across web pages now resides only in the Front Controller, it need not be repeated in worker components. Thus, multiple Front Controllers can reuse worker components.

### *Category*

Since the Front Controller pattern is concerned with communication with other components, it falls in the category of behavioral pattern.

In the J2EE pattern catalog, the Front Controller pattern is kept under the presentation tier because it directly deals with the client's requests and dispatches them to the appropriate handler or worker components.

### *Points to remember*

A Front Controller, or Front Component, is a component that provides a common point of entry for all client requests. In this way, the controller unifies and streamlines authentication and authorization, and dispatches the work to appropriate worker components, thereby facilitating use case management.

Pay special attention to the following words, phrases, or terms appearing in the problem statement:

- Dispatch requests
- Manage workflow of a web application
- Manage the sequence of steps
- Manage use cases

Many times, developers confuse the two design patterns—MVC and Front Controller. Remember that MVC is more of an architectural pattern, with three subsystems—Model, View, and Controller—and each of these may consist of multiple components. For example, the Controller subsystem may be made up of several intercommunicating servlets, and one or more of these servlets may act as the Front Controllers for different sequences or sets of steps.

### 17.2.7 Putting it all together

Let's now look at the big picture. Figure 17.8 shows the five design patterns that we've discussed, together with a few other patterns and the tiers in which they exist. It will give you an overview of the way the J2EE design patterns interact with one another and how we use them to create enterprise applications.

As we can see, the components in the diagram are divided into four parts: the client-tier components, the presentation-tier components, the business- and integration-tier components, and the resource-tier components. (Since the business-tier and integration-tier components usually reside on the same JVM, we have grouped them together here.) The dark dotted lines serve as a boundary separating the tiers. The client and presentation tiers communicate over the Internet using the HTTP protocol. The presentation, business, and resource tiers are usually part of an intranet within an organization, while some components of the resource tier, such as business partner services, can reside on an extranet.

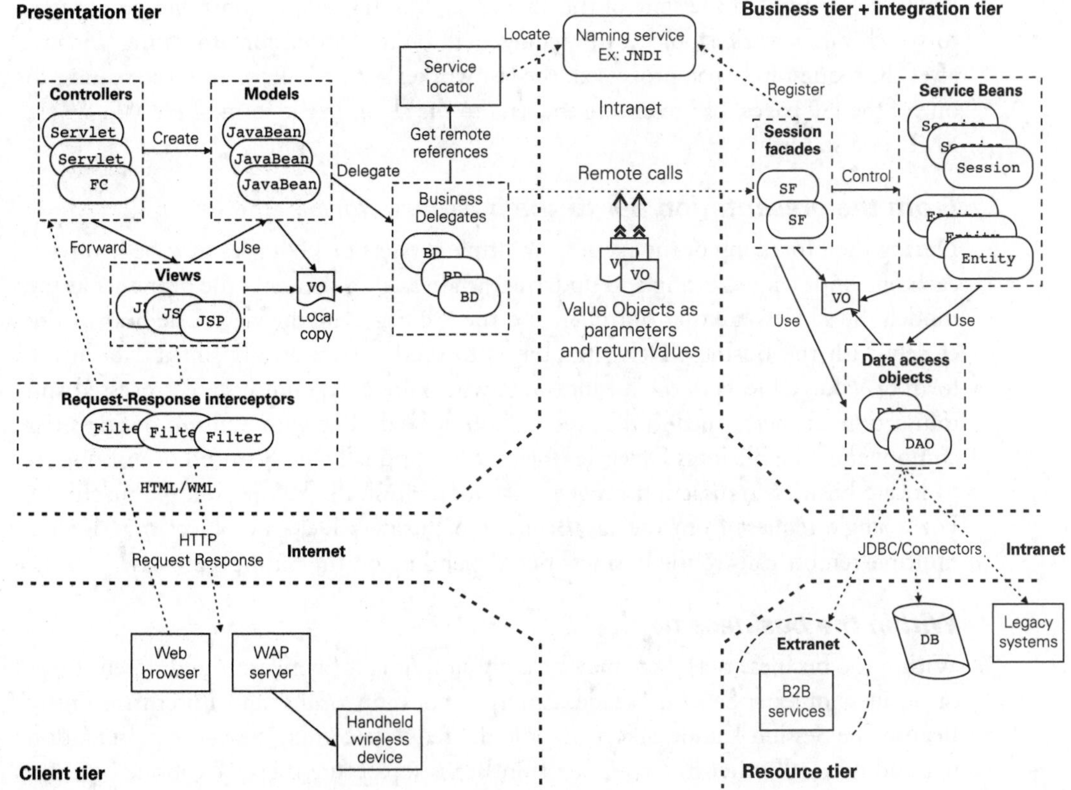


**Figure 17.8 The J2EE architecture patterns and tiers.**

### *From the client tier to the presentation tier*

The client-tier components always send their requests to the presentation-tier components. The first entity that handles the requests is usually a set of filters. As we will explain in the next chapter, *filters* are special types of components designed to intercept requests from and responses to the clients and perform various conversion tasks on the data. The J2EE pattern catalog has a separate pattern named Intercepting Filter that helps us solve pre- and post-processing of requests and responses in a uniform fashion across all requests to all components.

### *Within the presentation tier*

After passing through one or more filter objects, the request reaches the target component. This component is the Front Controller, usually implemented as a servlet. The Front Controller then authenticates the request itself or delegates the work of authentication and authorization to another component. It may also use JavaBeans to access the information from the database that is required to authenticate the request. Then, depending on the state of the client's session, the Front Controller determines to which other worker objects the request will be forwarded for processing. Finally, after the request has been processed, the last worker servlet will forward the request to one of the JSP pages for presenting the data to the client in the form of HTML, WML, XML, and so forth.

### *From the presentation tier to the business tier*

During the processing of the request, multiple servlets or JSP pages may be involved, each one optionally creating and updating JavaBeans. In this case, the beans act as the model, the servlets are the controller, and the JSP pages are the view. The beans work closely with the Business Delegate objects to send and receive business data in the form of Value Objects to the business tier, where these data objects are processed and transactions are performed. If the presentation tier is dealing with multiple business-tier components, the Business Delegate objects can optionally use Service Locator objects to locate business transaction services that may physically be on multiple machines. For a single request from the JavaBeans, the Business Delegate object may invoke multiple remote calls to the business tier, depending on the business use case.

### *Within the business tier*

Within the business tier, there may be a division of labor between the different types of business objects: Session Facade, Enterprise Session Beans, and Enterprise Entity Beans. The Session Facade objects handle the requests coming from the presentation tier and may call other Enterprise Session Beans to execute the application's business logic. The Enterprise Session Beans perform the transactions, while the Enterprise Entity Beans represent the business data as a collection of attributes.

All these business objects then make use of Data Access Objects, which are logically a part of the integration tier, to fetch and update data from the data store. The DAO shields the business objects from the management chores of the data stores. Note that the objects of the business and integration tiers reside in the same JVM.

#### *Back to the client from the business tier via the presentation tier*

If everything goes well, then the results of the business logic transactions are sent back to the presentation tier via Value Objects, where their values are cached within the Business Delegates and JavaBeans. The scriptlets and the custom tags within the JSP pages then query the JavaBeans and Business Delegate objects and present the client with the desired data formatted as HTML, XML, or WML.

## 17.3 SUMMARY

Design patterns induce abstraction, division of labor, and reusability in software systems. Consistent use of design patterns results in scalable and maintainable systems. We briefly looked at 15 design patterns of the J2EE architecture, classified into three tiers: presentation, business, and integration. Then we examined in depth the four design patterns that are specified by the exam objectives—Value Object, MVC, Data Access Object, and Business Delegate—and a fifth pattern, the Front Controller.

If you are interested in learning more about design patterns, various books and articles on patterns related to all kinds of domains are available. There are books on design patterns in compiler writing, design patterns on parallel computing, design patterns specifically for the Java programming language, and so forth. During your explorations, you may soon find yourself lost in a jungle of patterns, as you discover that some of them do the same thing but have different names, and that many of them provide similar solutions but different implementations.

If you are planning to study for the Sun Certified Enterprise Architect (SCEA) exam in addition to becoming a Sun Certified Web Component Developer (SCWCD), then we suggest you become familiar with all the J2EE patterns and the various specifications that are part of the J2EE family of architectures.

As for the SCWCD, with the end of this chapter, you are now ready to answer the questions based on the important design patterns: Value Object, MVC, Data Access Object, Business Delegate, and Front Controller.

## 17.4 REVIEW QUESTIONS

1. What are the benefits of using the Data Access Object pattern? (Select two)

   **a** The type of the actual data source can be specified at deployment time.
   **b** The data clients are independent of the data source vendor API.
   **c** It increases the performance of data-accessing routines.
   **d** It allows the clients to access the data source through EJBs.
   **e** It allows resource locking in an efficient way.

2. Which design pattern allows you to decouple the business logic, data representation, and data presentation? (Select one)

   **a** Model-View-Controller
   **b** Value Object
   **c** Bimodal Data Access
   **d** Business Delegate

3. Which of the following are the benefits of using the Value Object design pattern? (Select two)

   **a** It improves the response time for data access.
   **b** It improves the efficiency of object operations.
   **c** It reduces the network traffic.
   **d** It reduces the coupling between the data access module and the database.

4. Which of the following statements are correct? (Select two)

   **a** The Value Object pattern ensures that the data is not stale at the time of use.
   **b** It is wise to make the Value Object immutable if the Value Object represents read-only data.
   **c** Applying the Value Object pattern on EJBs helps to reduce the load on enterprise beans.
   **d** A Value Object exists only on the server side.

5. What are the benefits of using the Business Delegate pattern? (Select three)

   **a** It implements the business service functionality locally to improve performance.
   **b** It shields the clients from the details of the access mechanism, such as CORBA or RMI, of the business services.
   **c** It shields the clients from changes in the implementation of the business services.
   **d** It provides the clients with a uniform interface to the business services.
   **e** It reduces the number of remote calls and reduces network overhead.

6. You are designing an application that is required to display the data to users through HTML interfaces. It also has to feed the same data to other systems through XML as well as WAP interfaces. Which design pattern would be appropriate in this situation? (Select one)

   **a** Interface Factory
   **b** Session Facade
   **c** Value Object
   **d** Model-View-Controller
   **e** Factory

7. You are automating a computer parts ordering business. For this purpose, your web application requires a controller component that would receive the requests and dispatch them to appropriate JSP pages. It would also coordinate the request processing among the JSP pages, thereby managing the workflow. Finally, the behavior of the controller component is to be loaded at runtime as needed. Which design pattern would be appropriate in this situation? (Select one)

   **a** Front Controller
   **b** Session Facade
   **c** Value Object
   **d** Model-View-Controller
   **e** Data Access Object

8. You are building the server side of an application and you are finalizing the interfaces that you will provide to the presentation layer. However, you have not yet finalized the access details of the business services. Which design pattern should you use to mitigate this concern? (Select one)

   **a** Model-View-Controller
   **b** Data Access Object
   **c** Business Delegate
   **d** Facade
   **e** Value Object

C H A P T E R 18

# *Using filters*



The topics discussed in this chapter are currently not included in the exam objectives. However, in case these topics are included in the exam at some time in the future, we've created some possible objectives for these topics.

## POTENTIAL OBJECTIVES

1 Identify the interfaces (or classes) and methods used in each of the following:
   - Implement a filter.
   - Initialize a filter.
   - Handle the filter life-cycle events.

   (Section 18.2)

2 Identify the web application deployment descriptor element names used to accomplish the following actions:
   - Declare a filter.
   - Declare filter initialization parameters.
   - Associate a filter with a resource.
   - Associate a filter with a URL pattern.

   (Section 18.3)

**3** Identify the interfaces or classes that are used to achieve the following:

- Alter requests from clients.
- Alter responses from resources.

(Section 18.4)

## INTRODUCTION

Filters are a new addition in the Servlet Specification 2.3. The current version of the exam does not cover them, but we have provided this chapter in anticipation of the topic being included in the next version of the exam.

# 18.1 WHAT IS A FILTER?

In technical terms, a *filter* is an object that intercepts a message between a data source and a data destination, and then filters the data being passed between them. It acts as a guard, preventing undesired information from being transmitted from one point to another. For example, a Digital Subscriber Line (DSL) filter sits between the DSL line and the telephone equipment, and allows normal telephone frequencies to pass through the phone line to the telephone but blocks the frequencies meant for DSL modems. A filter in your email system allows genuine email messages to reach your inbox while blocking spam. These filters screen out undesired parts of the original messages. Another example of a filter is in data transmissions over TCP/IP; as it receives the data packets, the lower layer (IP) removes the information that was intended just for that layer from the data packets before sending the packets to the upper layer (TCP).

For a web application, a *filter* is a web component that resides on the web server and filters the requests and responses that are passed between a client and a resource.

Figure 18.1 illustrates the general idea of a filter in a web application. It shows the request passing through a filter on its way to a servlet. The servlet generates the response as usual; the response also passes through the filter on its way to the client. The filter can thus monitor the request and the response before they reach their destination. As shown in figure 18.1, the existence of a filter is transparent to the client as well as to the servlet.

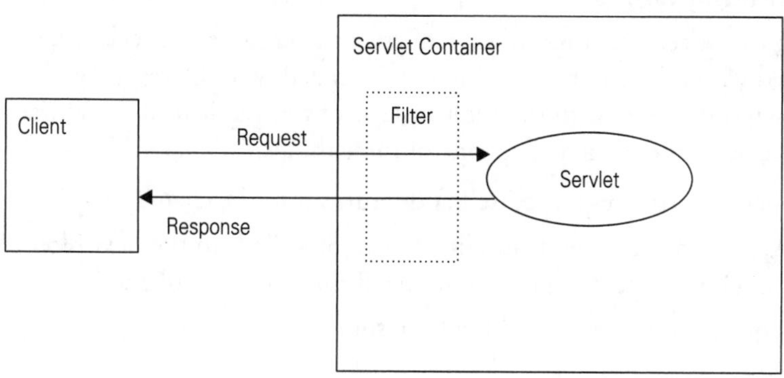


**Figure 18.1 A single filter**

We can also employ a chain of filters, if necessary, in which each filter processes the request and passes it on to the next filter in the chain (or to the actual resource if it is the last filter in the chain). Similarly, each filter processes the response in the reverse order before the response reaches the client. This process is illustrated in figure 18.2. Observe that a request will be processed by the filters in this order: Filter1, Filter2, and Filter3. However, the response will be processed by the filters in this order: Filter3, Filter2, and Filter1.

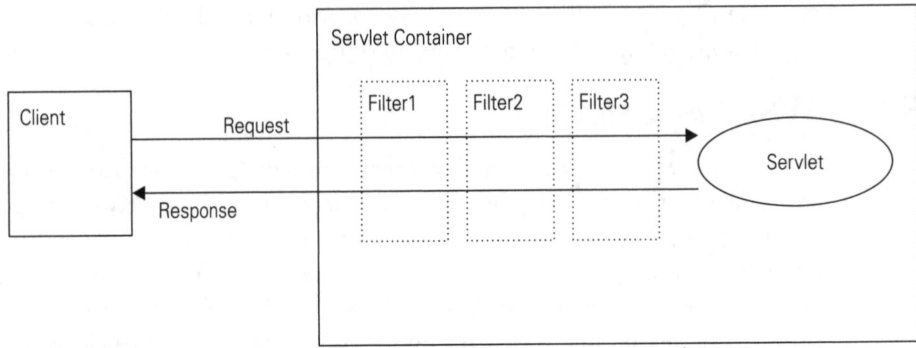


**Figure 18.2 Using multiple filters**

This is a very simple explanation of filters. As we will learn in the following sections, filters can do much more than just monitor the communication between the client and the server. In general, filters allow us to:

- Analyze a request and decide whether to pass on the request to the resource or create a response on its own.
- Manipulate a request, including a request header, by wrapping it into a customized request object before it is delivered to a resource.
- Manipulate a response by wrapping it into a customized response object before it is delivered to the client.

### 18.1.1 How filtering works

When a servlet container receives a request for a resource, it checks whether a filter is associated with this resource. If a filter is associated with the resource, the servlet container routes the request to the filter instead of routing it to the resource. The filter, after processing the request, does one of three things:

- It generates the response itself and returns it to the client.
- It passes on the request (modified or unmodified) to the next filter in the chain (if any) or to the designated resource if this is the last filter.
- It routes the request to a different resource.

As it returns to the client, the response passes back through the same set of filters in the reverse order. Each filter in the chain may modify the response.

### 18.1.2 Uses of filters

Some of the common applications of filters identified by the Servlet specification are:

- Authentication filters
- Logging and auditing filters
- Image conversion filters
- Data compression filters
- Encryption filters
- Tokenizing filters
- Filters that trigger resource access events
- XSL/T filters
- MIME-type chain filters

### 18.1.3 The Hello World filter

To get a feel for filters, let's write a simple Hello World filter. In this section, we will look at the four steps—coding, compiling, deploying, and running—involved in developing and using a filter. This filter will intercept all of the requests matching the URI pattern /filter/* and will respond with the `Hello Filter World` message.

#### *Code*

All filters implement the `javax.servlet.Filter` interface. Listing 18.1 shows the code for `HelloWorldFilter.java`. It declares one class, `HelloWorldFilter`, that implements the `Filter` interface and defines three methods—`init()`, `doFilter()`, and `destroy()`—that are declared in the `Filter` interface.

**Listing 18.1 HelloWorldFilter.java**

```
import java.io.*;
import javax.servlet.*;

public class HelloWorldFilter implements Filter
{
   private FilterConfig filterConfig;
   public void init(FilterConfig filterConfig)
   {
      this.filterConfig = filterConfig;
   }

   public void doFilter(
                  ServletRequest request,
                  ServletResponse response,
                  FilterChain filterChain
                 ) throws ServletException, IOException
```

```
    {
        PrintWriter pw = response.getWriter();
        pw.println("<html>");
        pw.println("<head>");
        pw.println("</head>");
        pw.println("<body>");
        pw.println("<h3>Hello Filter World!</h3>");
        pw.println("</body>");
        pw.println("</html>");
    }

    public void destroy()
    {
    }
}
```

The code that implements the filter in listing 18.1 is similar to the code that implements a servlet. First, we import the required packages, `javax.servlet` and `java.io`. The `ServletRequest`, `ServletResponse`, `ServletException`, `FilterConfig`, `Filter`, and `FilterChain` classes and interfaces belong to the `javax.servlet` package, while the `PrintWriter` and `IOException` classes belong to the `java.io` package. Since we are not using HTTP-specific features in this code, we don't need to import the `javax.servlet.http` package.

Next, we declare the `HelloWorldFilter` class. It implements all of the methods declared in the `Filter` interface. We will learn more about these methods in section 18.2.

### *Compilation*

As usual, we include the `servlet.jar` (located under the directory `c:\jakarta-tomcat4.0.1\common\lib\`) in the classpath and compile the `HelloWorldFilter.java` file.

### *Deployment*

Just like with a Servlet, the deployment of a filter is a two-step process:

1. Copy the file `HelloWorldFilter.class` to the `WEB-INF\classes` directory of the web application corresponding to this chapter:

    ```
    c:\jakarta-tomcat4.0.1\webapps\chapter18\WEB-INF\classes
    ```

2. Specify the filter class and map the required request URLs to this filter in the deployment descriptor:

```
<web-app>

  <!-- specify the Filter name and the Filter class -->
  <filter>
     <filter-name>HelloWorldFilter</filter-name>
```

```
        <filter-class>HelloWorldFilter</filter-class>
    </filter>

    <!-- associate the Filter with a URL pattern -->
    <filter-mapping>
        <filter-name>HelloWorldFilter</filter-name>
        <url-pattern>/filter/*</url-pattern>
    </filter-mapping>

</web-app>
```

We will see the details of these elements in section 18.4.

You could also copy the `chapter18` directory directly from the accompanying CD to your `c:\jakarta-tomcat4.0.1\webapps` directory. This directory contains all the files needed to run the example.

### *Execution*

Start Tomcat and enter this URL in your browser's navigation bar:

```
http://localhost:8080/chapter18/filter
```

The browser should display the message `Hello Filter World!`. Notice that we have not put any resource on the server with the above URL. You can enter any URL matching the pattern `/filter/*` and the filter will still execute without any problem. Thus, the resource to which a filter is mapped does not have to exist if the filter does not propagate the request to the designated resource and generates a response on its own.

## 18.2 THE FILTER API

The Filter API is not in a separate package. The set of classes and interfaces used by filters is part of the `javax.servlet` and `javax.servlet.http` packages. Table 18.1 describes the three interfaces and four classes used by filters.

**Table 18.1 Interfaces used by filters**

| Interface/Class | Description |
|---|---|
| **Interfaces of the package javax.servlet** | |
| javax.servlet.Filter | We implement this interface to write filters. |
| javax.servlet.FilterChain | The servlet container provides an object of this interface to the filter developer at request time. This object gives the developer a view into the invocation chain of a filtered request for a resource. |
| javax.servlet.FilterConfig | Similar to ServletConfig. The servlet container provides a FilterConfig object that contains initialization parameters for this filter. |

*continued on next page*

**Table 18.1 Interfaces used by filters *(continued)***

| Interface/Class | Description |
|---|---|
| **Classes of the package javax.servlet** | |
| javax.servlet.ServletRequestWrapper | Provides a convenient implementation of the ServletRequest interface that can be subclassed by developers wanting to adapt the request to a Servlet/JSP. |
| javax.servlet.ServletResponseWrapper | Provides a convenient implementation of the ServletResponse interface that can be subclassed by developers wanting to adapt the response from a Servlet/JSP. |
| **Classes of the package javax.servlet.http** | |
| javax.servlet.http.HttpServletRequestWrapper | Provides a convenient implementation of the HttpServletRequest interface that can be subclassed by developers wanting to adapt the request to a Servlet/JSP. |
| javax.servlet.http.HttpServletResponseWrapper | Provides a convenient implementation of the HttpServletResponse interface that can be subclassed by developers wanting to adapt the response from a Servlet/JSP. |

## 18.2.1 The Filter interface

This is the heart of the Filter API. Just as all servlets must implement the `javax.servlet.Servlet` interface (either directly or indirectly), all filters must implement the `javax.servlet.Filter` interface. It declares three methods, as shown in table 18.2.

**Table 18.2 Methods of the javax.servlet.Filter interface**

| Method | Description |
|---|---|
| void init(FilterConfig) | Called by the container during application startup |
| void doFilter(ServletRequest, ServletResponse, FilterChain) | Called by the container for each request whose URL is mapped to this filter |
| void destroy() | Called by the container during application shutdown |

The three methods of the `Filter` interface are also the life-cycle methods of a filter. Since, unlike the Servlet API, the Filter API does not provide any implementation for the `Filter` interface, all filters must implement all three methods explicitly.

### *The init() method*

The servlet container calls the `init()` method on a filter instance once and only once during the lifetime of the filter. The container does not dispatch any request to a filter before this method finishes. This method gives the filter object a chance to initialize itself if required. Here is the signature of the `init()` method:

```
public void init(FilterConfig filterConfig)
                 throws ServletException;
```

This method is analogous to the `init(ServletConfig)` method of the `Servlet` interface. This method is typically implemented to save for later use the `FilterConfig` object passed in a parameter. (We will learn more about `FilterConfig` in section 18.2.2.) If the initialization fails, the `init()` method may throw a `ServletException` or a subclass of the `ServletException` to indicate the problem as per application requirements.

### *The doFilter() method*

The `doFilter()` method is analogous to the `service()` method of the `Servlet` interface. The servlet container calls this method for each request with the URL that is mapped to this filter. This is the signature of the `doFilter()` method:

```
public void doFilter(ServletRequest request,
                     ServletResponse response,
                     FilterChain chain)
            throws java.io.IOException, ServletException;
```

This gives the `Filter` object a chance to process the request, forward the request to the next component in the chain, or reply to the client itself.

Note that the `request` and `response` parameters are declared of type `ServletRequest` and `ServletResponse`, respectively. Thus, the Filter API is not restricted to only HTTP servlets. However, if the filter is used in a web application, which uses the HTTP protocol, these variables refer to objects of type `HttpServletRequest` and `HttpServletResponse`, respectively. Casting these parameters to their corresponding HTTP types before using them is a typical implementation of this method.

The uses of this method vary from filter to filter, based on the requirements. A simple auditing filter may retrieve the request URL, the request parameters, and the request headers, and then log them to a file. A security filter may authenticate the request and decide to either forward the request to the resource or reject access to the designated resource. Yet another type of filter may wrap the `ServletRequest` and `ServletResponse` parameter objects with wrapper classes, and alter the request and response messages partially or completely.

A rather odd implementation is to route the request to another resource using the `include()` and `forward()` methods of `RequestDispatcher`. The `RequestDispatcher` object can be obtained using `request.getRequestDispatcher()`.

In case of an irrecoverable error during the processing, `doFilter()` may decide to throw an `IOException`, a `ServletException`, or a subclass of either of these exceptions.

### *The destroy() method*

The `destroy()` method of the `Filter` interface is analogous to the `destroy()` method of the `Servlet` interface. The servlet container calls this method as the last method on the filter object. This is the signature of the `destroy()` method:

```
public void destroy();
```

This gives the filter object a chance to release the resources acquired during its lifetime and to perform cleanup tasks, if any, before it goes out of service. This method does not declare any exceptions.

## 18.2.2 The FilterConfig interface

Just as a servlet has a `ServletConfig`, a filter has a `FilterConfig`. This interface provides the initialization parameters to the filter. It declares four methods, as shown in table 18.3.

**Table 18.3 Methods of the javax.servlet.FilterConfig interface**

| Method | Description |
|---|---|
| String getFilterName() | Returns the name of the filter specified in the deployment descriptor. |
| String getInitParameter(String) | Returns the value of the parameter specified in the deployment descriptor. |
| Enumeration getInitParameterNames() | Returns the names of all the parameters specified in the deployment descriptor. |
| ServletContext getServletContext() | Returns the ServletContext object associated with the web application. Filters can use it to get and set application-scoped attributes. |

The servlet container provides a concrete implementation of the `FilterConfig` interface. It creates an instance of this implementation class, initializes it with the initialization parameter values, and passes it as a parameter to the `Filter.init()` method. The name and initialization parameters are specified in the deployment descriptor, which we will discuss in section 18.3.

Most important, `FilterConfig` also provides a reference to the `ServletContext` in which the filter is installed. A filter can use the `ServletContext` to share application-scoped attributes with other components of the web application.

## 18.2.3 The FilterChain interface

The `FilterChain` interface has just one method, described in table 18.4.

**Table 18.4 The javax.servlet.FilterChain interface method**

| Method | Description |
|---|---|
| void doFilter(ServletRequest, ServletResponse); | We call this method from the doFilter() method of a Filter object to continue the process of filter chaining. It passes the control to the next filter in the chain or to the actual resource if this is the last filter in the chain. |

The servlet container provides an implementation of this interface and passes an instance of it in the `doFilter()` method of the `Filter` interface. Within the `doFilter()` method, we can use this interface to pass the request to the next component in the chain, which is either another filter or the actual resource if this is the last filter in the chain. The two parameters of type `ServletRequest` and `ServletResponse` that we pass in this method are received by the next component in the chain in its `doFilter()` or `service()` method.

### 18.2.4 The request and response wrapper classes

`ServletRequestWrapper` and `HttpServletRequestWrapper` provide a convenient implementation of the `ServletRequest` and `HttpServletRequest` interfaces, respectively, that we can subclass if we want to alter the request before sending it to the next component of the filter chain. Similarly, `ServletResponseWrapper` and `HttpServletResponseWrapper` are used if we want to alter the response received from the previous component. These objects can be passed as parameters to the `doFilter()` method of the `FilterChain` interface. We will see how to do this in section 18.4.

## 18.3 CONFIGURING A FILTER

A filter is configured using two deployment descriptor elements: `<filter>` and `<filter-mapping>`. Each `<filter>` element introduces a new filter into the web application, while each `<filter-mapping>` element associates a filter with a set of request URIs. Both elements directly come under `<web-app>` and are optional. These elements are similar to the `<servlet>` and `<servlet-mapping>` elements.

### 18.3.1 The <filter> element

Here is the definition of the `<filter>` element:

```
<!ELEMENT filter (icon?, filter-name, display-name?, description?,
                  filter-class, init-param*)>
```

As you can see from the above definition, each filter requires a `<filter-name>` and a `<filter-class>` that implements the filter. Other elements—`<icon>`, `<display-name>`, `<description>`, and `<init-param>`—serve the usual purposes and are optional.

The following example illustrates the use of the `<filter>` element:

```
<filter>
   <filter-name>ValidatorFilter</filter-name>
   <description>Validates the requests</description>
   <filter-class>com.manning.filters.ValidatorFilter</filter-class>
   <init-param>
      <param-name>locale</param-name>
      <param-value>USA</param-value>
   </init-param>
</filter>
```

This code introduces a filter named `ValidatorFilter`. The servlet container will create an instance of the `com.manning.filters.ValidatorFilter` class and associate it with this name. At the time of initialization, the filter can retrieve the `locale` parameter by calling `filterConfig.getParameterValue("locale")`.

### 18.3.2 The <filter-mapping> element

This element works exactly like the `<servlet-mapping>` element that we discussed in detail in chapter 5, "Structure and deployment." The `<filter-mapping>` element is defined as follows:

```
<!ELEMENT filter-mapping (filter-name, (url-pattern | servlet-name))>
```

The `<filter-name>` element is the name of the filter as defined in the `<filter>` element, `<url-pattern>` is used to apply the filter to a set of requests identified by a particular URL pattern, and `<servlet-name>` is used to apply the filter to all the requests that are serviced by the servlet identified by this servlet name. In the case of `<url-pattern>`, the pattern matching follows the same rules for servlet mapping that we described in chapter 5.

The following examples illustrate the use of the `<filter-mapping>` element:

```
<filter-mapping>
   <filter-name>ValidatorFilter</filter-name>
   <url-pattern>*.doc</url-pattern>
</filter-mapping>

<filter-mapping>
   <filter-name>ValidatorFilter</filter-name>
   <servlet-name>reportServlet</servlet-name>
</filter-mapping>
```

The first filter mapping shown above associates `ValidatorFilter` with all the requests that try to access a file with the extension `.doc`, while the second filter mapping associates `ValidatorFilter` with all the requests that are to be serviced by the servlet named `reportServlet`. The servlet name used here must refer to a servlet defined using the `<servlet>` element in the deployment descriptor.

### 18.3.3 Configuring a filter chain

In some cases, you may need to apply multiple filters to the same request. Such filter chains can be configured using multiple `<filter-mapping>` elements. When the servlet container receives a request, it finds all the filter mappings with a URL pattern that matches the request URI. This becomes the first set of filters in the filter chain. Next, it finds all the filter mappings with a servlet name that matches the request URI. This becomes the second set of filters in the filter chain. In both sets, the order of the filters is the order in which they appear in the deployment descriptor.

To understand this process, consider the filter mappings and servlet mapping in the `web.xml` file shown in listing 18.2.

**Listing 18.2 A web.xml file for illustrating filter chaining**

```
<web-app>

   <filter>
      <filter-name>FilterA</filter-name>
      <filter-class>TestFilter</filter-class>
   </filter>
   <filter>
      <filter-name>FilterB</filter-name>
      <filter-class>TestFilter</filter-class>
   </filter>
   <filter>
      <filter-name>FilterC</filter-name>
      <filter-class>TestFilter</filter-class>
   </filter>
   <filter>
      <filter-name>FilterD</filter-name>
      <filter-class>TestFilter</filter-class>
   </filter>
   <filter>
      <filter-name>FilterE</filter-name>
      <filter-class>TestFilter</filter-class>
   </filter>

<!-- associate FilterA and FilterB to RedServlet -->
   <filter-mapping>
      <filter-name>FilterA</filter-name>
      <servlet-name>RedServlet</servlet-name>
   </filter-mapping>
   <filter-mapping>
      <filter-name>FilterB</filter-name>
      <servlet-name>RedServlet</servlet-name>
   </filter-mapping>

<!-- associate FilterC to a request matching /red/* -->
   <filter-mapping>
      <filter-name>FilterC</filter-name>
      <url-pattern>/red/*</url-pattern>
   </filter-mapping>

<!-- associate FilterD to a request matching /red/red/* -->
   <filter-mapping>
      <filter-name>FilterD</filter-name>
```

```
        <url-pattern>/red/red/*</url-pattern>
    </filter-mapping>

<!-- associate FilterE to a request matching *.red -->
    <filter-mapping>
        <filter-name>FilterE</filter-name>
        <url-pattern>*.red</url-pattern>
    </filter-mapping>

    <servlet>
        <servlet-name>RedServlet</servlet-name>
        <servlet-class>RedServlet</servlet-class>
    </servlet>

    <servlet-mapping>
        <servlet-name>RedServlet</servlet-name>
        <url-pattern>/red/red/red/*</url-pattern>
    </servlet-mapping>
    <servlet-mapping>
        <servlet-name>RedServlet</servlet-name>
        <url-pattern>*.red</url-pattern>
    </servlet-mapping>

<web-app>
```

In the above `web.xml`, we have associated:

1 `FilterA` and `FilterB` with `RedServlet` using the servlet name in the filter mapping elements
2 `FilterC` to a request whose URI matches `/red/*`
3 `FilterD` to a request whose URI matches `/red/red/*`
4 `FilterE` to a request whose URI matches `*.red`

We have also configured `RedServlet` to service requests having the URI pattern of `/red/red/red/*` and `*.red`.

Table 18.5 shows the order of filter invocations for various request URIs. We have not shown the base URIs for any of the request URIs in the table, since it is the same for all: `http://localhost:8080/chapter18/`.

**Table 18.5 Order of filter invocation in filter chaining**

| Request URI | Filter Invocation Order | Reason | | |
|---|---|---|---|---|
| | | Request Serviced by RedServlet Because Of | Matching Filter Mappings with URL Pattern | Matching Filter Mappings with Servlet Name |
| aaa.red | FilterE, FilterA, FilterB | *.red | FilterE | FilterA, FilterB |
| red/aaa.red | FilterC, FilterE, FilterA, FilterB | *.red | FilterC, FilterE | FilterA, FilterB |

*continued on next page*

**Table 18.5 Order of filter invocation in filter chaining *(continued)***

| Request URI | Filter Invocation Order | Reason | | |
|---|---|---|---|---|
| | | Request Serviced by RedServlet Because Of | Matching Filter Mappings with URL Pattern | Matching Filter Mappings with Servlet Name |
| red/red/aaa.red | FilterC, FilterD, FilterE, FilterA, FilterB | *.red | FilterC, FilterD, FilterE | FilterA, FilterB |
| red/red/red/aaa.red | FilterC, FilterD, FilterE, FilterA, FilterB | *.red and /red/red/red/* | FilterC, FilterD, FilterE, | FilterA, FilterB |
| red/red/red/aaa | FilterC, FilterD, FilterA, FilterB | /red/red/red/* | FilterC, FilterD | FilterA, FilterB |
| red/red/aaa | FilterC, FilterD | NONE (404 Error) | FilterC, Filter D | |
| red/aaa | FilterC | NONE (404 Error) | FilterC | |
| red/red/red/aaa.doc | FilterC, FilterD, FilterA, FilterB | /red/red/red/* | FilterC, FilterD | FilterA, FilterB |
| aaa.doc | None | NONE (404 Error) | | |

In table 18.5, observe the following points:

- The container will call the filters that match the request URI (`url-pattern`) before it calls the filters that match the servlet name to which the request will be delegated (`servlet-name`). Thus, `FilterC`, `FilterD`, and `FilterE` are always called before `FilterA` and `FilterB`.
- Whenever called, `FilterC`, `FilterD`, and `FilterE` are always called in this order since they are configured in this order in the `web.xml` file.
- Whenever `RedServlet` is invoked, `FilterA` and `FilterB` are called in this order, since they are configured in this order in the `web.xml` file.

We have provided this test application on the accompanying CD. You can try it out with different request URIs and see the results.

## 18.4 ADVANCED FEATURES

In addition to monitoring the communication between the clients and the web application components, filters can manipulate the requests and alter the responses. In this section, we will learn about these features.

### 18.4.1 Using the request and response wrappers

All four wrapper classes—`ServletRequestWrapper`, `ServletResponseWrapper`, `HttpServletRequestWrapper`, and `HttpServletResponseWrapper`—work in the same way. They take a request or a response object in their constructor and delegate all the method calls to that object. This allows us to extend these classes and override any methods to provide a customized behavior.

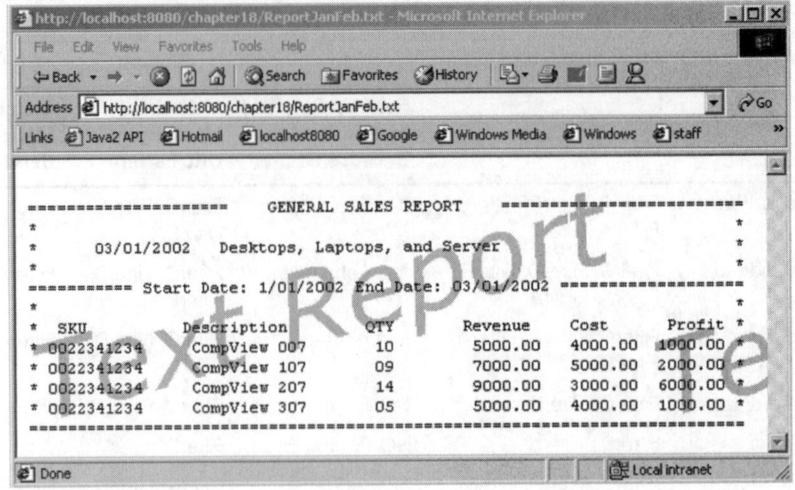


**Figure 18.3 A sample report with a background image.**

In this section, we will use these classes in a filter to solve a simple problem. We have a legacy system that generates reports in a plain ASCII text format and stores them in a text file with an extension of `.txt`. We want these reports to be accessible from browsers with an image displayed as the background of the report. For example, figure 18.3 shows how a sample report should display on the browser.

At the same time, we also do not want the browser to cache the report files. These two problems can be easily solved if we are able to do the following:

1 Embed the text of the report into `<html>` and `<body>` tags with an appropriate image as the background:

```
<html>
   <body background="textReport.gif">
   <pre>
      text of the report here.
   </pre>
   </body>
</html>
```

The `background` attribute of the `<body>` element will display the given image as the background of the report, while the `<pre>` tag will keep the formatting of the textual data intact.

2 Override the `If-Modified-Since` header. Browsers send this header so that the server can determine whether the resource needs to be sent. If the resource has not been modified after the period specified by the `If-Modified-Since` value, then the server does not send the resource at all.

For this purpose, we will filter all the requests for files with the extension `.txt`. Our filter will do two things:

1 Wrap the request into an `HttpServletRequestWrapper` and override the `getHeader()` method to return `null` for the `If-Modified-Since` header. A `null` value for this header ensures that the server does send the file.

2 Wrap the response object into an `HttpServletResponseWrapper` so that the filter can modify the response and append the required HTML before sending it to the client.

Let's now look at the code that implements this. Listing 18.3 shows the code for `NonCachingRequestWrapper.java`, which customizes the behavior of `HttpServletRequestWrapper`.

**Listing 18.3 Wrapping a request to hide a header value**

```
import javax.servlet.*;
import javax.servlet.http.*;
public class NonCachingRequestWrapper extends HttpServletRequestWrapper
{
   public NonCachingRequestWrapper(HttpServletRequest req)
   {
       super(req);
   }

   public String getHeader(String name)
   {
      // hide only the If-Modified-Since header
      // and return the actual value for other headers
      if(name.equals("If-Modified-Since"))
      {
            return null;
      }
      else
      {
            return super.getHeader(name);
      }
   }
}
```

The code for `NonCachingRequestWrapper` is quite simple. It overrides the `getHeader()` method and returns null for the `If-Modified-Since` header. Since this class extends from `HttpServletRequestWrapper`, all other methods are delegated to the underlying request object that is passed in the constructor.

Listing 18.4 shows the code for `TextResponseWrapper`, which customizes the behavior of `HttpServletResponseWrapper`.

**Listing 18.4 Wrapping a response to buffer text data**

```
import java.io.*;
import javax.servlet.*;
import javax.servlet.http.*;

public class TextResponseWrapper
         extends HttpServletResponseWrapper
{
   //This inner class creates a ServletOutputStream that
   //dumps everything that is written to it to a byte array
   //instead of sending it to the client.
   private static class ByteArrayServletOutputStream
         extends ServletOutputStream
   {
      ByteArrayOutputStream baos;
      ByteArrayServletOutputStream(ByteArrayOutputStream baos)
      {
         this.baos = baos;
      }

      public void write(int param) throws java.io.IOException
      {
         baos.write(param);
      }
   }

   //the actual ByteArrayOutputStream object that is used by
   //the PrintWriter as well as ServletOutputStream
   private ByteArrayOutputStream baos
                                 = new ByteArrayOutputStream();

   //This print writer is built over the ByteArrayOutputStream.
   private PrintWriter pw = new PrintWriter(baos);

   //This ServletOutputStream is built over the ByteArrayOutputStream.
   private ByteArrayServletOutputStream basos
                        = new ByteArrayServletOutputStream(baos);


   public TextResponseWrapper(HttpServletResponse response)
   {
      super(response);
   }

   public PrintWriter getWriter()
   {
      //Returns our own PrintWriter that writes to a byte array
      //instead of returning the actual PrintWriter associated
      //with the response.
      return pw;
   }

   public ServletOutputStream getOutputStream()
```

```
    {
        //Returns our own ServletOutputStream that writes to a
        //byte array instead of returning the actual
        //ServletOutputStream associated with the response.

        return basos;
    }

    byte[] toByteArray()
    {
        return baos.toByteArray();
    }
}
```

The code for TextResponseWrapper looks complicated but is actually very straightforward. It creates a ByteArrayOutputStream to store all the data that is written by the server. It overrides the getWriter() and getOutputStream() methods of HttpServletResponse to return the customized PrintWriter and ServletOutputStream that are built over the same ByteArrayOuptut-Stream. Thus, no data is sent to the client.

Listing 18.5 shows the code for TextToHTMLFilter.java, which converts a textual report into a presentable HTML format as required.

**Listing 18.5 Code for TextToHTMLFilter.java**

```
import java.io.*;
import javax.servlet.*;
import javax.servlet.http.*;

public class TextToHTMLFilter implements Filter
{
   private FilterConfig filterConfig;

   public void init(FilterConfig filterConfig)
   {
      this.filterConfig = filterConfig;
   }

   public void doFilter(
                  ServletRequest request,
                  ServletResponse response,
                  FilterChain filterChain
                 ) throws ServletException, IOException
   {

      HttpServletRequest req = (HttpServletRequest) response;
      HttpServletResponse res = (HttpServletResponse) response;

      NonCachingRequestWrapper ncrw
                  = new NonCachingRequestWrapper( req );
      TextResponseWrapper trw = new TextResponseWrapper(res);

      //Passes on the dummy request and response objects
```

```
        filterChain.doFilter(ncrw, trw);

        String top = "<html><body background=\"textReport.gif\"><pre>";
        String bottom = "</pre></body></html>";

        //Embeds the textual data into <html>, <body>, and <pre> tags.
        StringBuffer htmlFile = new StringBuffer(top);
        String textFile = new String(trw.toByteArray());
        htmlFile.append(textFile);
        htmlFile.append("<br>"+bottom);

        //Sets the content type to text/html
        res.setContentType("text/html");

        //Sets the content type to new length
        res.setContentLength(htmlFile.length());

        //Writes the new data to the actual PrintWriter
        PrintWriter pw = res.getWriter();
           pw.println(htmlFile.toString());
    }
    public void destroy()
    {
    }
}
```

The code in listing 18.5 wraps the actual request and response objects into the `NonCachingRequestWrapper` and `TextResponseWrapper` objects, respectively, and then passes them on to the next component of the filter chain using the `doFilter()` method.

When the `filterChain.doFilter()` call returns, the text report is already written to the `TestResponseWrapper` object. Our filter retrieves the text data from this object and embeds it into the appropriate HTML tags. Finally, it writes the data to the actual `PrintWriter` object that sends the data to the client.

### *Deploying the filter*

As explained earlier, deploying this filter requires two steps:

1. Copy all the class files to the `WEB-INF\classes` directory.
2. Set the filter and the filter mapping in the `web.xml` file of the web application as shown here:

```
<filter>
   <filter-name>TextToHTML</filter-name>
   <filter-class>TextToHTMLFilter</filter-class>
</filter>

<filter-mapping>
   <filter-name>TextToHTML</filter-name>
   <url-pattern>*.txt</url-pattern>
</filter-mapping>
```

If you have copied the chapter18 directory to the webapps directory of your Tomcat installation, you can open the given web.xml file and see these settings.

### *Running the application*

To run the application, restart Tomcat and request any text file that is available in this web application from the browser. For testing purposes, we have provided a sample text file and a GIF image. You can view them through this URL:

```
http://localhost:8080/chapter18/ReportJanFeb.txt
```

## 18.4.2 Important points to remember about filters

You need to understand these points when using filters:

- Like servlets, filters are by default executed in the multithreaded model. There is one filter per <filter> entry in the web.xml file, per virtual machine. A servlet container is free to run multiple threads on the same filter object to service multiple requests simultaneously. Unlike with servlets, however, there is no way to configure filters to run in the single-threaded model.
- Filters associated with a resource are not executed when a request is sent to the resource through a RequestDispatcher. This is done in order to prevent a filter calling itself and thus entering into a livelock.
- As an extension of the second point, filters associated with error pages are not executed.

## 18.4.3 Using filters with MVC

As we discussed in chapter 2, "Understanding JavaServer Pages," the JSP Model 2 architecture is based on the MVC design pattern. It breaks a web application down into three distinct areas where the JavaBeans act as the model, the JSP pages act as the view, and the servlets act as the controller. A request, or a group of related requests, is actually handled by a servlet, which retrieves the data and creates JavaBeans to hold the data. After creating the beans, it uses a RequestDispatcher object to forward the request to an appropriate JSP page. The JSP page uses the beans and generates the view.

This approach works well when the view to be displayed is determined by the business rules. For example, the page that should be displayed after a user logs in may depend on the access rights she has. Therefore, the final presentation depends on the servlet code that decides which JSP page the request is to be forwarded to.

Now consider another situation. An application is required to display some reports in either XML or HTML format as requested by the client. For this purpose, you develop two JSP pages: xmlView.jsp and htmlView.jsp. You also develop a servlet that generates the data needed by both the JSP pages. In the Model 2 architecture, the client request would go to this servlet. The servlet would retrieve the data and then dispatch the request to either xmlView.jsp or htmlView.jsp. The problem with this solution is that the servlet needs an extra parameter in the request that will indicate which view is being requested. Furthermore, the servlet will have to hard-code the names of the JSP pages. This means that adding a new view will require a code change in the servlet.

Filters are very useful in the situation described above. We can code the servlet's logic of retrieving the data and creating JavaBeans in a filter and apply this filter to both views. The user can directly request the `xmlView.jsp` or `htmlView.jsp` page. Since the filter will be executed first, the necessary beans will be available when the request reaches the JSP page. This architecture eliminates the need for an extra parameter to inform the filter about the view; this information is already present in the name of the resource given in the request. It also provides a clean way of adding a new view. For example, if we need to provide a text view, we can develop a `textView.jsp` file and apply the same filter on this JSP page. There is no code change in the filter. Thus, in such situations filters are a better choice for controllers than servlets.

## 18.5 SUMMARY

Filters add value to a web application by monitoring the requests and responses that are passed between the client and the server. With filters, we can analyze, manipulate, and redirect requests and responses.

In this chapter, we learned about the Filter API, including the three interfaces—`Filter`, `FilterConfig`, and `FilterChain`—and we saw how to configure filters in the deployment descriptor. We then looked at the way we can use a filter to wrap a request or a response in a customized object before delivering it to its destination. Within the MVC model, filters, rather than servlets, can better play the role of a controller in some situations.

APPENDIX A

# *Installing Tomcat 4.0.1*



You'll need to install Tomcat to test the sample code that we have developed in the chapters. This appendix will help you install Tomcat.

## A.1 PREREQUISITES

You should have JDK 1.2 or higher installed and working on your machine.

## A.2 GETTING TOMCAT

For your convenience, we've provided Tomcat version 4.0.1 on the accompanying CD. It is a binary file named `jakarta-tomcat-4.0.1.exe` present in the `tomcat` directory of the CD. If you wish, you can download the latest version from `http://jakarta.apache.org`.

## A.3 INSTALLATION

Installing Tomcat is pretty easy. The following sections will help you install and set up Tomcat on Windows 98/NT/2000.

### A.3.1 Extracting files

Double-click on `jakarta-tomcat-4.0.1.exe` to start installing the files. When you are asked for the installation directory name, avoid using long names or names with spaces. For older versions (before version 4.0.1), this directory was referred as `TOMCAT_HOME`. However, from version 4.0.1 on, it is referred to as `CATALINA_HOME`. We have used `C:\jakarta-tomcat-4.0.1`.

### A.3.2 Setting environment variables

To run Tomcat, you need to set two environment variables: `CATALINA_HOME` and `JAVA_HOME`. `CATALINA_HOME` refers to the installation directory, and `JAVA_HOME` refers to the JDK1.2 installation directory. To be able to compile your servlet classes, you need the Servlet API classes in the `CLASSPATH` environment variable. Servlet API classes are packaged in `c:\jakarta-tomcat-4.0.1\common\lib\servlet.jar`. You need to add this file to your classpath.

On Windows 98, open `c:\autoexec.bat` and add the following three lines:

```
SET CATALINA_HOME=c:\jakarta-tomcat-4.0.1
SET JAVA_HOME=c:\jdk1.2.2
SET CLASSPATH=%CLASSPATH%;c:\jakarta-tomcat-4.0.1\common\lib\servlet.jar
```

Be sure to substitute the appropriate directory for `c:\jdk1.2.2`. You'll need to restart your machine.

In Windows 2000/NT, go to Start|Settings|Control Panel|System. Then select the Advanced tab and in the Environment Variables section, set the above two variables as either System variables or User variables. You can also modify the `CLASSPATH` variable here. You do not need to restart your machine, but you will need to close all the DOS windows and open a new DOS window to see the newly set variables.

## A.4 DIRECTORY STRUCTURE

After you've installed Tomcat, your `jakarta-tomcat-4.0.1` directory should look like the one shown in figure A.1.

There are three important directories under the `jakarta-tomcat-4.0.1` directory.

#### *The bin directory*

This directory contains the executable batch files, such as `startup.bat` and `shutdown.bat`, for Windows, and shell files, such as `startup.sh` and `shutdown.sh`, for Unix.

#### *The conf directory*

This directory contains several configuration files, such as `server.xml` and `tomcat-users.xml`.

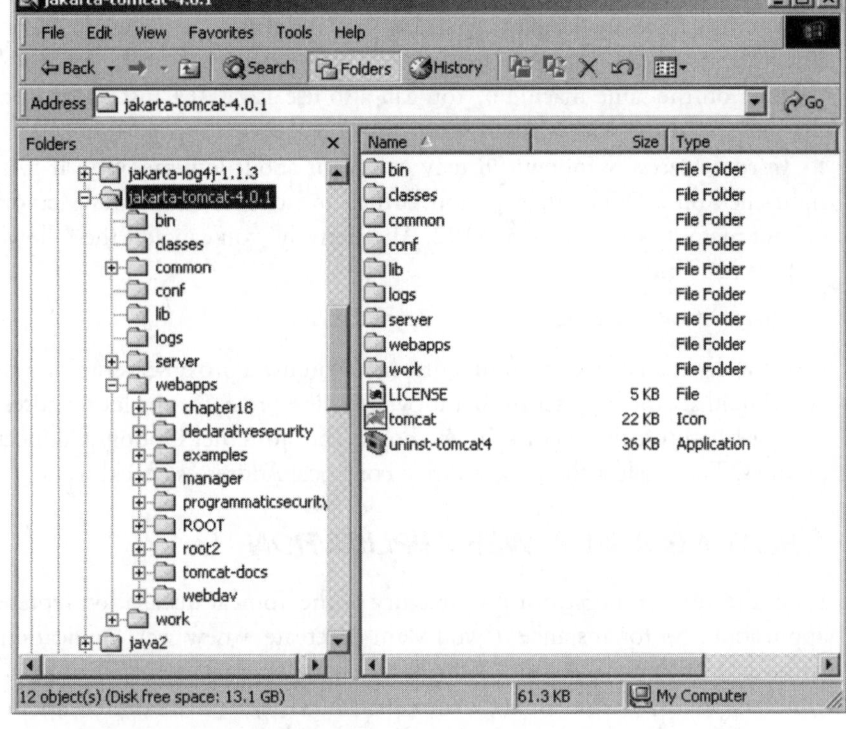


**Figure A.1 Tomcat directory structure.**

### *The webapps directory*

Tomcat keeps all the web applications in this directory. Each directory that you see under the `c:\jakarta-tomcat-4.0.1\webapps` directory actually corresponds to a web application. The directory named `ROOT` refers to the default web application.

## A.5 RUNNING TOMCAT

Open up a DOS prompt and go to `c:\jakarta-tomcat-4.0.1\bin`. If the environment variables are set properly, you should be able to see them from this DOS window. You can check these variables by typing the following commands:

```
C:\jakarta-tomcat-4.0.1\bin> echo %JAVA_HOME%
C:\jakarta-tomcat-4.0.1\bin> echo %CATALINA_HOME%
```

Now, type the following command to start Tomcat:

```
C:\jakarta-tomcat-4.0.1\bin>startup
```

This should start Tomcat in a separate window. To shut it down, you can use the `shutdown` command:

```
C:\jakarta-tomcat-4.0.1\bin>shutdown
```

To check whether Tomcat is running, go to `http://localhost:8080` from your browser. You'll see the default page saying your installation is successful. Here, the name `localhost` means that you are connecting to your own machine (since Tomcat is running on the same machine). You can also use 127.0.0.1 instead of `localhost`, that is, `http://127.0.0.1:8080`.

In some cases, Windows 98 may complain about low memory. If this happens, right-click on a DOS window's top border and choose Properties|Memory. Set the default memory from Auto to 8192. Alternatively, you can add the following line in `autoexec.bat`:

```
SHELL=C:/windows/command.com /E:8192 /P
```

If you work in an office environment where you use a proxy server to browse the web, you should set the browser so that it bypasses the proxy for the local addresses. To do this for Microsoft Internet Explorer, choose Tools|Internet Options|Connections|LAN Settings. Then, select the Bypass Proxy For Local Addresses checkbox.

## A.6 CREATING A NEW WEB APPLICATION

Each directory in the `webapps` directory of the Tomcat installation represents a web application. So for instance, if you want to create a new web application with the name `helloapp`, you create a directory by that name in the `webapps` directory. You can put static files directly into this directory and then view them from the browser. For example, if you put in a file named `myhomepage.html`, you can view it through the following URL:

```
http://localhost:8080/helloapp/myhomepage.html
```

However, before you add servlets and JSP pages, you should read the discussion about the directory structure of a web application in chapter 5, "Structure and deployment."

**NOTE** The above method works with Tomcat 3.2, but with Tomcat 4.0.1, you will also have to create a `WEB-INF` directory, which may be empty, under the application's document root directory.

## A.7 SECURITY

By default, Tomcat runs in a non-secure mode. This means that a web application class can access anything on the system. For example, a malicious servlet class or a JSP page can delete files from your system. You can prevent this by running Tomcat in the secure mode:

```
C:\jakarta-tomcat4.0.1\bin>startup -security
```

The `–security` option forces Tomcat to use a security manager. This security manager uses the policies specified in the `conf/catalina.policy` file. You can customize this policy file by granting rights to specific web applications as per the application requirements. If an application tries to access anything for which it does not have the appropriate rights, it will be denied access and the server will throw a `java.security.AccessControlException`.

Security is especially important when you want to run a readymade third-party web application under your Tomcat installation; running Tomcat in the secure mode will protect your system. Also, service providers often use a shared Tomcat instance for hosting multiple web applications, in which case running it in the secure mode becomes a necessity.

APPENDIX B

# An introduction to XML



In this appendix, we will give you a brief introduction to XML. If you are not familiar with XML at all, you might have difficulty understanding some of the topics covered in this book that assume a basic knowledge of XML. Our objective here is to make you comfortable with XML so that you can understand such topics easily.

## B.1 What is XML?

XML stands for EXtensible Markup Language. It is a markup language that is used for describing data. In structure, it is very similar to HTML. However, there is a basic difference between the two: while HTML is meant to *display* the data, XML is meant to *describe* the data. For example, the following XML snippet describes an address:

```
<address>
   <street>Cheryl Dr</street>
   <city>Iselin</city>
   <state>NJ</state>
   <zip>08830</zip>
   <country>USA</country>
 </address>
```

Our sample XML code does not describe how to display (font, color, etc.) the address data. It merely provides an address in a structured manner using XML tags. In this example, `<address>`, `<number>`, `<street>`, and so forth are XML tags, which hold the actual data. The data is contained between the start tag and the end tag. It's important to remember that XML includes no predefined tags; we must define our own tags according to our needs. Thus, in this example, we could easily add another tag named `<apartment-number>`.

Since an XML document itself describes the structure of the data that it contains, it can be easily communicated across multiple systems. However, while the structure of the data is evident from an XML document, the meaning of the data elements is not. This is because any system can invent the tags on its own. These tags may not make any sense to other systems. Therefore, for one system to understand the data sent by another system, it is essential that both systems be aware of the tags used to describe the data. This brings us to the concept of a *Document Type Definition (DTD)*. A DTD is a separate document that describes the tags used by an XML document. An XML document usually carries with it a reference to a DTD that contains information about the tags used in that XML document. For example, a complete listing of an XML file that stores a person's address may look like the one shown in listing B.1.

**Listing B.1 myaddress.xml**

```
<?xml version="1.0" encoding="ISO-8859-1"?>
<!DOCTYPE address SYSTEM "address.dtd">
<address id="231">
   <street>Cheryl Dr</street>
   <city>Iselin</city>
   <state>NJ</state>
   <zip>08830</zip>
   <country>USA</country>
</address>
```

The second line of the XML document specifies that this XML file follow the rules defined in the `address.dtd` file. We will discuss the DTD file in section B.3.

## B.2 XML SYNTAX

All XML documents must strictly follow certain syntax rules:

- The first line in the document is the XML declaration. It defines the XML version and the character encoding used in the document. In listing B.1, the declaration specifies that this document conforms to the XML Specification 1.0 and uses the ISO-8859-1 character set. This line is not considered to be a part of the data.

- The second line should specify the DTD of the XML document, but it is optional. If present, it specifies the root node of this XML document, the place where the DTD can be found, and the name of the DTD file. In listing B.1, the root node is address, the location of the DTD is SYSTEM, and the name of the DTD is "address.dtd". This line is also not considered to be a part of the data.
- All XML documents must start with a root tag that encompasses the whole document. If a DTD is specified, the root tag must be the one that is specified by the DTD declaration. In listing B.1, <address> is the root tag.
- All XML elements must have a closing tag. Unlike in HTML, where you can get away with not including a closing tag, it is illegal to omit the closing tags in XML. A closing tag is written with a / before the name of the tag. For example, the closing tag for <address> is </address>.
- All XML elements must be properly nested—that is, a tag may contain other elements inside it; however, a tag that starts first must end last. For example, the following is illegal:

```
<street><aptNo>65</street></aptNo>
```

- XML tags are case sensitive. Therefore, <address> and <Address> are not the same. We must be careful to ensure that the closing tag matches the opening tag.
- Tags may have attributes. In listing B.1, id is an attribute of the <address> tag and 123 is the value of the attribute. We can include as many attributes as the document's DTD allows.
- Tag attributes must be enclosed within quotes. For example, although <form name=login> is valid in HTML, it must be written as <form name="login"> in XML. However, both single quotes and double quotes are valid.
- White space is preserved. For example, <b>Hello    World!</b> will be displayed as Hello World! in HTML because HTML replaces all the white spaces with a single space. However, this is not the case in XML.

In the following sections, we will learn more about the components of an XML document.

### B.2.1 XML elements

Elements are the building blocks of an XML document. Each element describes a part of the data. For example, a document containing the résumé of a person may consist of multiple elements, such as <personal-information>, <qualification>, and <experience>. These elements may, in turn, be composed of other elements. Therefore, a document essentially becomes a hierarchical structure of elements in which the outer element is called the *parent* element and the inner element is called the *child* element. Elements at the same level are called *siblings*. The root node, of course, does not have a parent.

### *Extensibility*

Over time, an XML element may not be able to completely represent the data. For example, an <address> element may have another element, <pobox>, which is not described in the current DTD. To allow the XML documents to evolve, XML elements are permitted to be extensible. This means that an older application will still work with an XML document in which an <address> element contains an extra element, such as <pobox>. Of course, it will not be able to understand the new element, but it will not break—it will just ignore the new element.

### *Element types*

An XML tag is often referred to as an XML element, but technically, an XML element consists of its start tag and its end tag, and everything in between. For example, in `<id>123</id>`, `<id>` is the tag and `<id>123</id>` is the element. An XML element may contain the following:

- *Elemental content.* The element contains one or more child elements, but does not contain any free content; that is, all of the element's content is inside the child elements. For example, the <address> element shown in listing B.1 contains elemental content, since all the contents are embedded inside other XML tags.
- *Simple or text content.* The contents of an element are not embedded in child elements. For example, the <number> element in `<number>214</number>` contains simple content.
- *Mixed content.* The element consists of elemental as well as simple content. For example, the <address> element in `<address>214<street>Cheryl </street></address>` contains mixed contents.

### *Element naming rules and conventions*

When naming XML elements, we must follow these rules:

- Names can contain letters, numbers, and other characters.
- They must not start with a number or punctuation character.
- They must not start with the letters *xml* (or *XML* or *Xml* or any combination of case).
- They cannot contain spaces.

Based on these rules, <a123> and <a&2-;> are valid, while <2a>, <a b>, and <xml> are invalid.

In general, element names are supposed to describe the data that they contain. Therefore, the names should be easy to understand and should not be cryptic.

## B.2.2 Attributes

Attributes are used to convey additional information about tags. This is similar to HTML, where we use attributes to specify information about the HTML tags, such as:

```
<form action="/servlet/testServlet" method="POST">
```

Information conveyed by attributes is usually not a part of the data, but it is a kind of meta-information about the data. In this example, the `action` attribute specifies only that the actual data is to be sent to `/servlet/TestServlet`, and the `method` attribute specifies only that the actual data is to be sent via an HTTP POST request. None of the parts of an attribute's value is a part of the actual data, though.

Attribute values are usually enclosed within double quotes, but single quotes are also valid. Using single quotes is necessary when the attribute value itself contains double quotes.

#### Attributes or elements

Here's a good rule of thumb: data goes in elements and metadata goes in attributes. For example, `<address aptNo="214" street="cheryl dr">` is valid, but keeping the data in the attributes is not a good practice.

Similarly,

```
<file>
   <type>text</type>
   <content>file content here</content>
</file>
```

is better written as:

```
<file type="text">
   <content>file content here</content>
</file>.
```

## B.3 The Document Type Definition

An XML document that follows all the syntax rules we've explained is called a *well-formed document.* However, to communicate information between multiple systems, a well-formed document is not enough. All the systems participating in the conversation must be able to validate that the document they are sending or have received follows the rules that all the systems agreed on. As we mentioned earlier, these rules are defined in the DTD of an XML document. In practical terms, a DTD defines the document structure with a list of legal elements. An XML document that is verified according to the document's DTD is called a *valid document.* Validating an XML file is a fairly automated task. Many standard software packages are available that parse an XML document and validate its elements using its associated DTD.

### B.3.1 Understanding a DTD

To validate an XML document, you should know how the rules are specified in the DTD. Understanding a DTD is also important because various configuration files, such as `web.xml` and TLD files, are validated by using their respective DTDs. You also need to understand the DTD in order to write a valid XML file.

Let's start with an example. Listing B.2 shows the DTD for `address.xml`.

**Listing B.2 address.dtd**

```
<!DOCTYPE address [

<!ELEMENT address (street, city, state, zip, country)>
<!ELEMENT street (#CDATA)>
<!ELEMENT city (#CDATA)>
<!ELEMENT state (#CDATA)>
<!ELEMENT zip (#CDATA)>
<!ELEMENT country (#CDATA)>

]>
```

All XML documents are made up of the following building blocks:

- *Elements.* As we saw earlier, these are the main components of an XML document. They contain the actual data. Elements can contain plain text or other elements, or they can be empty.
- *Tags.* Tags mark up the elements. For example, in <p>hello <b>world</b> </p>, <p> is the start tag and </p> is the end tag. The text hello <b> world </b> is the element marked up by this tag. Of course, the element itself contains text, other tags, and child elements.
- *Attributes.* As we mentioned earlier, attributes provide meta-information about the elements.
- *Entities and entity references.* Entities are variables used to define common text. Entity references are references to entities from within the XML documents. If you have used   in HTML, you know what this means. This special set of characters instructs the browser to display one non-breaking white space. When an HTML page is displayed, all the consecutive white spaces are collapsed into one; therefore, for example, if we want to display two consecutive spaces, we must write    instead of two space characters. Thus, entities are expanded to their actual value when an XML parser parses a document. The entities shown in table B.1 are predefined in XML.

**Table B.1 Predefined entities**

| Entity References | Character |
|---|---|
| < | < |
| > | > |
| & | & |
| " | " |
| ' | ' |

- *PCDATA.* This stands for Parsed Character **Data**. This is the text contained between the start and end tags of an XML element. As the name suggests, this text is parsed by a parser and the tags inside the text are treated as normal XML markup. At the same time, the entities are also expanded.
- *CDATA.* This stands for Character **Data**. This is also the text contained between the start and end tags of an XML element. However, this text is not parsed by a parser and is used as is.

In our earlier example, `<street>`, `<city>`, `<state>`, `<zip>`, and `<country>` are all elements that contain CDATA—that is, normal text that will not be parsed.

In the following sections, we will explain how elements and attributes are defined.

## B.3.2 Defining elements

XML elements are declared with an element declaration. An element declaration has the following syntax:

```
<!ELEMENT element-name category>
```

or

```
<!ELEMENT element-name (element-content)>
```

Here, `category` can be `EMPTY` or ANY. `EMPTY` means that the element does not contain any data. For example, `<!ELEMENT distributable EMPTY>`. ANY means that the element may contain data that can be parsed. An example is `<!ELEMENT anydata ANY>`.

The value of `element-content` can be `#PCDATA`, `#CDATA`, a list of child elements, or a combination of these. For example, `<!ELEMENT description (#CDATA)>` specifies that the `<description>` element can contain any character data. The definition `<!ELEMENT address (street, city, state, zip, country)>` specifies that the `<address>` element must contain `<street>`, `<city>`, `<state>`, `<zip>`, and `<country>`. These child elements must occur in the same sequence given in the element list.

### *Understanding repeatability of child elements*

We can specify how many times a child element can occur by using `+`, `*`, and `?`. The `+` sign means the element can occur one or more number of times, the `*` sign means the element can occur zero or more number of times, and the `?` sign means the element is optional but can occur at most once. The absence of a sign means the element must occur once and only once. For specifying an either-or situation, we use the `|`.

Let's take some element declarations from the DTD of `web.xml` and see what they mean:

- `<!ELEMENT listener (listener-class)>`

  This means that the `<listener>` element can only contain a `<listener-class>` element. Further, since no sign is appended to `<listener-class>`, it must occur once and only once.

- `<!ELEMENT context-param (param-name, param-value, description?)>`

  This means that `<context-param>` must contain a `<param-name>` element, a `<param-value>` element, and an optional description.

- `<!ELEMENT error-page ((error-code | exception-type), location)>`

  This means that the `<error-page>` element can contain either `error-code` or `exception-type` but not both. Since there is no sign after `(error-code | exception-type)`, it must occur exactly once.

- ```
  <!ELEMENT security-constraint (display-name?,
     web-resource-collection+, auth-constraint?,
     user-data-constraint?)>
  ```

  This means that the `<security-constraint>` element can contain an optional `<display-name>`, one or more `<web-resource-collection>` elements, an optional `<auth-constraint>` element, and an optional `<user-data-constraint>` element.

- ```
  <!ELEMENT servlet (icon?, servlet-name, display-name?, description?,
    (servlet-class|jsp-file), init-param*, load-on-startup?, run-as?,
     security-role-ref*)>
  ```

  This means that the `<servlet>` element can contain an optional icon, exactly one `<servlet-name>`, an optional `<display-name>`, an optional description, either `<servlet-class>` or `<jsp-file>`, any number of `<init-param>` elements, an optional `<load-on-startup>` element, an optional `<run-as>` element, and any number of `<security-role-ref>` elements.

### B.3.3 Defining attributes

Attributes are declared with an `ATTLIST` declaration. It has the following syntax:

```
<!ATTLIST element-name attribute-name attribute-type default-value>
```

Here, `element-name` is the name of the element for which this attribute is being defined, `attribute-name` is the name of the attribute, `attribute-type` is the type of the attribute, and `default-value` specifies the default value, if any.

Table B.2 explains how `attribute-type` is used.

**Table B.2 Attribute types and their meaning**

| attribute-type value | Meaning |
|---|---|
| CDATA | The value is character data. |
| (val1\|val2\|val3\|...) | The value must be one from an enumerated list of values. |
| ID | This value uniquely identifies the element. |
| IDREF | The value is a reference to a uniquely identifiable value. |
| IDREFS | A list of comma-separated IDREF values. |

*continued on next page*

**Table B.2 Attribute types and their meaning *(continued)***

| attribute-type value | Meaning |
|---|---|
| NMTOKEN | The value is a valid XML name. |
| NMTOKENS | A list of comma-separated NMTOKEN values. |
| ENTITY | The value is an entity. |
| ENTITIES | A list of comma-separated ENTITY values. |
| NOTATION | The value is a name of a notation. |
| xml: | The value is a predefined XML value. |

Table B.3 explains how `default-value` is used.

**Table B.3 default-value**

| default-value value | Meaning |
|---|---|
| Value | The attribute's default value. |
| #DEFAULT value | The attribute's default value. |
| #REQUIRED | The attribute value must be included in the element. |
| #IMPLIED | The attribute does not have to be included. |
| #FIXED | The attribute value is fixed. |

The following declaration shows how the values from tables B.2 and B.3 can be used:

```
<!ELEMENT item (name)>
<!ATTLIST item
   price CDATA #REQUIRED
   currency (USD|EUR) "USD"
   category CDATA #IMPLIED
   tax_id CDATA #FIXED "22314">
```

The `<item>` element may have four attributes: `price`, `currency`, `category`, and `tax_id`. The `price` attribute is required, and there is no default value. The `currency` attribute can have only one of two values: `USD` and `EUR`, where `EUR` is the default. The `category` attribute is optional. The `tax_id` attribute always has the value `22314`.

## B.4 Further reading

We have only skimmed the surface of XML. After reading this appendix, you should be able to decipher the DTDs for `web.xml` and tag library descriptors. However, there is much more to XML than this. You can learn more about XML by visiting `www.xml.org`. We also recommend the book *J2EE and XML Development* (ISBN 1930110308), by Kurt A. Gabrick and David B. Weiss, available from Manning Publications.

APPENDIX C

# *A sample web.xml file*

The following listing of a sample `web.xml` file illustrates the use of various elements of a deployment descriptor. We have explained the elements that you are required to know for the exam throughout the book. This code listing is just for a quick recap.

```
<?xml version="1.0" encoding="ISO-8859-1"?>

<!DOCTYPE web-app
    PUBLIC "-//Sun Microsystems, Inc.//DTD Web Application 2.3//EN"
    "http://java.sun.com/dtd/web-app_2_3.dtd">

<web-app>
    <display-name>Test Webapp</display-name>

    <description>This is a sample deployment descriptor that shows
                 the use of important elements.
    </description>

    <!-- Presence of this element indicates that this
         WebApp is distributable. -->
    <distributable/>

    <!-- Defines WebApp initialization parameters.-->
    <context-param>
        <param-name>locale</param-name>
        <param-value>US</param-value>
    </context-param>
    <context-param>
        <param-name>DBName</param-name>
        <param-value>Oracle</param-value>
    </context-param>
```

```
<!-- Defines filters and specifies filter mapping -->
<filter>
    <filter-name>Test Filter</filter-name>
    <description>Just for test</description>
    <filter-class>filters.TestFilter</filter-class>
    <init-param>
        <param-name>locale</param-name>
        <param-value>US</param-value>
    </init-param>
</filter>

<filter-mapping>
    <filter-name>Test Filter</filter-name>
    <servlet-name>TestServlet</servlet-name>
</filter-mapping>

<!-- Defines application events listeners -->
<listener>
    <listener-class>listeners.MyServletContextListener
    </listener-class>
</listener>
<listener>
    <listener-class>listeners.MySessionCumContextListener
    </listener-class>
</listener>

<!-- Defines servlets -->
<servlet>
    <servlet-name>TestServlet</servlet-name>
    <description>Just for test</description>
    <servlet-class>servlets.TestServlet</servlet-class>
</servlet>
<servlet>
    <servlet-name>HelloServlet</servlet-name>
    <servlet-class>servlets.HelloServlet</servlet-class>
    <init-param>
        <param-name>locale</param-name>
        <param-value>US</param-value>
    </init-param>
    <load-on-startup>1</load-on-startup>
    <security-role-ref>
        <!-- role-name is used in
             HttpServletRequest.isUserInRole(String role)
             method. -->
        <role-name>manager</role-name>
        <!-- role-link is one of the role-names specified in
             security-role elements. -->
        <role-link>supervisor</role-link>
    <security-role-ref>
</servlet>

<!-- Defines servlet mappings -->
<servlet-mapping>
```

```
        <servlet-name>TestServlet</servlet-name>
        <url-pattern>/test/*</url-pattern>
    </servlet-mapping>
    <servlet-mapping>
        <servlet-name>HelloServlet</servlet-name>
        <url-pattern>*.hello</url-pattern>
    </servlet-mapping>

    <session-config>
        <!--specifies session timeout as 30 minutes. -->
        <session-timeout>30</session-timeout>
    <session-config>


    <mime-mapping>
        <extension>jar</extension>
        <mime-type>application/java-archive</mime-type>
    </mime-mapping>
    <mime-mapping>
        <extension>conf</extension>
        <mime-type>text/plain</mime-type>
    </mime-mapping>

    <welcome-file-list>
        <welcome-file>index.html</welcome-file>
        <welcome-file>home.html</welcome-file>
        <welcome-file>welcome.html</welcome-file>
    </welcome-file-list>

    <error-page>
        <error-code>404</error-code>
        <location>notfoundpage.jsp</location>
    </error-page>
    <error-page>
        <exception-type>java.sql.SQLException</exception-type>
        <location>sqlexception.jsp</location>
    </error-page>

    <taglib>
        <taglib-uri>http://abc.com/testlib</taglib-uri>
        <taglib-location>
           /WEB-INF/tlds/testlib.tld
        </taglib-location>
    </taglib>
    <taglib>
        <taglib-uri>/examplelib</taglib-uri>
        <taglib-location>
           /WEB-INF/tlds/examplelib.tld
        </taglib-location>
    </taglib>

    <security-constraint>
      <display-name>Example Security Constraint</display-name>
      <web-resource-collection>
```

```
      <web-resource-name>Protected Area</web-resource-name>
      <url-pattern>/test/*</url-pattern>
      <!-- only POST method is protected -->
      <http-method>POST</http-method>
    </web-resource-collection>

    <web-resource-collection>
      <web-resource-name>Another Protected Area</web-resource-name>
      <url-pattern>*.hello</url-pattern>
      <!-- All methods are protected as no http-method is
      specified -->
    </web-resource-collection>

    <auth-constraint>
      <!-- Only the following roles can access the above resources.
           The role must be defined in security-role. -->
      <role-name>supervisor</role-name>
    </auth-constraint>

    <user-data-constraint>
      <!-- Specifies the type of communication
           between the client and the server.
           It can be: NONE, INTEGRAL, or CONFIDENTIAL -->
      <transport-guarantee>INTEGRAL</transport-guarantee>
    </user-data-constraint>

  </security-constraint>


  <login-config>
    <!-- auth-method can be: BASIC, FORM, DIGEST, or CLIENT-CERT -->
    <auth-method>FORM</auth-method>
    <realm-name>sales</realm-name>
    <form-login-config>
      <form-login-page>/formlogin.html</form-login-page>
      <form-error-page>/formerror.jsp</form-error-page>
    </form-login-config>
  </login-config>

  <!-- Specifies the roles that are defined in the application
       server. For example, Tomcat defines it in
       conf\tomcat-users.xml -->
  <security-role>
      <role-name>supervisor</role-name>
  </security-role>
  <security-role>
      <role-name>worker</role-name>
  </security-role>

</web-app>
```

APPENDIX D

# Review Q & A

## CHAPTER 4—THE SERVLET MODEL

1. Which method in the `HttpServlet` class services the HTTP POST request? (Select one)

   a `doPost(ServletRequest, ServletResponse)`
   b `doPOST(ServletRequest, ServletResponse)`
   c `servicePost(HttpServletRequest, HttpServletResponse)`
   d `doPost(HttpServletRequest, HttpServletResponse)`

   *Answer: d*

   ***Explanation***

   Remember that `HttpServlet` extends `GenericServlet` and provides HTTP-specific functionality. Thus, all its methods take `HttpServletRequest` and `HttpServletResponse` objects as parameters.

   Also, the method names follow the standard Java naming convention—for example, the method for processing POST requests is `doPost()` and not `doPOST()`.

2. Consider the following HTML page code:

```
<html><body>
<a href="/servlet/HelloServlet">POST</a>
</body></html>
```

   Which method of `HelloServlet` will be invoked when the hyperlink displayed by the above page is clicked? (Select one)

   a `doGet`
   b `doPost`
   c `doForm`

**d** doHref

**e** serviceGet

*Answer: a*

***Explanation***

Don't get confused by the text POST displayed by the hyperlink. A click on a hyperlink always generates an HTTP GET request, which is handled by the `doGet()` method. You can generate a POST request through a hyperlink by using JavaScript. For example:

```
<html>
<script lanaguage="JavaScript">
function sendPost()
{
  dummyform.submit();
}
</script>
<body>
<form name="dummyform" action=
            "/servlet/HelloServlet" method="POST">
<input type="text" name="name">
</form>
<a href="" onClick="javascript:sendPost();">POST</a>
</body>
</html>
```

This HTML code executes the JavaScript function `sendPost()` whenever the hyperlink is clicked. This function submits the `dummyform`, causing a POST request to be sent.

**3.** Consider the following code for the `doGet()` method:

```
public void doGet(HttpServletRequest req,
                  HttpServletResponse res)
{
   PrintWriter out = res.getWriter);
   out.println("<html><body>Hello</body></html>");
   //1
   if(req.getParameter("name") == null)
   {
      res.sendError(HttpServletResponse.SC_UNAUTHORIZED);
   }
}
```

Which of the following lines can be inserted at `//1` so that the above code does not throw any exception? (Select one)

**a** if ( ! res.isSent() )

**b** if ( ! res.isCommitted() )

**c** if ( ! res.isDone() )

**d** if ( ! res.isFlushed() )

**e** if ( ! res.flush() )

*Answer: b*

***Explanation***

The question is based on the concept that the `ServletRequest.sendError()` method throws an `IllegalStateException` if the response has already been sent to the client. The `ServletRequest.isCommitted()` method checks whether or not the response is committed.

**4.** Which of the following lines would initialize the `out` variable for sending a Microsoft Word file to the browser? (Select one)

**a** `PrintWriter out = response.getServletOutput();`

**b** `PrintWriter out = response.getPrintWriter();`

**c** `OutputStream out = response.getWriter();`

**d** `PrintWriter out = response.getOuputStream();`

**e** `OutputStream out = response.getOuputStream();`

**f** `ServletOutputStream out = response.getServletOutputStream();`

*Answer: e*

***Explanation***

For sending any data other than text, you need to get the `OutputStream` object. `ServletResponse.getOutputStream()` returns an object of type `ServletOutputStream`, where `ServletOutputStream` extends `OutputStream`.

**5.** You need to send a GIF file to the browser. Which of the following lines should be called after (or before) a call to `response.getOutputStream()`? (Select one)

**a** `response.setContentType("image/gif"); Before`

**b** `response.setContentType("image/gif"); After`

**c** `response.setDataType("image/gif"); Before`

**d** `response.setDataType("image/gif"); After`

**e** `response.setStreamType("image/gif"); Before`

**f** `response.setStreamType("image/gif"); After`

*Answer: a*

***Explanation***

You need to set the content type of the response using the `ServletResponse.setContentType()` method *before* calling the `ServletResponse.getOutputStream()` method.

**6.** Consider the following HTML page code:

```
<html><body>
<form name="data" action="/servlet/DataServlet" method="POST">
<input type="text" name="name">
<input type="submit" name="submit">
</form>
</body></html>
```

Identify the two methods that can be used to retrieve the value of the `name` parameter when the form is submitted.

a `getParameter("name");`

b `getParameterValue("name");`

c `getParameterValues("name");`

d `getParameters("name");`

e `getValue("name");`

f `getName();`

*Answers: a and c*

***Explanation***

`ServletRequest` provides two methods to retrieve input parameters:

- `getParameter("name")`: Returns a `String` or `null`.
- `getParameterValues("name")`: Returns a `String` array containing all the values for the `name` parameter or `null`.

Besides these two, `ServletRequest` also provides a `getParameterNames()` method that returns an `Enumeration` object of all the parameter names present in the request, or an empty `Enumeration` if the request does not contain any parameter.

7. Which of the following methods would you use to retrieve header values from a request? (Select two)

a `getHeader()` of `ServletRequest`

b `getHeaderValues()` of `HttpServletRequest`

c `getHeaderValue()` of `ServletRequest`

d `getHeader()` of `HttpServletRequest`

e `getHeaders()` of `ServletRequest`

f `getHeaders()` of `HttpServletRequest`

*Answers: d and f*

***Explanation***

Headers are a feature of the HTTP protocol. Thus, all the header-specific methods belong to `HttpServletRequest`. `getHeader()` returns a `String` (or `null`), while `getHeaders()` returns an `Enumeration` of all the values for that header (or an empty `Enumeration`).

8. Consider the following code:

```
public void doGet(HttpServletRequest req,
                  HttpServletResponse res)
                  throws IOException
{

  if(req.getParameter("switch") == null)
  {
    //1
  }
```

```
        else
        {
            //other code
        }
    }
```

Which of the following lines can be inserted at `//1` so that the request is redirected to the `collectinfo.html` page? (Select one)

**a** `req.sendRedirect("collectinfo.html");`
**b** `req.redirect("collectinfo.html");`
**c** `res.direct("collectinfo.html");`
**d** `res.sendRedirect("collectinfo.html");`
**e** `this.sendRedirect("collectinfo.html");`
**f** `this.send("collectinfo.html");`

*Answer: d*

***Explanation***

You can redirect the client to another resource using the `HttpServletResponse.sendRedirect()` method.

**9.** Consider the following code:

```
public void doGet(HttpServletRequest req,
                  HttpServletResponse res)
{
    HttpSession session = req.getSession();
    ServletContext ctx = this.getServletContext();

    if(req.getParameter("userid") != null)
    {
        String userid = req.getParameter("userid");
        //1
    }
}
```

You want the `userid` parameter to be available only to the requests that come from the same user. Which of the following lines would you insert at `//1`? (Select one)

**a** `session.setAttribute("userid", userid);`
**b** `req.setAttribute("userid", userid);`
**c** `ctx.addAttribute("userid", userid);`
**d** `session.addAttribute("userid", userid);`
**e** `this.addParameter("userid", userid);`
**f** `this.setAttribute("userid", userid);`

*Answer: a*

***Explanation***

Attributes stored in the session scope are available only for the requests from the same client. Attributes stored in the context scope are available for all the requests to the same web application from all the clients. Attributes stored in the request scope are available only for the request in which it is stored.

10. Which of the following lines would you use to include the output of `DataServlet` into any other servlet? (Select one)

a
```
RequestDispatcher rd = request.getRequestDispatcher(
    "/servlet/DataServlet"); rd.include(request, response);
```

b
```
RequestDispatcher rd = request.getRequestDispatcher(
    "/servlet/DataServlet"); rd.include(response);
```

c
```
RequestDispatcher rd = request.getRequestDispatcher();
    rd.include("/servlet/DataServlet", request, response);
```

d
```
RequestDispatcher rd = request.getRequestDispatcher();
    rd.include("/servlet/DataServlet", response);
```

e
```
RequestDispatcher rd = request.getRequestDispatcher();
    rd.include("/servlet/DataServlet");
```

*Answer: a*

***Explanation***

To forward or include a request to another resource, first you need to get a `RequestDispatcher` object from either `ServletRequest` or `ServletContext`. Then you can call `include()` or `forward()` and pass the current request and response objects as parameters.

## CHAPTER 5—STRUCTURE AND DEPLOYMENT

1. Which element is used to specify useful information about an initialization parameter of a servlet in the deployment descriptor? (Select one)

a `param-description`

b `description`

c `info`

d `param-info`

e `init-param-info`

*Answer: b*

***Explanation***

Remember that the `description` element is used for all the elements that can take a description (useful information about that element). This includes `servlet`, `init-param`, and `context-param`, among others. For a complete list of the elements that can take a description, please read the DTD for `web.xml`.

2. Which of the following deployment descriptor snippets correctly associates a servlet implemented by a class named `com.abc.SalesServlet` with the name `SalesServlet`? (Select one)

a
```
<servlet>
  <servlet-class>com.abc.SalesServlet</servlet-class>
  <servlet-name>SalesServlet</servlet-name>
</servlet>
```

**b**
```
<servlet>
    <servlet-name>SalesServlet</servlet-name>
    <servlet-package>com.abc.SalesServlet</servlet-package>
</servlet>
```

**c**
```
<servlet>
    <servlet-name>SalesServlet</servlet-name>
    <servlet-class>com.abc.SalesServlet</servlet-class>
</servlet>
```

**d**
```
<servlet name="SalesServlet" class="com.abc.SalesServlet">
    <servlet>
    <servlet-class name="SalesServlet">
        com.abc.SalesServlet
    </servlet-class>
</servlet>
```

**e**
```
<servlet>
    <servlet-name class="com.abc.SalesServlet">
        SalesServlet
    </servlet-name>
</servlet>
```

*Answer: c*

### Explanation

A servlet is configured using the `servlet` element. Here is the definition of the `servlet` element:

```
<!ELEMENT servlet ( icon?, servlet-name, display-name?,
                                               description?,
                                    (servlet-class|jsp-file), init-param*,
                                       load-on-startup?,
                                    run-as?, security-role-ref* ) >
```

Observe that `servlet-name` must occur before `servlet-class`. Thus, answer a is invalid.

3. A web application is located in a directory named `sales`. Where should its deployment descriptor be located? (Select one)

**a** `sales`
**b** `sales/deployment`
**c** `sales/WEB`
**d** `sales/WEB-INF`
**e** `WEB-INF/sales`
**f** `WEB-INF`
**g** `WEB/sales`

*Answer: d*

### Explanation

The deployment descriptor is always located in the `WEB-INF` directory of the web application.

4. What file is the deployment descriptor of a web application named `BankApp` stored in? (Select one)

   a `BankApp.xml`

   b `bankapp.xml`

   c `server.xml`

   d `deployment.xml`

   e `WebApp.xml`

   f `web.xml`

   *Answer: f*

   ***Explanation***

   The deployment descriptor of a web application is always kept in a file named `web.xml`, no matter what the name of the web application is.

5. Your servlet class depends on a utility class named `com.abc.TaxUtil`. Where would you keep the `TaxUtil.class` file? (Select one)

   a `WEB-INF`

   b `WEB-INF/classes`

   c `WEB-INF/lib`

   d `WEB-INF/jars`

   e `WEB-INF/classes/com/abc`

   *Answer: e*

   ***Explanation***

   All the classes that are not packaged in a JAR file must be kept in the `WEB-INF/classes` directory with its complete directory structure, as per the package of the class. The servlet container automatically adds this directory to the classpath of the web application.

6. Your web application, named `simpletax`, depends on a third-party JAR file named `taxpackage.jar`. Where would you keep this file? (Select one)

   a `simpletax`

   b `simpletax/WEB-INF`

   c `simpletax/WEB-INF/classes`

   d `simpletax/WEB-INF/lib`

   e `simpletax/WEB-INF/jars`

   f `simpletax/WEB-INF/thirdparty`

   *Answer: d*

   ***Explanation***

   All the classes that are packaged in a JAR file must be kept in the `WEB-INF/lib` directory. The servlet container automatically adds all the classes in all the JAR files kept in this directory to the classpath of the web application.

7. Which of the following deployment descriptor elements is used to specify the initialization parameters for a servlet named `TestServlet`? (Select one)

**a** No element is needed because initialization parameters are specified as attributes of the `<servlet>` element.

**b** `<servlet-param>`

**c** `<param>`

**d** `<initialization-param>`

**e** `<init-parameter>`

**f** `<init-param>`

*Answer: f*

***Explanation***

Each initialization must be specified using a separate `<init-param>` element:

```
<!ELEMENT init-param (param-name, param-value, description?)>
```

The following is an example of a servlet definition that specifies two initialization parameters:

```
<servlet>
  <servlet-name>TestServlet</servlet-name>
  <servlet-class>com.abc.TestServlet</servlet-class>
  <init-param>
    <param-name>MAX</param-name>
    <param-value>100</param-value>
    <description>maximum limit</description>
  </init-param>
  <init-param>
    <param-name>MIN</param-name>
    <param-value>10</param-value>
  </init-param>

</servlet>
```

8. Assume that the following servlet mapping is defined in the deployment descriptor of a web application:

```
<servlet-mapping>
   <servlet-name>TestServlet</servlet-name>
   <url-pattern>*.asp</url-pattern>
</servlet-mapping>
```

Which of the following requests will not be serviced by `TestServlet`? (Select one)

**a** `/hello.asp`

**b** `/gui/hello.asp`

**c** `/gui/hello.asp/bye.asp`

**d** `/gui/*.asp`

**e** `/gui/sales/hello.asp`

**f** `/gui/asp`

*Answer: f*

***Explanation***

Here, any request that ends with `.asp` will be directed to `TestServlet`. Thus, only answer f will not be serviced by `TestServlet`. We suggest that you identify the context path, servlet path, and path info for all the above options according to the rules given in section 5.2.4.

## CHAPTER 6—THE SERVLET CONTAINER MODEL

1. Which of the following methods will be invoked when a `ServletContext` is destroyed? (Select one)

   **a** `contextDestroyed()` of `javax.servlet.ServletContextListener`
   **b** `contextDestroyed()` of `javax.servlet.HttpServletContextListener`
   **c** `contextDestroyed()` of `javax.servlet.http.ServletContextListener`
   **d** `contextDestroyed()` of `javax.servlet.http.HttpServletContextListener`

   *Answer: a*

   ***Explanation***

   Remember that the concept of servlet context applies to all the servlets and not just `HttpServlets`. Therefore, interfaces related to servlet context belong to the `javax.servlet` package.

2. Which of the following methods will be invoked when a `ServletContext` is created? (Select one)

   **a** `contextInstantiated()` of `javax.servlet.ServletContextListener`
   **b** `contextInitialized()` of `javax.servlet.ServletContextListener`
   **c** `contextInited()` of `javax.servlet.ServletContextListener`
   **d** `contextCreated()` of `javax.servlet.ServletContextListener`

   *Answer: b*

   ***Explanation***

   On the exam, you will be asked questions that require you to know the method names for all the methods of the servlet API. As in this question, the options may be very confusing.

3. Consider the following class:

```
import javax.servlet.*;
public class MyListener implements ServletContextAttributeListener
{
   public void attributeAdded(ServletContextAttributeEvent scab)
   {
      System.out.println("attribute added");
   }
   public void attributeRemoved(ServletContextAttributeEvent scab)
   {
      System.out.println("attribute removed");
   }
}
```

Which of the following statements about the above class is correct? (Select one)

**a** This class will compile as is.

**b** This class will compile only if the `attributeReplaced()` method is added to it.

**c** This class will compile only if the `attributeUpdated()` method is added to it.

**d** This class will compile only if the `attributeChanged()` method is added to it.

*Answer: b*

***Explanation***

`ServletContextAttributeListener` also declares the `public void attributeReplaced(ServletContextAttributeEvent scab)` method, which is called when an existing attribute is replaced by another one.

**4.** Which method is used to retrieve an attribute from a `ServletContext`? (Select one)

**a** `String getAttribute(int index)`

**b** `String getObject(int index)`

**c** `Object getAttribute(int index)`

**d** `Object getObject(int index)`

**e** `Object getAttribute(String name)`

**f** `String getAttribute(String name)`

**g** `String getObject(String name)`

*Answer: e*

***Explanation***

Since we can store any type of object in a servlet context, the `getAttribute` method returns an Object. You can then cast the returned object to whatever type you expect it to be.

**5.** Which method is used to retrieve an initialization parameter from a `ServletContext`? (Select one)

**a** `Object getInitParameter(int index)`

**b** `Object getParameter(int index)`

**c** `Object getInitParameter(String name)`

**d** `String getInitParameter(String name)`

**e** `String getParameter(String name)`

*Answer: d*

***Explanation***

Initialization parameters are specified in the deployment descriptor. Since we can only specify strings in the deployment descriptor, the `getInitParameter()` method returns a String.

**6.** Which deployment descriptor element is used to specify a `ServletContextListener`? (Select one)

**a** `<context-listener>`

**b** `<listener>`

**c** `<servlet-context-listener>`

**d** `<servletcontextlistener>`

**e** `<servletcontext-listener>`

*Answer: b*

***Explanation***

All the listeners that are specified in the deployment descriptor are specified using the `<listener>` element:

```
<listener>
  <listener-class>com.abc.MyServletContextListener</listener-class>
</listener>
```

The servlet container automatically figures out the type of interface that the specified class implements.

7. Which of the following `web.xml` snippets correctly specify an initialization parameter for a servlet context? (Select one)

**a**
```
<context-param>
    <name>country</name>
    <value>USA</value>
<context-param>
```

**b**
```
<context-param>
    <param name="country" value="USA" />
<context-param>
```

**c**
```
<context>
    <param name="country" value="USA" />
<context>
```

**d**
```
<context-param>
    <param-name>country</param-name>
    <param-value>USA</param-value>
<context-param>
```

*Answer: d*

***Explanation***

Initialization parameters for the servlet context are specified using the `<context-param>` element, which contains exactly one `<param-name>` and exactly one `<param-value>` element.

8. Which of the following is *not* a requirement of a distributable web application? (Select one)

**a** It cannot depend on the notification events generated due to changes in the `ServletContext` attribute list.

**b** It cannot depend on the notification events generated due to changes in the session attribute list.

**c** It cannot depend on the notification events generated when a session is activated or passivated.

**d** It cannot depend on the notification events generated when `ServletContext` is created or destroyed.

**e** It cannot depend on the notification events generated when a session is created or destroyed.

*Answer: c*

***Explanation***

A servlet container may not propagate `ServletContextEvents` (generated when a context is created or destroyed) and `ServletContextAttributeEvents` (generated when the attribute list of a context changes) to listeners residing in other JVMs. This means that your web application cannot depend on these notifications. The same is true for events generated when a session is created or destroyed and when the attribute list of a session changes.

A session resides in only one JVM at a time. So, all the session attributes that implement `HttpSessionActivationListener` receive notifications when the session is activated or passivated.

**9.** Which of the following is a requirement of a distributable web application? (Select one)

**a** It cannot depend on `ServletContext` for sharing information.
**b** It cannot depend on the `sendRedirect()` method.
**c** It cannot depend on the `include()` and `forward()` methods of the `RequestDispatcher` class.
**d** It cannot depend on cookies for session management.

*Answer: a*

***Explanation***

Since each JVM has a separate instance of a servlet context for each web application (except the default one), the attribute set in a `ServletContext` on one JVM will not be visible in the `ServletContext` for the same application on another JVM.

## CHAPTER 7—HANDLING SERVER-SIDE EXCEPTIONS

**1.** Your servlet encounters an exception while processing a request. Which method would you use to send an error response to the browser? (Select two)

**a** `sendError(int errorCode)` of `HttpServlet`
**b** `sendError(int errorCode)` of `HttpServletRequest`
**c** `sendError(int errorCode)` of `HttpServletResponse`
**d** `sendError(String errorMsg)` of `HttpServletRequest`
**e** `sendError(int errorCode, String errorMsg)` of `HttpServletResponse`

*Answers: c and e*

***Explanation***

The `sendError(int code)` and `sendError(int code, String msg)` methods of `HttpServletResponse` are used to send error codes to the browser. These error codes are defined in the `HttpServletResponse` interface.

2. Consider the following `doPost()` method of a servlet:

```
public void doPost (HttpServletRequest request,
                    HttpServletResponse response)
                    throws ServletException, IOException
{
   System.out.println("Inside doPost");
   PrintWriter out = response.getWriter();
   out.println("Hello, ");
   out.flush();
   String name = getNameFromDBSomeHow();
   if(name == null)
   {
      response.sendError(HttpServletResponse.SC_NOT_FOUND,
                         "Unable to get name.");
   }
   out.println(name);
}
```

Assuming that `getNameFromDBSomeHow()` returns `null`, which of the following statements regarding this code are correct? (Select one)

**a** It will throw an `InvalidStateException` while serving a request.
**b** It will throw a `ServletException` while serving a request.
**c** It will throw a `NullPointerException` while serving a request.
**d** It will throw an `IllegalStateException` while serving a request.
**e** It will not throw an exception.

*Answer: d*

***Explanation***

When the `sendError()` method is called, the response is assumed to be committed. If you write anything to the response after it gets committed, an `IllegalStateException` is thrown. In this case, `sendError()` is called if the name is null. This commits the response. However, after the `if` condition, we have `out.println(name)`, which will cause the `IllegalStateException` to be thrown.

3. You want to send a status message of `HttpServletResponse.SC_OK` after successfully processing a request. Which of the following methods would you use? (Select one)

**a** `HttpServletResponse.setStatus(HttpServletResponse.SC_OK)`
**b** `HttpServletResponse.setStatusCode(HttpServletResponse.SC_OK)`
**c** `HttpServletResponse.sendStatus(HttpServletResponse.SC_OK)`
**d** `HttpServletResponse.sendStatusCode(HttpServletResponse.SC_OK)`
**e** `HttpServletRequest.sendStatus(HttpServletResponse.SC_OK)`
**f** `HttpServletRequest.setStatus(HttpServletResponse.SC_OK)`

*Answer: a*

***Explanation***

The `setStatus(int code)` method is declared in the `HttpServletResponse` interface.

**4.** Which deployment descriptor element contains the `<exception-type>` element? (Select one)

**a** `<error>`

**b** `<error-mapping>`

**c** `<error-page>`

**d** `<exception-mapping>`

**e** `<exception-page>`

*Answer: c*

***Explanation***

The `<error-page>` element is used for specifying the mapping for an exception type and a page. Here is the definition of the `<error-page>` element:

```
<!ELEMENT error-page ((error-code | exception-type), location)>
```

**5.** Your servlet may throw a business logic exception named `AccountFrozenException` that extends from `RuntimeException`. Which of the following `web.xml` snippets correctly maps this exception to `accounterror.html` so that whenever the servlet throws this exception, `accounterror.html` is displayed? (Select one)

**a**
```
<error-page>
    <exception-type>AccountFrozenException</exception-type>
    <page-location >accounterror.html</page-location >
</error-page>
```

**b**
```
<error>
    <exception-type>AccountFrozenException</exception-type>
    <location>accounterror.html</location>
</error>
```

**c**
```
<error-page>
    <exception>AccountFrozenException</exception>
    <location>accounterror.html</location>
</error-page>
```

**d**
```
<error-page>
    <exception-type>AccountFrozenException</exception-type>
    <location>accounterror.html</location>
 </error-page>
```

**e**
```
<error-page>
    <exception-type>AccountFrozenException</exception-type>
    <page>accounterror.html</page>
</error-page>
```

*Answer: d*

***Explanation***

For mapping an exception to an error page, we need to define an `<error-page>` mapping with the `<exception-type>` and `<location>` subelements.

6. Which of the following is true about the business logic exceptions thrown by a servlet? (Select one)

**a** Error-page mapping can be specified only for exceptions that extend from `ServletException`.
**b** Error-page mapping can be specified only for exceptions that extend from `ServletException` or `IOException`.
**c** Error-page mapping can be specified only for exceptions that extend from `RuntimeException`.
**d** Error-page mapping can be specified for any exception.

*Answer: d*

***Explanation***

You can specify a mapping for any exception in the deployment descriptor. However, for exceptions that do not extend from `ServletException`, `IOException`, or `RuntimeException`, you have to wrap them into `ServletException`.

7. Instead of displaying the standard `HTTP 404- NOT FOUND` message for all bad requests to a web application, you want to display a customized page. Which of the following is the correct way to do this? (Select one)

**a** You have to check the servlet container documentation and change the default error message file.
**b** You have to change your servlets to redirect the responses to your customized error message file.
**c** You have to specify the mapping of the error-code (404) and the customized error page in `web.xml`.
**d** You cannot do it in a standard way.

*Answer: c*

***Explanation***

You can map error codes to error pages just as you map exception types to error pages. The following `web.xml` snippet maps `404` to `customnotfoundpage.html`:

```
<error-page>
   <error-code>404</exception-type>
   <location>customnotfoundpage.html</location>
</error-page>
```

8. Consider the following servlet code:

```
public class LogTestServlet extends HttpServlet
{
   public void service(HttpServletRequest req,
                       HttpServletResponse res)
                       throws ServletException, IOException
   {
      String logMsg = "LogTestServlet.service():Probe message";

      //1
   }
}
```

Which of the following statements can be inserted at //1 so that logMsg may be entered into the servlet log file? (Select three)

**a** `log(logMsg);`

**b** `req(logMsg);`

**c** `getServletConfig().log(logMsg);`

**d** `getServletContext().log(logMsg);`

**e** `getServletConfig().getServletContext().log(logMsg);`

**f** `res.log(logMsg);`

**g** `req.getSession().log(logMsg);`

*Answers: a, d, and e*

***Explanation***

The log() methods are provided only by GenericServlet and ServletContext. Answer a is valid since HttpServlet extends GenericServlet. Answers d and e are valid since GenericServlet and ServletConfig both provide the getServletContext() method, which returns ServletContext.

All other options are invalid because ServletRequest, ServletResponse, ServletConfig, and HttpSession do not provide any methods for logging.

**9.** Consider the following code for the doGet() method of a servlet:

```
public void doGet(HttpServletRequest req, HttpServletResponse res)
          throws ServletException, IOException
  {
  String userId = null;
  try
  {
     userId = loginUser(req);
  }
  catch(Exception e)
  {
     // 1:  log "Unknown User" and the exception to the log file.
  }
  if(userId != null)
  {
     //do something.
  }
}
```

Which of the following statements can be inserted at //1 to write a message as well as the exception stack trace to the log file? (Select one)

**a** `req.log(e, "Unknown User");`

**b** `this.log(e, "Unknown User")`

**c** `this.getServletContext().log("Unknown User", e);`

**d** `this.getServletContext().log(e, "Unknown User");`

**e** The stack trace of the exception cannot be logged using any of the log() methods.

*Answer: c*

#### *Explanation*

`GenericServlet` and `ServletContext` both provide `log(String msg)` and `log(String, Throwable)` methods that write error messages to a log file. The only difference between the `GenericServlet` version and the `ServletContext` version is that the `GenericServlet` version also prepends the servlet name to the error message before writing it to the log file.

## CHAPTER 8—SESSION MANAGEMENT

**1.** Which of the following interfaces or classes is used to retrieve the session associated with a user? (Select one)

**a** `GenericServlet`
**b** `ServletConfig`
**c** `ServletContext`
**d** `HttpServlet`
**e** `HttpServletRequest`
**f** `HttpServletResponse`

*Answer: e*

#### *Explanation*

The session associated with a user can only be retrieved using the `HttpServletRequest.getSession()` method.

**2.** Which of the following code snippets, when inserted in the `doGet()` method, will correctly count the number of GET requests made by a user? (Select one)

**a**
```
HttpSession session = request.getSession();
     int count = session.getAttribute("count");
     session.setAttribute("count", count++);
```

**b**
```
HttpSession session = request.getSession();
     int count = (int) session.getAttribute("count");
     session.setAttribute("count", count++);
```

**c**
```
HttpSession session = request.getSession();
    int count = ((Integer) session.getAttribute("count")).intValue();
     session.setAttribute("count", count++);
```

**d**
```
HttpSession session = request.getSession();
    int count = ((Integer) session.getAttribute("count")).intValue();
     session.setAttribute("count", new Integer(count++));
```

*Answer: d*

#### *Explanation*

Remember that the `setAttribute()` and `getAttribute()` methods only work with Objects and not with primitive data types. The `getAttribute()` method returns an Object and so you need to cast the returned value to the actual type (Integer, in this case). Similarly, you need to wrap the count variable into an Integer object and pass it to the `setAttribute()` method.

3. Which of the following methods will be invoked on a session attribute that implements `HttpSessionBindingListener` when the session is invalidated? (Select one)

   **a** `sessionDestroyed`

   **b** `valueUnbound`

   **c** `attributeRemoved`

   **d** `sessionInvalidated`

   *Answer: b*

   ***Explanation***

   When a session is invalidated, all the session attributes are unbound from the session. In the process, if an attribute implements `HttpSessionBindingListener`, the `valueUnbound()` method will be called on the attribute.

4. Which of the following methods will be invoked on a session attribute that implements appropriate interfaces when the session is invalidated? (Select one)

   **a** `sessionDestroyed` of `HttpSessionListener`

   **b** `attributeRemoved` of `HttpSessionAttributeListener`

   **c** `valueUnbound` of `HttpSessionBindingListener`

   **d** `sessionWillPassivate` of `HttpSessionActivationListener`

   *Answer: c*

   ***Explanation***

   The `HttpSessionListener` and `HttpSessionAttributeListener` are configured in the deployment descriptor. Therefore, even if a session attribute implements these interfaces, the `sessionDestroyed()` and `attributeRemoved()` methods will not be called on that attribute.

   An `HttpSessionActivationListener` is also configured in the deployment descriptor, and it is used when a session is passivated or activated.

5. Which of the following methods will expunge a session object? (Select one)

   **a** `session.invalidate();`

   **b** `session.expunge();`

   **c** `session.destroy();`

   **d** `session.end();`

   **e** `session.close();`

   *Answer: a*

   ***Explanation***

   The `invalidate()` method of `HttpSession` invalidates (or expunges) the session object.

6. Which of the following method calls will ensure that a session will never be expunged by the servlet container? (Select one)

   **a** `session.setTimeout(0);`

   **b** `session.setTimeout(-1);`

**c** `session.setTimeout(Integer.MAX_VALUE);`

**d** `session.setTimeout(Integer.MIN_VALUE);`

**e** `None of these`

*Answer: e*

***Explanation***

The correct method is `HttpSession.setMaxInactiveInterval(int seconds);`. A negative value (for example, `setMaxInactiveInterval(-1)`) ensures that the session is never invalidated. However, calling this method affects only the session on which it is called. All other sessions behave normally.

**7.** How can you make sure that none of the sessions associated with a web application will ever be expunged by the servlet container? (Select one)

**a** `session.setMaxInactiveInterval(-1);`

**b** Set the session timeout in the deployment descriptor to –1.

**c** Set the session timeout in the deployment descriptor to `0` or `-1`.

**d** Set the session timeout in the deployment descriptor to `65535`.

**e** You have to change the timeout value of all the sessions explicitly as soon as they are created.

*Answer: c*

***Explanation***

The `setMaxInactiveInterval(-1)` method will only affect the session on which it is called. The `<session-config>` element of `web.xml` affects all the sessions of the web application. A value of 0 or less ensures that the sessions are never invalidated.

```
<web-app>
...
   <session-config>
      <session-timeout>0</session-timeout>
   </session-config>
...
</web-app>
```

**8.** In which of the following situations will a session be invalidated? (Select two)

**a** No request is received from the client for longer than the session timeout period.

**b** The client sends a `KILL_SESSION` request.

**c** The servlet container decides to invalidate a session due to overload.

**d** The servlet explicitly invalidates the session.

**e** A user closes the active browser window.

**f** A user closes all of the browser windows.

*Answers: a and d*

***Explanation***

Sessions will be invalidated only in two cases: when no request comes from the client for more than the session timeout period or when you call the `session.invalidate()` method on a session. Closing the browser windows does not actually invalidate the session. Even if you close all the browser windows, the session will still be active on the server. The servlet container will only invalidate the session after the timeout period of the session expires.

**9.** Which method is required for using the URL rewriting mechanism of implementing session support? (Select one)

**a** `HttpServletRequest.encodeURL()`
**b** `HttpServletRequest.rewriteURL()`
**c** `HttpServletResponse.encodeURL()`
**d** `HttpServletResponse.rewriteURL()`

*Answer: c*

***Explanation***

In URL rewriting, the session ID has to be appended to all the URLs. The `encodeURL(String url)` method of `HttpServletResponse` does that.

**10.** The users of your web application do not accept cookies. Which of the following statements are correct? (Select one)

**a** You cannot maintain client state.
**b** URLs displayed by static HTML pages may not work properly.
**c** You cannot use URL rewriting.
**d** You cannot set session timeout explicitly.

*Answer: b*

***Explanation***

If cookies are not supported, you can maintain the state using URL rewriting. Thus, answers a and c are incorrect. URL rewriting requires the session ID to be appended to all the URLs; however, static HTML pages will not have any session ID in the URLs that they display, so they may not work properly. Thus, answer b is correct.

Once the session is available, it does not matter whether it is maintained using cookies or URL rewriting. You can call all the methods as you would normally would, including `session.setMaxInactiveInterval()`. Therefore, answer d is wrong.

## CHAPTER 9—DEVELOPING SECURE WEB APPLICATIONS

**1.** Which of the following correctly defines data integrity? (Select one)

**a** It guarantees that information is accessible only to certain users.
**b** It guarantees that the information is kept in encrypted form on the server.
**c** It guarantees that unintended parties cannot read the information during transmission between the client and the server.
**d** It guarantees that the information is not altered during transmission between the client and the server.

*Answer: d*

2. What is the term for determining whether a user has access to a particular resource? (Select one)

   a Authorization
   b Authentication
   c Confidentiality
   d Secrecy

   *Answer: a*

3. Which one of the following must be done before authorization takes place? (Select one)

   a Data validation
   b User authentication
   c Data encryption
   d Data compression

   *Answer: b*

   ***Explanation***

   First, a user is authenticated. Once the identity of the user is determined using any of the authentication mechanisms, authorization is determined on a per-resource basis.

4. Which of the following actions would you take to prevent your web site from being attacked? (Select three)

   a Block network traffic at all the ports except the HTTP port.
   b Audit the usage pattern of your server.
   c Audit the Servlet/JSP code.
   d Use HTTPS instead of HTTP.
   e Design and develop your web application using a software engineering methodology.
   f Use design patterns.

   *Answers: a, c, and d*

   ***Explanation***

   Answer a is correct because this will prevent network congestion and will close all possible entry points to the server except HTTP. Answer b seems correct, but it is wrong because auditing the usage pattern will help you in finding out the culprits only *after* the site has been attacked—it will not prevent an attack. Answer c is correct because auditing the Servlet/JSP code will ensure that no malicious code exists inside your server that can open a backdoor for hackers. Answer d is correct because HTTPS will prevent hackers from sniffing the communication between the clients and the server, thereby preventing the leakage of sensitive information such as usernames and passwords. Answers e and f are good for developing an industrial-strength system but are not meant for making a system attack proof.

5. Identify the authentication mechanisms that are built into the HTTP specification. (Select two)

   a Basic
   b Client-Cert

**c** FORM
**d** Digest
**e** Client-Digest
**f** HTTPS

*Answers: a and d*

***Explanation***

The HTTP specification only defines Basic and Digest authentication mechanisms.

6. Which of the following deployment descriptor elements is used for specifying the authentication mechanism for a web application? (Select one)

**a** `security-constraint`
**b** `auth-constraint`
**c** `login-config`
**d** `web-resource-collection`

*Answer: c*

***Explanation***

The authentication mechanism is specified using the `login-config` element; for example:

```
<login-config>
  <auth-method>FORM</auth-method>
  <realm-name>sales</realm-name>

  <form-login-config>
    <form-login-page>/formlogin.html</form-login-page>
    <form-error-page>/formerror.html</form-error-page>
  </form-login-config>
</login-config>
```

The `security-constraint`, `auth-method`, and `web-resource-collection` elements are used for specifying the authorization details of the resources.

7. Which of the following elements are used for defining a security constraint? Choose only those elements that come directly under the `security-constraint` element. (Select three)

**a** `login-config`
**b** `role-name`
**c** `role`
**d** `transport-guarantee`
**e** `user-data-constraint`
**f** `auth-constraint`
**g** `authorization-constraint`
**h** `web-resource-collection`

*Answers: e, f, and h*

***Explanation***

Remember that, logically, you need three things to define a security constraint: a collection of resources (i.e., `web-resource-collection`), a list of roles who are authorized to access the collection of resources (i.e., `auth-constraint`), and finally, the way the application data has to be transmitted between the clients and the server (i.e., `user-data-constraint`).

The following is the definition of the `security-constraint` element:

```
<!ELEMENT security-constraint (display-name?,
                    web-resource-collection+,
                    auth-constraint?, user-data-constraint?)>
```

**8.** Which of the following `web.xml` snippets correctly identifies all HTML files under the `sales` directory? (Select two)

**a**
```
<web-resource-collection>
    <web-resource-name>reports</web-resource-name>
    <url-pattern>/sales/*.html</url-pattern>
</web-resource-collection>
```

**b**
```
<resource-collection>
   <web-resource-name>reports</web-resource-name>
    <url-pattern>/sales/*.html</url-pattern>
</resource-collection>
```

**c**
```
<resource-collection>
    <resource-name>reports</resource-name>
    <url-pattern>/sales/*.html</url-pattern>
</resource-collection>
```

**d**
```
<web-resource-collection>
   <web-resource-name>reports</web-resource-name>
    <url-pattern>/sales/*.html</url-pattern>
    <http-method>GET</http-method>
</web-resource-collection>
```

*Answers: a and d*

***Explanation***

A collection of web resources is defined using the `web-resource-collection` element, which is defined as follows:

```
<!ELEMENT web-resource-collection (web-resource-name, description?,
                                   url-pattern*, http-method*)>
```

Observe that `http-method` is optional. The absence of the `http-method` element is equivalent to specifying all HTTP methods.

**9.** You want your `PerformanceReportServlet` to be accessible only to managers. This servlet generates a performance report based on a FORM submitted by a user. Which of the following correctly defines a security constraint for this purpose? (Select one)

**a**
```
<security-constraint>
     <web-resource-collection>
     <web-resource-name>performance report</web-resource-name>
     <url-pattern>/servlet/PerformanceReportServlet</url-pattern>
     <http-method>GET</http-method>
     </web-resource-collection>

     <auth-constraint>

     <role-name>manager</role-name>
     </auth-constraint>

     <user-data-constraint>
     <transport-guarantee>NONE</transport-guarantee>
     </user-data-constraint>
</security-constraint>
```

**b**
```
<security-constraint>
     <web-resource-collection>
     <web-resource-name>performance report</web-resource-name>
     <url-pattern>/servlet/PerformanceReportServlet</url-pattern>

     <http-method>*</http-method>
     </web-resource-collection>

     <accessibility>
     <role-name>manager</role-name>
     </accessibility>

     <user-data-constraint>
     <transport-guarantee>CONFIDENTIAL</transport-guarantee>
     </user-data-constraint>

</security-constraint>
```

**c**
```
<security-constraint>
     <web-resource-collection>
     <web-resource-name>performance report</web-resource-name>
     <url-pattern>/servlet/PerformanceReportServlet</url-pattern>
     <http-method>POST</http-method>
     </web-resource-collection>

     <accessibility>
     <role-name>manager</role-name>
     </accessibility>

     <user-data-constraint>
     <transport-guarantee>CONFIDENTIAL</transport-guarantee>
     </user-data-constraint>

     </security-constraint>
```

**d**
```
<security-constraint>
     <web-resource-collection>
     <web-resource-name>performance report</web-resource-name>
```

```
<url-pattern>/servlet/PerformanceReportServlet</url-pattern>
<http-method>POST</http-method>
</web-resource-collection>

<auth-constraint>
<role-name>manager</role-name>
</auth-constraint>
```

*Answer: d*

***Explanation***

Since the question states that the servlet generates the report based on the submission of a form, either the `<http-method>` must specify POST or there should be no `<http-method>` (which means the restriction applies to all the methods). Thus, answer a is incorrect. Further, the question states that the report should be accessible only to managers. This needs to be specified using the `<auth-constraint>` element. There is no such element as `<accessibility>`. Therefore, answers b and c are incorrect. Answer d is correct because both of the above requirements are satisfied. The question does not say anything about the `<user-data-constraint>` element, which is optional anyway.

**10.** Which of the following statements regarding authentication mechanisms are correct? (Select two)

- **a** The HTTP Basic mechanism transmits the username/password "in the open."
- **b** The HTTP Basic mechanism uses HTML FORMs to collect usernames/passwords.
- **c** The transmission method in the Basic and FORM mechanisms is the same.
- **d** The method of capturing the usernames/passwords in the Basic and FORM mechanisms is the same.

*Answers: a and c*

***Explanation***

The HTTP Basic mechanism uses a browser-specific way (usually a dialog box) to capture the username and password, while the FORM mechanism uses an HTML FORM to do the same. However, both mechanisms transmit the captured values in clear text without any encryption. Therefore, answers a and c are correct.

**11.** Which of the following statements are correct for an unauthenticated user? (Select two)

- **a** `HttpServletRequest.getUserPrincipal()` returns `null`.
- **b** `HttpServletRequest.getUserPrincipal()` throws `SecurityException`.
- **c** `HttpServletRequest.isUserInRole()` returns `false`.
- **d** `HttpServletRequest.getRemoteUser()` throws a `SecurityException`.

*Answers: a and c*

***Explanation***

None of the three methods—`getUserPrincipal()`, `isUserInRole()`, and `getRemoteUser()`—throws an exception. We suggest you read the description of these methods in the JavaDocs.

## *CHAPTER 10—DEVELOPING THREAD-SAFE SERVLETS*

**1.** Consider the following servlet code:

```
public class TestServlet extends HttpServlet
{
   private static StringBuffer staticVar = new StringBuffer();
   private StringBuffer instanceVar = new StringBuffer();
  public void doGet(HttpServletRequest req, HttpServletResponse res)
   {
      private StringBuffer localVar = new StringBuffer();
   }
}
```

Which of the variables used in the above servlet reference objects is thread safe? (Select one)

**a** `staticVar`

**b** `instanceVar`

**c** `localVar`

**d** None

*Answer: c*

***Explanation***

Static variables are never thread safe, so answer a is incorrect. Instance variables are not thread safe for servlets that do not implement the `SingleThreadModel` interface; therefore, answer b is also wrong. Objects created in and referred to only from local scope are always thread safe, which makes answer c the correct choice.

**2.** Consider the following servlet code:

```
public class TestServlet extends HttpServlet
{
   public void doGet(HttpServletRequest req, HttpServletResponse res)
    {
       private HttpSession session = req.getSession();
       private ServletContext ctx = getServletContext();

    }
}
```

Which of the variables used in the above servlet reference objects that are thread safe? (Select two)

**a** `req`

**b** `res`

**c** `session`

**d** `ctx`

*Answers: a and b*

### Explanation

Request and response objects are accessible only for the lifetime of a request, and so they are thread safe. Session and context objects can be accessed from multiple threads while processing multiple requests, which means they are not thread safe.

**3.** Consider the following servlet code:

```
public class TestServlet extends HttpServlet
                         implements SingleThreadModel
{
   private static Hashtable staticHash = new StringBuffer();
   private Hashtable instanceHash = new StringBuffer();

  public void doGet(HttpServletRequest req, HttpServletResponse res)
  {
      StringBuffer sb = new StringBuffer()

      HttpSession session = req.getSession();
      ServletContext ctx = getServletContext();

      // 1
  }
}
```

Which of the following lines can be inserted at `//1` so that the `StringBuffer` object referred to by the variable `sb` can only be accessed from a single thread at a time? (Select two)

**a** `staticHash.put("sb", sb);`
**b** `instanceHash.put("sb", sb);`
**c** `session.setAttribute("sb", sb);`
**d** `ctx.setAttribute("sb", sb);`
**e** `req.setAttribute("sb", sb);`

*Answers: b and e*

### Explanation

Answer b is correct because instance variables are thread safe if the servlet implements the `SingleThreadModel` interface. Answer e is correct because request and response objects are accessible only for the lifetime of a request. All the remaining ones can be accessed from multiple threads simultaneously.

**4.** Which of the following statements is correct? (Select one)

**a** By default, the servlets are executed in the single-threaded model.
**b** The threading model of a servlet can be set through the deployment descriptor.
**c** The threading model of a servlet depends on the interfaces that it implements.
**d** Servlets developed for the multithreaded model are not thread safe while servlets developed for the single-threaded model are.
**e** A servlet can be made thread safe by running it in the single-threaded model.

*Answer: c*

***Explanation***

A servlet is run in the single-threaded model if it implements the `javax.servlet.SingleThreadModel` interface. By default—that is, if the servlet does not implement this interface—it is run in the multithreaded model. There is no setting in the deployment descriptor for this purpose.

Implementing `SingleThreadModel` does not automatically make a servlet thread safe. All it guarantees is that the servlet container will not execute the servlet instance methods in multiple threads simultaneously. However, the servlet container may maintain a pool of servlet instances, which makes static variables thread unsafe.

In general, servlets developed for any model are not necessarily thread safe or unsafe. It is possible to write a thread-safe or -unsafe servlet for both the threading models. It depends on how a servlet is coded.

**5.** Which of the following statements is correct for a servlet that implements `SingleThreadModel`? (Select one)

**a** The servlet container cannot handle multiple requests simultaneously.
**b** The servlet container cannot create multiple instances of the servlet class.
**c** The servlet container will not run multiple threads on one instance simultaneously.
**d** It is thread safe.

*Answer: c*

***Explanation***

Answer c is the only statement guaranteed to be correct if your servlet implements `SingleThreadModel`. The servlet container can handle multiple requests simultaneously by maintaining a pool of servlet instances.

**6.** What is the requirement for a servlet that implements the `SingleThreadModel` interface? (Select one)

**a** Its `service(HttpServletRequest, HttpServletResponse)` must be synchronized.
**b** It must implement the `service(HttpServletRequest, HttpServletResponse)` method.
**c** It must implement the `release()` method.
**d** It must implement the `destroy()` method.
**e** None of the above.

*Answer: e*

***Explanation***

The `SingleThreadModel` interface is just a tag interface and does not declare any methods.

## CHAPTER 11—THE JSP TECHNOLOGY MODEL—THE BASICS

**1.** Consider the following code and select the correct statement about it from the options below. (Select one)

```
<html><body>
   <%! int aNum=5 %>
   The value of aNum is <%= aNum %>
</body></html>
```

**a** It will print `"The value of aNum is 5"` to the output.
**b** It will flag a compile-time error because of an incorrect declaration.
**c** It will throw a runtime exception while executing the expression.
**d** It will not flag any compile time or runtime errors and will not print anything to the output.

*Answer: b*

***Explanation***
It will flag a compile-time error because the variable declaration `<%! int aNum=5 %>` is missing a `;` at the end. It should be:

```
<%! int aNum=5; %>
```

**2.** Which of the following tags can you use to print the value of an expression to the output stream? (Select two)

**a** `<%@     %>`
**b** `<%!     %>`
**c** `<%      %>`
**d** `<%=     %>`
**e** `<%--  --%>`

*Answers: c and d*

***Explanation***
You can use a JSP expression to print the value of an expression to the output stream. For example, if the expression is `x+3`, you can write `<%= x+3 %>`. Answer d is a JSP expression and is therefore the correct answer. But you can also use a scriptlet to print the value of an expression to the output stream as `<% out.print(x+3); %>`. Answer c is a scriptlet and is therefore also correct. If the exam asks you to select one correct option, then select the expression syntax, as in answer d. But if the exam asks for two correct answers, then select the scriptlet syntax as well.

**3.** Which of the following methods is defined by the JSP engine? (Select one)

**a** `jspInit()`
**b** `_jspService()`
**c** `_jspService(ServletRequest, ServletResponse)`
**d** `_jspService(HttpServletRequest, HttpServletResponse)`
**e** `jspDestroy()`

*Answer: d*

#### *Explanation*

The `_jspService()` method of the `javax.servlet.jsp.HttpJspPage` class is defined by the JSP engine. `HttpJspPage` is meant to serve HTTP requests, and therefore the `_jspService()` method accepts the `javax.servlet.http.HttpServletRequest` and `javax.servlet.http.HttpServletResponse` parameters.

4. Which of the following exceptions may be thrown by the `_jspService()` method? (Select one)

   **a** `javax.servlet.ServletException`
   **b** `javax.servlet.jsp.JSPException`
   **c** `javax.servlet.ServletException` and javax.servlet.jsp.JSPException
   **d** `javax.servlet.ServletException` and `java.io.IOException`
   **e** `javax.servlet.jsp.JSPException` and `java.io.IOException`

   *Answer: d*

   #### *Explanation*

   The `_jspService()` method may throw a `javax.servlet.ServletException`, a `java.io.IOException`, or a subclass of these two exception classes. Note that the `_jspService()` method does not define `javax.servlet.jsp.JspException` in its `throws` clause.

5. Write the name of the method that you can use to initialize variables declared in a JSP declaration in the space provided. (Write only the name of the method. Do not write the return type, parameters, or parentheses.)

   [____________]

   *Answer:* `jspInit`

   #### *Explanation*

   The `jspInit()` method is the first method called by the JSP engine on a JSP page. It is called only once to allow the page to initialize itself. You can use this method to initialize variables declared in JSP declarations (`<%! %>`).

6. Which of the following correctly declares that the current page is an error page and also enables it to take part in a session? (Select one)

   **a** `<%@ page pageType="errorPage" session="required" %>`
   **b** `<%@ page isErrorPage="true" session="mandatory" %>`
   **c** `<%@ page errorPage="true" session="true" %>`
   **d** `<%@ page isErrorPage="true" session="true" %>`
   **e** None of the above.

   *Answer: d*

   #### *Explanation*

   The `isErrorPage` attribute accepts a Boolean value (`true` or `false`) and indicates whether the current page is capable of handling errors. The `session` attribute accepts a Boolean value (`true` or `false`) and indicates whether the current page must take part in a session. Therefore, answer d is correct. Since the `pageType` attribute is not a valid attribute for a `page` directive, answer a is not correct. The `mandatory` value is not a valid value for the `session` attribute, which means answer b is not correct. The `errorPage` attribute is a valid attribute, but it is used for specifying another page as an error handler for the current page. Therefore, answer c is also incorrect.

## CHAPTER 12—THE JSP TECHNOLOGY MODEL—ADVANCED TOPICS

**1.** What will be the output of the following code? (Select one)

```
<html><body>
   <%  x=3;       %>
   <%  int x=5; %>
   <%! int x=7; %>
   x = <%=x%>, <%=this.x%>
</body></html>
```

**a** `x = 3, 5`
**b** `x = 3, 7`
**c** `x = 5, 3`
**d** `x = 5, 7`
**e** Compilation error

*Answer: c*

***Explanation***

The above code will translate to servlet code similar to the following:

```
public class ...
{
   int x = 7;

   public void _jspService(...)
   {
      ...
      out.print("<html><body>");
      x = 3;
      int x = 5;
      out.write("x = "); out.print(x);
      out.write(","); out.print(this.x);
      out.print("</body></html>");
   }
}
```

The declaration will create a member variable `x` and initialize it to `7`. The first scriptlet, `x=3`, will change its value to `3`. Then, the second scriptlet will declare a local variable `x` and initialize it to `5`. The first expression refers to the local variable `x` and will therefore print `5`. The second expression uses the keyword `this` to refer to the member or instance variable `x`, which was set to `3`. Thus, the correct answer is c, `x = 5, 3`.

2. What will be the output of the following code? (Select one)

```
<html><body>
    The value is <%=""%>
</body></html>
```

**a** Compilation error
**b** Runtime error
**c** `The value is`
**d** `The value is null`

*Answer: c*

***Explanation***

The expression is converted to

```
out.print("");
```

Thus, the correct answer is c.

3. Which of the following implicit objects is not available to a JSP page by default? (Select one)

**a** `application`
**b** `session`
**c** `exception`
**d** `config`

*Answer: c*

***Explanation***

The implicit variables `application` and `config` are always available to a JSP page. The implicit variable `session` is available if the value of the `page` directive's `session` attribute is set to `true`. Since it is set to `true` by default, the implicit variable `session` is also available by default. The implicit variable `exception` is available only if the value of the `page` directive's `isErrorPage` attribute is set to `true`. It is set to `false` by default, so the implicit variable `exception` is not available by default. We have to explicitly set it to `true`:

```
<%@ page isErrorPage="true" %>
```

The correct answer, therefore, is c.

4. Which of the following implicit objects can you use to store attributes that need to be accessed from all the sessions of a web application? (Select two)

**a** `application`
**b** `session`
**c** `request`
**d** `page`
**e** `pageContext`

*Answers: a and e*

### Explanation

To store attributes that are accessible from all the sessions of a web application, we have to put them in the application scope. To achieve this, we have to use the implicit object `application`. If the exam asks you to select one answer, then select `application`. If the exam asks for two correct answers, then read the question carefully. It says, "Which of the following implicit objects *can you use* to store attributes that need to be accessed from all the sessions of a web application?" We can also use `pageContext` to store objects in the application scope as `pageContext.setAttribute("name", object, PageContext.APPLICATION_SCOPE);` and `pageContext.getAttribute("name", PageContext.APPLICATION_SCOPE);`.

**5.** The implicit variable `config` in a JSP page refers to an object of type: (Select one)

**a** `javax.servlet.PageConfig`
**b** `javax.servlet.jsp.PageConfig`
**c** `javax.servlet.ServletConfig`
**d** `javax.servlet.ServletContext`

*Answer: c*

The implicit variable `config` in a JSP page refers to an object of type `javax.servlet.ServletConfig`.

**6.** A JSP page can receive context initialization parameters through the deployment descriptor of the web application.

**a** True
**b** False

*Answer: a*

### Explanation

Context initialization parameters are specified by the `<context-param>` tags in `web.xml`. These parameters are for the whole web application and not specific to any servlet or JSP page. Thus, all components of a web application can access context initialization parameters.

**7.** Which of the following will evaluate to `true`? (Select two)

**a** `page == this`
**b** `pageContext == this`
**c** `out instanceof ServletOutputStream`
**d** `application instanceof ServletContext`

*Answers: a and d*

### Explanation

The implicit variable `page` refers to the current servlet, and therefore answer a will evaluate to `true`. The `application` object refers to an object of type `ServletContext`, which means answer d will also evaluate to `true`. The `pageContext` object refers to an object of type `PageContext` and not to the servlet, which means answer b will evaluate to `false`. The `out` implicit variable refers to an instance of `javax.servlet.jsp.JspWriter` and not to an instance of `javax.servlet.ServletOutputStream`, so answer c evaluates to `false`. Note that `JspWriter` is derived from `java.io.Writer`, while `ServletOutputStream` is derived from `java.io.OutputStream`.

**8.** Select the correct statement about the following code. (Select one)

```
<%@ page language="java" %>
<html><body>
out.print("Hello ");
out.print("World ");
</body></html>
```

**a** It will print `Hello World` in the output.
**b** It will generate compile-time errors.
**c** It will throw runtime exceptions.
**d** It will only print `Hello`.
**e** None of above.

*Answer: e*

***Explanation***

The lines `out.print("Hello ")` and `out.print("World ")` are not contained in a scriptlet (`<%...%>`). The JSP engine assumes they are a part of the template text and sends them to the browser without executing them on the server. Therefore, it will print the two statements in the browser window:

```
out.print("Hello ");out.print("World ");
```

**9.** Select the correct statement about the following code. (Select one)

```
<%@ page language="java" %>
<html><body>
<%
   response.getOutputStream().print ("Hello ");
   out.print("World");
%>
</body></html>
```

**a** It will print Hello World in the output.
**b** It will generate compile-time errors.
**c** It will throw runtime exceptions.
**d** It will only print `Hello`.
**e** None of above.

*Answer: c*

***Explanation***

As explained in chapter 4, "The Servlet model," the `OutputStream` of a response object is used for sending binary data to the client while the `Writer` object is used for sending character data. However, we cannot use both on the same response object. Since the JSP engine automatically gets the `JspWriter` from the response object to output the content of the JSP as character data, the call to `getOutputStream()` throws a `java.lang.IllegalStateException`. Thus, the correct answer is c.

**10.** Which of the following implicit objects does not represent a scope container? (Select one)

**a** `application`
**b** `session`
**c** `request`
**d** `page`
**e** `pageContext`

*Answer: d*

***Explanation***

The implicit objects `application`, `session`, and `request` represent the containers for the scopes, *application*, *session*, and *request*, respectively. The implicit object `page` refers to the generated Servlet and does not represent any scope container. The implicit object `pageContext` represents the page scope container, so the correct answer is d.

**11.** What is the output of the following code? (Select one)

```
<html><body>
    <% int i = 10 ;%>
    <%  while(--i>=0) { %>
        out.print(i);
    <% } %>
</body></html>
```

**a** `9876543210`
**b** 9
**c** 0
**d** None of the above

*Answer: d*

***Explanation***

The statement `out.print(i)` is not inside a scriptlet and is part of the template text. The above JSP page will print

```
out.print(i);out.print(i);out.print(i);......
```

ten times.

When in doubt, always convert a JSP code to its equivalent servlet code step by step:

```
out.write("<html><body>");
int i = 10;
while (--i>=) {
    out.write("out.print(i); ");
}
out.write("<html><body>");
```

12. Which of the following is not a valid XML-based JSP tag? (Select one)

a `<jsp:directive.page    />`
b `<jsp:directive.include />`
c `<jsp:directive.taglib  />`
d `<jsp:declaration></jsp:declaration>`
e `<jsp:scriptlet></jsp:scriptlet>`
f `<jsp:expression></jsp:expression>`

*Answer: c*

***Explanation***

The tag `<jsp:directive.taglib>` is not a valid XML-based tag. Remember that tag library information is provided in the `<jsp:root>` element.

13. Which of the following XML syntax format tags do not have an equivalent in JSP syntax format? (Select two)

a `<jsp:directive.page/>`
b `<jsp:directive.include/>`
c `<jsp:text></jsp:text>`
d `<jsp:root></jsp:root>`
e `<jsp:param/>`

*Answers: c and d*

***Explanation***

The equivalent of `<jsp:directive.page/>` is `<%@ page %>`. The equivalent of `<jsp:directive.include/>` is `<%@ include %>`. The `<jsp:param/>` tag is the same for both the syntax formats. Thus, the correct answers are c and d. The tags `<jsp:text>` and `<jsp:root>` have no equivalent in the JSP syntax format.

14. Which of the following is a valid construct to declare that the implicit variable session should be made available to the JSP page? (Select one)

a `<jsp:session>true</jsp:session>`
b `<jsp:session required="true" />`
c
```
<jsp:directive.page>
    <jsp:attribute name="session" value="true" />
</jsp:directive.page>
```
d `<jsp:directive.page session="true" />`
e `<jsp:directive.page attribute="session" value="true" />`

*Answer: d*

***Explanation***

The correct way to declare that the implicit variable `session` should be made available to the JSP page in XML format is shown in answer d: `<jsp:directive.page session="true" />`.

## CHAPTER 13—REUSABLE WEB COMPONENTS

1. Which of the following JSP tags can be used to include the output of another JSP page into the output of the current page at request time? (Select one)

   **a** `<jsp:insert>`
   **b** `<jsp:include>`
   **c** `<jsp:directive.include>`
   **d** `<jsp:directive:include>`
   **e** `<%@ include %>`

   *Answer: b*

   ***Explanation***
   The tags in answers a and d are not valid JSP tags. Answers c and e are valid tags in XML syntax and JSP syntax, respectively, but they are directives and include other JSP pages or HTML/XML files at translation time. Answer b is the right answer because it includes the output of another component, JSP page, or Servlet at request time.

2. Consider the contents of the following two JSP files:

   File 1: `test1.jsp`

```
<html><body>
      <% String message = "Hello"; %>

      //1 Insert LOC here.

      The message is <%= message %>
</body></html>
```

   File 2: `test2.jsp`

```
<% message = message + " world!"; %>
```

   Which of the following lines can be inserted at `//1` in `test1.jsp` so that it prints `"The message is Hello world!"` when requested? (Select one)

   **a** `<%@ include  page="test2.jsp" %>`
   **b** `<%@ include  file="test2.jsp" />`
   **c** `<jsp:include page="test2.jsp" />`
   **d** `<jsp:include file="test2.jsp" />`

   *Answer: b*

   ***Explanation***
   Since the `test2.jsp` file does not declare or define the variable `message`, it cannot compile on its own. This rules out dynamic inclusion using the `<jsp:include>` action. The file `test1.jsp` could print `"Hello world"` if it statically included `test2.jsp`. This could be done using the `include` directive: `<%@ include %>`. For the `include` directive, the valid attribute is `file` and not `page`, so answer b is correct.

3. Which of the following is a correct way to pass a parameter equivalent to the query string `user=mary` at request time to an included component? (Select one)

a
```
<jsp:include page="other.jsp" >
    <jsp:param paramName="user" paramValue="mary" />
</jsp:include>
```

b
```
<jsp:include page="other.jsp" >
    <jsp:param name="mary" value="user" />
</jsp:include>
```

c
```
<jsp:include page="other.jsp" >
   <jsp:param value="mary" name="user" />
</jsp:include>
```

d
```
<jsp:include page="other.jsp" >
    <jsp:param param="user" value="mary"/>
</jsp:include>
```

e
```
<jsp:include page="other.jsp" >
    <jsp:param user="mary" />
</jsp:include>
```

*Answer: c*

***Explanation***

The only valid attributes that a `<jsp:param>` tag can have are `name` and `value`. This rules out answers a, d, and e. Answer b, `<jsp:param name="mary" value="user" />`, is equivalent to the query string `mary=user`. In the included component, a call to `request.getParameter("mary");` will return `"user"`. Answer c, `<jsp:param value="mary" name="user" />`, is equivalent to the query string `user=mary`. In the included component, a call to `request.getParameter("user");` will return `"mary"`. Therefore, answer c is the correct answer.

4. Identify the JSP equivalent of the following code written in a servlet. (Select one)

```
RequestDispatcher rd = request.getRequestDispatcher("world.jsp");
rd.forward(request, response);
```

a `<jsp:forward page="world.jsp"/>`

b `<jsp:action.forward page="world.jsp"/>`

c `<jsp:directive.forward page="world.jsp"/>`

d `<%@ forward file="world.jsp"%>`

e `<%@ forward page="world.jsp"%>`

*Answer: a*

***Explanation***

The action tags in answers b through e are all invalid JSP tags. Answer a, `<jsp:forward page="relativeURL" />`, is the only valid way to write a forward action.

5. Consider the contents of two JSP files:

File 1: `test1.jsp`

```
<html><body>
   <% pageContext.setAttribute("ninetyNine", new Integer(99)); %>

   //1

</body></html>
```

File 2: `test2.jsp`

```
The number is <%= pageContext.getAttribute("ninetyNine") %>
```

Which of the following, when placed at line `//1` in the `test1.jsp` file, will allow the `test2.jsp` file to print the value of the attribute when `test1.jsp` is requested? (Select one)

a `<jsp:include page="test2.jsp" />`
b `<jsp:forward page="test2.jsp" />`
c `<%@ include file="test2.jsp" %>`
d None of the above because objects placed in `pageContext` have the page scope and cannot be shared with other components.

*Answer: c*

***Explanation***

Objects placed in `pageContext` have the `page` scope and are accessible within a single translation unit. Since files included statically using the `include` directive become an integral part of the same translation unit as the including file, they can share objects in the `page` scope via the `PageContext` container. So the correct answer is c: `<%@ include file="test2.jsp" %>`.

6. Consider the contents of two JSP files:

File 1: `this.jsp`

```
<html><body><pre>
   <jsp:include page="that.jsp" >
      <jsp:param name="color" value="red" />
      <jsp:param name="color" value="green" />
   </jsp:include>
</pre></body></html>
```

File 2: `that.jsp`

```
<%
   String colors[] = request.getParameterValues("color");
   for (int i=0; i<colors.length; i++)
   {
  out.print(colors[i] + " ");
   }
%>
```

What will be the output of accessing the `this.jsp` file via the following URL? (Select one)

```
http://localhost:8080/chapter13/this.jsp?color=blue
```

**a** `blue`

**b** `red green`

**c** `red green blue`

**d** `blue red green`

**e** `blue green red`

*Answer: c*

***Explanation***

The parameters passed via the `<jsp:param>` tag to an included component tag take precedence over the parameters already present in the request object of the including component. Also, the order of values passed via the `<jsp:param>` tag is the same as the order in which the tags appear. Thus, the correct answer is c. The output will be `red green blue`.

7. Consider the contents of two JSP files:

File 1: `this.jsp`

```
<html><body>

   <%= request.getParameter("color")  %>

   <jsp:include page="that.jsp" >
      <jsp:param name="color" value="red" />
   </jsp:include>

   <%= request.getParameter("color")  %>

</body></html>
```

File 2: `that.jsp`

```
<%= request.getParameter("color")  %>
```

What will be the output of accessing the `this.jsp` file via the following URL? (Select one)

```
http://localhost:8080/chapter13/this.jsp?color=blue
```

**a** `blue red blue`

**b** `blue red red`

**c** `blue blue red`

**d** `blue red null`

*Answer: a*

***Explanation***

The first call to `request.getParameter("color")` in the `this.jsp` file returns `blue`. This file then includes the `that.jsp` file and passes a value of `red` for the color attribute. Since, the values passed via `<jsp:param>` take precedence over the original values, a call to `request.getParameter("color")` in `that.jsp` returns `red`. However, this new value exists and is available only within the included component—that is, `that.jsp`. So, after the `that.jsp` page finishes processing, a call to request.getParameter("color") in the this.jsp file again returns blue. Thus, the correct answer is a. The output will be blue red blue.

**8.** Consider the contents of three JSP files:

File 1: one.jsp

```
<html><body><pre>

   <jsp:include page="two.jsp" >
      <jsp:param name="color" value="red" />
   </jsp:include>

</pre></body></html>
```

File 2: two.jsp

```
<jsp:include page="three.jsp" >
   <jsp:param name="color" value="green" />
</jsp:include>
```

File 3: three.jsp

```
<%= request.getParameter("color")  %>
```

What will be the output of accessing the one.jsp file via the following URL? (Select one)

```
http://localhost:8080/chapter13/one.jsp?color=blue
```

**a** red
**b** green
**c** blue
**d** The answer cannot be determined.

*Answer: b*

***Explanation***
The output is generated by the three.jsp file. Since the two.jsp file calls three.jsp and provides a value of green, this value takes precedence over all the previous values passed to one.jsp and two.jsp. Thus, the correct answer is b. The output will be green.

## CHAPTER 14—USING JAVABEANS

**1.** Which of the following is a valid use of the <jsp:useBean> action? (Select one)

**a** `<jsp:useBean id="address" class="AddressBean" />`
**b** `<jsp:useBean name="address" class="AddressBean"/>`
**c** `<jsp:useBean bean="address" class="AddressBean" />`
**d** `<jsp:useBean beanName="address" class="AddressBean" />`

*Answer: a*

***Explanation***

name and bean are not valid attributes for a `<jsp:useBean>` tag. Thus, answers b and c are incorrect. The beanName and class attributes cannot be used together, which means answer d is incorrect. Further, the id attribute is the mandatory attribute of `<jsp:useBean>` and is missing from answers b, c, and d. Therefore, only answer a is correct.

**2.** Which of the following is a valid way of getting a bean's property? (Select one)

**a** `<jsp:useBean action="get" id="address" property="city" />`
**b** `<jsp:getProperty id="address" property="city" />`
**c** `<jsp:getProperty name="address" property="city" />`
**d** `<jsp:getProperty bean="address" property="*" />`

*Answer: c*

***Explanation***

The `<jsp:getProperty>` action has only two attributes—name and property—and both are mandatory. Therefore, answer c is correct.

**3.** Which of the following are valid uses of the `<jsp:useBean>` action? (Select two)

**a**
```
<jsp:useBean id="address" class="AddressBean" name="address"          />
```
**b**
```
<jsp:useBean id="address" class="AddressBean"
     type="AddressBean"      />
```
**c**
```
<jsp:useBean id="address" beanName="AddressBean"
     class="AddressBean"    />
```
**d**
```
<jsp:useBean id="address" beanName="AddressBean"
     type="AddressBean"     />
```

*Answers: b and d*

***Explanation***

Answer a is not correct because name is not a valid attribute in `<jsp:useBean>`. Answer c is not correct because beanName and class cannot be used together.

**4.** Which of the following gets or sets the bean in the ServletContext container object? (Select one)

**a** `<jsp:useBean id="address" class="AddressBean" />`
**b** `<jsp:useBean id="address" class="AddressBean" scope="application" />`
**c** `<jsp:useBean id="address" class="AddressBean" scope="servlet" />`
**d** `<jsp:useBean id="address" class="AddressBean" scope="session" />`
**e** None of the above

*Answer: b*

***Explanation***

The correct answer is b, because the ServletContext container represents the application scope. Answer a is not correct because if the scope is not specified, then the page scope is assumed by default.

5. Consider the following code:

```
<html><body>
<jsp:useBean id="address" class="AddressBean" scope="session" />
state = <jsp:getProperty name="address" property="state" />
</body></html>
```

Which of the following are equivalent to the third line above? (Select three)

```
a <% state = address.getState();                                %>
b <% out.write("state = "); out.print(address.getState());      %>
c <% out.write("state = "); out.print(address.getstate());      %>
d <% out.print("state = " + address.getState());                %>
e state = <%= address.getState()                                %>
f state = <%! address.getState();                               %>
```

*Answers: b, d, and e*

***Explanation***

The third line in the code prints `"state = "` followed by the actual value of the property in the output HTML. Answer a is incorrect, because it is inside a scriptlet and does not print any output. Answer c is incorrect because the standard convention that the beans follow is to capitalize the first character of the property's name. Therefore, it should be `getState()` and not `getstate()`. Answer f is incorrect because the method call `address.getState()` is in a declaration instead of an expression. Answers b, d, and e all do the same thing and are all equivalent to the third line of the code.

6. Which of the options locate the bean equivalent to the following action? (Select three)

```
<jsp:useBean id="address" class="AddressBean" scope="request" />
```

```
a request.getAttribute("address");
b request.getParameter("address");
c getServletContext().getRequestAttribute("address");
d pageContext.getAttribute("address",PageContext.REQUEST_SCOPE);
e pageContext.getRequest().getAttribute("address");
f pageContext.getRequestAttribute("address");
g pageContext.getRequestParameter("address");
```

*Answers: a, d, and e*

***Explanation***

Answer b is not correct because beans cannot be *get* or *set* as request parameters. They can be *get* and *set* as request attributes. Answer c is incorrect because `getServletContext()` returns an object of type `ServletContext` and `ServletContext` has nothing to do with the request scope. Answers f and g are incorrect because the methods `getRequestAttribute()` and `getRequestParameter()` do not exist in `PageContext`. Answer a is the simplest way to do that. Answers d and e achieve the same result using the `PageContext` object. `PageContext` is explained in chapter 12, "The JSP technology model—advanced topics."

7. Consider the following code for address.jsp:

```
<html><body>
<jsp:useBean id="address" class="AddressBean" />
<jsp:setProperty name="address" property="city" value="LosAngeles" />
<jsp:setProperty name="address" property="city" />
<jsp:getProperty name="address" property="city" />
</body></html>
```

What is the output if the above page is accessed via the URL

```
http://localhost:8080/chap14/address.jsp?city=Chicago&city=Miami
```

Assume that the city property is not an indexed property. (Select one)

**a** LosAngeles
**b** Chicago
**c** Miami
**d** ChicagoMiami
**e** LosAngelesChicagoMaimi
**f** It will not print anything because the value will be null or "".

*Answer: b*

***Explanation***

The first <jsp:setProperty> action sets the value of the city property explicitly to LosAngeles using the value attribute. The second <jsp:setProperty> action overwrites this value with the value from the request parameter. Since it is not an indexed property, only the first value from the parameter is used. Thus, the correct answer is b, Chicago.

8. Consider the following code:

```
<html><body>

<%{%>
<jsp:useBean id="address" class="AddressBean" scope="session" />
<%}%>

//1

</body></html>
```

Which of the following can be placed at line //1 above to print the value of the street property? (Select one)

**a** `<jsp:getProperty name="address" property="street" />`
**b** `<% out.print(address.getStreet()); %>`
**c** `<%= address.getStreet() %>`
**d** `<%= ((AddressBean)session.getAttribute( "address")).getStreet() %>`
**e** None of the above; the bean is nonexistent at this point.

*Answer: d*

### *Explanation*

The `<jsp:useBean>` declaration puts an object of type `AddressBean` in the session scope. The pair of curly braces ({ and }) marks the scope of the variable `address` and, therefore, we cannot use answers a, b, and c. However, the object is still existent and is available in the session scope. This means we can use the implicit variable `session` to get the `address` object, typecast the returned value to `AddressBean`, and call its `getStreet()` method to print the `street` property. Therefore, answer d is correct.

**9.** Consider the following code:

```
<html><body>

<%{%>
<jsp:useBean id="address" class="AddressBean" scope="session" />
<%}%>

<jsp:useBean id="address" class="AddressBean" scope="session" />
<jsp:getProperty name="address" property="street" />

</body></html>
```

Which of the following is true about the above code? (Select one)

**a** It will give translation-time errors.
**b** It will give compile-time errors.
**c** It may throw runtime exceptions.
**d** It will print the value of the `street` property.

*Answer: a*

### *Explanation*

A translation time error will occur if we use the same ID more than once in the same translation unit.

**10.** Consider the following servlet code:

```
//...

public void service (HttpServletRequest request,
                     HttpServletResponse response)
        throws IOException, ServletException
   {
   //1
   }
```

Which of the following can be used at `//1` to retrieve a JavaBean named `address` present in the application scope? (Select one)

**a** `getServletContext().getAttribute("address");`
**b** `application.getAttribute("address");`
**c** `request.getAttribute("address",APPLICATION_SCOPE);`
**d** `pageContext.getAttribute("address",APPLICATION_SCOPE);`

*Answer: a*

***Explanation***

The implicit variables are automatically available in the `_jspService()` method of a JSP page but are not defined automatically in a Servlet class. We cannot use the implicit variables `application` and `pageContext` because the code is part of a servlet's `service()` method and not of a JSP page. So, answers b and d are not correct. There is no such method as `getAttribute(String, int)` in `HttpServletRequest` that accepts an integer to identify scopes. Therefore, answer c is also incorrect.

**11.** Consider the following code, contained in a file called `this.jsp`:

```
<html><body>
<jsp:useBean id="address" class="AddressBean" />
<jsp:setProperty name="address" property="*"  />
<jsp:include page="that.jsp"   />
</body></html>
```

Which of the following is true about the `AddressBean` instance declared in this code? (Select one)

**a** The bean instance will not be available in `that.jsp`.

**b** The bean instance may or may not be available in `that.jsp`, depending on the threading model implemented by `that.jsp`.

**c** The bean instance will be available in `that.jsp`, and the `that.jsp` page can print the values of the beans properties using `<jsp:getProperty />`.

**d** The bean instance will be available in `that.jsp` and the `that.jsp` page can print the values of the bean's properties using `<jsp:getProperty />` only if `that.jsp` also contains a `<jsp:useBean/>` declaration identical to the one in `this.jsp` and before using `<jsp:getProperty/>`.

*Answer: a*

***Explanation***

By default, the scope is page, so the bean is not available in `that.jsp`. If it were any other scope, the answer would have been d.

**12.** Consider the following code contained in a file named `this.jsp` (the same as above, except the fourth line):

```
<html><body>
<jsp:useBean id="address" class="AddressBean" />
<jsp:setProperty name="address" property="*"  />
<%@ include file="that.jsp"   %>
</body></html>
```

Which of the following is true about the `AddressBean` instance declared in the above code? (Select one)

**a** The bean instance will not be available in `that.jsp`.

**b** The bean instance may or may not be available in `that.jsp`, depending on the threading model implemented by `that.jsp`.

**c** The bean instance will be available in `that.jsp`, and the `that.jsp` page can print the values of the bean's properties using `<jsp:getProperty />`.

**d** The bean instance will be available in `that.jsp`, and the `that.jsp` page can print the values of the bean's properties using `<jsp:getProperty />` only if `that.jsp` also contains a `<jsp:useBean/>` declaration identical to the one in `this.jsp` and before using `<jsp:getProperty/>`.

*Answer: c*

***Explanation***

The `that.jsp` page is included using a directive. Thus, it is a static inclusion, and the two pages form a single translation unit.

## CHAPTER 15—USING CUSTOM TAGS

**1.** Which of the following elements are required for a valid `<taglib>` element in `web.xml`? (Select two)

**a** `uri`
**b** `taglib-uri`
**c** `tagliburi`
**d** `tag-uri`
**e** `location`
**f** `taglib-location`
**g** `tag-location`
**h** `tagliblocation`

*Answers: b and f*

***Explanation***

The `<taglib>` element is defined as follows:

```
<!ELEMENT taglib (taglib-uri, taglib-location)>
```

As you can see, both `taglib-uri` and `taglib-location` are required elements.

**2.** Which of the following `web.xml` snippets correctly defines the use of a tag library? (Select one)

**a**
```
<taglib>
    <uri>http://www.abc.com/sample.tld</uri>
    <location>/WEB-INF/sample.tld</location>
</taglib>
```

**b**
```
<tag-lib>
    <taglib-uri>http://www.abc.com/sample.tld</taglib-uri>
    <taglib-location>/WEB-INF/sample.tld</taglib-location>
</tag-lib>
```

**c**
```
<taglib>
    <taglib-uri>http://www.abc.com/sample.tld</taglib-uri>
   <taglib-location>/WEB-INF/sample.tld</taglib-location>
</taglib>
```

**d**
```
<tag-lib>
    <taglib>http://www.abc.com/sample.tld</taglib-uri>
    <taglib>/WEB-INF/sample.tld</taglib-location>
</tag-lib>
```

*Answer: c*

***Explanation***

The use of a tag library is defined using the `<taglib>` element:

```
<!ELEMENT taglib (taglib-uri, taglib-location)>
```

**3.** Which of the following is a valid `taglib` directive? (Select one)

**a** `<% taglib uri="/stats" prefix="stats" %>`

**b** `<%@ taglib uri="/stats" prefix="stats" %>`

**c** `<%! taglib uri="/stats" prefix="stats" %>`

**d** `<%@ taglib name="/stats" prefix="stats" %>`

**e** `<%@ taglib name="/stats" value="stats" %>`

*Answer: b*

***Explanation***

A directive starts with `<%@`, so answers a and c are invalid. A `taglib` directive requires `uri` and `prefix` attributes, so only answer b is correct.

**4.** Which of the following is a valid `taglib` directive? (Select one)

**a** `<%@ taglib prefix="java" uri="sunlib"%>`

**b** `<%@ taglib prefix="jspx" uri="sunlib"%>`

**c** `<%@ taglib prefix="jsp" uri="sunlib"%>`

**d** `<%@ taglib prefix="servlet" uri="sunlib"%>`

**e** `<%@ taglib prefix="sunw" uri="sunlib"%>`

**f** `<%@ taglib prefix="suned" uri="sunlib"%>`

*Answer: f*

***Explanation***

The JSP specification does not allow us to use the names `jspx`, `java`, `javax`, `servlet`, `sun`, and `sunw` as a value for the `prefix` attribute. Therefore, only answer f is valid.

**5.** Consider the following `<taglib>` element, which appears in a deployment descriptor of a web application:

```
<taglib>
  <taglib-uri>/accounting</taglib-uri>
  <taglib-location>/WEB-INF/tlds/SmartAccount.tld</taglib-location>
</taglib>
```

Which of the following correctly specifies the use of the above tag library in a JSP page? (Select one)

**a** `<%@ taglib uri="/accounting" prefix="acc"%>`

**b** `<%@ taglib uri="/acc" prefix="/accounting"%>`

**c** `<%@ taglib name="/accounting" prefix="acc"%>`

**d** `<%@ taglib library="/accounting" prefix="acc"%>`

**e** `<%@ taglib name="/acc" prefix="/accounting"%>`

*Answer: a*

***Explanation***

The `taglib` directive contains two attributes, `uri` and `prefix`:

- `uri`: The value of the `uri` attribute in a JSP page must be the same as the value of the `<taglib-uri>` subelement of the `<taglib>` element in `web.xml`. If the entries in `web.xml` are not used, then the value of the `uri` attribute in a JSP page can directly point to the TLD file using a root-relative URI, as in `uri="/WEB-INF/tlds/SmartAccount.tld"`.
- `prefix`: This can be any string allowed by the XML naming specification. It is similar to an alias and is used in the rest of the page to refer to this tag library.

**6.** You are given a tag library that has a tag named `printReport`. This tag may accept an attribute, `department`, which cannot take a dynamic value. Which of the following are correct uses of this tag? (Select two)

**a** `<mylib:printReport/>`

**b** `<mylib:printReport department="finance"/>`

**c** `<mylib:printReport attribute="department" value="finance"/>`

**d**
```
<mylib:printReport attribute="department"
    attribute-value="finance"/>
```

**e**
```
<mylib:printReport>
    <jsp:attribute name="department" value="finance" />
</mylib:printReport>
```

*Answers: a and b*

***Explanation***

Answer a is correct because the `department` attribute is not required. Answer b is syntactically correct, but the rest of the answers are syntactically wrong.

**7.** You are given a tag library that has a tag named `getMenu`, which requires an attribute, `subject`. This attribute can take a dynamic value. Which of the following are correct uses of this tag? (Select two)

**a** `<mylib:getMenu />`

**b** `<mylib:getMenu subject="finance"/>`

**c**
```
<% String subject="HR";%>
<mylib:getMenu subject="<%=subject%>"/>
```

**d** `<mylib:getMenu> <jsp:param subject="finance"/> </mylib:getMenu>`

**e**
```
<mylib:getMenu>
    <jsp:param name="subject" value="finance"/>
</mylib:getMenu>
```

*Answers: b and c*

***Explanation***

Answer a is wrong because `subject` is a required attribute (as the question states). Answer b is correct because a static value can be specified for an attribute that takes a dynamic value (but the reverse is not true). Answer c is correct because the `subject` attribute takes a dynamic value. Answers d and e do not make sense.

**8.** Which of the following is a correct way to nest one custom tag inside another? (Select one)

**a**
```
<greet:hello>
    <greet:world>
    </greet:hello>
</greet:world>
```
**b**
```
<greet:hello>
    <greet:world>
    </greet:world>
</greet:hello>
```
**c**
```
<greet:hello
    <greet:world/>
/>
```
**d**
```
<greet:hello>
    </greet:hello>
    <greet:world>
</greet:world>
```

*Answer: b*

***Explanation***

The inner tag should exist completely within the outer tag; therefore, answer a is not valid. We cannot use a tag as an attribute to another tag. Thus, answer c is incorrect. Answer d does not have any kind of nesting at all.

**9.** Which of the following elements can you use to import a tag library in a JSP document? (Select one)

**a** `<jsp:root>`
**b** `<jsp:taglib>`
**c** `<jsp:directive.taglib>`
**d** `<jsp:taglib.directive>`
**e** We cannot use custom tag libraries in XML format.

*Answer: a.*

***Explanation***

In the XML syntax, the tag library information is included in the `<jsp:root>` element:

```
<jsp:root
    xmlns:jsp="http://java.sun.com/JSP/Page"
    xmlns:test="sampleLib.tld"
    version="1.2" >

    ...JSP PAGE...

</jsp:root>
```

## CHAPTER 16—DEVELOPING CUSTOM TAG LIBRARIES

1. Which of the following is not a valid subelement of the `<attribute>` element in a TLD? (Select one)

   **a** `<name>`
   **b** `<class>`
   **c** `<required>`
   **d** `<type>`

   *Answer: b*

   ***Explanation***
   The valid subelements of the `<attribute>` element are as shown below:

   ```
   <!ELEMENT attribute (name, required? , rtexprvalue?,
                        type?, description?) >
   ```

   Thus, the correct answer is b. `<class>` is not a valid subelement of the `<attribute>` element in a TLD.

2. What is the name of the tag library descriptor element that declares that an attribute can have a request-time expression as its value?
   [_______________]

   *Answer:* `rtexprvalue`

   ***Explanation***
   The `<rtexprvalue>` element specifies whether or not an attribute can take a request-time expression as its value. Its value can be either `true` or `false`. By default, it is `false`.

3. Consider the following code in a JSP page.

   ```
   <% String message = "Hello "; %>

   <test:world>
      How are you?
      <% message = message + "World! " %>
   </test:world>

   <%= message %>
   ```

   If `doStartTag()` returns `EVAL_BODY_BUFFERED` and `doAfterBody()` clears the buffer by calling `bodyContent.clearBody()`, what will be the output of the above code? (Select one)

   **a** `Hello`
   **b** `Hello How are you?`
   **c** `Hello How are you? World!`
   **d** `Hello World!`
   **e** `How are you World!`

   *Answer: d*

### Explanation

If `doStartTag()` returns `EVAL_BODY_BUFFERED`, then the body is executed and the output is buffered. The text `How are you?` is inserted into the current `JspWriter` buffer and the scriptlet `<% message = message + "World! " %>` assigns the value `Hello World!` to the message `String`. However, the scriptlet only assigns the new value; it does not print the value using the `out` variable. Therefore, only the text `How are you?` goes into the buffer. The `doAfterBody()` method discards the body contents by calling `bodycontent.clearBody()`. So, the actual output of the JSP page does not contain the text. After the tag is over, the expression `<%=message%>` prints the value of the `String message`, which now contains the text `Hello World!`. Thus, the correct answer is d, `Hello World!`.

**4.** Which of the following interfaces are required at a minimum to create a simple custom tag with a body? (Select one)

**a** `Tag`
**b** `Tag` and `IterationTag`
**c** `Tag`, `IterationTag`, and `BodyTag`
**d** `TagSupport`
**e** `BodyTagSupport`

*Answer: a*

### Explanation

The `Tag` interface is all you need to create a simple custom tag with a body. You do not have to implement the `BodyTag` interface in order to specify a body for a tag. The `BodyTag` interface is required only when the evaluation of the tag body needs to be buffered. Answers d and e are classes and not interfaces.

**5.** At a minimum, which of the following interfaces are required to create an iterative custom tag? (Select one)

**a** `Tag`
**b** `Tag` and `IterationTag`
**c** `Tag`, `IterationTag`, and `BodyTag`
**d** `TagSupport`
**e** `BodyTagSupport`

*Answer: b*

### Explanation

To create an iterative tag, we need to implement `IterationTag`. `IterationTag` extends `Tag`. Hence, the correct answer is b.

**6.** Which of the following methods is never called for handler classes that implement only the `Tag` interface? (Select one)

**a** `setParent()`
**b** `doStartTag()`
**c** `doAfterbody()`
**d** `doEndTag()`

*Answer: c*

***Explanation***

The `doAfterBody()` method is defined in `IterationTag`. The other three methods are defined in the `Tag` interface. Thus, the correct answer is c; `doAfterBody()` is never called on a tag that implements only the `Tag` interface.

**7.** Which of the following is a valid return value for `doAfterBody()`? (Select one)

**a** `EVAL_BODY_INCLUDE`
**b** `SKIP_BODY`
**c** `EVAL_PAGE`
**d** `SKIP_PAGE`

*Answer: b*

***Explanation***

The constant in answer a, `EVAL_BODY_INCLUDE`, is valid only for the `doStartTag()` method. The constants in answers c, `EVAL_PAGE`, and d, `SKIP_PAGE`, are valid only for the `doEndTag()` method.

The method `doAfterBody()` can return the following three values:

- `EVAL_BODY_AGAIN`, to reevaluate the body
- `EVAL_BODY_BUFFERED`, to reevaluate the body (only if the tag implements `BodyTag`)
- `SKIP_BODY`, to skip the body

Thus, the correct answer is b, `SKIP_BODY`.

**8.** Which element would you use in a TLD to indicate the type of body a custom tag expects?

[____________________]

*Answer:* `<body-content>`

***Explanation***

The `<body-content>` element is a subelement of the `<tag>` element in a TLD that indicates the type of body a custom tag expects. The valid values are `empty`, `JSP`, and `tagdependent`. JSP is the default value if `<body-content>` is not specified.

**9.** If the `doStartTag()` method returns `EVAL_BODY_INCLUDE` one time and the `doAfterBody()` method returns `EVAL_BODY_AGAIN` five times, how many times will the `setBodyContent()` method be called? (Select one)

**a** Zero
**b** One
**c** Two
**d** Five
**e** Six

*Answer: a*

***Explanation***

If the doStartTag() method returns EVAL_BODY_INCLUDE, then the evaluation of the body is not buffered. Thus, setBodyContent() is never called. The correct answer is a, zero times.

**10.** If the doStartTag() method returns EVAL_BODY_BUFFERED one time and the doAfterBody() method returns EVAL_BODY_BUFFERED five times, how many times will the setBodyContent() method be called? Assume that the body of the tag is not empty. (Select one)

**a** Zero
**b** One
**c** Two
**d** Five
**e** Six

*Answer: b*

***Explanation***

If the doStartTag() method returns EVAL_BODY_BUFFERED, then the evaluation of the body is buffered. But setBodyContent() is called only once—before the first time the body is evaluated. This happens only after the doStartTag() method returns EVAL_BODY_BUFFERED. It is not called after every call to doAfterBody() regardless of the return value of doAfterBody(). The correct answer is b, one time.

**11.** How is the SKIP_PAGE constant used? (Select one)

**a** doStartTag() can return it to skip the evaluation until the end of the current page.
**b** doAfterBody() can return it to skip the evaluation until the end of the current page.
**c** doEndTag() can return it to skip the evaluation until the end of the current page.
**d** It is passed as a parameter to doEndTag() as an indication to skip the evaluation until the end of the current page.

*Answer: c*

***Explanation***

The SKIP_PAGE constant is defined in the Tag interface as a return value for the doEndTag() method. It indicates that evaluation of the page from the end of the current tag until the end of the current page must be skipped. The correct answer is c.

**12.** Which of the following can you use to achieve the same functionality as provided by findAncestorWithClass()? (Select one)

**a** getParent()
**b** getParentWithClass()
**c** getAncestor()
**d** getAncestorWithClass()
**e** findAncestor()

*Answer: a*

***Explanation***

`findAncestorWithClass(Tag currentTag, Class klass)` is a convenient way to get a reference to an outer tag that is closest to the specified `Class` object. This can also be achieved by calling `getParent()` on the current tag to get its immediate parent and then again calling `getParent()` on the returned reference, working our way up the nested hierarchy until we find the tag with the desired `Class` object. Thus, the correct answer is a, `getParent()`. The methods shown in all the other answers are not valid methods of any interface.

**13.** Consider the following code in a tag handler class that extends `TagSupport`:

```
public int doStartTag()
{
   //1
}
```

Which of the following can you use at `//1` to get an attribute from the application scope? (Select one)

**a** `getServletContext().getAttribute("name");`
**b** `getApplication().getAttribute("name");`
**c** `pageContext.getAttribute("name",PageContext.APPLICATION_SCOPE);`
**d** `bodyContent.getApplicationAttribute("name");`

*Answer: c*

***Explanation***

The only implicit object made available to tag handler classes by the engine is `PageContext` via the `setPageContext()` method. To access all other implicit objects and user-defined objects in other scopes, we must save the reference to `pageContext` passed in as a parameter to the `setPageContext()` method and use the saved object in other methods. The `TagSupport` class implements `setPageContext()` and maintains this reference in a protected member named `pageContext`. We can use this member in the methods of the classes that extend `TagSupport`. Thus, the correct answer is c, `pageContext.getAttribute("name",PageContext.APPLICATION_SCOPE);`.

**14.** Which types of objects can be returned by `PageContext.getOut()`? (Select two)

**a** An object of type `ServletOutputStream`
**b** An object of type `HttpServletOutputStream`
**c** An object of type `JspWriter`
**d** An object of type `HttpJspWriter`
**e** An object of type `BodyContent`

*Answers: c and e*

***Explanation***

The return type of `pageContext.getOut()` is `JspWriter`. If the exam asks you to select only one correct option, select `JspWriter`. However, `BodyContent` extends `JspWriter`, and the return value of the `pageContext.getOut()` is an object of type `BodyContent` if `doStartTag()` returns `EVAL_BODY_BUFFERED`. Thus, if the exam asks you to select two correct options, then select `BodyContent` as well.

15. We can use the directive `<%@ page buffer="8kb" %>` to specify the size of the buffer when returning `EVAL_BODY_BUFFERED` from `doStartTag()`.

   **a** True
   **b** False

   *Answer: b*

   ***Explanation***
   The `page` directive attribute buffer specifies the size of the buffer to be maintained by the actual output stream that is meant for the whole page. It has nothing to do with the buffer maintained by `BodyContent`, which is meant for a particular tag when the `doStartTag()` method returns `EVAL_BODY_BUFFERED`. The buffer size of a `BodyContent` object is unlimited. Therefore, the correct answer is b, false.

## CHAPTER 17—DESIGN PATTERNS

1. What are the benefits of using the Data Access Object pattern? (Select two)

   **a** The type of the actual data source can be specified at deployment time.
   **b** The data clients are independent of the data source vendor API.
   **c** It increases the performance of data-accessing routines.
   **d** It allows the clients to access the data source through EJBs.
   **e** It allows resource locking in an efficient way.

   *Answers: a and b*

   ***Explanation***
   This pattern is used to decouple business logic from data access logic. It hides the data access mechanism from the business objects so that the data source can be changed easily and transparently to the business objects.

2. Which design pattern allows you to decouple the business logic, data representation, and data presentation? (Select one)

   **a** Model-View-Controller
   **b** Value Object
   **c** Bimodal Data Access
   **d** Business Delegate

   *Answer: a*

   ***Explanation***
   In the Model-View-Controller pattern, Model is the data representation, View is the data presentation, and Controller is the implementation of business logic.

3. Which of the following are the benefits of using the Value Object design pattern? (Select two)

   a It improves the response time for data access.
   b It improves the efficiency of object operations.
   c It reduces the network traffic.
   d It reduces the coupling between the data access module and the database.

   *Answers: a and c*

   ***Explanation***

   The Value Object pattern allows you to retrieve all the data elements in one remote call instead of making multiple remote calls; therefore, it reduces the network traffic and improves the response time since the subsequent calls to the object are local.

4. Which of the following statements are correct? (Select two)

   a The Value Object pattern ensures that the data is not stale at the time of use.
   b It is wise to make the Value Object immutable if the Value Object represents read-only data.
   c Applying the Value Object pattern on EJBs helps to reduce the load on enterprise beans.
   d A Value Object exists only on the server side.

   *Answers: b and c*

   ***Explanation***

   Answer a is wrong because just the reverse is true. For instance, this pattern is not used when the attributes of an EJB are volatile, such as stock quotes. Answer b is correct because making the Value Object immutable reinforces the idea that the Value Object is not a remote object and any changes to its state will not be reflected on the server. Answer c is correct because clients require a fewer number of remote calls to retrieve attributes. Answer d is wrong because a Value Object is created on the server and sent to the client.

5. What are the benefits of using the Business Delegate pattern? (Select three)

   a It implements the business service functionality locally to improve performance.
   b It shields the clients from the details of the access mechanism, such as CORBA or RMI, of the business services.
   c It shields the clients from changes in the implementation of the business services.
   d It provides the clients with a uniform interface to the business services.
   e It reduces the number of remote calls and reduces network overhead.

   *Answers: b, c, and d*

   ***Explanation***

   Answer a is wrong because a Business Delegate does not implement any business service itself. It calls remote methods on the business services on behalf of the presentation layer. Answer b is correct because the clients delegate the task of calling remote business service methods to the Business Delegate. Thus, they are shielded by the Business Delegate from the access mechanism of the business services. Answer c is correct because the Business Delegate is meant for shielding the clients from the implementation of the business services. Answer d is also correct because this is one of the goals of this pattern. Answer e is not correct because the Business Delegate does not reduce the number of remote calls. It calls the remote methods on behalf of the client components.

6. You are designing an application that is required to display the data to users through HTML interfaces. It also has to feed the same data to other systems through XML as well as WAP interfaces. Which design pattern would be appropriate in this situation? (Select one)

   **a** Interface Factory
   **b** Session Facade
   **c** Value Object
   **d** Model-View-Controller
   **e** Factory

   *Answer: d*

   ***Explanation***
   The application requires multiple views (HTML, XML, and WAP) for the same data; therefore, MVC is the correct answer.

7. You are automating a computer parts ordering business. For this purpose, your web application requires a controller component that would receive the requests and dispatch them to appropriate JSP pages. It would also coordinate the request processing among the JSP pages, thereby managing the workflow. Finally, the behavior of the controller component is to be loaded at runtime as needed. Which design pattern would be appropriate in this situation? (Select one)

   **a** Front Controller
   **b** Session Facade
   **c** Value Object
   **d** Model-View-Controller
   **e** Data Access Object

   *Answer: a*

   ***Explanation***
   This is a standard situation for the Front Controller pattern. The Front Controller receives all the requests and dispatches them to the appropriate JSP pages. This is not the MVC pattern, because the question only asks about controlling the workflow. You would choose the MVC pattern if it asked about controlling and presenting the data in multiple views.

8. You are building the server side of an application and you are finalizing the interfaces that you will provide to the presentation layer. However, you have not yet finalized the access details of the business services. Which design pattern should you use to mitigate this concern? (Select one)

   **a** Model-View-Controller
   **b** Data Access Object

**c** Business Delegate
**d** Facade
**e** Value Object

*Answer: c*

***Explanation***

You already know the services that you have to provide, but the implementation of the service access mechanism for the services has not yet been decided. The Business Delegate pattern gives you the flexibility to implement the access mechanism any way you want. The presentation-tier components—servlets and JSP pages—can use the interface provided by the Business Delegate object to access the business services. Later, when the decision about access mechanism changes, only the Business Delegate object needs to be modified. Other components will remain unaffected.

APPENDIX E

# *Exam Quick Prep*

This appendix provides a quick recap of all the important concepts that are covered in the exam objectives. It also notes important points regarding the concepts, which may help you answer the questions correctly during the exam. You should go through this appendix a day before you take the exam.

We have grouped the information according to the exam objectives given by Sun. Therefore, the numbering of the objectives corresponds to the numbering given to the objectives on Sun's web site. The objectives are listed with the chapters in which they are discussed. However, since the first three chapters of this book do not correspond to any exam objectives, the objectives start with chapter 4. Also, since the topics of chapter 18 are not currently mentioned in the exam objectives, we have created some hypothetical objectives for that chapter.

## *CHAPTER 4—THE SERVLET MODEL*

### *Objectives 1.1–1.6*

**1.1** *For each of the HTTP methods, GET, POST, and PUT, identify the corresponding method in the HttpServlet class.*

| **Important concepts** | **Exam tips** |
|---|---|
| ✧ For HTTP method *XXX*, HttpServlet's do*XXX*(HttpServletRequest, HttpServletResponse) is called. | Servlet container calls the service(ServletRequest, ServletResponse) method of the Servlet interface. |
| ✧ For example, for GET, HttpServlet's doGet() is called. | HttpServlet.service(HttpServletRequest, HttpServletResponse) interprets the HTTP request and calls the appropriate do*XXX*() method. |

**1.2** *For each of the HTTP methods, GET, POST, and HEAD, identify triggers that might cause a browser to use the method, and identify benefits or functionality of the method.*

| **Important concepts** | **Exam tips** |
|---|---|
| ✧ Triggers for GET request:<br>• Clicking on a hyperlink<br>• Browsing through the browser's address field | The default method of the HTML FORM element is GET. |
| ✧ Triggers for POST request:<br>• Submitting an HTML FORM, ONLY if its method attribute is POST | Parameters sent via GET are visible in the URL. Parameters sent via POST are not visible in the URL, and so it is used to send data such as the user ID/password. |
| ✧ Triggers for HEAD request:<br>• Clicking a menu option that makes the browser synchronize offline content with the web site | GET supports only text data.<br>POST supports text as well as binary data. The HTTP protocol does not limit the length of the query string, but many browsers and HTTP servers limit it to 255 chars.<br>POST is used to send large amounts of data. |

**1.3** *For each of the following operations, identify the interface and method name that should be used:*

- *Retrieve HTML form parameters from the request*
- *Retrieve a servlet initialization parameter*
- *Retrieve HTTP request header information*
- *Set an HTTP response header; set the content type of the response*
- *Acquire a text stream for the response*
- *Acquire a binary stream for the response*
- *Redirect an HTTP request to another URL*

| **Important concepts** | **Exam tips** |
|---|---|
| ✧ HTML FORM parameters or parameters embedded in query string can be retrieved using:<br>• String ServletRequest.getParameter(String paramName)<br>• String[] ServletRequest.getParameterValues(String param) | ServletConfig allows you to get Init parameters. You cannot set anything into it.<br>sendRedirect is not transparent to the browser. |
| ✧ Servlet initialization parameters can be retrieved using:<br>• String ServletConfig.getInitParameter(String paramName)<br>• Enumeration ServletConfig.getInitParameterNames() | ServletConfig allows you to get Init parameters. You cannot set anything into it.<br>sendRedirect is not transparent to the browser. |
| ✧ HTTP request headers can be retrieved using:<br>• String HttpServletRequest.getHeader(String headerName)<br>• Enumeration HttpServletRequest.getHeaderValues(String headerName) | |
| ✧ HTTP response headers can be set using:<br>• HttpServletResponse.setHeader(String headerName, String value)<br>• HttpServletResponse.addHeader(String headerName, String value) | |
| ✧ Content-Type for HTTP response can be set using:<br>• ServletResponse.setContentType(String value) | |
| ✧ ServletConfig provides the following methods to retrieve initialization parameters for a servlet:<br>• String getInitParameter(String name)<br>• Enumeration getInitParameterNames() | |
| ✧ To acquire a text stream to send character data to the response, use:<br>• PrintWriter ServletResponse.getWriter() | |

*continued on next page*

| Important concepts | Exam tips |
|---|---|
| ✧ To acquire a binary stream to send any data to the response, use:<br>• ServletOutputStream ServletResponse.getOutputStream()<br><br>✧ To redirect an HTTP request to another URL, use:<br>• HttpServletResponse.sendRedirect(String newURL) | |

**1.4** ***Identify the interface and method to access values and resources and to set object attributes within the following three web scopes:***

- *Request*
- *Session*
- *Context*

| Important concepts | Exam tips |
|---|---|
| ✧ ServletContext provides the following methods to access a resource in a location independent manner:<br>• java.net.URL getResource(String path)<br>• java.io.InputStream getResourceAsStream(String path)<br><br>✧ ServletRequest, HttpSession, and ServletContext provide the following methods to share data among coordinating servlets:<br>• setAttribute(String name, Object value)<br>• Object getAttribute(String name)<br>• Enumeration getAttributeNames() | Request scope is provided by the ServletRequest object.<br>Session scope is provided by the HttpSession object.<br>Context scope is provided by the ServletContext object. |

**1.5** *Given a life-cycle method: init, service, or destroy, identify correct statements about its purpose or about how and when it is invoked.*

| Important concepts | Exam tips |
|---|---|
| ✧ Following are the servlet life-cycle methods:<br>• init(ServletConfig): Guaranteed to be called once and only once on a Servlet object by the servlet container before putting the servlet into service.<br>• service(ServletRequest, ServletResponse): Called by the servlet container for each request.<br>• destroy(): Called by the servlet container after it takes the servlet out of service. It is called only once. But it may not be called if the servlet container crashes. | The init() method is called once per servlet object. You can have multiple servlet objects of the same servlet class.<br>You can configure multiple servlets using the same servlet class but with different names to provide multiple sets of initialization parameters. |

**1.6** *Use a RequestDispatcher to include or forward to a web resource.*

| Important concepts | Exam tips |
|---|---|
| ✧ The RequestDispatcher interface provides the following methods to forward the request to another servlet or to include the partial response generated by another servlet:<br>• RequestDispatcher.forward(ServletRequest, ServletResponse)<br>• RequestDispatcher.include(ServletRequest, ServletResponse)<br>✧ ServletRequest and ServletContext provide the following method to get a RequestDispatcher:<br>• getRequestDispatcher(String path)<br>✧ Additionally, ServletContext also provides the following method:<br>• getNamedDispatcher(String servletName) | RequestDispatcher.forward() is transparent to the browser, unlike HttpServletResponse.sendRedirect().<br>The path string passed to ServletContext.getRequestDispatcher() must start with /.<br>ServletRequest.getRequestDispatcher supports relative paths while ServletContext.getRequestDispatcher does not. |

## CHAPTER 5—STRUCTURE AND DEPLOYMENT

### *Objectives 2.1 and 2.2*

**2.1** *Identify the structure of a Web Application and Web Archive file, the name of the WebApp deployment descriptor, and the name of the directories where you place the following:*

- *The WebApp deployment descriptor*
- *The WebApp class files*
- *Any auxiliary JAR files*

| Important concepts | Exam tips |
|---|---|
| ✧ Directory structure of a web application:<br><br>webappname<br>  \|-all html, gif, jsp, etc. files<br>  \|-WEB-INF<br>    \|-web.xml<br>    \|-classes<br>    \|-lib<br><br>A WAR file is nothing but the web application directory packaged in a JAR file. At the time of deployment, the name of the web application is assumed to be the name of the WAR file. | The name of the deployment descriptor file is web.xml, and it should be in the WEB-INF directory.<br>Class files should be in the WEB-INF/classes directory.<br>JAR files should be in the WEB-INF/lib directory. |

**2.2** *Match the name with a description of purpose or functionality, for each of the following deployment descriptor elements:*

- *Servlet instance*
- *Servlet name*
- *Servlet class*
- *Initialization parameters*
- *URL to named servlet mapping*

**Important concepts**

- ✧ A servlet container creates a servlet instance for each <servlet> element.
  The <servlet-name> element is used to give a name to a servlet.
  The <servlet-class> element specifies the fully qualified Java class name for the servlet.
  Each <init-param> element specifies an initialization parameter.
  Each <servlet-mapping> element specifies a URI to the servlet mapping.

- ✧ Sample Servlet definition:

```
<servlet>
  <servlet-name>
    TestServlet
  </servlet-name>
  <servlet-class>
    com.abc.TestServlet
  </servlet-class>
  <init-param>
     <param-name>region</param-name>
     <param-value>USA</param-value>
  </init-param>
</servlet>
```

- ✧ Sample URL-to-Servlet mapping:

```
<servlet-mapping>
  <servlet-name>
    ColorServlet
   </servlet-name>
  <url-pattern>*.col</url-pattern>
</servlet-mapping>
```

**Exam tips**

You can define two servlets using the same servlet class but different servlet names to provide multiple sets of initialization parameters.

## *CHAPTER 6—THE SERVLET CONTAINER MODEL*

### *Objectives 3.1–3.3*

**3.1** *Identify the uses for and the interfaces (or classes) and methods to achieve the following features:*

- *Servlet context init parameters*
- *Servlet context listener*
- *Servlet context attribute listener*
- *Session attribute listeners*

| Important concepts | Exam tips |
|---|---|
| ✧ ServletContext init parameters can be retrieved using ServletContext.getInit-Parameter(String). | javax.servlet.GenericServlet implements the ServletConfig interface. |
| ✧ ServletContextListener has two methods:<br>• contextInitialized(ServletContextEvent)<br>• contextDestroyed(ServletContextEvent) | ServletContextEvent defines only one method: getServletContext(). |
| ✧ ServletContextAttributeListener has three methods:<br>• attributeAdded(ServletContextAttribute-Event)<br>• attributeRemoved(ServletContextAttribute-Event)<br>• attributeReplaced(ServletContextAttribute-Event) | ServletContextAttributeEvent extends Servlet-ContextEvent and defines two methods: get-Name() and getValue(). They return the name and value of the attribute that was added, removed, or replaced. |
| ✧ HttpSessionAttributeListener has three methods:<br>• attributeAdded(HttpSessionBindingEvent)<br>• attributeRemoved(HttpSessionBinding-Event)<br>• attributeReplaced(HttpSessionBinding-Event) | HttpSessionEvent defines only one method: HttpSession getSession().<br>HttpSessionBindingEvent extends HttpSession-Event and defines two methods: getName() and getValue(). |

**3.2** *Identify the WebApp deployment descriptor element name that declares the following features:*

- *Servlet context init parameters*
- *Servlet context listener*
- *Servlet context attribute listener*
- *Session attribute listeners*

| Important concepts | Exam tips |
|---|---|
| ✧ The following is a web.xml code snippet showing ServletContext init parameters and a listener configuration:<br>`<web-app>`<br>`  ...`<br>`  <context-param>`<br>`    <param-name>locale</param-name>`<br>`    <param-value>US</param-value>`<br>`  </context-param>`<br>`  <listener>`<br>`    <listener-class>`<br>`      com.xyz.MySessionContextListener`<br>`    </listener-class>`<br>`  </listener>`<br>`  <listener>`<br>`    <listener-class>com.xyz.SomeListener`<br>`      </listener-class>`<br>`  </listener>`<br>`  ...`<br>`</web-app>` | The <listener> element is used to configure ServletContextListener, ServletContext-AttributeListener, and HttpSessionAttribute-Listener.<br>You do not specify the listener interface that the configured class implements. The servlet container automatically figures it out.<br>You can configure multiple classes to receive the same notification. However, only one instance of each of the classes is created.<br>You can implement more than one listener interface in one class. In this case as well, only one instance of the class is created. The same instance will be sent all the relevant notifications. |

**3.3** *Distinguish the behavior of the following in a distributable environment:*

- *Servlet context init parameters*
- *Servlet context listener*
- *Servlet context attribute listener*
- *Session attribute listeners*

| Important concepts | Exam tips |
|---|---|
| ✧ There is one ServletContext for each web application on each JVM. However, ServletContext for the default web application exists on only one JVM.<br>HttpSession exists on only one JVM at a time but may be migrated across the JVMs.<br>HttpSession attributes should implement the java.io.Serializable interface; otherwise, setAttribute() may throw an IllegalArgumentException. | ServletContext init parameters are available on all the JVMs.<br>ServletContext attributes are not visible across the JVMs.<br>ServletContextEvent, ServletContextAttribute-Event, and HttpSessionAttributeEvent may not be propagated across the JVMs. Therefore, a distributable web application should not depend on the notification of changes to the attribute list of either ServletContext or HttpSession. |

The following table summarizes the properties of all the application life-cycle event listeners:

| Listener interface | Methods |
|---|---|
| javax.servlet.ServletContextListener<br>• Configured in the deployment descriptor.<br>• Used to listen for creation and destruction of the servlet context.<br>• Should not depend on this in a distributed environment. | void contextDestroyed(ServletContextEvent sce)<br>Called when the servlet context is about to be destroyed.<br><br>void contextInitialized(ServletContextEvent sce)<br>Called when the web application is ready to process requests. |
| javax.servlet.ServletContextAttributeListener<br>• Configured in the deployment descriptor.<br>• Used to listen for changes in the attribute list of the servlet context.<br>• Should not depend on this in a distributed environment. | void attributeAdded(ServletContextAttributeEvent scae)<br>Called when a new attribute is added to the servlet context.<br><br>void attributeRemoved(ServletContextAttributeEvent scae)<br>Called when an attribute is removed from the servlet context.<br><br>void attributeReplaced(ServletContext-AttributeEvent scae)<br>Called when an attribute on the servlet context is replaced. |
| javax.servlet.http.HttpSessionListener<br>• Configured in the deployment descriptor.<br>• Used to listen for changes in the list of sessions of a web application.<br>• Should not depend on this in a distributed environment. For example, if a session is created on one machine, this may not trigger a call to sessionCreated() on another machine. | void sessionCreated(HttpSessionEvent se)<br>Called when a session is created.<br><br>void sessionDestroyed(HttpSessionEvent se)<br>Called when a session is invalidated. |
| javax.servlet.http.HttpSessionAttributeListener<br>• Configured in the deployment descriptor.<br>• Used to listen for changes in the attribute list of sessions of a web application.<br>• Should not depend on this in a distributed environment because the HttpSession-AttributeListener instances will be present on all the JVMs but the session will be present on only one JVM. Thus, the HttpSessionBindingEvents will be delivered only to the listener instance that is present on the session's JVM. | void attributeAdded(HttpSessionBindingEvent se)<br>Called when an attribute is added to a session.<br><br>void attributeRemoved(HttpSessionBindingEvent se)<br>Called when an attribute is removed from a session.<br><br>void attributeReplaced(HttpSessionBindingEvent se)<br>Called when an attribute is replaced in a session. |

*continued on next page*

| Listener interface | Methods |
|---|---|
| javax.servlet.http.HttpSessionBindingListener<br>• NOT Configured in the deployment descriptor.<br>• An attribute should implement this interface if it wants to be notified when it is added or removed from a session.<br>• Can depend on this in a distributed environment, since a session resides on only one machine at a time. | void valueBound(HttpSessionBindingEvent event)<br>Called on the object when it is being bound to a session.<br><br>void valueUnbound(HttpSessionBindingEvent event)<br>Called on the object when it is being unbound from a session. |
| javax.servlet.http.HttpSessionActivationListener<br>• NOT Configured in the deployment descriptor.<br>• An attribute should implement this interface if it wants to be notified when the session is migrated.<br>• Can depend on this in a distributed environment, because a session resides on only one machine at a time. | void sessionDidActivate(HttpSessionEvent se)<br>Called on all the attributes that implement this interface after the session is activated.<br><br>void sessionWillPassivate(HttpSessionEvent se)<br>Called on all the attributes that implement this interface just before the session is passivated. |

## CHAPTER 7—HANDLING SERVER-SIDE EXCEPTIONS

### Objectives 4.1–4.3

**4.1** *For each of the following cases, identify correctly constructed code for handling business logic exceptions, and match that code with correct statements about the code's behavior:*

- *Return an HTTP error using the sendError response method*
- *Return an HTTP error using the setStatus method*

| Important concepts | Exam tips |
|---|---|
| ✧ Programmatic handling of error conditions:<br>`try`<br>`{`<br>`  //application code`<br>`}`<br>`catch(XXXException e)`<br>`{`<br>`  resp.sendError(resp.SC_XXX, "message");`<br>`  //OR : resp.sendError(resp.SC_XXX);`<br>`  //OR: resp.setStatus(resp.SC_XXX);`<br>`}`<br><br>If an error-code/error-page mapping is specified, the servlet container uses the specified page to generate a response. | sendError(int code) / sendError(int code, String message)<br>Throws IllegalStateException if the response is already committed.<br>A response should be assumed to be committed after a call to this method.<br>Triggers the container to generate a default HTML page if an error-code/error-page mapping is not specified.<br>setStatus(int code)<br>A call to this method is ignored if the response is already committed.<br>Should only be used to set status codes that do not represent an error.<br>DOES NOT trigger the container to generate a default HTML page if no error-code/error-page mapping is specified.<br>setStatus(int code, String message) is deprecated. |

**4.2** *Given a set of business logic exceptions, identify the following:*

- *The configuration that the deployment descriptor uses to handle each exception*
- *How to use a RequestDispatcher to forward the request to an error page*
- *Specify the handling declaratively in the deployment descriptor*

| **Important concepts** | **Exam tips** |
|---|---|
| ✧ Three steps to handle standard or business logic exceptions declaratively:<br><br>1. Specify the mapping in the deployment descriptor:<br><br><web-app><br>...<br><error-page><br><error-code>403</error-code><br><location>/errorpages/securityerror.html<br></location><br></error-page><br><error-page><br><exception-type>com.abc.MyException<br></exception-type><br><location>/servlet/exceptionHandlerServlet<br></location><br></error-page><br>...<br></web-app><br><br>2. Throw the exception wrapped inside a ServletException:<br><br>try<br>{<br>//application code<br>}<br>catch(com.abc.MyException e)<br>{<br>throw new ServletException("message", e);<br>}<br><br>3. Implement the error handler (if the mapping specifies a servlet or a JSP page) to generate the appropriate page. | Only subclasses of ServletException, IOException, or RuntimeException can be thrown from the servlet code. All other business exceptions must be wrapped inside a ServletException.<br><br>javax.servlet.ServletOutputStream extends java.io.OutputStream. |
| ✧ Use RequestDispatcher.forward() to forward a request to an error-handler page. In case of an exception, set javax.servlet.error.exception_type, javax.servlet.error.request_uri, and javax.servlet.error.servlet_name in the request, and in case of an error condition, set javax.servlet.error.error_code, javax.servlet.error.request_uri, and javax.servlet.error.servlet_name in the request before forwarding the request. | |

*continued on next page*

| Important concepts | Exam tips |
|---|---|
| ✧ Rules for exceptions thrown by an included or forwarded resource using the RequestDispatcher interface:<br>1. If the exception thrown by the included or forwarded resource is a RuntimeException, a ServletException, or an IOException, it is thrown as is by the include() or forward() method.<br>2. Otherwise, the exception is wrapped in a ServletException as the rootCause, and the ServletException is thrown by the include() or forward() method. | |

**4.3** *Identify the method used for the following:*

- *Write a message to the WebApp log*
- *Write a message and an exception to the WebApp log*

| Objective | Exam tips |
|---|---|
| ✧ javax.servlet.GenericServlet and javax.servlet.ServletContext provide the following two methods for logging:<br>• void log(String message);<br>• void log(String message, Throwable t) | GenericServlet.log() methods prepend the message with the servlet name, but ServletContext.log() methods do not. |

## *CHAPTER 8—SESSION MANAGEMENT*

### *Objectives 5.1–5.3*

**5.1** *Identify the interface and method for each of the following:*

- *Retrieve a session object across multiple requests to the same or different servlets within the same WebApp*
- *Store objects into a session object*
- *Retrieve objects from a session object*
- *Respond to the event when a particular object is added to a session*
- *Respond to the event when a session is created and destroyed*
- *Expunge a session object*

| **Important concepts** | **Exam tips** |
|---|---|
| ✧ Methods to retrieve a session while processing a user request:<br>• request.getSession(boolean createFlag)<br>• request.getSession(): This is same as request.getSession(true)<br><br>✧ Methods to get and store attributes from and to HttpSession:<br>• Object getAttribute(String name);<br>• void setAttribute(String name, Object value)<br><br>✧ HttpSessionBindingListener is used by objects to receive notifications when they are added to or removed from a session. It has two methods:<br>• void valueBound(HttpSessionBindingEvent e)<br>• void valueUnound(HttpSessionBindingEvent e)<br><br>✧ HttpSessionListener is used to receive notifications when any session is created or destroyed. It has two methods:<br>• void sessionCreated(HttpSessionEvent e)<br>• void sessionDestroyed(HttpSessionEvent e)<br><br>✧ A session can be explicitly expunged using the session.invalidate() method. | HttpSessionListener is configured in the deployment descriptor while HttpSessionBindingListener is not.<br><br>HttpSessionAttributeListener and HttpSessionBindingListener are similar, but their scopes are different. HttpSessionAttributeListener is configured in the deployment descriptor and is used to listen for application-wide HttpSessionBindingEvents. HttpSessionBindingListener is not configured in the deployment descriptor and is implemented by classes, objects of which are to be stored in a session.<br><br>HttpSessionEvent has only one method:<br><br>HttpSession getSession()<br><br>HttpSessionBindingEvent extends HttpSessionEvent and adds methods:<br><br>String getName()<br><br>Object getValue()<br><br>The sessionDestroyed() method of HttpSessionListener is called after the session is invalidated, so you cannot retrieve anything from the session in this method. |

**5.2** *Given a scenario, state whether a session object will be invalidated.*

| Important concepts | Exam tips |
|---|---|
| ✧ Session timeout is specified in the deployment descriptor:<br><web-app><br>...<br><session-config><br><session-timeout>30</session-timeout><br></session-config><br>...<br></web-app><br><br>A session is invalidated if no request comes from the client for session-timeout minutes or if session.invalidate() is called. | Session timeout (in web.xml) is specified in minutes. A value of 0 or less means the sessions will never expire (unless explicitly expunged using session.invalidate()).<br><br>Session timeout for a particular session can be changed using HttpSession.setMaxInactiveInterval(int seconds). This method takes the interval in number of seconds (unlike the deployment descriptor, which takes minutes). It does not affect other sessions. Any negative value prevents the session from being timed out. |

**5.3** *Given that URL-rewriting must be used for session management, identify the design requirement on session-related HTML pages.*

| Important concepts | Exam tips |
|---|---|
| ✧ All the URLs displayed by all the pages of the application must have the session ID attached.<br><br>✧ HttpServletResponse.encodeURL(String url) appends the session ID to the URL only if it is required.<br><br>✧ HttpServletResponse.encodeRedirectURL(String url) should be used to rewrite URLs that are to be passed to the response.sendRedirect() method. | None of the static HTML pages that contain URLs can be served directly to the client. They must be parsed in a servlet and the session ID must be attached to the URLs. |

## *CHAPTER 9—DEVELOPING SECURE WEB APPLICATIONS*

### *Objectives 6.1–6.3*

**6.1** *Identify correct descriptions or statements about the security issues:*

- *Authentication*
- *Authorization*
- *Data integrity*
- *Auditing*
- *Malicious code*
- *Web site attacks*

| Important concepts | Exam tips |
|---|---|
| ✧ Authentication: Verifying that the user is who he claims to be. Performed by asking for the username and password. | |
| ✧ Authorization: Verifying that the user has the right to access the requested resource. Performed by checking with an access control list. | |
| ✧ Data integrity: Verifying that the data is not modified in transit. Performed using cryptography. | |
| ✧ Confidentiality: Making sure that unintended parties cannot make use of the data. Performed using encryption. | |
| ✧ Auditing: Keeping logs that can be used to hold users responsible for their actions. | |
| ✧ Malicious code: Code that performs actions without the user's permission and knowledge. Malicious code may be avoided by using signed code. | |
| ✧ Web site attacks: Mainly denial-of-service attacks, which hog the server resources and prevent genuine users from using the services. May be prevented by monitoring access patterns continuously and by blocking misbehaving clients. | |

**6.2** *Identify the deployment descriptor element names, and their structure, that declare the following:*

- *A security constraint*
- *A Web resource*
- *The login configuration*
- *A security role*

| Important concepts | Exam tips |
|---|---|
| ✧ Three things are used to define a security constraint:<br>1. web-resource-collection (at least one is required)<br>2. auth-constraint (optional)<br>3. user-data-constraint (optional) | Values for transport-guarantee:<br>NONE implies HTTP<br>CONFIDENTIAL, INTEGRAL imply HTTPS<br>Values for auth-method: BASIC, FORM, DIGEST, and CLIENT-CERT. |
| ✧ Sample security constraint: | |

```
<security-constraint>

  <web-resource-collection>
    <web-resource-name>declarativetest
      </web-resource-name>
    <url-pattern>/servlet/SecureServlet
      </url-pattern>
    <http-method>POST</http-method>
  </web-resource-collection>

  <auth-constraint>
    <role-name>supervisor</role-name>
  </auth-constraint>

  <user-data-constraint>
    <transport-guarantee>NONE
      </transport-guarantee>
  </user-data-constraint>

</security-constraint>
```

✧ Login config is used to authenticate the users. Sample login configuration:

```
<login-config>
  <auth-method>FORM</auth-method>
  <form-login-config>
    <form-login-page>/formlogin.html
      </form-login-page>
    <form-error-page>/formerror.html
      </form-error-page>
  </form-login-config>
</login-config>
```

*continued on next page*

| Important concepts | Exam tips |
|---|---|
| ✧ Sample security role:<br><security-role><br><role-name>supervisor</role-name><br></security-role><br><br>✧ Programmatic security requires role names that are hard-coded in the servlet to be specified in the security-role-ref element. An example:<br><br><servlet><br><servlet-name>SecureServlet</servlet-name><br><servlet-class>cgscwcd.chapter9.SecureServlet<br></servlet-class><br><security-role-ref><br><role-name>manager</role-name><br><role-link>supervisor</role-link><br></security-role-ref><br></servlet><br><br>In this example, manager will be hard-coded in the servlet while supervisor is the actual role name in the deployment environment. | Values for transport-guarantee:<br>NONE implies HTTP<br>CONFIDENTIAL, INTEGRAL imply HTTPS<br><br>Values for auth-method: BASIC, FORM, DIGEST, and CLIENT-CERT. |

**6.3** *Given an authentication type: BASIC, DIGEST, FORM, and CLIENT-CERT, identify the correct definition of its mechanism.*

| Important concepts | Exam tips |
|---|---|
| ✧ BASIC: Performed by sending the username and password in Base64 encoding.<br>Advantages:<br>• Very easy to set up<br>• Supported by all browsers<br>Disadvantages:<br>• It is not secure, since the username and password are not encrypted.<br>• You cannot customize the look and feel of the dialog box. | |
| ✧ DIGEST: Performed by sending a digest of the password in an encrypted form.<br>Advantages:<br>• Secure<br>Disadvantages:<br>• Not supported by all browsers | |
| ✧ FORM: Performed by sending username and password in Base64 encoding. The username and password are captured using a customized HTML FORM.<br>Advantages:<br>• Easy to set up<br>• Supported by all browsers<br>• Customized look and feel<br>Disadvantages:<br>• It is not secure, since the username and password are not encrypted unless HTTPS is used. | |
| ✧ Client-Cert:<br>Advantages:<br>• Very secure<br>• Supported by all browsers<br>Disadvantages:<br>• Costly to implement | |

## CHAPTER 10—DEVELOPING THREAD-SAFE SERVLETS

### Objectives 7.1–7.3

**7.1** *Identify which attribute scopes are thread-safe:*

- *Local variables*
- *Instance variables*
- *Class variables*
- *Request attributes*
- *Session attributes*
- *Context attributes*

| Important concepts | Exam tips |
|---|---|
| ✧ Local variables: Always thread safe<br>Instance variables: Thread safe only for SingleThreadModel<br>Class or Static variables: NEVER thread safe | |
| ✧ Request attributes: Always thread safe<br>Session attributes and Context attributes: NEVER thread safe | |

**7.2** *Identify correct statements about differences between the multi-threaded and single-threaded servlet models.*

| Important concepts | Exam tips |
|---|---|
| ✧ Multithreaded model<br>• Only one instance of the servlet class is created.<br>• Multiple threads can execute the service() method simultaneously.<br>• Requests are serviced in parallel by a single instance. | |
| ✧ Single-threaded model<br>• Multiple instances of the servlet class may be created.<br>• Only one thread executes the service() method of one instance.<br>• Multiple requests may be serviced concurrently by multiple instances.<br>• One instance services only one request at a time. | |

**7.3** *Identify the interface used to declare that a servlet must use the single thread model.*

| Important concepts | Exam tips |
|---|---|
| ✧ The javax.servlet.SingleThreadModel interface ensures that only one thread executes the service() method at a time. | There is no such interface as MultiThreadModel. The default behavior *is* multithreaded.<br>Implementing SingleThreadModel does not ensure that the servlet is thread safe. |

## Chapter 11—The JSP Technology Model—The Basics

**Objectives 8.1, 8.2, 8.4 and 8.5**

**8.1** *Write the opening and closing tags for the following JSP tag types:*

- *Directive*
- *Declaration*
- *Scriptlet*
- *Expression*

| Important concepts | Exam tips |
|---|---|
| ✧ Directives use @<br><%@ page attribute list %><br><%@ include file="relativeURL" %><br><%@ taglib prefix="" uri="" %><br>Declaration use !<br><%! int count; %><br><%!<br>int getCount()<br>{<br>return count;<br>}<br>%><br>Scriptlets have no special character<br><%<br>//some Java code<br>%><br>Expressions use =<br><%= request.getParameter("paramName") %> | • Tag names, their attributes, and their values are case sensitive.<br>• Unknown attributes or invalid values result in errors and are caught during the translation phase.<br>• Page directives can be placed anywhere in a page but apply to the entire translation unit.<br>• Variable declarations end with a semicolon; methods do not.<br>• Expressions must not end with a semicolon.<br>• <%! String name="SCWCD"%> is an instance variable declared outside _jspService().<br>• <% String name="SCWCD"%> is a local variable declared inside _jspService(). |

**8.2** *Given a type of JSP tag, identify correct statements about its purpose or use.*

| Important concepts | Exam tips |
|---|---|
| ✧ Directive<br>Specifies translation time instructions to the JSP engine. | |
| ✧ Declaration<br>Declares and defines methods and variables. | |
| ✧ Scriptlet<br>Used for writing free-form Java code. | |

*continued on next page*

| Important concepts | Exam tips |
|---|---|
| ✧ Expression<br>Used as a shortcut to print values in the generated page. | |
| ✧ Action<br>Provides request time instructions to the JSP engine. | |
| ✧ Comment<br>Used to comment out parts of JSP code. | |

**8.4** *Identify the page directive attribute, and its values, that:*

- *Import a Java class into the JSP page*
- *Declare that a JSP page exists within a session*
- *Declare that a JSP page uses an error page*
- *Declare that a JSP page is an error page*

| Important concepts | Exam tips |
|---|---|
| ✧ To import a Java class into the page, use the import attribute:<br><br>`<%@ page import="java.util.* " %>`<br><br>✧ To declare that a JSP page exists within a session, use the attribute session and set it to true:<br><br>`<%@ page session="true" %>`<br><br>✧ To declare that a JSP uses an error page, use the errorPage attribute and supply the relative URL:<br><br>`<%@ page errorPage="myErrorPage.jsp" %>`<br><br>✧ To declare that a JSP is itself an error page, use the isErrorPage attribute and set it to true:<br><br>`<%@ page isErrorPage="true" %>` | Whether specified explicitly or not, by default, the following four packages are always imported:<br>java.lang.*<br>javax.servlet.*<br>javax.servlet.http.*<br>javax.servlet.jsp*<br><br>The default value of the session attribute is true.<br><br>The default value of errorPage is null.<br><br>The default value of isErrorPage is false. |

**8.5** *Identify and put in sequence the following elements of the JSP page lifecycle:*

- *Page translation*
- *JSP page compilation*
- *Load class*
- *Create instance*
- *Call jspInit*
- *Call _jspService*
- *Call jspDestroy*

| Important concepts | Exam tips |
|---|---|
| ✧ The life-cycle phases occur in the following order: | jspInit() and jspDestroy() are defined in the javax.servlet.jsp.JspPage interface. |
| 1. Page translation | _jspService() is defined in the javax.servlet.jsp.HttpJspPage interface. |
| 2. Page compilation | |
| 3. Load class | jspInit() and jspDestroy() are called only once. |
| 4. Create instance | _jspService() is called multiple times, once for every request for this page. |
| 5. Call jspInit() | JSP declarations are used to declare jspInit() and jpsDesctoy(). |
| 6. Call _jspService() | |
| 7. Call jspDestroy() | We never declare _jspService() explicitly. The JSP engine automatically declares it. |
| | The return type of all the three methods is void. |
| | jspInit() and jspDestroy() take no arguments. |
| | jspInit() and jspDestroy() do not throw any exceptions. |
| | _jspService() takes two arguments:<br>HttpServletRequest<br>HttpServletResponse |
| | _jspService() throws two exceptions:<br>ServletException<br>IOException |

## CHAPTER 12—THE JSP TECHNOLOGY MODEL—ADVANCED TOPICS

### *Objectives 8.3, 8.6 and 8.7*

**8.3** *Given a JSP tag type, identify the equivalent XML-based tags.*

| Important concepts | Exam tips |
|---|---|
| ✧ XML syntax for directives:<br><jsp:directive.page attribute list /><br><jsp:directive.include file="relativeURL" /> | • The rules for tag names, attributes, and values are the same in XML and JSP formats. |
| ✧ XML syntax for declarations:<br><jsp:declaration><br>int count;<br></jsp:declaration><br><jsp:declaration><br>int getCount(){<br>return count;<br>}<br></jsp:declaration> | • The semantics of placement of the tags are the same in XML and JSP formats.<br>• All XML-based pages should have a root tag named <jsp:root>. Thus, the page ends with </jsp:root>.<br>• There is no taglib directive in XML. Taglibs are specified in <jsp:root>. |
| ✧ XML syntax for scriptlets:<br><jsp:scriptlet><br>//some Java code<br></jsp: scriptlet> | |
| ✧ XML syntax for expressions:<br><jsp:expression><br>request.getParameter("paramName")<br></jsp:expression> | |

**8.6** *Match correct descriptions about purpose, function, or use with any of the following implicit objects:*

- *request*
- *response*
- *out*
- *session*
- *config*
- *application*
- *page*
- *pageContext*
- *exception*

| Implicit object | Purpose, Function, or Uses |
|---|---|
| ✧ request | Object of type javax.servlet.http.HttpServletRequest. Passed in as a parameter to _jspService(). Used for getting HTTP header information, cookies, parameters, etc. Also used for getting and setting attributes into the request scope. |

*continued on next page*

| Implicit object | Purpose, Function, or Uses |
|---|---|
| ✧ response | Object of type javax.servlet.http.HttpServletResponse. Passed in as a parameter to _jspService(). Used to send a response to the client. Used for setting HTTP header information, cookies, etc. |
| ✧ out | Object of type javax.servlet.jsp.JspWriter; used for writing data to the output stream |
| ✧ session | Object of type javax.servlet.http.HttpSession. Used for storing and retrieving session related information and sharing objects across multiple requests and pages within the same HTTP session. |
| ✧ config | Object of type javax.servlet.ServletConfig. Used to retrieve initialization parameters for a JSP page. |
| ✧ application | Object of type javax.servlet.ServletContext. Used for storing and retrieving application related information and sharing objects across multiple sessions, requests, and pages within the same web application. |
| ✧ page | Refers to the generated Servlet class. Not used much because it is declared as of type java.lang.Object. |
| ✧ pageContext | Object of type javax.servlet.jsp.PageContext. Used for storing and retrieving page-related information and sharing objects within the same translation unit and same request. Also used as a convenience class that maintains a table of all the other implicit objects. |
| ✧ exception | Object of type java.lang.Throwable. Only available in pages that have the page directive isErrorPage set to true. |

**8.7** *Distinguish correct and incorrect scriptlet code for:*

- *A conditional statement*
- *An iteration statement*

| Important concepts | Exam tips |
|---|---|

✧ Sample code for a conditional statement:

```
<% if (someCondition)
    {%>
       regular HTML/JSP code
 <%}
     else
     { %>
       regular HTML/JSP code
 <%} %>
```

✧ Sample code for an iterative statement:

```
<% for(int i=0; i<10; i++)
    {%>
       regular HTML/JSP code
 <%} %>
```

## *CHAPTER 13—REUSABLE WEB COMPONENTS*

### *Objective 9.1*

**9.1** *Given a description of required functionality, identify the JSP page directive or standard tag in the correct format with the correct attributes required to specify the inclusion of a Web component into the JSP page.*

| Important concepts | Exam tips |
|---|---|
| ✧ To include a component statically, use the include directive:<br><br><%@ include file="relativeURL" %> | Points to remember for the include directive:<br>• There is only one attribute: *file.*<br>• The file attribute is mandatory.<br>• The file attribute's value is a relative path. We cannot specify a protocol, hostname, or port number.<br>• The attribute cannot point to a servlet. |
| ✧ To include a component dynamically, use the include action:<br><br><jsp:include page="relativeURL" flush="true" /> | Points to remember for <jsp:include>:<br>• There are two attributes: *page* and *flush.*<br>• The page attribute is mandatory.<br>• The flush attribute is optional. The default value of flush is false.<br>• The name of the attribute is *page*–not *url* or *file.*<br>• The value of the page attribute is a relative path. We cannot specify a protocol, hostname, or port number.<br>• Even though the name of the attribute is *page*, it can point to a servlet.<br>• You can also include an HTML file dynamically. |
| ✧ To forward a request to another component dynamically, use the forward action:<br><br><jsp:forward page="relativeURL" /> | Points to remember for <jsp:forward>:<br>• There is only one attribute: *page.* There is no *flush* attribute in <jsp:forward>.<br>• The name of the attribute is *page* and not *url.*<br>• The attribute's value is a relative path. We cannot specify a protocol, hostname, or port number.<br>• Even though the name of the attribute is *page*, the value can point to a servlet.<br>• You can also forward to an HTML file dynamically. |

**Include Directive vs. Include Action**

| | Include directive | Include action |
|---|---|---|
| Syntax | <%@ include<br>file='relativeURL'%> | <jsp:include<br>page='relativeURL'<br>flush='true\|false' /> |
| | The attribute name is *file* and not *page*. | The attribute name is *page* and not *file*. |
| relativeURL | It can point to any file—JSP, HTML, text, XML, etc. However:<br>• It *cannot* point to a servlet.<br>• It *cannot* be a request-time expression. | It can point to any file—JSP, HTML, text, XML, etc. Also:<br>• It *can* point to a servlet.<br>• It *can* be a request-time expression.<br><%=expr%> |
| Parameters | The including JSP file *cannot* pass new parameters to the included JSP files. The following is *not* valid: | The including JSP page *can* pass new parameters to the included JSP pages and servlets using <jsp:param> as |
| | <%@ include<br>file='other.jsp?abc=123'%> | <jsp:include page='other.jsp' ><br><jsp:param name='abc'<br>value='123' /><br></jsp:include> |
| | However, the included files can access the original parameters available in the request to the including JSP file. | The included pages can also access the original parameters present in the request to the including JSP page. |
| Inclusion | Inclusion is static. | Inclusion is dynamic. |
| | Inclusion of the included file happens at translation time. | Inclusion of the output of the included component happens each time the including page is requested. |
| Translation Unit | The including page and the included pages *become* a part of a single translation unit. | The including page and the including pages *do not become* a part of a single translation unit. |
| | The page directives in any of the components—including or included JSP pages—affect the entire translation unit. | The page directives in the including page do not affect the included components, and vice versa. |
| If included file changes | The changes are not reflected unless all the including pages are re-translated. | The changes are reflected automatically each time the pages are requested. |
| Uses | Files that do not change very often are included using directives. | Components that do change often are included using actions. |
| | Examples include copyright information and navigational bars. | Examples include news headlines and advertisement bars. |

**<jsp:include> vs. <jsp:forward>**

| | **<jsp:include>** | **<jsp:forward>** |
|---|---|---|
| Syntax | <jsp:include<br>page='relativeURL'<br>flush='true\|false' /> | <jsp:forward<br>page='relativeURL' /> |

## CHAPTER 14—USING JAVABEANS

### Objectives 10.1–10.3

**10.1** *For any of the following tag functions, match the correctly constructed tag, with attributes and values as appropriate, with the corresponding description of the tag's functionality:*

- *Declare the use of a JavaBean component within the page.*
- *Specify, for jsp:useBean or jsp:getProperty tags, the name of an attribute.*
- *Specify, for a jsp:useBean tag, the class of the attribute.*
- *Specify, for a jsp:useBean tag, the scope of the attribute.*
- *Access or mutate a property from a declared JavaBean.*
- *Specify, for a jsp:getProperty tag, the property of the attribute.*
- *Specify, for a jsp:setProperty tag, the property of the attribute to mutate, and the new value.*

| Important concepts | Exam tips |
|---|---|
| ✧ To declare a JavaBean component, use the <jsp:useBean> action:<br>`<jsp:useBean attribute-list />`<br><br>Valid attributes: id, scope, class, type, and beanName. The attribute id is mandatory, while scope is optional. At least one of the following combinations of class, type, and beanName must be present: class, type, class and type, beanName and type.<br><br>The body of the <jsp:useBean> action can be used to initialize its properties. Example:<br>`<jsp:useBean id="address" scope="session"`<br>`  class="AddressBean" >`<br>`  <jsp:setProperty name="address"`<br>`    property="street" value="123 Main" />`<br>`</jsp:useBean>` | • The default value of the scope attribute is page.<br>• The beanName attribute can also be a JSP expression.<br>• beanName can be used to instantiate a class or a serialized object whereas class is only for a class.<br>• class uses the new keyword to instantiate a class and beanName uses java.beans.Beans.instantiate()<br>• Using beanName and class together is illegal. |

*continued on next page*

| Important concepts | Exam tips |
|---|---|
| ✧ To set a bean's property, use <jsp:setProperty>:<br><jsp:setProperty name="address" property="city" value="Albany" /><br><br>Valid attributes: name, property, param, and value.<br><br>The attributes name and property are mandatory, while others are optional. The name attribute must refer to a bean that is already declared using a useBean action.<br><br>Examples:<br><br><jsp:setProperty name="aName" property="*" /> : Sets all the properties for which there is a matching parameter in the request.<br><br><jsp:setProperty name="aName" property="aProp" /> : Sets aProp using the parameter of the same name in the request.<br><br><jsp:setProperty name="aName" property="aProp" param="aParam"/>: Sets aProp using the parameter named aParam in the request.<br><br><jsp:setProperty name="aName" property="aProp" value="aValue"/>:<br>Sets aProp to the value aValue.<br><br><jsp:setProperty name="aName" property="aProp" value="<%=JSPExpression%>"/>:<br>Sets aProp to the value returned by the expression. | Using param and value together is illegal. |
| ✧ To access a JavaBean property, use <jsp:getProperty>. Valid attributes: name and property. Both are mandatory. | <jsp:getProperty> prints out the value. |

**10.2** *Given JSP page attribute scopes: request, session, application, identify the equivalent servlet code.*

| Scope | Usage |
|---|---|
| ✧ request | Use the request object passed in as parameter to the service() method:<br><br>public void service (HttpServletRequest request, HttpServletResponse response)<br>{<br>request.setAttribute()<br>request.getAttribute()<br>} |

*continued on next page*

| Scope | Usage |
|---|---|
| ✧ session | Get the session object from the request object as:<br><br>HttpSession session = request.getSession();<br><br>session.setAttribute();<br>session.getAttribute(); |
| ✧ application | Get the ServletContext object from the servlet object as:<br><br>ServletContext servletContext = this.getServletContext ();<br><br>servletContext.setAttribute();<br>servletContext.getAttribute(); |

**10.3** *Identify techniques that access a declared JavaBean component.*

| Important concepts | Exam tips |
|---|---|
| ✧ Once the use of a JavaBean is declared using a <jsp:useBean> action, a variable by the given name is automatically declared in the servlet code. Therefore, besides the setProperty and getProperty actions, the bean can also be accessed through this variable in the scripting elements.<br><br>Example:<br><jsp:useBean id="user"<br>class="UserBean"<br>scope="session" /><br><br><%<br>//The bean is used in a scriptlet here.<br>//You can call methods on the object<br>//referred to by the user variable.<br>user.initialize();<br>out.println(user.getName());<br>%> | |

## *CHAPTER 15—USING CUSTOM TAGS*

### *Objectives 11.1–11.3*

**11.1** *Identify properly formatted tag library declarations in the Web application deployment descriptor.*

| Important concepts | Exam tips |
|---|---|
| ✧ A sample taglib declaration:<br>`<web-app>`<br>`<!--...other stuff -->`<br>`<taglib>`<br>`  <taglib-uri>`<br>`    http://www.manning.com/sampleLib`<br>`  </taglib-uri>`<br>`  <taglib-location>`<br>`    /WEB-INF/sampleLib.tld`<br>`  </taglib-location>`<br>`</taglib>`<br>`<!--...other stuff -->`<br>`</web-app>` | Remember the following points:<br>• Each taglib element maps one URI to one location.<br>• Remember the syntax of <taglib> carefully. There is no hyphen in <taglib>, but there is a hyphen in <taglib-uri> and <taglib-location>.<br>• The value of <taglib-uri> can be an absolute URI, a root-relative URI, or a non-root-relative URI.<br>• The value of <taglib-location> can be either a root-relative URI or a non-root-relative URI. It cannot be an absolute URI.<br>• The value of <taglib-uri> must be unique in the deployment descriptor.<br>• The value of <taglib-location> must point to a valid TLD resource path. It can be either a TLD file or a JAR file containing the TLD file at location META-INF/taglib.tld. |

**11.2** *Identify properly formatted taglib directives in a JSP page.*

| Important concepts | Exam tips |
|---|---|
| ✧ The syntax of the taglib directive is:<br>`<%@ taglib`<br>`    prefix="test"`<br>`    uri="http://www.manning.com/sampleLib" %>`<br>✧ In XML syntax, a tag library is introduced in the <jsp:root> element:<br>`<jsp:root`<br>`  xmlns:jsp="http://java.sun.com/JSP/Page"`<br>`  xmlns:test=" http://www.manning.com/`<br>`    sampleLib "`<br>`  version="1.2" >`<br>`  ...JSP PAGE...`<br>`</jsp:root>` | Understand the syntax of a taglib directive thoroughly. |

**11.3** *Given a custom tag library, identify properly formatted custom tag usage in a JSP page. Uses include:*

- *An empty custom tag*
- *A custom tag with attributes*
- *A custom tag that surrounds other JSP code*
- *Nested custom tags*

**Important concepts**

✧ An empty tag:

```
<test:required />
    or
<test:required></test:required>
```

✧ A tag with attributes:

```
<test:greet user="john"/>
```

✧ A tag that surrounds JSP code:

```
<test:debug>
  Some code here
</test:debug>
```

✧ Nested custom tags:

```
<test:switch>
  <test:case>
    Some JSP code Here
  </test:case>
  <test:default>
    Some JSP code Here too
  </test:default>
</test:switch>
```

**Exam tips**

You cannot nest a custom tag in the attribute list of another custom tag like this:

```
<test:tag1 name="<test:tag2 />" />
```

In this case, the JSP engine may assume "<test:tag2/">" as a String value passed to the name attribute. It will not execute tag2.

## CHAPTER 16—DEVELOPING CUSTOM TAG LIBRARIES

### Objectives 12.1–12.8

**12.1** *Identify the tag library descriptor element names that declare the following:*

- *The name of the tag*
- *The class of the tag handler*
- *The type of content that the tag accepts*
- *Any attributes of the tag*

| Important concepts | Exam tips |
|---|---|
| ✧ To declare the name of a tag use: <name>SimpleTag</name> | The name element is mandatory. |
| ✧ To declare the class of tag use : <tag-class>com.abc.MyTagClass</tag-class> | The tag-class element is mandatory. |
| ✧ To declare the type of content use: <body-content>JSP</body-content> Its values can be any one of the three: empty, JSP, or tagdependent. | The <body-content> element is not mandatory. The default value for <body-content> is JSP. |
| ✧ To declare the attributes of the tag use <attribute> and its subelements. | There may be zero or more attributes in a tag. |

**12.2** *Identify the tag library descriptor element names that declare the following:*

- *The name of a tag attribute*
- *Whether a tag attribute is required*
- *Whether or not the attribute's value can be dynamically specified*

| Important concepts | Exam tips |
|---|---|
| ✧ The <attribute> element has the following structure<br><tag><br><attribute><br><name>anyName</name><br><required>true\|false</required><br><rtexprvalue>true\|false</rtexprvalue><br></attribute><br></tag> | The <name> element is mandatory. For each attribute, the container calls the setXXX() method. The <required> element is not mandatory. The default value of the <required> element is false. When set to true, the attribute is mandatory. The <rtexprvalue> element is not mandatory. The default value of <rtexprvalue> element is false. When set to true, the attribute's value can be specified dynamically. |

**12.3** *Given a custom tag, identify the necessary value for the body-content TLD element for any of the following tag types:*

- *Empty-tag*
- *Custom tag that surrounds other JSP code*
- *Custom tag that surrounds content that is used only by the tag handler*

| Important concepts | Exam tips |
|---|---|
| ✧ The <body-content> element can take any one of the following values:<br><body-content>empty</body-content><br><body-content>JSP</body-content><br><body-content>tagdependent</body-content> | The <body-content> element is not mandatory.<br>The default value for <body-content> is JSP.<br>If <body-content> is specified as empty, the actual tag usage cannot have a body.<br>However, if <body-content> is specified as JSP or tagdependent, the actual tag usage may choose not to have a body. |

**12.4** *Given a tag event method (doStartTag, doAfterBody, and doEndTag), identify the correct description of the method's trigger.*

| Important concepts | Exam tips |
|---|---|
| ✧ doStartTag() is called after the JSP engine completely parses the opening tag. Before calling doStartTag(), the JSP engines calls the following methods:<br>1. setPageContext()<br>2. setParent()<br>3. setter methods for attributes | |

*continued on next page*

| Important concepts | Exam tips |
|---|---|
| ✧ doAfterBody() is called after the JSP engine completely evaluates the entire body of the tag. This happens the first time only if:<br><br>1. The tag implements IterationTag and doStartTag() returns EVAL_BODY_INCLUDE.<br><br>OR<br><br>2. The tag implements BodyTag and doStartTag() returns EVAL_BODY_INCLUDE.<br><br>OR<br><br>3. The tag implements BodyTag and doStart-Tag() returns EVAL_BODY_BUFFERED. | doAfterBody() is not called for tags that implement only the Tag interface. |
| ✧ The body of the tag is evaluated again (repeatedly), that is, the doAfterBody() is called repeatedly, only if:<br><br>1. The tag implements IterationTag and the previous call to doAfterBody() returns EVAL_BODY_AGAIN.<br><br>OR<br><br>2. The tag implements BodyTag and the previous call to doAfterBody() returns EVAL_BODY_AGAIN.<br><br>OR<br><br>3. The tag implements BodyTag and the previous call to doAfterBody() returns EVAL_BODY_BUFFERED. | |
| ✧ doEndTag() is always called at the end of processing a tag. | |

**12.5** *Identify valid return values for the following methods:*

- *doStartTag*
- *doAfterBody*
- *doEndTag*
- *PageConext.getOut*

| Important concepts | Exam tips |
|---|---|
| ✧ doStartTag() can return three values:<br>1. SKIP_BODY<br>Do not process the content of the body. Ignore it completely.<br>2. EVAL_BODY_INCLUDE<br>Process the contents of the body as with the normal JSP code.<br>3. EVAL_BODY_BUFFERED<br>Process the contents of the body as with the normal JSP code, but the output should be buffered and not sent to the client. The JSP engine uses a stack of javax.servlet.jsp.tagext.BodyContent objects for buffering. | The Tag interface defines doStartTag().<br>Implementations classes of Tag interface can return only two values in doStartTag():<br>SKIP_BODY or EVAL_BODY_INCLUDE<br>The IterationTag interface extends the Tag interface, but does not add any new return values for doStartTag(). Implementations classes of the IterationTag interface can return only one of the two values in doStartTag(): SKIP_BODY or EVAL_BODY_INCLUDE.<br>The BodyTag interface extends the IterationTag interface, and adds a new return value, EVAL_BODY_BUFFERED, for doStartTag(). Implementation classes of BodyTag interface can return any one of the three values in doStartTag(): SKIP_BODY, EVAL_BODY_INCLUDE, or EVAL_BODY_BUFFERED.<br>Thus, doStartTag() can return EVAL_BODY_BUFFERED *only if* the handler class implements the BodyTag interface. |
| ✧ doAfterBody() can return three values:<br>1. EVAL_BODY_AGAIN<br>Evaluate the body of the tag again. Do not use buffering.<br>2. EVAL_BODY_BUFFERED<br>Evaluate the body of the tag again, but the output of the tag should be buffered.<br>3. SKIP_BODY<br>Do not process the content of the body again. Ignore it. The loop is over and doAfterBody() is not called again. | The Tag interface does not have doAfterBody().<br>The IterationTag interface defines doAfterBody().<br>Implementation classes of the IterationTag interface can return only one of two values in doAfter():<br>EVAL_BODY_AGAIN or SKIP_BODY.<br>The BodyTag interface extends the IterationTag interface, and adds a new return value, EVAL_BODY_TAG, for doAfterBody(). EVAL_BODY_TAG is deprecated in JSP 1.2. Implementations classes of the BodyTag interface can return three values in doAfterBody(): EVAL_BODY_AGAIN, EVAL_BODY_BUFFERED, or SKIP_BODY.<br>Thus, doAfterBody() can return EVAL_BODY_BUFFERED *only if* the handler class implements the BodyTag interface. |
| ✧ doEndTag() can return two values:<br>1. SKIP_PAGE<br>Do not process the rest of the JSP page. Ignore it completely.<br>2. EVAL_PAGE<br>Process the rest of the JSP page as with the normal JSP code. | The Tag interface defines doEndTag().<br>Implementation classes of the Tag interface can return two values in doEndTag(): SKIP_PAGE or EVAL_PAGE<br>IterationTag and BodyTag inherit doEndTag().<br>They do not add any new return values. Implementation classes of IterationTag and BodyTag also can return one of the two values in doEndTag(): SKIP_PAGE or EVAL_PAGE.<br>doEndTag() is always called at the end of processing a tag regardless of the interfaces implemented and regardless of the return values from doStartTag() and doAfterBody() |

*continued on next page*

| Important concepts | Exam tips |
|---|---|
| ✧ The return value for PageContext.getOut() is JspWriter. However, at request time, if the doStartTag() returns EVAL_BODY_BUFFERED, PageContext.getOut() returns an object of type BodyContent (which extends JspWriter) when it is called from within the body of the tag. | |

**12.6** *Given a "BODY" or "PAGE" constant, identify a correct description of the constant's use in the following methods:*

- *doStartTag*
- *doAfterBody*
- *doEndTag*

| Constants | doStartTag() | doAfterBody() | doEndTag() |
|---|---|---|---|
| ✧ BODY Constants | | | |
| EVAL_BODY_INCLUDE | Includes the body of the tag for the first time. | N/A | N/A |
| EVAL_BODY_AGAIN | N/A | Includes the body of the tag for the second and further times in a loop. | N/A |
| EVAL_BODY_BUFFERED | Allows processing of the tag body for the first time. Uses buffering.<br><br>Valid only for tags implementing the BodyTag interface. | Allows processing of the tag body repeatedly in a loop.<br><br>Valid only for tags implementing the BodyTag interface. | N/A |
| SKIP_BODY | Does not include or process the body of the tag even for the first time. | Does not include or process the body of the tag the next time. | N/A |
| ✧ PAGE Constants | | | |
| EVAL_PAGE | N/A | N/A | Continue processing the rest of the page. |
| SKIP_PAGE | N/A | N/A | Do not process the rest of the page. Skip everything from the end of this tag to the end of the page. |

N/A = Not Applicable. The specified method cannot return the specified constant.

**12.7** *Identify the method in the custom tag handler that accesses:*

- *A given JSP page's implicit variable*
- *The JSP page's attributes*

**Getting Implicit Objects in the Tag Handler**

| Implicit objects | Getting implicit objects | |
|---|---|---|
| | **Using convenience methods** | **Using constants** |
| application | pageContext.getServletContext() | pageContext.getAttribute(PageContext.APPLICATION) |
| session | pageContext.getSession() | pageContext.getAttribute(PageContext.SESSION) |
| request | pageContext.getRequest() | pageContext.getAttribute(PageContext.REQUEST) |
| response | pageContext.getResponse() | pageContext.getAttribute(PageContext.RESPONSE) |
| out | pageContext.getOut() | pageContext.getAttribute(PageContext.OUT) |
| config | pageContext.getConfig() | pageContext.getAttribute(PageContext.CONFIG) |
| page | pageContext.getPage() | pageContext.getAttribute(PageContext.PAGE) |
| pageContext | | pageContext.getAttribute(PageContext.PAGECONTEXT) |
| exception | pageContext.getException() | pageContext.getAttribute(PageContext.EXCEPTION) |

**Getting Page Attributes in the Tag Handler**

| Scope | Getting attributes in different scopes | |
|---|---|---|
| | **Using implicit objects** | **Using constants** |
| application | pageContext.getServletContext().getAttribute("name") | pageContext.getAttribute( "name", PageContext.APPLICATION_SCOPE) |
| session | pageContext.getSession().getAttribute("name") | pageContext.getAttribute( "name", PageContext.SESSION_SCOPE) |
| request | pageContext.getRequest().getAttribute("name") | pageContext.getAttribute( "name", PageContext.REQUEST_SCOPE) |
| page | pageContext.getAttribute("name") | pageContext.getAttribute( "name", PageContext.PAGE_SCOPE) |

**12.8** *Identify methods that return an outer tag handler from within an inner tag handler.*

| Important concepts | Exam tips |
|---|---|
| ✧ The Tag interface has two methods:<br><br>public void setParent(Tag parentTag)<br>public Tag getParent()<br><br>The container calls setParent() before calling doStartTag(). It is the responsibility of the tag implementation class to save this reference in a private member for later use.<br><br>When the getParent() method is called, the tag returns its parent tag (the outer handler). | |
| ✧ The TagSupport class implements the Tag interface and provides implementation for the setParent() and getParent() methods.<br><br>So a class derived from the TagSupport class need not maintain its own parent, nor does it need to implement these methods. It can call getParent() to retrieve the outer handler, and subsequently call getParent() on the returned value to get ancestors. | |
| ✧ The TagSupport class also provides a new convenience method:<br><br>public static final Tag<br>findAncestorWithClass(Tag from, java.lang.Class klass)<br><br>This method works outward within the nested tags and gets the instance of a given class type that is closest to the given tag instance. | The findAncestorWithClass() is a static method. Hence, it is *not* necessary to subclass TagSupport to use this method. Even simple tag handlers that directly implement the Tag interface can use TagSupport.findAncestorWithClass(). |

## *CHAPTER 17—DESIGN PATTERNS*

### *Objectives 13.1 and 13.2*

**13.1** *Given a scenario description with a list of issues, select the design pattern (Value Objects, MVC, Data Access Object, or Business Delegate) that would best solve those issues.*

| Issues | Pattern |
|---|---|
| • Small object<br>• Grouped information<br>• Read-only data<br>• Reduce network traffic<br>• Increase response time<br>• Transfer data across networked tiers | Value Object |
| • Flexible design<br>• Provide services to different clients: web client, WAP client, etc.<br>• Multiple views, such as HTML or WML<br>• Single controller | Model-View-Controller (MVC) |
| • Uniform access to the database<br>• Transparent access to the database<br>• Centralized access to the database<br>• Reduce dependency on the type of database<br>• Reduce dependency on the database access mechanism<br>• Reduce coupling between the enterprise beans and the database<br>• Reduce coupling between the business objects and the database<br>• Easier migration of data from one database to another<br>• Multiple data sources, such as database systems on the intranet, database systems | Data Access Object (DAO) |
| • Reduce coupling between presentation and business tiers<br>• Proxy for the client<br>• Client-side facade<br>• Cache business service references for presentation-tier components<br>• Cache business service results for presentation-tier components<br>• Encapsulate business service lookup<br>• Encapsulate business service access<br>• Decouple clients from business service API | Business Delegate |
| • Dispatch requests<br>• Manage workflow of a web application<br>• Manage the sequence of steps<br>• Manage use cases | Front Controller |

**13.2** *Match design patterns with statements describing potential benefits that accrue from the use of the pattern, for any of the following patterns:*

- *Value Objects*
- *MVC*
- *Data Access Object*
- *Business Delegate*

| Important concepts | Exam tips |
|---|---|
| ✧ Value Objects<br><br>A Value Object is a small-sized serializable Java object that is used for transferring data over the network in a distributed application. | The potential benefits of VO are:<br><br>• Less communication overhead<br>• Fewer number of remote calls<br>• Reduction in network traffic<br>• Increased response time |
| ✧ Model-View-Controller (MVC)<br><br>The Model-View-Controller design pattern is applicable in situations where the same data (Model) is to be presented in different formats (Views), but is to be managed centrally by a single controlling entity (Controller). | The potential benefits of MVC are:<br><br>• Flexible design<br>• Centrally managed data<br>• Multiple ways of presentation |
| ✧ Data Access Objects (DAO)<br><br>A Data Access Object provides other application components with a clean, simple, and common interface to access the data from various multiple data stores.<br><br>DAO talks to the actual underlying database and takes care of the different types of data access mechanism. | The potential benefits of DAO are:<br><br>• Reduced dependency of other components on the details of using the database<br>• Access to database unified, centralized, and made transparent to the business-tier components<br>• Reduced dependency on type of database<br>• Reduced dependency on database access mechanism<br>• Reduced coupling between the enterprise beans and the database<br>• Reduced coupling between the business objects and the database<br>• Migration of data from one database to another made easier |
| ✧ Business Delegate<br><br>A Business Delegate is an object that communicates with the business service components on behalf of the client components.<br><br>The client-side components delegate the work of accessing the business services to the Business Delegate object. | The potential benefits of Business Delegate are:<br><br>• Reduced coupling between presentation and business tiers<br>• Cached business service results for presentation-tier components.<br>• Business service lookup encapsulated<br>• Business service access encapsulated<br>• Decoupled clients from business service API |

## *CHAPTER 18—USING FILTERS*

Since this topic is currently not required for the exam, we have created some potential objectives.

### *Objectives P.1–P.3*

**P.1** *Identify the uses for and the interfaces (or classes) and methods to achieve the following features:*

- *Implementing a filter*
- *Using FilterConfig to initialize a filter*
- *Understanding the filter life cycle*

| Important concepts | Exam tips |
|---|---|
| ✧ All filters implement the javax.servlet.Filter interface. | |
| ✧ javax.servlet.FilterConfig provides initialization parameters to a filter through:<br>1. getInitParameter(String name)<br>2. getInitParameterNames()<br>FilterConfig also contains a reference to the ServletContext object, which can be retrieved through the getServletContext() method. | |
| ✧ Filter life-cycle methods:<br>1. init(FilterConfig): Called by the container during application startup.<br>2. doFilter(ServletRequest, ServletResponse): Called by the container for each request whose URL is mapped to this filter.<br>3. destroy(): Called by the container during application shutdown. | |

**P.2** *Identify the WebApp deployment descriptor element names that declare the following features:*

- *Declaring a filter*
- *Declaring filter initialization parameters*
- *Associating a filter with a resource*
- *Associating a filter with a URL pattern*

| Important concepts | Exam tips |
|---|---|
| ✧ The following is a sample filter declaration: | |

```
<filter>
  <filter-name>ValidatorFilter</filter-name>
  <description>Validates the requests
    </description>
  <filter-class>com.abc.filters.ValidatorFilter
    </filter-class>
  <init-param>
    <param-name>locale</param-name>
    <param-value>USA</param-value>
  </init-param>
</filter>
```

*continued on next page*

| Important concepts | Exam tips |
|---|---|
| ✧ The following is a sample filter mapping that associates ValidatorFilter with a *.doc URL pattern:<br><filter-mapping><br><filter-name>ValidatorFilter</filter-name><br><url-pattern>*.doc</url-pattern><br></filter-mapping> | |
| ✧ The following is a sample filter mapping that associates ValidatorFilter with TestServlet:<br><filter-mapping><br><filter-name>ValidatorFilter</filter-name><br><servlet-name>TestServlet</servlet-name><br></filter-mapping> | |

**P.3** *Identify the uses for and the interfaces (or classes) and methods to achieve the following feature:*

- *Wrap requests and response to intercept and alter the client request and resource response.*

| Important concepts | Exam tips |
|---|---|
| ✧ The javax.servlet package defines the ServletRequestWrapper and ServletResponseWrapper classes. | |
| ✧ The javax.servlet.http package defines the HttpServletRequestWrapper and HttpServletResponseWrapper classes. | |
| ✧ All four classes delegate the method calls to the underlying request or response object. | |

# index

## Symbols

## D



## E

## F



## G



## H

## I

## J



## L

## T

## U



## V



## W



## X



## Z

## The SCWCD Exam Study Kit
## CD-ROM contents

### System requirements:

The CD-ROM will run on Windows and Unix operating systems. The minimum system requirements for running the CD_ROM are:

- 64 MB of RAM
- Java 2 environment
- Pentium or better processor (or equivalent on other platforms)
- At least 50 MB of free space on your hard drive for the Tomcat installation

To view the CD contents, insert it into your CD-ROM drive. An auto-run program will start and display the opening screen. From there, you can browse the CD. If your system does not launch the opening screen, you can display the contents of the CD-ROM by manually opening index.html in a browser. From there you can navigate through the contents of the CD.

### About the examples:

The code examples in the book are organized into separate web applications for each chapter. To run the examples, just copy the web applications into Tomcat's webapps directory.

### About Tomcat:

Tomcat is a free, open-source implementation of Java Servlet and JavaServer Pages technologies developed by the Jakarta project at the Apache Software Foundation. Appendix A explains how to install Tomcat on a Windows operating system. For non-windows operating systems, extract jakarta-tomcat-4.0.1.tar.gz and follow the instructions in the readme.txt file. Updates are made to Tomcat frequently; you can download the latest version from http://jakarta.apache.org/tomcat/.

### About JWebPlus:

JWebPlus is a popular exam simulator from Enthuware that allows you to evaluate your readiness for the exam. The abridged version of JWebPlus included on this CD contains three practices exams with all new questions that are not in the book. Each exam is timed to last 90 minutes and contains 60 questions. If you don't have a full 90 minutes to devote to the exam, you can even save it when you stop and continue later. Some of the features of JWebPlus include:

- **180 questions of varying degrees of toughness**

  The questions are based on the concepts presented in the Servlet 2.3 and JSP 1.2 Specifications, and thoroughly cover all of the exam objectives.
- **Detailed explanations**

  The explanations of the questions are broad enough to cover the whole concept, and also contain tips and warnings. We also explain why the individual choices are right or wrong.
- **Detailed results and analysis**

  The analysis tells you not only which sections you need to work on but also the level of difficulty you have mastered. You can track your progress by saving the results for future reference.

### Running JWebPlus:

*Prerequisites.* You must have JDK1.2 or higher installed on your machine.

*For Windows.* Double click startjwebplus.bat in the JWebPlus directory of the CD.

*For non-Windows.* Execute the startjwebplus.sh in the JWebPlus directory of the CD.

If you have problems running JWebPlus, please refer to the help text at http://www.enthuware.com/jwebplus/commonproblems.html.

### LICENSE AGREEMENTS

Any use of the contents of the CD (including the software and any standard documents) are subject to the License Agreements which are contained in the CD.

***Apache Software Foundation.*** The CD includes software developed by the Apache Software Foundation (http://www.apache.org/). Redistribution and use in source and binary forms, with or without modification, are permitted provided that the conditions contained in the License Agreement, which is included on the CD, are met. By opening the CD package, you are agreeing to be bound by the terms and conditions of the Agreement.

***Sun Microsystems, Inc.*** The CD includes software developed by Sun Microsystems, Inc (http://java.sun.com). Use of Sun software is subject to the Sun Microsystems, Inc. Binary Code License Agreement which is contained in the CD. By opening this CD package, you are agreeing to be bound by the terms and conditions of the agreement.